W9-ADS-835

This rich and varied portrait of the drama from 1660 to 1714 provides students with essential information about playwrights, staging, and genres, situating them in the social and political culture of the time. No longer seen as a privileged arena for select dramatists and élite courtiers, the Restoration theatre is revealed in all of its tumult, energy, and conflict.

Fourteen contributors examine the theatre, paying attention to major playwrights such as Dryden, Wycherley, and Congreve and also to more minor works and to plays by the first professional female dramatists. The book begins with chapters on staging and performance, continues with the main dramatic genres, progresses to historical and cultural contexts, and concludes with a chapter on the canon of Restoration drama.

The volume also includes a thorough chronology and biographies and bibliographies of dramatists.

THE CAMBRIDGE
COMPANION TO
ENGLISH RESTORATION
THEATRE

CAMBRIDGE COMPANIONS TO LITERATURE

The Cambridge Companion to Thomas Hardy
edited by Dale Kramer

*The Cambridge Companion to American
Women Playwrights*
edited by Brenda Murphy

CAMBRIDGE COMPANIONS TO CULTURE

*The Cambridge Companion to Modern German
Culture*
edited by Eva Kolinsky and Wilfried van der
Will

*The Cambridge Companion to Modern Spanish
Culture*
edited by David T. Gies

*The Cambridge Companion to Modern Russian
Culture*
edited by Nicholas Rzhevsky

THE CAMBRIDGE
COMPANION TO
ENGLISH
RESTORATION
THEATRE

EDITED BY
DEBORAH PAYNE FISK

CAMBRIDGE
UNIVERSITY PRESS

PUBLISHED BY THE PRESS SYNDICATE OF THE UNIVERSITY OF CAMBRIDGE
The Pitt Building, Trumpington Street, Cambridge, United Kingdom

CAMBRIDGE UNIVERSITY PRESS
The Edinburgh Building, Cambridge CB2 2RU, United Kingdom
http://www.cup.cam.ac.uk
40 West 20th Street, New York, NY 10011–3211, USA
http://www.cup.org
10 Stamford Road, Oakleigh, Melbourne 3166, Australia
Ruiz de Alarcón 13, 28014 Madrid, Spain

First published 2000

Printed in the United Kingdom at the University Press, Cambridge

Typeset in 10/13pt Sabon   [CE]

A catalogue record for this book is available from the British Library

ISBN 0 521 58215 6 hardback
ISBN 0 521 58812 X paperback

CONTENTS

ix

CONTENTS

ILLUSTRATIONS

NOTES ON CONTRIBUTORS

MICHAEL CORDNER is Senior Lecturer in the Department of English and Related Literature at the University of York. He is the editor of George Farquhar's *The Beaux' Stratagem* (1976), *The Plays of George Etherege* (1982), *Four Comedies* of John Vanbrugh (1989), *Four Restoration Marriage Plays* (1995), and *Selected Plays* of Richard Brinsley Sheridan (1998). He is the co-editor, with Peter Holland and John Kerrigan, of *English Comedy* (1994). Currently he is writing a book on the comedy of marriage, 1660–1737.

BRIAN CORMAN is Professor and Chair of English at the University of Toronto. He has published articles on the plays of Behn, Centlivre, Cibber, Congreve, Dryden, Etherege, Shadwell, Tate, and Wycherley. He is the author of *Genre and Generic Change in English Comedy, 1660–1710* (1993). His current project is a reception history of female novelists before Jane Austen. He is editor of the *University of Toronto Quarterly*.

MICHAEL DOBSON is Professor of Renaissance Drama at the Roehampton Institute, London. Among his books are *The Making of the National Poet: Shakespeare, Adaptation and Authorship, 1660–1769* (1992) and, with Nicola Watson, *England's Elizabeth: the Virgin Queen in National Mythology, 1603–1990* (forthcoming). He has published widely on Shakespeare and seventeenth-century theatre and edited Middleton and Rowley's *Wit at Several Weapons for The Complete Oxford Middleton*.

DEBORAH PAYNE FISK is Associate Professor of Literature of American University. She edited, with J. Douglas Canfield, *Cultural Readings of Restoration and Eighteenth-Century English Theatre* (1995), and is currently editing *Four Restoration Libertine Plays* for Oxford University Press. The author of scholarly articles on Wycherley, Behn, Pope, and Restoration drama and theatre, she has just completed a book-length study of authorship and the theatrical marketplace during the Restoration.

PAT GILL is an Associate Professor in the Institute of Communications Research at the University of Illinois in Champaign-Urbana. She is the author of *Interpreting*

Ladies: Women, Wit, and Morality in the Restoration Comedy of Manners (1994), and the co-editor, with Tom DiPiero, of *Illicit Sex: Identity Politics in Early Modern Culture* (1996). She has written articles on the plays of Wycherley, Otway, Lee, and Behn, in addition to essays on film and feminism.

PETER HOLLAND is Director of the Shakespeare Institute in Stratford-upon-Avon. He is the author of *The Ornament of Action: Text and Performance in Restoration Comedy* (1979) and *English Shakespeares: Shakespeare on the English Stage in the 1990s* (1997). He is the co-editor, with Hanna Scolnicov, of *Reading Plays: Interpretation and Reception* (1991) and, with Michael Cordner and John Kerrigan, of *English Comedy* (1994). In addition, he has edited *A Midsummer Night's Dream* (1994).

DEREK HUGHES is a reader in English at the University of Warwick. He has published many articles on Restoration drama, and is the author of *Dryden's Heroic Plays* (1981) and *English Drama, 1660–1700* (1996). He has also published on German opera, and is currently working on a study of literary and operatic representations of human sacrifice.

EDWARD A. LANGHANS is Professor Emeritus at the University of Hawaii. In addition to having published dozens of articles, reviews, and book chapters between 1949 and 1999, he is the author of *Restoration Promptbooks* (1981) and *Eighteenth-Century British and Irish Promptbooks* (1987). Professor Langhans co-authored, along with Philip H. Highfill and Kalman A. Burnim, *A Biographical Dictionary of Actors, Actresses, Musicians, Dancers, Managers, and Other Stage Personnel in London, 1660–1800* (1973–93). He also edited *Five Restoration Theatrical Adaptations* (1980) and co-edited *An International Dictionary of Theatre Language* (1985).

NANCY KLEIN MAGUIRE is the author of *Regicide and Restoration: English Tragicomedy, 1660–1671* (1992) and the editor of *Renaissance Tragicomedy: Explorations in Genre and Politics* (1987). She has contributed essays on the relationship of theatre and politics to various journals and collections of essays. She is currently working on Anglo-French relations during the reign of Charles II.

JEAN I. MARSDEN is Associate Professor of English at the University of Connecticut. She is the author of *The Re-Imagined Text: Shakespeare, Adaptation and Eighteenth-Century Literary Theory* (1995) and the editor of *The Appropriation of Shakespeare: Post-Renaissance Reconstructions of the Works and the Myth* (1991). She has published widely on Restoration and eighteenth-century drama and is currently completing a study of women and the eighteenth-century stage.

ROBERT MARKLEY is Jackson Distinguished Chair of British Literature at West Virginia University and editor of *The Eighteenth Century: Theory and Interpretation*. Among his books are *Two-Edg'd Weapons: Style and Ideology in the*

Comedies of Etherege, Wycherley, and Congreve (1988), *Fallen Languages: Crises of Representation in Newtonian England* (1993), and *Dying Planet: Mars and the Anxieties of Ecology from the Canals to Terraformation* (2000).

JESSICA MUNNS is Professor of English at the University of Denver. She is the author of *Restoration Politics and Drama: The Plays of Thomas Otway* (1995) and the co-editor of two volumes, *A Cultural Studies Reader: History, Theory, and Practice* (1996), and *The Clothes that Wear Us: Dressing and Transgressing in Eighteenth-Century Culture* (1999). Currently she is working on an edition of Otway's *Venice Preserv'd* and a book on Restoration drama.

SUSAN J. OWEN teaches English literature at the University of Sheffield. The author of numerous articles on Restoration drama, Behn, Marvell, and the relationship between literary and chaos theory, she has also written *Restoration Theatre and Crisis* (1996). She is the editor of *A Babel of Bottles: Drink, Drinkers, and Drinking Places in Literature* (forthcoming).

JOSEPH ROACH is Professor of English and Theater Studies at Yale University. He is the author of *The Player's Passion: Studies in the Science of Acting* (1993) and *Cities of the Dead: Circum-Atlantic Performance* (1996), which won the James Russell Lowell Prize for best critical book from the Modern Language Association in 1997. He is the co-editor, with Janelle G. Reinelt, of *Critical Theory and Performance* (1992).

CHRISTOPHER J. WHEATLEY is Professor of English at The Catholic University. He is the author of *Without God or Reason: The Plays of Thomas Shadwell and Secular Ethics in the Restoration* (1993) and *Beneath Iérne's Banners: Irish Protestant Drama of the Restoration and Eighteenth Century* (1999). Currently he is editing the *Dictionary of Literary Biography for Twentieth-Century American Drama* and, with Keven Donovan, an anthology of Irish plays from the seventeenth and eighteenth centuries.

PREFACE

Over the last two decades our notion of Restoration theatre has broadened considerably. Earlier critics, ignoring the rich variety of plays written between 1660 and 1714, focused almost exclusively on one genre, the "comedy of manners," written by a handful of canonical dramatists, Etherege, Wycherley, and Congreve. Dryden, by all estimates the most important writer of the period, was also studied, although his plays did not easily fit this generic designation. The witty language of Restoration comedies was thought to be its jewel; that wit, moreover, supposedly paid homage to the courtiers and roués who attended these plays. Since then scholars have realized the heterogeneity of Restoration theatre: its rich variety of dramatic forms, its innovations in staging and architecture, its complex representations of political and social events, its appeal to people from all walks of life. A vital theatre, it attracted talented men and women, mainly from the professional classes, to tread its boards and create its words. Long overshadowed by Shakespeare and the Renaissance stage, the Restoration theatre need no longer apologize for its considerable claims on our attention at the close of the twentieth century.

That attention shows in several ways. Despite the difficulties of staging Restoration plays, theatre companies in Britain and the United States regularly mount productions. Restoration prose, especially the sinewy similes of a Behn, Wycherley, or Congreve, demands vocal control more typical of opera singers than actors accustomed to the pauses afforded by Shakespearean blank verse. Modern ears unfamiliar with the Restoration penchant for balance and antithesis, both in the verse and prose, might find it "artificial" or, in the case of the tragedies and tragicomedies, "bombastic," another difficulty to overcome in staging. Settings and stories also seem alien to a modern sensibility accustomed to realism and psychologism. Restoration tragedies and tragicomedies favor the courts of distant lands – no mythic Arden or Illyria here – while the comedies prefer the fashionable drawing-rooms and bedrooms of London. The stories tell of kings deposed and restored, of citizens jilted and cuckolded, of wives bedded and avenged. Even the familiar plot of romantic comedy – young lovers overcoming familial and social obstacles to their union – often occupies a mere corner of the play, leaving the larger spaces to tales of deceit and adultery.

The plays, despite their strangeness, continue to be popular with audiences. The last decade alone has seen productions of perennial favorites, plays such as *The Man of Mode*, *The Way of the World*, and *The Plain Dealer*. More surprising, though, has been the interest in lesser-known Restoration plays. The rediscovery of Aphra Behn as an important dramatist – which the Restoration knew all along – has accounted for numerous productions of *The Rover*, now a repertory favorite. Vanbrugh figures more frequently in repertory as well (witness recent productions of *The Relapse* and *The Provok'd Wife*). Even fairly obscure – to modern eyes, at least – dramatists such as Edward Ravenscroft and Thomas Southerne have enjoyed attention: both *The London Cuckolds* and *The Wives' Excuse* were hits in recent London seasons. Several factors might account for this recent popularity. Modern audiences, inured to sex and violence, would hardly object to, much less register, the "obscene" nature of Restoration plays that so offended the Victorians. And, while plots and settings might seem alien, arguably there are aspects of Restoration plays that speak strongly to us at the close of the twentieth century. To an age obsessed with themes of gender and class, Restoration plays make "cultural sense": the plays question endlessly the "natural" hierarchies underpinning the family and society. The 1980s and 1990s have also witnessed a stratification in wealth and privilege, especially in the west; more than one director has used a Restoration play to comment sardonically on our own greed and to show us an unflattering portrait of ourselves via the late seventeenth century. Victorians accustomed to the social commentary of a Dickens or early moderns habituated to the social criticism of an Ibsen probably would not see that reflection. Sadly, Restoration plays that, on the one hand, celebrate privilege and deceit and, on the other, cynically analyze the workings of wealth and chicanery, speak all too well to our own times. In many senses, we are the Restoration *redux*, as Edward Bond reminds us in his 1980s play of the same name. The enduring appeal of Restoration drama also shows in the recent attention to critical editions of the plays: Janet Todd has published in a fine scholarly edition the complete plays of Aphra Behn; Harold Love has done the same for Thomas Southerne; and Kathleen Lesko has forthcoming the first scholarly edition of the plays of John Wilson. The canonical playwrights continue to receive attention: Wycherley, Etherege, and Congreve are available in multiple editions. And increasingly presses such as Penguin and Oxford are making accessible paperback editions for use in the classroom. Even the standard anthology of Restoration and eighteenth-century plays edited by George Winchester Stone nearly sixty years ago will be replaced by a far more timely collection of plays edited by J. Douglas Canfield. For the student or scholar interested in Restoration drama and theatre, this is a good time to be working in the field.

In organizing this volume I have tried to reflect recent approaches to the field. Once upon a time a volume such as this would have been organized along the lines of authorship, with requisite chapters on Dryden, Etherege, Wycherley, Congreve, and (perhaps) Vanbrugh. Increasingly, though, studies of Restoration drama and theatre focus on historical contexts, on material culture, on gender and class rather than individual authors (although the last still appear occasionally). Accordingly, in this volume the first two chapters treat the staging of plays, the next five chapters survey dramatic types, and the remaining seven examine important ideas and themes in the plays. This mode of organization was intended to convey something of the literary richness and historical tumult of this period. Readers will encounter in the succeeding chapters a wide range of playwrights, plays, and topics.

As with any volume of this nature, there are, of course, arbitrary omissions and limits. The years span 1660 to 1714; the *terminus ad quem* is conveniently framed by the Restoration itself, the year that reinstated the monarchy and restored the professional theatre to London. The final date is more difficult. Some scholars now posit 1688 for the end of the Restoration. This makes sense in political terms although less so in theatrical terms. Dryden continued to write plays well into the 1690s that share marked affinities with his earlier works. A playwright like Southerne, also writing in the 1690s, could easily have written his plays in the 1670s. And even though one can make a case for a shift toward "softer" or more "humane" comedy by the first decade of the eighteenth century, arguably the transformation to sentimental comedy does not stabilize until well after Queen Anne's reign. Tragedies written and produced in the early eighteenth century also do not seem that far removed from the Restoration. Ending the volume at 1714 strikes a balance between continuity and change.

Constraints of space imposed certain limitations. The volume focuses exclusively on London theatre; however, readers should be aware that a theatre opened in Smock Alley, Dublin, shortly after the Restoration and that throughout the period bands of traveling players performed in Britain and abroad. This volume also does not treat Restoration opera or the occasional music composed for the theatre; but excellent studies have been published on the subject. Curtis Price has written extensively on Restoration music for the theatre; in addition, the mid-nineties, because of the tercentenary of Purcell's death, saw a wealth of scholarship produced on baroque opera. The final omission concerns the entr'acte entertainments that were a staple of any performance at the theatre. For more information about these, the reader is advised to consult *The London Stage*.

I should like to offer thanks to everyone who helped me with this project. I am especially grateful to the Folger Shakespeare Library for assisting with illustrations and for providing the most pleasant of working conditions; I am also indebted to the British Library and to the Huntington Library for the use of their collections. For their good advice I should like to thank Kathy Lesko, Chris Wheatley, Peter Holland, Bob Markley, Jessica Munns, and Ann Kelly. Sarah Stanton proved the most indefatigable and patient of editors, even when I ran into delays or difficulties. Shannon Mariotti has been the most stalwart of research assistants from the beginning to the end of this project; Jenny Fast also gave valuable assistance in proofreading text.

To my husband, Rodney Harald Fisk, is this book affectionately dedicated.

ABBREVIATIONS

AEB	*Analytical and Enumerative Bibliography*
BJRL	*Bulletin of the John Rylands University Library of Manchester*
BNYPL	*Bulletin of the New York Public Library*
BWVACET	*Bulletin of the West Virginia Association of College English Teachers*
CLAJ	*College Language Association Journal*
CollL	*College Literature*
CompD	*Comparative Drama*
CultCrit	*Cultural Critique*
DR	*Drama: The Quarterly Theatre Review*
DramS	*Drama Survey*
DUJ	*Durham University Journal*
ECent	*The Eighteenth Century: Theory and Interpretation*
ECLife	*Eighteenth-Century Life*
ECS	*Eighteenth-Century Studies*
EIC	*Essays in Criticism*
EiT	*Essays in Theatre*
ELH	*English Literary History*
ELR	*English Literary Renaissance*
ELWIU	*Essays in Literature (Macomb, Ill.)*
EM	*English Miscellany*
ES	*English Studies*
HLQ	*Huntington Library Quarterly*
ISJR	*Iowa State Journal of Research*
JDTC	*Journal of Dramatic Theory and Criticism*
JEGP	*Journal of English and Germanic Philology*
JES	*Journal of European Studies*
JNT	*Journal of Narrative Technique*
JWCI	*Journal of the Warburg and Courtauld Institutes*
L&H	*Literature and History*
LC	*The Library Chronicle (Philadelphia, Penn.)*
MHLS	*Mid-Hudson Language Studies*
MLQ	*Modern Language Quarterly*

MLR	*Modern Language Review*
MLS	*Modern Language Studies*
MP	*Modern Philology*
N&Q	*Notes and Queries*
NCTR	*Nineteenth-Century Theatre*
PAPA	*Publications of the Arkansas Philological Association*
PBSA	*Papers of the Bibliographical Society of America*
PLL	*Papers in Language and Literature*
PMLA	*Publications of the Modern Language Association*
PQ	*Philological Quarterly*
PubHist	*Publishing History*
RECTR	*Restoration and Eighteenth-Century Theatre Research*
RES	*Review of English Studies*
RLC	*Revue de Littérature Comparée*
SAQ	*South Atlantic Quarterly*
SECC	*Studies in Eighteenth-Century Culture*
SEL	*Studies in English Literature, 1500–1900*
ShS	*Shakespeare Survey*
SlitI	*Studies in the Literary Imagination*
SN	*Studia Neophilologica*
SoAR	*South Atlantic Review*
SE	*Studies in English*
SP	*Studies in Philology*
SQ	*Shakespeare Quarterly*
SSJ	*Southern Speech Journal*
SVEC	*Studies on Voltaire and the Eighteenth Century*
ThS	*Theatre Survey*
TJ	*Theatre Journal*
TN	*Theatre Notebook*
TRI	*Theatre Research International*
TSL	*Tennessee Studies in Literature*
TSLL	*Texas Studies in Language and Literature*
UDR	*University of Dayton Review*
UTQ	*University of Toronto Quarterly*
W&L	*Women & Literature*
WS	*Women's Studies*
YES	*Yearbook of English Studies*

CHRONOLOGY

Like other Protestant countries, England was reluctant to adopt the new calendar devised by Pope Gregory XIII, the so-called "Gregorian" or "new style" calendar, which began the new year on 1 January and changed the number of days in the year. Not until 1752 was legislation passed in England that made mandatory all legal and public transactions in this new style. The Restoration and early eighteenth century still employed the "old style" calendar, which reckoned the year from Lady Day (25 March) rather than 1 January. Furthermore, dates in English documents were ten days (eleven after 28 February 1700) behind those on the Continent. Some editors retain old-style dating for events occurring between 1 January and 25 March; thus, the date on which the Theatre Royal in Drury Lane burned down would be indicated as 25 January 1671/2. For the convenience of students, I employ new-style dating throughout. I take the incineration of the Theatre Royal to have occurred on 25 January 1672. Nonetheless, students should be aware of the old-style convention.

The dates of plays derive from première, not publication, unless the play was never produced on the stage.

1660	Declaration of Breda; Charles Stuart enters London; execution of regicides; grants given to Thomas Killigrew and William Davenant to establish, respectively, the King's Company and the Duke's Company; Defoe b.; Southerne b. Pepys, *Diary* (begun); Evelyn begins his "Kalendarium," the eventual source for his diary
1661	Coronation of Charles II; Venner's Rebellion; Lincoln's Inn Fields (for the Duke's Company) opens; actresses appear on the stage Cowley, *Cutter of Coleman Street*

1662	Establishment of the Royal Society; Act of Uniformity; Licensing Act Howard, *The Committee*
1663	Theatre Royal (for the King's Company) opens in Drury Lane Tuke, *The Adventures of Five Hours*; Dryden, *The Wild Gallant*; Wilson, *The Cheats*
1664	Conventicle Act; Vanbrugh b. Evelyn, *Sylva*; Dryden and Howard, *The Indian Queen*; Dryden, *The Rival Ladies*; Etherege, *The Comical Revenge*; Lacy, *The Old Troop*; Orrery, *The Generall* and *Henry V*
1665	Second Dutch War; Great Plague Dryden, *The Indian Emperour*; Orrery, *Mustapha*
1666	Great Fire of London
1667	Treaty of Breda ending the Second Dutch War; Cowley d.; Swift b. Milton, *Paradise Lost*; Dryden, *Annus Mirabilis*, *Secret Love*; Dryden and Newcastle, *Sir Martin Mar-all*; Dryden and Davenant, *The Tempest*
1668	Triple Alliance between England, Holland, and Sweden; William Davenant d.; Dryden appointed Poet Laureate Dryden, *An Essay of Dramatic Poesy* and *An Evening's Love*; Etherege, *She Wou'd If She Cou'd*; Sedley, *The Mulberry-Garden*; Shadwell, *The Sullen Lovers*
1669	Pepys, *Diary* (ends); Dryden, *Tyrannick Love*
1670	Secret Treaty of Dover with France; Congreve b. Dryden, *The Conquest of Granada, Part I*
1671	Duke's Company moves to new playhouse in Dorset Garden Milton, *Paradise Regained* and *Samson Agonistes*; Dryden, *The Conquest of Granada*, Part II; Buckingham, *The Rehearsal*; Wycherley, *Love in a Wood*
1672	Declaration of Indulgence; Third Dutch War; burning of the Theatre Royal; Addison b.; Steele b.

Wycherley, *The Gentleman Dancing-Master*; Shadwell, *Epsom-Wells*; Dryden, *Marriage-A-la-Mode* and *The Assignation*; Ravenscroft, *The Citizen turn'd Gentleman*; Howard, *All Mistaken*

1673 The Test Act
Behn, *The Dutch Lover*; Settle, *The Empress of Morocco*; Dryden, *Amboyna*; Ravenscroft, *The Careless Lovers*

1674 Third Dutch War ends; opening of the new Theatre Royal at Drury Lane; Milton d.
Lee, *The Tragedy of Nero*; Shadwell *et al.*, *The Tempest* (opera); Howard, *The English Monsieur*

1675 Establishment of the Royal Observatory at Greenwich; Proclamation Concerning Coffee-Houses
Dryden, *Aureng-Zebe*; Wycherley, *The Country Wife*; Shadwell, *The Libertine* and *Psyche*; Lee, *Sophonisba*; Crowne, *Calisto*; Otway, *Alcibiades*

1676 Secret treaty between Charles II and Louis XIV
Etherege, *The Man of Mode*; Wycherley, *The Plain-Dealer*; Shadwell, *The Virtuoso*; Behn, *The Town-Fopp*; Otway, *Don Carlos, Titus and Berenice*, and *The Cheats of Scapin*; Durfey, *Madam Fickle* and *The Fool turned Critick*

1677 Behn, *The Rover, The Counterfeit Bridegroom*, and *The Debauchee*; Dryden, *All for Love* and *The State of Innocence*; Durfey, *A Fond Husband*; Lee, *The Rival Queens*; Banks, *The Rival Kings*

1678 Popish Plot; Marvell d.; Farquhar b.
Bunyan, *The Pilgrim's Progress*; Rymer, *Tragedies of the Last Age Considered*; Behn, *Sir Patient Fancy*; Otway, *Friendship in Fashion*; Dryden and Lee, *Oedipus*; Dryden, *The Kind Keeper*; Lee, *Mithridates*; Durfey, *Trick for Trick*, Shadwell, *A True Widow*

1679 Duke of York sent abroad; Exclusion Bill; Hobbes d.; Orrery d.
Behn, *The Feign'd Curtezans*; Dryden, *Troilus and Cressida*; Lee, *Caesar Borgia*; Shadwell, *The Woman-Captain*

1680	Exclusion Crisis: Duke of York returns; Second Exclusion Bill rejected by the Lords; Rochester d.
	Rochester, *Poems*; Otway, *The Orphan, Caius Marius*, and *The Soldier's Fortune*; Lee, *The Princess of Cleve, Theodosius* and *Lucius Junius Brutus*; Dryden, *The Spanish Friar*
1681	Charles II dissolves Parliament; Shaftesbury committed to the Tower
	Dryden, *Absalom and Achitophel*; Marvell, *Poems*; Banks, *The Unhappy Favourite*; Behn, *The Roundheads, The False Count*, and *The Rover, Part II*; Ravenscroft, *The London Cuckolds*; Shadwell, *The Lancashire Witches*
1682	Establishment of the United Company; the company uses both Drury Lane and Dorset Garden
	Dryden, *Religio Laici*; *The Medal*, and *MacFlecknoe*; Otway, *Venice Preserv'd*; Behn, *The City Heiress*; Dryden and Lee, *The Duke of Guise*; Ravenscroft, *The London Cuckolds*; Banks, *Vertue Betray'd*
1683	Rye House Plot; Killigrew d.
	Crowne, *City Politicks*; Otway, *The Atheist*; Lee, *Constantine the Great*
1684	Corneille d.
	Dryden, *The History of the League*; Tonson, *Miscellany Poems*; Rochester, *Valentinian*
1685	Charles II d.; coronation of James II; Monmouth's Rebellion; execution of the Duke of Monmouth; Otway d.
	Crowne, *Sir Courtly Nice*; Dryden, *Albion and Albanius*
1686	Dryden converts to Catholicism
	Behn, *The Lucky Chance*
1687	Duke of Buckingham d.
	Dryden, *The Hind and the Panther*; Newton, *Principia Mathematica*; Sedley, *Bellamira*; Behn, *The Emperor of the Moon*
1688	Declaration of Indulgence; Glorious Revolution; James II flees to France; Dryden loses the post of Poet Laureate, which

is awarded to Thomas Shadwell; Dryden also loses the post of Historiographer Royal; Bunyan d.; Pope b.
Shadwell, *The Squire of Alsatia*

1689 Coronation of William of Orange and Mary; Toleration Act; War declared on the French; Behn d.; Richardson b.
Dryden, *Don Sebastian*; Shadwell, *Bury Fair*; Behn, *The Widow Ranter*; Purcell/Tate, *Dido and Aeneas*

1690 Battle of the Boyne
Locke, *Two Treatises of Government* and *An Essay Concerning Human Understanding*; Southerne, *Sir Anthony Love*; Dryden, *Amphitryon*

1691 Etherege d.
Langbaine, *An Account of the English Dramatick Poets*; Congreve, *Incognita*; Dryden/Purcell, *King Arthur*; Durfey, *Love for Money*; Southerne, *The Wives' Excuse*

1692 Shadwell d.; Tate becomes Poet Laureate
Durfey, *The Marriage-Hater Match'd*; Dryden, *Cleomenes*; Settle/Purcell, *The Fairy Queen*; Shadwell, *The Volunteers*

1693 Sir Thomas Skipwith and Christopher Rich consolidate control over the United Company
Rymer, *A Short View of Tragedy*; Congreve, *The Old Batchelor* and *The Double Dealer*

1694 Bank of England founded; Queen Mary d.; Voltaire b.
Dryden, *Love Triumphant*; Durfey, *Don Quixote*; Southerne, *The Fatal Marriage*

1695 Beginning of the Whig junto and party government; Thomas Betterton, Elizabeth Barry, and Anne Bracegirdle break away from the United Company, beginning their own company in Lincoln's Inn Fields; Purcell d.
Locke, *The Reasonableness of Christianity*; Congreve, *Love for Love*; Southerne, *Oroonoko*; Trotter, *Agnes de Castro*

1696 Vanbrugh, *The Relapse*; Cibber, *Love's Last Shift*; Manley, *The Lost Lover* and *The Royal Mischief*; Pix, *Ibrahim*

1697	Treaty of Ryswick ending the war with France; Hogarth b. Dryden, *Alexander's Feast* and translation of *Virgil*; Defoe, *An Essay upon Projects*; Congreve, *The Mourning Bride*; Vanbrugh, *The Provok'd Wife*; Pix, *The Innocent Mistress* and *The Deceiver Deceiv'd*
1698	Collier, *A Short View of the Immorality and Profaneness of the English Stage*; Behn, *The Histories and Novels*; Farquhar, *Love and a Bottle*; Trotter, *The Fatal Friendship*
1699	Gildon, *The Lives and Characters of the English Dramatick Poets*; Durfey, *The Rise and Fall of Massaniello*; Farquhar, *The Constant Couple*
1700	Dryden d. Congreve, *The Way of the World*; Dryden, *Fables*; Rowe, *The Ambitious Stepmother*; Trotter, *Love at a Loss*; Centlivre, *The Perjur'd Husband*
1701	James II d.; Act of Settlement securing the Hanoverian succession; Sedley d. Defoe, *True-born Englishman*; Rowe, *Tamerlane*; Farquhar, *Sir Harry Wildair*
1702	William III d.; coronation of Queen Anne; War of Spanish Succession [Gildon], *A Comparison Between the Two Stages*; Defoe, *The Shortest Way with Dissenters*; Centlivre, *The Stolen Heiress*; Farquhar, *The Inconstant*
1703	Pepys d. Rowe, *The Fair Penitent*; Steele, *The Lying Lover*
1704	Battle of Blenheim; Locke d. Newton, *Optics*; Swift, *Tale of a Tub* and *Battle of the Books*; Cibber, *The Careless Husband*
1705	Queen's Theatre (later known as the King's Theatre) opens in Haymarket where it is used by Betterton's Company Steele, *The Tender Husband*; Centlivre, *The Gamester*, *The Basset-table*, and *Love at a Venture*; Rowe, *Ulysses*; Vanbrugh, *The Mistake* and *The Confederacy*

1706	Evelyn d. Farquhar, *The Recruiting Officer*; Centlivre, *The Platonick Lady*
1707	Union Treaty with Scotland; Farquhar d.; Fielding b. Farquhar, *The Beaux' Stratagem*; Rowe, *The Royal Convert*
1708	Downes, *Roscius Anglicanus*
1709	Copyright Act; Act for the Encouragement of Learning; Dorset Garden Theatre demolished; Johnson b. Manley, *The New Atalantis*; Steele, *The Tatler*; Centlivre, *The Busie Body*; Rowe, edition of Shakespeare
1710	Companies united at Drury Lane under Colley Cibber; Wren finishes St. Paul's Cathedral; Betterton d. Berkeley, *Principles of Human Knowledge*; Centlivre, *Marplot in Lisbon*
1711	Pope, *Essay on Criticism*; Shaftesbury, *Characteristics*; Addison, *The Spectator*; Swift, *Miscellanies in Prose and Verse*
1713	Treaty of Utrecht ending the War of the Spanish Succession; Sterne b.; Scriblerus Club formed Pope, *Windsor Forest*; Addison, *Cato*
1714	Queen Anne d.; coronation of George I; Lincoln's Inn Fields renovated by John Rich Pope, *Rape of the Lock*; Mandeville, *Fable of the Bees*; Rowe, *Jane Shore*; Centlivre, *The Wonder! A Woman keeps a Secret*

I

EDWARD A. LANGHANS

The theatre

Our will and pleasure is that you prepare a Bill for our signature to passe our Greate Seale of England, containing a Grant unto our trusty and well beloved Thomas Killegrew Esquire, one of the Groomes of our Bed-chamber and Sir William Davenant Knight, to give them full power and authoritie to erect Two Companys of Players consisting respectively of such persons as they shall chuse and apoint; and to purchase or build and erect at their charge as they shall thinke fitt Two Houses or Theaters.[1]

So began the draft of a warrant, dated 19 July 1660, allowing two courtiers of Charles II to have shared control of the London public theatre. The document went on to authorize Killigrew and Davenant to give performances with scenery and music, to establish ticket prices and employee salaries, and to suffer no rival companies. This draft, written, remarkably, by Davenant himself, served as the basis for a warrant a month later stating essentially the same thing and directing the two new managers to be their own censors of plays. By 1663 they had been granted definitive patents not only empowering them to run the only official theatres in London but giving that authority to their heirs or assigns. Not until 1843 were the patents rescinded, and even today Drury Lane Theatre and the Royal Opera House, Covent Garden, derive their rights from the royal grants of the 1660s.

That Davenant was allowed to draft a document giving powers to himself and Killigrew shows the strength of their position. Killigrew, called the King's jester, had the court connections; Davenant, who held an unused patent from 1639, had the theatrical experience. There were other theatrical companies in England in 1660; only one, under George Jolly, posed a threat, and he ended up running, for the two patentees, a "nursery" for young actors. These courtiers, then, were largely responsible for what the early Restoration theatres were like, who came to them, and what kind of drama was encouraged. They were each allotted specific pre-1660 plays to perform and allowed to decide what new plays would be produced. The theatre world was all before them.

The companies

England had been without official theatrical activity for eighteen years, though there had been sporadic attempts at illegal performing. Gone, or nearly gone, was the general enthusiasm for theatre that in earlier days had encouraged entrepreneurs to build seven public theatres between 1576 and 1605 in a London of 200,000 people. Though greater London by 1660 had a population of about 500,000, the potential audience after years of Puritan dominance was probably small. The theatres used by various transient companies just before and after the Restoration of the monarchy were leftovers from before the Civil War – the Red Bull, Salisbury Court, and the Cockpit or Phoenix in Drury Lane. Killigrew and Davenant worked temporarily in those relics but elected not to make them permanent theatrical homes. Instead, they opened new playhouses seating about 400 and built within the walls of roofed tennis courts. These were tiny – as small as 25 feet wide by 75 feet long (about the size of a modern court) and no larger than 42 feet by 106 feet – with spectator benches along one side and private seating at one end.[2] Davenant and Killigrew may have selected small buildings in reputable neighborhoods because they anticipated a limited, aristocratic audience that would prefer intimacy and would not fill larger houses. Having both spent time on the Continent during the civil strife in England, they were surely familiar with the tennis-court theatres that were popular across the channel.

The two managers approached their building renovations in different ways. Killigrew chose to construct within his tennis court in Vere Street a sceneryless stage, with U-shaped seating on perhaps two levels, and a benched pit on the auditorium floor. His alterations must have been minimal, for he had his King's Company performing there by 8 November 1660, only two months after the Crown granted him permission to proceed. It could hardly have been a very fancy or even comfortable theatre, though the diarist Samuel Pepys praised it as "the finest play-house, I believe, that ever was in England."[3] (We should remember, however, that Pepys had precious little playgoing experience at the time.) The first dramas Killigrew staged were old, since no new plays were available. He even began with males playing the women's roles, just as in the old public theatre days.[4] Killigrew, who grew up in Shakespeare's London and is said to have played bit parts at the Red Bull when he was a boy, may have assumed that the new theatre of the Restoration would be pretty much like the old. Or he may just have been anxious to get his business going quickly. In any case, the Vere Street Theatre probably looked something like the old "private" theatre in the Blackfriars that Shakespeare's troupe had used for winter performances, though Killigrew had had no special connection with that playhouse. His decisions must have seemed sensible at the time, but within a year after opening his Vere Street house he had to lay plans for a new theatre, built from the ground up.

Sir William Davenant's approach was different, though he, too, thought small. He also converted a tennis court into a playhouse, but he followed not the private theatre tradition of earlier days but that of the court theatre, which had featured scenery. Davenant's choice meant that preparing his theatre in Lincoln's Inn Fields would take time. His Duke's Company did not begin performing there until 28 June 1661, over six months after Killigrew had opened at Vere Street. Sir William had known the public and private theatres of pre-war London but had also worked, in 1640, with the court masque designer Inigo Jones on the last of the great Caroline extravaganzas, Davenant's own *Salmacida Spolia*. Just as Killigrew may have intended to use the old private theatres as a model, Davenant seems to have made a conscious effort to introduce to the public the characteristics of the old court productions and in that way bring the English-speaking theatre in line with the mainstream theatrical developments on the Continent. He also elected to have women playing female roles, again as in the court theatres, and four of the eight actresses he hired in 1660 he housed in his own home, which was attached to the tennis court he remodeled. Ironically, Killigrew apparently introduced Restoration audiences to actresses first, at Vere Street as early as 8 December 1660, when a woman played Desdemona in *Othello*.

Though the managers were assured from the beginning of royal patronage and a virtual theatrical monopoly, to fill their houses they had to attract members of the middle social class. Perhaps that helped Davenant decide to equip his theatre with scenery. As Pepys' *Diary* makes clear, the novelty proved irresistible. Killigrew had to follow suit; his plans for a new theatre included scenes and machines. These managerial decisions were fraught with financial dangers, for roofed theatres and scenic spectacles were expensive. Looking back on the pre-war theatre, an observer wrote "That tho' the Town was then, perhaps, not much more than half so Populous as now, yet then the Prices were small (there being no Scenes) and better order kept among the Company that came."[5]

Davenant and Killigrew seem not to have seriously considered the inexpensive route of restoring the sceneryless, open-air playhouses of Shakespeare's day. Perhaps that kind of theatre could not have been successfully revived in the 1660s, especially with two courtiers holding the patents during the reign of a monarch more familiar with French than English entertainments. The continental roofed playhouses, scenery, and actresses were by the mid-seventeenth century so firmly established that Shakespeare's Globe could hardly have been thought of by Davenant and Killigrew as a model for the future – if it was thought of at all. Had the patentees chosen to revive the old public theatre tradition, and had King Charles supported them (neither supposition very likely), the course of English drama might have been very different. The managers and their monarch probably did not stop to consider what effect on the future their decisions would have. By 1667 Killigrew boasted "That the stage is now by his pains a thousand times better and more glorious then ever heretofore. Now, wax-candles, and many of them; then, not above 3*lb.* of tallow. Now, all things civil, no rudeness anywhere; then, as in a bear-garden. Then, two or three fiddlers; now, nine or ten of the best."[6] He did not seem much concerned with the drama, only the show.

Restoration acting companies were organized much like those in Shakespeare's day. Davenant and Killigrew were the masters, but though they held royal patents, they did not own the troupes. The companies were businesses, and shares in them were sold to raise the money needed to furnish theatres, hire personnel, and produce plays. Shares could be purchased in the company as an organization, and the holders, mostly the actors themselves, prospered if the troupe thrived. Shares were also sold in their playhouse, but the speculators were often non-theatrical people.

Each company had a permanent cadre of performers who were engaged for the theatrical season, September to June. Following the medieval guild system, master performers helped train the younger ones. Many members of a troupe, along with the house and backstage personnel, were hirelings – employees in a variety of theatrical capacities working for fixed wages. Before the end of the seventeenth century some employees – at first performers only – were granted benefit performances that could, if successful, provide them with extra income. Theatre personnel might also augment their salaries by playing in London or touring the provinces in the summers. Bartholomew and Southwark fairs in August and early September provided further opportunities for performers if they did not mind acting at a "booth" theatre next door to a troupe of rope dancers or prize fighters or conjurers.

The repertory system used by the players gave audiences a variety of theatrical fare in a given week, for a different production was usually offered each day. Long runs were unheard of, though a play that "took" with the crowd might run several days in succession. The system placed heavy demands on players, for a performer had to hold dozens of roles in his head and be ready to play any one of them on short notice. An advantage was that a company could avoid losing money on an unsuccessful new play or revival, for the bill could be switched and a flop dropped in a hurry. For a new work, playwrights received the profits of a third performance (if it took place), but if the production failed, the play and pay to the author could disappear. Extra expenditure on a lavish new production was a financial strain, though costs could be made up by using scenery from that show to enhance another. The system allowed successful works to support weak ones and encouraged managers to take risks they might otherwise avoid. It was an economical and time-tested way of running a theatre, and new playwrights had a fair chance of being produced.

Davenant was a capable proprietor, and although he died in 1668 and did not live to see the new Dorset Garden Theatre, his company prospered under the leadership of his widow and the fine actor Thomas Betterton. Killigrew, on the other hand, was inept, and his group was in such financial difficulty by 1682 that the Duke's players absorbed the King's, and for over ten years London had only one patent troupe, the United Company. More theatrical outsiders, finding theatre an attractive, though chancy, investment, began buying shares or portions of shares. Control came into the hands of a wily lawyer, Christopher Rich, and his almost silent partner, Sir Thomas Skipwith. The older actors rebelled and set up their own company at the Lincoln's Inn Fields playhouse, where they operated under a license, since Rich and Skipwith, after the King's and Duke's companies merged in 1682, held both of the royal patents. At the beginning of the eighteenth century London had two theatrical companies, but they struggled to survive under Queen Anne, who had little of her uncle Charles's interest in theatre. Further, it was a period of moral soul-searching that altered the tone of playwriting. Audiences were changing as more middle-class patrons were attracted to the playhouses; they preferred greater variety on a typical theatrical bill instead of the performance of just a single play. The trend was toward less risqué dramatic offerings, greater visual spectacle, more song and dance entr'actes, bigger theatres, and larger but less sophisticated audiences. Aristocratic patrons became attracted to Italian opera which, for different reasons, also required larger theatres, greater spectacle, and the expensive talents of singers and dancers. By 1710, when the composer Handel began his London career, the theatre Pepys and King Charles had known and loved was only a memory.

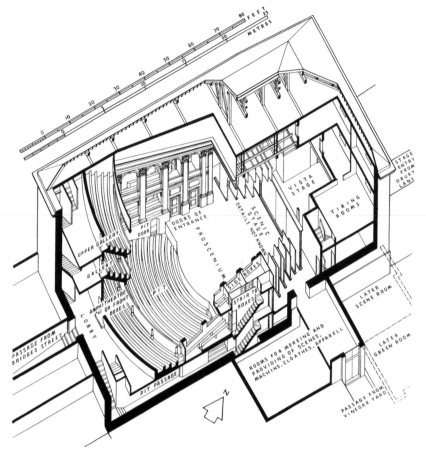

Figure 1 Isometric reconstruction of Drury Lane Theatre, 1674, by Richard Leacroft

The playhouses

The competition between Davenant and Killigrew in the 1660s became lopsided after the Duke's Company opened their Lincoln's Inn Fields Theatre with scenes and machines; the King's troupe needed a new playhouse, fully equipped to compete with their rivals. In 1663 the Bridges Street Theatre opened; eight years later the Duke's Company countered with a larger theatre in Dorset Garden, the most elegant of all the Restoration playhouses; and in 1674, after the Bridges Street building burned to the ground, the King's Company inaugurated, on the same site, Drury Lane (figs. 1 and 2). Not until 1705 did London see another new theatre, though Lincoln's Inn Fields was refurbished in 1695 and brought back into service. The new playhouse, the Queen's Theatre in the Hay-

Figure 2 Reconstruction of interior of Drury Lane Theatre, 1674, by Richard Leacroft

market, was designed by the playwright Vanbrugh but needed renovations before it became acoustically acceptable for plays. In time, it became a home for opera.

An important characteristic of all Restoration theatres, and unique to England, was an apron or forestage – an acting area forward of the curtain, thrusting well into the audience space, with permanent proscenium entrance doors on each side. Performers appearing on it stood in front of rather than in the scenic area, though they could, if they wished, move back and use the scenery as an environment instead of a decorative background. The forestage of Restoration playhouses was similar to the platform in Elizabethan public and private playhouses and to the performing space on the auditorium floor in front of court theatre stages. Regardless of the size or capacity of a theatre, an acting space that was part of the auditorium, close to the audience and flanked by spectators, contributed to the feeling of intimacy. The forestage was ideal for plays where words were important, and the retention of the area in Restoration playhouses meant that new authors were encouraged to write plays that were highly verbal and full of wit, with frequent soliloquies and asides to the audience. The forestage was variously called the platform, area, stage, theatre, scene, and proscenium. Colley Cibber, who began his acting at Drury Lane, later lamented the loss in the 1690s of that prized actor's space:

> It must be observ'd, then, that the Area or Platform of the old Stage, projected about four Foot forwarder, in a Semi-oval Figure, parallel to the Benches of the Pit; and that the former, lower Doors of Entrance for the Actors were brought down between the two foremost (and then only) Pilasters; in the Place of which Doors, now the two Stage-Boxes are fixt . . . By this Original Form, the usual Station of the Actors, in almost every Scene, was advanc'd at least ten Foot nearer to the Audience, than they now can be; because, not only from the Stage's being shorten'd in front, but likewise from the additional Interposition of those Stage-Boxes, the Actors (in respect to the Spectators, that fill them) are kept so much more backward from the main Audience than they us'd to be: But when the Actors were in Possession of that forwarder Space, to advance upon, the Voice was then more in the Centre of the House, so that the most distant Ear had scarce the least Doubt, or Difficulty in hearing what fell from the weakest Utterance...[7]

Occasionally plays required actors to withdraw from the forestage and relate more closely to the scenery. Some Restoration pieces specify entrances in the scenic area, and many ask for the scenery to open and discover characters already in place. Such action was seen by spectators through the picture frame or frontispiece formed by the proscenium arch. Consequently, stage directions sometimes refer to action "in the scene" – that is, not on the apron but within the scenic area. As the forestage was cut back to increase seating capacity, the unique proscenium doors were also lost, though the proscenium arch itself remained. Denied their forward acting area and its entrance doors, the actors had to retreat into the scenic stage, and that in time led to more realism in staging and acting.

When Davenant began performing in the summer of 1661 at his

Lincoln's Inn Fields playhouse, he offered scenery that Pepys found "very fine and magnificent."[8] How fine and magnificent was it, we might ask, for information on Restoration scenery is very scanty. What little evidence we have suggests that English scene painting was not as opulent as that in France and Italy, where opera had spurred great advances in stagecraft.[9] Still, scene designers and machinists in England and on the Continent worked in essentially the same fashion. Virtually everything then was painted in perspective, giving the illusion of depth and making it possible for Davenant in his little theatre in Lincoln's Inn Fields to show spectators what looked like a deep forest, seascape, or street. The scenery was not built in three dimensions but painted on flat, canvas-covered frames called wings, lined up on each side of the stage, with the view closed off about the middle of the scenic area with larger flats: shutters. The wings and shutters stood in grooves on the stage floor (steadied by matching grooves above) and could be slid offstage and on by teams of stagehands; a second set also stood in grooves, directly behind the first, so that when the first set was pulled off, the second was revealed. From these practices came stage directions in Restoration plays that may baffle or mislead a modern reader: scene opens, scene shuts, scene draws. Hanging above the wing positions were horizontal masking pieces, borders, that could be pulled up or down in coordination with the lateral movement of the wings. By the 1690s in England painted drops – large painted cloths, probably on rollers – began to replace the shutters.

To enhance the perspective effect, the stage floor in most Renaissance and baroque theatres was raked or sloped from front to back, thus giving us the terms upstage and downstage; similarly, the heights of the wings and shutters decreased. If the perspective was too forced, performers could not move upstage very far or they would ruin the visual effect. The painters adjusted the perspective accordingly by placing the vanishing point not at the back of the scenic area but far deeper, usually well behind the back wall of the theatre building. Most of the scenery any company owned could serve in several productions, though occasionally Restoration plays, especially musical pieces, were given some newly designed scenery to augment stock settings.

Scene shifting was normally accomplished in full view of the audience – *a vista* as the Italians dubbed it – for the changes were part of the show. They were like a dissolve in film-making and took only seconds, signaled by the sound of the prompter's whistle. The front curtain, hanging in British theatres between the scenic area and the forestage, just behind the proscenium opening, was lowered during the performance only when an elaborate tableau had to be arranged. Wing-shutter-border shifting was

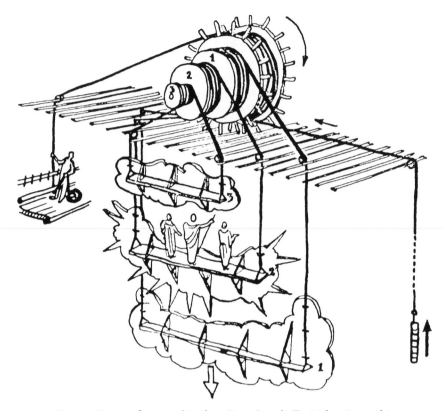

Figure 3 Baroque flying machine from Pierre Sonrel's *Traité de scénographie*

well suited to plays calling for many different locales and for episodes that lasted only a few lines. This meant that plays from the Shakespearean period could easily be produced with scenery and that new playwrights could ask for as many shifts as they wished. Today one can see the stunning effect of changeable scenery painted on wings, borders, and drops at such surviving baroque theatres as that at Drottningholm, Sweden.

Restoration theatres featured not only scenery but also machines for creating aerial flight, appearances from above and below, ocean waves, and other special effects (fig. 3). Many devices, such as cranes and trap doors, traced their roots back to the ancient Greeks, and almost all employed machines common in construction work through the ages. The London companies in their small theatres in the 1660s may not have been able to present London audiences with very elaborate shows, but their larger houses of the 1670s, Dorset Garden and Drury Lane, could handle striking painted and mechanical effects. Here is an example, from John Dryden's opera *Albion and Albanius*:

The Scene, is a Street of Palaces, which lead to the Front of the Royal Exchange; *the great Arch is open, and the view is continued through the open part of the* Exchange, *to the Arch on the other side, and thence to as much of the Street beyond, as could, properly be taken.*
Mercury descends in a Chariot drawn by Ravens.
He comes to Augusta, *and* Thamesis. *They lye on Couches, at a distance from each other, in dejected postures; She attended by Cities, He by Rivers.*
A double Pedestal rises: On the Front of it is painted, in Stone colour, two Women; one holding a double Fac'd Vizor; the other a Book, representing Hypocracy *and* Phanaticism … *they fall a sleep on the Pedestal, and it sinks with them.*

Then, after a dance of watermen in the King's and Duke's liveries,

The Clouds divide, and Juno *appears in a Machine drawn by Peacocks; while a Symphony is playing, it moves gently forward, and as it descends, it opens and discovers the Tail of the Peacock, which is so Large, that it almost fills the opening of the Stage between Scene and Scene.*[10]

And so it goes for four more acts, using borders that could be parted in the middle and pulled off to the sides, a crane and rolling platform that brought objects down from above and forward on the stage, trap doors through which objects on elevators were made to rise and sink, and quick changes of locale accomplished by shifting the wings, shutters, and borders. What Dryden asked for in *Albion and Albanius* the actor-manager Betterton could provide; such stage directions were common in operas, semi-operas, and "machine" plays in England and on the Continent.

Lighting, in this age before electricity, was not so changeable. To achieve what passed for darkness, stage candles could be dimmed by lowering perforated canisters over them, or chandeliers could be pulled higher above the stage, or footlights could be lowered in their troughs. Costumes were also an important part of the visual display. Davenant's *Love and Honour* in 1661, according to the prompter John Downes, "was Richly Cloath'd; The King giving Mr. *Betterton* his Coronation Suit, in which he Acted the Part of Prince *Alvaro*."[11] Musical theatre pieces often called for sumptuous costuming, but in many regular plays, except for special characters like the Ghost in *Hamlet*, the actors followed the Shakespearean custom and wore the fashions of the day. Most works were thus presented in "modern" dress, adding to the audience's sense of rapport with the world of the play.

Extravagant shows like *Albion and Albanius* were not the usual Restoration theatre fare. Far more common were plays requiring few special effects and mostly standard scenery. Wycherley's *The Country Wife*, for example, needs only five different settings: Horner's lodgings (a room setting), Pinchwife's house (a different room), the New Exchange and the Piazza of

Covent Garden (special exterior scenes depicting recognizable locales), and a bedchamber in Pinchwife's house (a third room). Playwrights sometimes gave no indication of locale in their stage directions, presumably because they knew the producer would supply from stock whatever seemed appropriate. Etherege in *The Man of Mode* described five locales but left six unspecified. The best plays of Congreve, Dryden, Etherege, Farquhar, Otway, Vanbrugh, and Wycherley do not call for much in the way of scenes and machines; Restoration authors of merit may not have wanted their dramas upstaged by the scenery. Plays with elaborate scenic demands were usually of a melodramatic or operatic nature, where a scenic feast was expected.

Audiences

Today we usually sit in theatres where most of the seats are oriented toward the stage, so that everyone has a good view of the performance. When the play is about to begin, the auditorium is darkened and the spectators quiet down. Though by the 1630s the Italians had devised ways of reducing the amount of light in the house, it was virtually impossible to plunge seventeenth-century spectators into darkness. An audience then was very conscious of itself and its part in the theatre event, whereas today, except in Brechtian productions, directors usually try to make an audience forget itself and succumb to the performance. A modern audience sitting in virtual darkness looking at a well-lit stage is lured into concentrating on whatever takes place there, simply because there is not much to see in the auditorium. The actors, under controlled lighting, can play in a small, realistic style, since they need not strain for the audience's attention. Imagine, by contrast, a house almost as well illuminated as the stage, where spectators could see one another throughout the performance. The seating arrangement placed many of them along each side of the auditorium, opera-house style, with a splendid view of other playgoers.

An audience in such a theatre will be less likely to remain quiet, and performers may be drawn toward a larger-than-life style. Further, many playgoers then did not attend a play to find out what happens next, for they already knew many of the plots. They did not come to see if Hamlet would revenge his father's murder but how this or that actor would play a familiar part. It was a performer's theatre, especially when old plays were revived, which they regularly were, and which spectators came to see again and again.

Pepys' *Diary* contains frequent references to playgoing. His affair with the theatre took place in the 1660s, when the Restoration stage was finding itself. What he liked was the act of going to the theatre, and if he was pleased with the play or the production, all the better. Often it was a social adventure:

> Thence ... with my wife by coach to the Duke of York's play-house, expecting a new play; so stayed not no more then other people, but to the King's to *The Mayds Tragedy*; but vexed all the while with two talking ladies and Sir Ch. Sidly, yet pleased to hear their discourse, he being a stranger; and one of the ladies would, and did, sit with her mask on all the play; and being exceeding witty as ever I heard woman, did talk most pleasantly with him; but was, I believe, a virtuous woman and of quality. He would fain know who she was, but she would not tell. Yet did give him many pleasant hints of her knowledge of him, by that means setting his brains at work to find out who she was; and did give him leave to use all means to find out who she was but pulling off her mask. He was mighty witty; and she also making sport with him very inoffensively, that a more pleasant rencontre I never heard. But by that means lost the pleasure of the play wholly.[12]

Other afternoons – for performances were after lunch – Pepys was less distracted. Even if he didn't particularly like a new play, he would often see it as many as three times in a month, partly because of his great curiosity and partly because he, like many others, was stage-struck. As the years passed, the audience became less fashionable, as Pepys noted in 1668: "Here a mighty company of citizens, prentices and others; and it makes me observe that when I begin first to be able to bestow a play on myself, I do not remember that I saw so many by half of the ordinary prentices and mean people in the pit."[13] The audience, more than the physical features of theatres, affects the course of drama, determining whether, in a given age, it is mostly serious or comic, frivolous, melodramatic, spectacular, lofty, or what have you. The actor needs no more than two boards and a passion, but the spectators may want more, and the audience, for better or worse, determines the theatre's fate and dictates what kind of theatre a period gets.

Sometimes for Pepys and others the play was not the thing. On 5 October 1667, for example, he went to

> the Duke of York's playhouse; but the House so full, it being a new play *The Coffee-house*, that we could not get in, and so to the King's House; and there going in, met with [the actress Elizabeth] Knipp and she took us up into the Tireing-rooms and to the women's Shift, where Nell [Gwyn] was dressing herself and was all unready; and is very pretty, prettier then I thought; and so walked all up and down the House above, and then below into the Scene-room [i.e. the Green Room or actors' lounge], and there sat down and she gave us fruit; and here I read the Qu's to Knepp while she answered me, through all her part of *Flora's Figarys*, which was acted today. But Lord, to

see how they were both painted would make a man mad – and did make me loath them – and what base company comes among them, and how lewdly they talk – and how poor the men are in clothes, and yet what a show they make on the stage by candle-light, is very observable. But to see how Nell cursed for having so few people in the pit was pretty, and the other House carrying away all the people at the new play, and is said nowadays to have generally most company, as being better players. By and by into the pit and there saw the play; which is pretty good.[14]

The easy access to backstage areas was not abused by Pepys, but some other patrons were not so well-behaved. Royal proclamations begged audience members not to interfere with the workings of the stage machinery, and actresses were not safe from bullies and hangers-on. The dashing actor-singer-dancer William Mountfort was killed by two young playgoers jealous of Mountfort's supposed attachment to the actress Anne Bracegirdle, who was nearly kidnapped by the culprits.

Many theatre patrons went to playhouses for lack of anything better to do or to impress others or to search for sexual game. The playwright Thomas Shadwell in *A True Widow* set the beginning of Act 4 in a playhouse and satirized the very people who paid to see his work at Dorset Garden Theatre in March 1678. After the main characters have arrived at the theatre,

> *Several more come in, Women mask'd, and Men of several sorts.*
> *Several young Coxcombs fool with the Orange-Women.*
> *Orange-Wo.* Oranges; Will you have any Oranges?
> *1 Bull.* What Play do they play? some confounded Play or other.
> *Prig.* A pox on't, Madam! what should we do at this damn'd Play-house? Let's send for some Cards, and play at Lang-trilloo in the Box; Pox on 'em! I ne'r saw a Play had any thing in't; some of 'em have Wit now and then, but what care I for Wit.
> *Self.* Does my Cravat sit well? I take all the care I can it should; I love to appear well. What Ladies are here in the Boxes? really I never come to a Play, but upon account of seeing the Ladies.
> *Car. Door-keeper*, are they ready to begin?
> *Door-keep.* Yes, immediately.
>
>   *   *   *
>
> *1 Bull.* Dam'me! When will these Fellows begin? Plague o'nt! here's a staying.
> *2 Man.* Whose Play is this?
> *3 Man.* One *Prickett's*, Poet *Prickett*.
> *1 Man.* Oh hang him! Pox on him! he cannot write; prithee let's to *White-hall.*
> *Enter several Ladies, and several Men.*
> *Door-keep.* Pray, Sir, pay me, my Masters will make me pay it.

3 Man. Impudent Rascal! Do you ask me for Money? Take that, Sirrah.

2 Door-keep. Will you pay me, Sir?

4 Man. No: I don't intend to stay.

2 Door-keep. So you say every day, and see two or three Acts for nothing.

4 Man. I'll break your Head, you Rascal.

1 Door-keep. Pray, Sir, pay me.

3 Man. Set it down, I have no Silver about me, or bid my Man pay you.

Theod. What, do Gentlemen run on tick for Plays?

Car. As familiarly as with their Taylors[.]

3 [Man]. Pox on you, Sirrah! go and bid 'em begin quickly.

                              [Ex. *Door-keeper.*

   They play the Curtain-[tune], then take their places.

Car. Now they'll begin.   [*Selfish and Young Maggot go to sit down.*[15]

Soon the play begins, with the "audience" paying attention for a few speeches and then interpolating comments, criticisms, and tomfoolery. Finally, swords are drawn and a fight begins. One of the actors enters out of character and says "We cannot go on with our Play, one of our young Women being frighted with the Swords, is fallen into a Fit, and carried homesick."[16] Shadwell may have been exaggerating for comic effect, but his satire would not have worked had he not based his scene on some facts of theatre life. For many Restoration spectators, theatre was a game, like the games played out in so many plays of the period, and patrons enjoyed watching these imitations of immorality that were comfortably (or uncomfortably) like the game of life they played themselves. How frequently spectators disrupted performances we cannot tell, but the conventions of playgoing and performing in the 1600s provided ample opportunities for the fops and ruffians to misbehave, especially if a play was poor enough not to warrant polite attention in the first place. In a period when characters frequently spoke lines to the audience, it should not be surprising if the audience talked back.

Though there is ample evidence of obstreperous behavior by patrons in Restoration theatres, we also know that the best actors could capture the attention of the crowd. Here is a description of Thomas Betterton at the climax of the closet scene in *Hamlet*:

And when *Hamlet* utters this Line, upon the Ghost's leaving the Stage (in Answer to his Mother's impatient Enquiry into the Occasion of his Disorder, and what he sees) – *See – where he goes – ev'n now – out at the Portal*: The whole Audience hath remain'd in a dead Silence for near a Minute, and then – as if recovering all at once from their Astonishment, have joined as one Man, in a Thunder of universal Applause.[17]

That was one of the things the audience came for: acting that could take their breath away.

Visitors from the Continent sometimes left accounts of playgoing experiences, and their comments also give us helpful pictures of Restoration theatres and audiences. In 1667 Samuel Chappuzeau called Lincoln's Inn Fields "admirably successful with machinery, and ... now equal to the Italians." He noted that the London theatres "are attended by well-to-do people, and above all by beautiful women; that their theatres are superb in decoration and [scene] changes; that the music there is excellent and the ballets magnificent; that they have not less than a dozen violins each for the preludes and the between-acts; that it would be a crime to use anything other than wax-light to illuminate the theatre."[18] Henri Misson in 1698 left us our best description of London theatres at the end of the Restoration period:

> There are two Theatres at *London*, one [Dorset Garden] large and handsome, where they sometimes act Opera's, and sometimes Plays; the other [Drury Lane] something smaller, which is only for Plays. The Pit is an Amphitheatre, fill'd with Benches without Backboards, and adorn'd and cover'd with green Cloth. Men of Quality, particularly the younger Sort, some Ladies of Reputation and Vertue, and abundance of Damsels that hunt for Prey, sit all together in this Place, Higgledy-piggledy, chatter, toy, play, hear, hear not. Farther up [at the back of the auditorium], against the Wall, under the first Gallery, and just opposite to the Stage, rises another Amphitheatre, which is taken up by Persons of the best Quality, among whom are generally very few Men. The Galleries, whereof there are only two Rows [i.e. tiers], are fill'd with none but ordinary People, particularly the Upper one.[19]

The chief fault foreigners found concerned not the theatres but the English playwrights' custom of ignoring the unities of time, place and action.[20]

The theatre experience for Restoration playgoers consisted of many things: the histrionics of the players, the contributions of the spectators as they enjoyed the social occasion and responded to the performance, the skill of the scene painters and technicians, the smell and flickering of the candles, the magic of the scene changes, the splendor of the costumes, the beauty of the music and dance, and the impact of the play – which was the thing for which all the rest was created. It was far more theatrical than what we usually get today and closer, perhaps, to Japanese Kabuki, which was developing in the seventeenth century. Any theatre form we are not accustomed to calls for a willing suspension of disbelief, as Coleridge called it, if we are to appreciate the unfamiliar form on its own terms rather than ours. But suspending disbelief needs to be assisted by our imaginations, especially when we do not have the help of a theatrical production. Plays from the Restoration period were written for theatrical conditions that we cannot easily revive, but we can imagine: relatively intimate theatres catering to a clientele largely from the leisured class, auditoria illuminated throughout a performance, spectators very conscious of their part in the theatre experience and able to relate to the characters and situations they witness, a prominent forestage where much of the acting took place, plays embellished with music and dance, scenery used more as a background than an environment, scene changes *a vista*, elaborate and fanciful machines ... Just imagine.

NOTES

1 Public Record Office, London, manuscript SP29/8/1.
2 Graham Barlow, "Gibbons's Tennis Court: Hollar v. Wilkinson," *TRI* 8 (1983), 130–46.
3 Samuel Pepys, *The Diary of Samuel Pepys* (1660–68), ed. Robert Latham and William Matthews, 11 vols. (Berkeley: University of California Press, 1970–83), I, 297.
4 Male domination of the acting profession goes back at least to the ancient Greeks. The good news is that it was largely responsible for the strong female characters created by Greek and Elizabethan playwrights. But England lagged far behind the Continent in accepting actresses on the public stage. For a study of Restoration actresses see Elizabeth Howe, *The First English Actresses* (Cambridge University Press, 1992).
5 [James Wright], *Historia Histrionica* (London, 1699), p. 5.
6 Pepys, *Diary*, VIII, 55. Compare with Wright's view, above, and Chappuzeau's, below.
7 Colley Cibber, *An Apology for the Life of Colley Cibber* (1740), ed. B. R. S. Fone (Ann Arbor: University of Michigan Press, 1968), p. 225.
8 Pepys, *Diary*, II, 131.
9 See Richard Southern, *Changeable Scenery* (London: Faber & Faber, 1952), Jocelyn Powell, *Restoration Theatre Production* (London: Routledge & Kegan Paul, 1984), and Per Bjurström, *Giacomo Torelli and Baroque Stage Design*, 2nd edn. (Stockholm: Almqvist & Wiksell, 1962).
10 John Dryden, *Albion and Albanius* (London, 1685), pp. 1–7 *passim*.
11 John Downes, *Roscius Anglicanus; or, An Historical Review of the Stage* (1708), ed. Judith Milhous and Robert D. Hume (London: Society for Theatre Research, 1987), p. 52.
12 Pepys, *Diary*, VIII, 71–72.
13 Ibid., IX, 2. Scholars argue about the makeup of Restoration audiences. It must have varied over the years and from one kind of production to another, but it is probably safe to say that the aristocrats in the audience were a strong influence on the companies and their managers. See Harold Love, "Who were the Restoration Audience?" *YES* 10 (1980), 21– 44.
14 Pepys, *Diary*, VIII, 463–64.
15 Thomas Shadwell, *A True Widow* (London, 1679), pp. 49–50.
16 Ibid., p. 55.

17 *The Laureat* (London, 1740), p. 31. Peter Holland in *The Ornament of Action* (Cambridge University Press, 1979) makes a case for Restoration acting style being more naturalistic than has usually been supposed. Given the performance circumstances, the style would probably not have been as "natural" as we see today, but perhaps not greatly exaggerated, either. In the eighteenth century, Garrick's style seemed naturalistic in comparison with the more formal style of his predecessors. Betterton's style may have seemed more natural than that used earlier in the seventeenth century.

18 Samuel Chappuzeau, *L'Europe vivante* (Paris, 1667), p. 214–15. Trans. C. Hodgson. Compare with Killigrew's boast, above.

19 *M. Misson's Memoirs and Observations in His Travels over England* (1698), trans. J. Ozell (London, 1719), pp. 219–20.

20 Extrapolating from Aristotle, Renaissance critics decreed: a play should have one action (plot), covering no more than twenty-four hours, in a single locale.

2

JOSEPH ROACH

The performance

Restoration actors and actresses worked very hard. Acting on approximately two hundred days of the year over the course of an eight- or nine-month season (not counting summer tours and fairs), key company members could each be expected to play on relatively short notice perhaps as many as thirty different roles. The bills changed quickly, alternating between stock plays, revivals from recent seasons, and new plays. In the face of sometimes fickle demand for drama (daily attendance at plays varied considerably throughout the period), the actors and actresses supplied a specialized and highly skilled service – the performance.[1]

Their business, practically speaking, was to embody the characters sketched by the playwrights, but their larger, unstated task was to provide their audiences with symbolic actions of various kinds. Whether they intended to or not, actors and actresses in Restoration England made themselves objects of public fantasy. According to Tom Brown, the acid-tongued observer of the London underworld, their workplace became known as the "Enchanted Island," and their job was to populate it with attractive (and compliant) natives. Brown's account of this indigenous population takes the form of a contemporary travel narrative of a voyage to an exotic paradise. On this "Enchanted Island," the natives will change into anything in order to keep the tourists coming back:

> The *Playhouse* was the *Land of Enchantment*, the *Country of Metamorphosis*, and perform'd it with the greatest speed imaginable. Here, in the twinkling of an Eye, you shall see Men transform'd into *Demi-gods*, and *Goddesses* made as true Flesh and Blood as our Common Women. Here *Fools* by slight of hand are converted into *Wits*, *Honest Women* into *errand Whores*, and which is most miraculous, *Cowards* into *valiant Heroes*, and rank *Coquet*s and *Jilts* into as chaste and virtuous *Mistresses* as a Man would desire to put his *Knife* into.[2]

The sexual violence of Brown's final image suggests the underlying ambivalence of the fantasies that the performers evoked. Although theirs was a marginal profession at or beyond the periphery of social respectability, which rendered them vulnerable to exploitation and abuse, paradoxically they did cultural work that featured glamorous representations of socially dominant roles, from royal surrogates to romantic or erotic icons. As their images and reputations began to circulate freely in the absence of their persons, actors and actresses became the first modern celebrities – popularly recognized public figures who were not also kings or queens, "Demigods" or "Goddesses," except by authority of their theatrical performances of those roles.

In 1660 this paradox of strength and vulnerability, which remains characteristic of celebrity performances to this day, ran upward to the titular head of the theatres, the royal sovereign himself. The original warrant issued by King Charles II to the eventual patentees spoke not only of the profanation and debauchery associated with the "acting and performance" of plays, but also of their redemptive power to offer "such kind of entertainments which if well managed might serve as moral instructions of human life."[3] The posthumous *Life* of the hardest-working actor of the age, Thomas Betterton (1635–1710), drew an explicit parallel between the fragility of the "Mimic State" or "Government" of the theatres and the dynastic state of the Stuart monarchy.[4] The son of an assistant cook in the service of Charles I, Betterton, who made his debut in 1659 with the Restoration of the Stuarts and died as their dynastic twilight approached, twice wore the borrowed coronation robes of Charles II as theatrical costumes. In his earlier years, Betterton wrote sexually explicit plays and acted the parts of rakes, but he was nevertheless remembered by the moralist Richard Steele as an exemplary figure for the actions he performed, not the least of which was his role in the early canonization of Shakespeare.[5] Alexander Pope wrote him an epitaph – "The Sweetest Part of Life well-lived is the Remembrance" – and painted a haunting version of his portrait by Kneller (fig. 4). Understanding the complex position held by this exceptional actor is the key to a general understanding of an institutional paradox: that the socially objectionable performer, whose art was by definition ephemeral, became the caretaker of cultural memory.

Remembering Betterton's art on the occasion of the interment of his body in the cloisters of Westminster Abbey in 1710, Steele compares the spectacle of the funerals of great and accomplished men to the sobering effect of public executions on the "rude and untaught Multitude." Both executions and burials are in their own ways morally edifying performances, *The Tatler* avows. Steele links them to the theatrical performances given by the great actor, "from whose Action I had received more strong Impressions of what is great and noble in Human Nature, than from the

Figure 4 Thomas Betterton, after Godfrey Kneller

Arguments of the most solid Philosophers, or the Descriptions of the most charming Poets I had ever read."[6] Like the contradictory and variegated roles played by the restored king himself,[7] the dramatic representations enacted on the stage explicitly drew attention to their dual nature as performances: they titillated the spectators with the weakness of human flesh while edifying them with its promised redemption in the continuity of "the body politic" or imagined community. This difficult job – of symbolically mediating between the one and the many – required majestic dramatic

Figure 5 Engraving of the Theatre Royal, 1698, from John Eccles's *Theater Musick*

"Action" performed in a space especially dedicated and provided with magical effects for the occasion – a "Theatre Royal."

Visual evidence showing performers actually at work together onstage (as opposed to their individual portraits) is scarce for the period 1660–1710. Historians must speculate on the basis of limited evidence, corroborating it where possible with stage directions from the plays and written descriptions from such sources as contemporary diaries and memoirs. Images that survive show the actors and actresses "opened out"; that is, mainly facing the audience, even when they are addressing each other, for which purpose they turn their heads to the side. The elaborate stage picture marked "The Theatre Royall," which appeared as the frontispiece to John Eccles's *Theater Musick* (1698), plagiarizes an engraving from a French opera but anglicizes it by inserting the title and motto from the Theatre Royal, Drury Lane (fig. 5).[8] This image, which may have been intended to puff the "Enchanted Wilderness" scene from Eccles's and John Dennis's forthcoming *Rinaldo and Armida* (1699) or the "temple of the palace" vista in Daniel Purcell's *The Island Princess* (1699), resembles in most respects the stage pictures for a spoken drama as represented by the oft-reproduced plates published as illustrations to Elkannah Settle's *The Empress of Morocco* of 1673 (fig. 6a–d). In both cases, *The Empress of Morocco* and "The Theatre Royall," scenery painted in perspective dominates the vista behind the proscenium arch. No furniture or other dimensional properties, however, encumber the stage. This economy facilitates not only the movement of the actors and actresses (the latter in flowing gowns and petticoats), but also the rapid shifting of the painted scenery, which was called into dynamic movement before the eyes of the audience by the prompter's audible whistle. Arranged in a line parallel to the apron of the stage, their bodies turned *contraposto*, weight unevenly distributed to make an interesting line of the body, the principal performers gesture broadly from their open stances.

This does not necessarily mean that actors and actresses performed in what is too frequently assumed to have been an "artificial style." Artifice is in the eye of the beholder, not to mention in the historical period of the beholder, and all stage performance is in some way stylized. Style, in fact, might be helpfully defined as social order as it is lived in the bodies of individual subjects. When individual subjects have lived with a style long enough, they begin to think of it as nature – until an innovator draws their attention to its artifice. Perhaps what makes Restoration performance seem particularly "stylized" is that the reciprocal construction of nature (passion and mortality) and second nature (manners and ceremony) is openly understood, acknowledged, and even celebrated in this period. The "Theatre

Figure 6 Four engravings of scenery from Settle's *Empress of Morocco*

Royall" engraving obviously records a moment of more than ordinary theatrical impact, no doubt well-motivated by the internal machinations of the dramatic action, but presented forthrightly to the spectators as a show. One character (the figure downstage right, or on the audience's left) has "taken stage," that is, he has conspicuously drawn attention to himself, evidently by having made a startling revelation. He has violently punctuated the moment by throwing his feathered helmet to the ground. The other figures respond uniformly in astonishment, as if by collective reflex action.

Astonishment is an oft-represented emotion in Restoration performance, perhaps because it was one of the most desired effects, akin to what the French dramatist Corneille called *admiration*, that the producers hoped to impart to the audience. The French source of the scene depicted as taking place in "The Theatre Royall" might further suggest such a kinship: *admiration*, a mixture of astonishment, awe, and mimetic desire, aptly describes the nature of the fantasies audiences entertained about Restoration heroes, heroines, and the flesh-and-blood performers who embodied them. The prevailing mode of that fantasy might be called public intimacy, the privilege of being present at scenes expressive of vulnerability poignantly juxtaposed to overwhelming strength. In the physical arrangements of Restoration spectatorship, audience members could be seated on the stage, and at times they were there in sufficient numbers to impede the actors' entrances and exits. Spectators could also move about freely during the acts as well as between the acts, buying fruit or meeting acquaintances, so every performance was at some level a test of how well the performers could gain and hold the admiring attention of the spectators. Betterton was especially revered for the way in which his commanding voice "enforc'd universal Attention, even from the *Fops* and the *Orange-girls*."[9] That the promotional image engraved to enhance Eccles's *Theater Musick* evoked the scene of an "enchanted wilderness" or perhaps the magical abode of an "island princess" might also suggest the sense of entitlement that audiences must have felt as they entered the precincts of "The Theatre Royall" and dared the natives to astonish them.

The emphatically performative (or presentational) nature of the Restoration theatre was reinforced by the prologues and epilogues, in which the performers addressed the audience directly and enlisted (if possible) their sympathetic participation, and by soliloquies and asides, in which the dramatic characters did the same. The playtexts record these moments of public intimacy. William Wycherley's *The Country Wife* (1675) begins with an aside, in which the scheming Horner, played by the same actor who had just spoken the prologue, takes the audience into his confidence without delay. In most plays of the period, the audience is flattered by being allowed to share in the knowledge possessed by the smartest and most attractive characters but withheld from the fops and fools. The intimate by-play necessary to savor the ironies of such discrepant awareness, which could include audience members answering back to the actors on the stage, required a playing space of a particular openness, flexibility, and proximity.

What "The Theatre Royall" engraving does not show (though the *Empress of Morocco* illustrations do) is the typical architectural arrangement of the forestage of the Restoration playhouse. This was a raised platform providing an open acting area flanked on either side by practical entrances known as "proscenium doors." The doors permitted efficient entrances and exits in convenient proximity to the downstage area, and this permanently imposed pattern of stage movement must have tended to draw the players downstage (away from the scenery), except in specialized scenes of concealment, discovery, or enclosure. The theatrical magic generated by the placement of the performers further forward in the midst of the spectators was defended by the actor Colley Cibber: he vehemently opposed alterations to the Drury Lane Theatre in 1696 that attenuated the forestage and moved the actors back closer to the scenes. His protest gives a hint at what he valued most in performance. The appearance of actors on the forestage, he argued, made visible "the minutest Motion of a Feature (properly changing with the Passion or Humour it suited)" and made audible "a voice scarce raised above the Tone of a Whisper." The loss of public intimacy described by Cibber must have been as much psychological as physical, for the reduction in question measured no more than ten feet.[10]

In performance the most important element of the unfolding action of the play was the grouping, which may be defined as the roll-call of characters assembled on the stage at a particular moment. In the French theatre, such a grouping constituted a scene, which changed with every exit or entrance. In the English theatre, the scene referred to the locale, which changed only when the scenery did. The performance of a Restoration play consisted of a series of continuous groupings – solos, duets, trios, quartets, etc. A reader of these plays today needs to be attentive to the by-play between characters in each grouping, including the presence of silent characters (who tend to be forgotten in reading, though not in performance). An example would be the continuous presence of Harriet's maid Busy in the "proviso scene," where the terms of Harriet's betrothal to Dorimant are wittily negotiated, in Act 5, scene 2 of *The Man of Mode; or, Sir Fopling Flutter* (1676).

Conventionally, the groupings ebbed and flowed across the playing space until a change of scene or the end of an act cleared the stage. To punctuate the continuous bustle of changing groupings and scenes, music played briefly between acts, and sometimes there was a dance or novelty act in these interludes. With the grouping as the dominant scenic element, entrances and exits were important events, marked by formal salutations or valedictions. This convention is simultaneously honored and mocked by William Congreve in *The Way of the World* (1700), when witty Mirabell welcomes even wittier Millamant by comparing her arrival in St. James Park accompanied by a fop to a great ship being piloted into harbor: "Here she comes, i'faith, full sail, with her fan spread and her streamers out, and a shoal of fools for tenders" (Act 2). In any well-written play, each grouping accelerates or deflects the on-going action by delivering new information or by complicating the existing circumstances. Millamant sails in with the news that she pins up her hair only in verse, never prose – and that she is fully apprised of the latest twist of Mirabell's plot to win her hand by blackmailing her superannuated guardian. "Sententious" (pompous) Mirabell makes the mistake of trying to persuade her "for one moment to be serious." Her abrupt exit with her maid in train leaves him sputtering in soliloquy, a mid-sentence transformation of a trio into a solo by the departure of a "whirlwind." Millamant, who entered as the fancied ship, has ended the grouping by taking the wind out of Mirabell's sails. In order to do their work effectively, performers had to know how to exploit such a rapidly changing panoply of dramatic opportunity.

The actors' and actresses' tools included voice, movement, histrionic sensibility (the capacity to express a wide range of emotions), and excellent memory. As Cibber suggested, it was a great advantage for the actor or actress to be able to register palpable transitions between emotional states, which were known as "Passions" and "Humours." Here the implied stage directions embedded in dramatic dialogue offer some extraordinary challenges to the actors, especially in tragedy. A number of these passages were later collected in the *Thesaurus Dramaticus* (1724). In each instance, the character draws attention to his or her emotional states or describes those of fellow characters. This happens in a context that obligates the performers to represent or somehow suggest the perturbations to which the attention of the audience has been drawn. In Thomas Otway's *The Orphan*, for instance, actors and audiences alike had to answer this question:

> Read'st thou not something in my Face, that speaks
> Wonderful Change, and Horror from within me?

In John Dryden's *Love Triumphant*, the spectators could not help but test their perceptions of the vascular metamorphoses explicitly promised to them:

See, the King reddens:
The Fear which seiz'd at Alphonso's Sight is vanish'd now;
And a new Tide returns upon his Cheeks,
And Rage, and Vengeance sparkle in his Eyes.

Not only the countenance of the performer but the action of his or her entire body could be similarly ventriloquized. An implied stage direction attributed by the *Thesaurus Dramaticus* to a play by John Dennis aspires to the condition of choreography:

In his Looks appears
A mild distracted Fierceness: I can read
Some dreadful Purpose in his Face.
Sometimes his Anger breaks thro' all Disguises,
And spares, nor Gods, nor Men: And then he seems
Jealous of all the World; suspects, and starts,
And looks behind him.

Even if the reader judiciously emends "mild" to read "wild," the dialogue directs the performer to represent radical alterations of action and expression while simultaneously alerting the audience to the obligatory effects. Like fancy directions for elaborate scenic effects in printed versions of plays, however, implied stage directions do not guarantee that the expressions there described were delivered exactly as specified in performance. For example, it is hard to imagine what Nathanial Lee really expected the actress to do with this line from *The Rival Queens*: "My Breasts grow bigger with the vast Delight."[11]

At the same time, representation of the changing Passions and Humours were as much a convention of Restoration performance as the changing scenery, and historians have to reckon with the fact that actors and actresses were tested on these "points." Indeed, the surviving anecdotal accounts attest to the extraordinary effectiveness of transformations of the Passions. *The Laureate* (1740), for instance, memorializes Betterton's response to the Ghost in the closet scene of *Hamlet*:

I have lately been told by a Gentleman who has frequently seen Mr. *Betterton* perform this part of *Hamlet*, that he has observ'd his Countenance (which was naturally ruddy and sanguin) in this Scene of the fourth Act where his Father's Ghost appears, thro' the violent and sudden Emotions of Amazement and Horror, turn instantly on the Sight of his Father's Spirit, as pale as his Neckcloth, when every Article of his Body seem'd to be affected with a Tremor inexpressible; so that, had his Father's Ghost actually risen before him; he could not have been seized with more real Agonies; and this was felt so strongly by the Audience, that the Blood seemed to shudder in their Veins likewise, and they in Some Measure partook of the Astonishment and Horror, with which they saw this excellent Actor affected.[12]

No one will ever know for certain if Betterton physically embodied this affect or whether he just made spectators think that he did. In either case, Betterton's Hamlet was his most enduring role, at least measured by the number and the intensity of the responses to it. Many historians believe that an illustration of the closet scene published in Rowe's *Shakespear* of 1709 depicts Betterton's staging (fig. 7). *The Life of Betterton* records some explicit instructions, attributed to the actor himself, which do correspond to the action depicted in the illustration:

> In all regular Gestures of the Hands, they ought perfectly to correspond with one another, as in starting in a Maze, on a sudden Fright, as *Hamlet* in the Scene betwixt him and his Mother, on the Appearance of his Father's Ghost – *Save me, and hover o'er me with your Wings, You Heavenly Guards!* This is spoke with Arms and Hands extended, and expressing his Concern, as well as his Eyes, and Whole Face.   (Gildon, *Life of Betterton*, p. 74)

Perhaps equally important for an understanding of the symbolic role of historic performance is the reverence with which Betterton's eloquence is inscribed in memory by *The Life of Betterton*, *The Laureate*, and other sources. A stage player and manager who was elsewhere compared unfavorably with shopkeepers and pimps (*Biographical Dictionary*, II, 84), Betterton became the first working professional whose actions were set down with the kind of detail that was previously reserved to record the behavior of kings.

The paradox of the performer's social standing intruded even on the most practical aspects of his or her job. Some of the physical skills required of actors and actresses belied their low status and generally humble origins: fencing was *de rigueur* for most of the men, who wore their own swords and had to know how to use them (though they could get into deep trouble for doing so);[13] so was graceful management of voluminous clothing for the women, who owned their own gowns and accessories and had to know how to use *them*. Ravishing good looks also helped, including unblemished skin and good teeth, as did the abilities to sing, to dance, and to execute specialized comic routines, even though some of the most prominent and beloved stars, including Betterton himself, showed marked deficiencies in each of these areas. Charismatic appeal was an attribute harder to specify but even more important in the longest and most brilliant careers.

With the reopening of the theatres at the Restoration, the most charismatic actors were those who had been displaced by the closing of the theatres in 1642, including Charles Hart and Michael Mohun. Steele

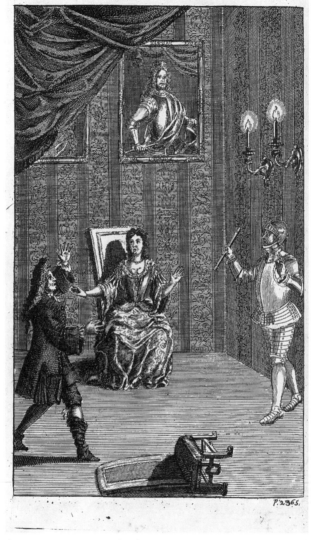

Figure 7 Thomas Betterton as Hamlet, frontispiece engraving to *Hamlet*, possibly from a Restoration production, in Rowe's *Works of Shakespear*, vol. VII

memorialized them by separating the qualities of natural and acquired virtuosity: "My old Friends, *Hart* and *Mohun*; the one by his natural and proper Force, the other by his great Skill and Art, never failed to send me Home full of such Idea's as affected my Behavior, and made me insensibly more courteous and humane to my Friends and Acquaintance" (*Tatler*, II, 108). The two had rallied to the cause of Charles I, the lamented "Royal Martyr" (Gildon, *Life of Betterton*, p. 18), Mohun rising to the rank of

Captain in the royal service. Hart had apprenticed as a boy actor, playing women's parts, including the Duchess in Shirley's *The Cardinal* (Thomas Wright, *Historia Histrionica*, in *Cibber*, i, xxiv), but in his adult career he undertook the leading roles of heroes and kings. Reversing the roles of Gildon's conception of the theatre as a "Mimic State," the old prompter John Downes recorded that "*Hart* might Teach any King on Earth how to Comport himself."[14]

One of the problems of the Restoration was coming to terms with what was possible or desirable to restore. The veteran actors carried over an historic performance tradition and adapted it to fit a substantially new political and cultural moment. Even before the triumphal return of Charles II, they were joined in improvised playing spaces by younger men, including Betterton and Edward Kynaston, and soon after the Restoration by the first English actresses, including Katherine Corey, Anne Marshall, and Mary Saunderson (later Mrs. Betterton). Later additions to the ranks of actresses included Nell Gwynn, Elizabeth Barry, and Anne Bracegirdle. The revolutionary introduction of women onto the English stage was a deliberate act of policy in the name of the reformation of morals, an act that was shared between the royal state and the "Mimic State," a clear instance of cultural authority improvising itself through reciprocal performances onstage and behind the scenes: "And we do likewise permit and give leave," the king nudged his patentees, "that all the women's parts to be acted in either of the said two companies for the time to come may be performed by women."[15] The King subsequently carried on sexual liaisons with some of the actresses, most notoriously Moll Davis and Nell Gwynn, which marked them in their public performances. Speaking the epilogue to Dryden's *Tyrannick Love* (1669), Gwynn was made to rhyme "Saint Cattern" (St. Catherine), the part she had just played in this tragedy, with "slattern," the popularly known role that she was then playing – and flaunting – in the royal service. The "Enchanted Island" of the London playhouse provided a stage for the lovers' actual adultery as it did for so many imaginary ones: the king's ledgers include the record of a payment to Nell Gwynn treating the actress and her friends to theatre tickets at the rival house (Hume and Milhous, *Register*, vol. i, document 862).

In hindsight, the introduction of actresses for the purpose of moral reform does seem counter-intuitive, but the royal warrants and patents responded strategically to objections to reopening the playhouses because they were likely to serve up cross-dressed boys as catalysts to "unnatural vice." John Dennis, in his defense of "The Usefulness of the Stage" (1698) against Jeremy Collier's moralistic attacks, touts its heteroerotic appeal as a bulwark against sodomy, even though the beautiful Kynaston had played both women and men with equally seductive effect. Certainly, cross-dressed women, showing off their legs in tight pants, made themselves indispensable to the convention of erotic disguise on the putatively reformed stage: of the 375 new plays or adaptations performed between 1660 and 1700, no fewer than 89 contained one or more "breeches" parts.[16]

The newly formed companies, the Duke of York's under Sir William Davenant and the King's under Thomas Killigrew, divided up the repertoire of pre-Restoration plays and put the actors and actresses to work in them. Davenant generally attracted the younger actors, including Betterton and eventually Elizabeth Barry, who was raised in the Davenant household, to the Duke's Company. The veterans Hart and Mohun were, along with Kynaston, King's Company actors. That division remained until the union of the companies in 1682, an arrangement which lasted until 1695, when Betterton and the established actors revolted against the mismanagement of Drury Lane by Christopher Rich and established their own rival company elsewhere. To appreciate the obligations of these performers to their companies it is necessary to understand the dynamics of the repertoire. Acting in a revolving repertory of plays in various genres, some of them hybrid and experimental, the players typically had to do their jobs in such a lively way as to keep audiences coming back to the afternoon performances while they rehearsed the next days' shows morning and night. Only success in the afternoon could turn characters on the page into enduring roles for the stage – the vessels of public memory and their companies' fortunes across the years. In this theatre, the material fact of performance predominated, and playwrights' names did not even appear on the advertising playbills until the 1690s.

If a show succeeded in winning a place in the permanent repertoire – if it was animated by what John Downes called "the life of Stock play" (*Roscius Anglicanus*, p. 100) – then the actors and actresses had to sustain their roles in memory over many years, in some cases over their entire professional lifetimes. Memory in this instance included not only the playwrights' words (and performers differed in their fidelity to the text), but also the physical delivery of those words with appropriate expressions, intonations, motions, gestures, and business. Downes believed that Betterton learned the business for his performance of the role of Hamlet from Sir William Davenant, who in turn had learned it from the actor Joseph Taylor, who had been instructed in the part by Shakespeare himself (*Roscius Anglicanus*, pp. 51–52). Downes constructs a similar genealogy of performance for Betterton's acting of Henry VIII: Davenant taught Betterton; John Lowin taught Davenant; Shakespeare taught Lowin (pp. 55–56). In testifying to these theatrical begats, Downes imagines a line of legitimate succession descending from an originary moment of canonical authority like a royal dynasty.

Drama is an art of actions in time. These actions are arranged – by the playwrights and actors as co-creators – in the form of a series of calculated impacts on an audience. During the Restoration period successful performances made carefully planned use of the three hours or so that audiences could spend at the playhouse – from the "first music," which summoned the spectators to their seats, to the announcement of the next day's offering, which ended the performance by inviting them back. In between there occurred a variety of exciting incidents calculated to stir involvement: in tragedy a rising pulse of lurid violence, frequently erotic; in comedy a concatenation of intrigues and cross-purposes, always erotic. The spirited action of the Restoration theatre is perhaps epitomized in Act 1, scene 2 of Aphra Behn's *The Rover* (1677), when the "wild" Helena, on probationary leave from a convent, gleefully preparing her disguise for carnival, speaks decisively in the imperative to her tempted but more timorous companions: "Let's ramble."

Hoping to draw a crowd, the playwrights often created characters with the aptitudes and attributes of particular actors and actresses in mind. John Dennis, for instance, retrospectively surveying the period as a whole, stated as a commonplace that playwrights "adapted their Characters to their Actors."[17] Occasionally playwrights would put into the mouth of a male character admiring descriptions of his beloved that anatomically matched the features of the actress intended for the part. Several comedians (John Lacy, Cave Underhill, and Joe Haines) and at least one swarthy villain (Samuel Sandford) became specialists in their lines. Charles Hart and Nell Gwynn were well matched as witty lovers, a liaison that blossomed into the "gay couple" pairing in a number of plays. Indeed, in some instances the performers became so firmly associated with their roles that the plays with which they were thus affiliated could not be revived without them. Looking back with deep nostalgia on the seventeenth-century stage, James Wright, writing in 1699, accounts for the disappearance of Ben Jonson's plays from the repertory "Because there are none now Living who can rightly Humour those Parts" (*Historia Histrionica*, p. xxiv). Making a living as players required living plays (that is, sure-fire draws), but the demands of audiences for novelty and variety pressured the actors to try new material, especially in times of intensified competition between the rival companies. More often than not, new plays closed after a handful of performances, never to be revived, frustrating a substantial investment in rehearsals and the private labor of memorization, but serving a vital purpose nonetheless in testing the taste of audiences on a weekly and even daily basis.

Actors "attempted" roles before a critical audience in the Restoration theatre, suggesting that the creation of a role, like the production of a new play in its entirety, was a kind of public test. The performer tested his or her action against the imagined prerequisites of the role, including the impressions that he or she had made in previous roles. Samuel Pepys, whose *Diary* affords many tantalizing glimpses into the expectations of a Restoration playgoer, typically anticipates and celebrates the actor's distinctive contribution. Pepys spoke of a performance as something that was "done," in the sense of bringing to completion or perfection. He spoke that way about Betterton's Hamlet, for instance, first in 1661: "And then I straight to the Opera and there saw *Hamlet Prince of Denmark*, done with scenes very well. But above all, Betterton did the prince's part beyond imagination"; and then again in 1663: "And so to the Duke's house and there saw *Hamlet* done, giving us fresh reason never to think enough of Betterton."[18] The fact that Betterton's Hamlet became what could be called a "living role," one that thrived in popular imagination as long as its creator drew breath (and even longer through anecdotal lore), is attested to by accounts of the actor's grip on the part fifty years after Pepys first saw him, by which time he was past seventy and tortured with gout. Writing in the persona of "Mr. Greenhat" in *The Tatler* number for 22 September 1709, Richard Steele memorialized what he termed "the Force of Action in Perfection":

> Your admir'd Mr. *Betterton* behav'd himself so well, that, tho' now about Seventy, he acted Youth; and by the prevalent Power of proper Manner, Gesture, and Voice, appear'd through the whole *Drama* a young Man of great Expectation, Vivacity, and Enterprize. The Soliloquy, where he began the celebrated Sentence of, *To be, or not to be*; the Expostulation where he explains with his Mother in her Closet, the noble Ardor after seeing his Father's Ghost, and his generous Distress for the Death of *Ophelia*; are each of them Circumstances which dwell strongly upon the Minds of the Audience, and which would certainly affect their Behavior on any parallel Occasions in their own Lives. (*Tatler*, I, 493)

Expectation, vivacity, and *enterprise* are words that could well describe the qualities of Restoration performers. Correct action in performance counted for more, evidently, than strict verisimilitude: the qualities that Betterton acted in Hamlet transcended the obvious unsuitability of his physical appearance in the role. The sequence of impacts described by *The Tatler* review suggests that the actor shaped the role to "perfect" an action of a particular kind: the redemptive transformation of bereavement into wisdom. He made Hamlet's grief seem "noble" and "generous" (not by any means the inevitable interpretive choice), so much so that Steele's

Mr. Greenhat proposes that Bettertonian deportment serve as a model for the moral performance of everyday life, even the "liberal Education" of youth, including his nephew: "let us have Virtue thus represented on the Stage with its proper Ornaments, or let these Ornaments be added to her in Places more sacred" (*Tatler*, 1, 493–94). Similarly, the full title of Gildon's *Life of Betterton* advertised its usefulness not only for the stage, but also for the *"Bar* and *Pulpit,"* extending the beneficial practices of Bettertonian elocution to more honored professions.

The cultural work of carrying the burden of a public's ideal self-conception, like the more practical work of turning a character into a role, can best be described as a process of substitution. This process may include (but need not be limited to) the substitution of the actor's specific physique and psyche for the character suggested by the disembodied "side" (or actor's part), of concrete business for the playwright's stage directions (sometimes explicitly noted, more often implicitly suggested by the dialogue), and, more subtly, of the imaginative embodiment of precise actions to fulfill the often unstated but nevertheless crucial expectations of the public. This is the connection between action and audience that Corneille defined with the word *admiration*. Anthony Aston noted that Betterton's septuagenarian Hamlet positively creaked when he tried to throw himself down at Ophelia's feet in the play scene. But Aston also had to concede that "no one else could have pleas'd the Town, he was so rooted in their Opinion" (Aston, in *Cibber*, II, 301). The process that Aston describes (substitution-as-public test) is in fact what most users intend when they say the word *performance*.

A vivid anecdote of such a test concerns the coaching that Elizabeth Barry, who became Betterton's co-star in many productions, received at the beginning of her career from the Earl of Rochester. Lady Davenant had tried to introduce Barry to the stage on three separate occasions: each time the neophyte, whose social origins were obscure, bombed. When "several Persons of Wit and Quality" ventured the opinion that she would never make an actress, Rochester took up her cause on a bet that he could transform her into "the finest Player on the Stage." Acting Pygmalion to her Galatea, he made her "enter into the nature of the each sentiment; perfectly changing herself, as it were, into the Person, not merely by the proper Stress or Sounding of the Voice, but feeling really, and being in the Humour, the Person she represented, was supposed to be in." Not trusting to raw emotion alone, unaided by technique, Rochester oversaw nearly thirty rehearsals onstage and twelve in the dress Barry was to wear in the part. Even her "Page was taught to manage her Train, in such a Manner, so as to give each Movement a peculiar Grace." Barry finally passed her test and

Rochester won his bet.[19] They did so by creating a presentable surrogate for a grand lady, substituting a grace and manner that Barry could put on in layers from the skin out, like the elaborate garments she acquired. The acquired costumes and the customs were both directed at the same end, recapitulating the relationship of the players to their audiences: the material embodiment – the performance – of a powerful patron's fantasies.

The cultural range of this process of substitution is suggested by the exoticism of some of the roles into which the English actors and actresses stepped. Betterton played no fewer than 183 parts over his illustrious career,[20] but Steele chose to eulogize him for his performance of Othello above all (*Tatler*, II, 423–24). The duality of such a substitution, the double mask of strength and vulnerability, is emphasized by the position of royalty or aristocracy often attributed to the racial other. The career of Anne Bracegirdle offers an occasion to sum up this as well as other tendencies of Restoration performance. Known as the "Romantick Virgin" because she kept her love-life discreetly but tantalizingly veiled, Bracegirdle was considered by many as the model of English beauty, her dark-brown hair and famous blush, an "involuntary Flushing in her Breast," setting off the transparent whiteness of her skin (Aston, in *Cibber*, II, 305). The most famous visual depiction of Bracegirdle, however, is of her exotic appearance in the role of "the Indian Queen." This famous image exists in two mezzotints, the less familiar portrait version of which is reproduced here (fig. 8). She wears the plumes and ornaments that popular imagination accepted as authentic Native American dress, and indeed some pieces of which may have been among those that the narrator of Aphra Behn's *Oroonoko* claims to have brought back from Surinam for use in the original production of Dryden and Howard's *The Indian Queen* (1664). Her right hand holds a flowing cloak to her bosom, while her head turns slightly to her left, as if she is sharing the scene with an unseen interlocutor.

In her befeathered glory Bracegirdle looks as if she has been recruited from the population of an enchanted island, and in fact she was adopted as a child and raised within ear-shot of the theatre by Thomas and Mary Betterton. The elaboration and the intensity of the fantasies she inspired are best studied in the fabulous roles that Congreve, who loved her passionately but probably asexually, wrote for her, including Mrs. Millamant in *The Way of World*. In his sardonic account of what contemporary gossips regarded as the unconsummated romance between Bracegirdle and Congreve, Tom Brown discloses his own fantasy about the teasingly available and yet ultimately uncapturable beauty. Pornographically, he places himself (and implicitly his reader) in the role of the bewitched but physically unrequited playwright:

Figure 8 Anne Bracegirdle as the Indian Queen, signed by Cooper

But 'tis *the way of the World*, to have an Esteem for the fair Sex, and She looks to a Miracle when She is acting a Part in one of his own Plays. . . . Look upon him once more I say, if She goes to her *Shift*, 'tis Ten to One but he follows her, not that I would say for never so much to take up her *Smock*; he Dines with her almost ev'ry day, yet She's a *Maid*, he rides out with her, and visits her in Publick and Private, yet She's a *Maid*; if I had not a particular respect for her, I should go near to say he lies with her, yet She's a *Maid*.

(Brown, in Nagler, *Source Book*, pp. 248–49)

This passage reiterates the process of mimetic desire out of which the intimate fantasy-world of the "Enchanted Island" perpetuated itself in the public imagination: the spectators, whose spokesperson is Tom Brown, learn to want what Congreve wants – that which he can't have himself, but which he alone can give them: the "Romantick Virgin" with his words on her lips.

Reading *The Way of the World* with Bracegirdle's performance of it in mind, especially the wonderful exits that Congreve wrote for the smiling "whirlwind" Millamant, recalls Anthony Aston's tender description of the actress: "having continually a chearful Aspect, and a fine Set of even white Teeth; never making an *Exit*, but she left her Audience in an Imitation of her pleasant Countenance" (305). Her retirement from the stage in 1708, the moment of her prime not yet past, followed shortly by the retirement of Elizabeth Barry and the death of Thomas Betterton in 1710, suggests a fairly clear terminus for the tradition of Restoration theatrical performance – the last transformation of the "the *Land of Enchantment*, the *Country of Metamorphosis*" over which they had reigned for fifty years. In death, as in life, the roles that they played linked the "Enchanted Island" or the microcosmic "Mimic State" to the dynastic memory of the larger island kingdom: Anne Bracegirdle's grave is in Westminster Abbey, near those of the Bettertons, Thomas and Mary, and the other kings and queens.

NOTES

1 Over the past twenty years, theatrical performance in the Restoration period has been the subject of four excellent book-length studies to which I am variously indebted: Peter Holland, *The Ornament of Action: Text and Performance in Restoration Comedy* (Cambridge University Press, 1979); Judith Milhous and Robert D. Hume, *Producible Interpretation: Eight English Plays 1675–1707* (Carbondale: Southern Illinois University Press, 1985); Jocelyn Powell, *Restoration Theatre Production* (London: Routledge & Kegan Paul, 1984); J. L. Styan, *Restoration Comedy in Performance* (Cambridge University Press, 1986). In that time there also appeared the great *Biographical Dictionary of Actors, Actresses, Musicians, Dancers, Managers, and Other Stage Personnel in London, 1660–1800*, eds. Philip J. Highfill, Jr., Kalman A. Burnim, and Edward A. Langhans (Carbondale: Southern Illinois University Press, 1973–93), which is indispensable to research in performance studies, particularly when it used in conjunction with the production calendars in *The London Stage 1660–1800* (Carbondale: Southern Illinois University Press, 1960–65). Also highly useful to students of theatre, particularly in its managerial aspects, are Milhous and Hume's *Register of Theatrical Documents 1660–1737* (Carbondale: Southern Illinois University Press, 1991) and David Thomas and Arnold Hare's *Restoration and Georgian England 1660–1788*, a volume in Cambridge's Theatre in Europe: A Documentary History.

2 Tom Brown, *Amusements Serious and Comical, Calculated for the Meridian of*

London (1700), cited in A. M. Nagler, *A Source Book in Theatrical History* (New York: Dover Publications, 1952), pp. 247, 250.

3 "Warrant granted by Charles II to Killigrew and Davenant, 21 August 1660," cited in David Thomas and Arnold Hare, eds., *Restoration and Georgian England, 1660–1788: A Documentary History* (Cambridge University Press, 1989), p. 12.

4 Charles Gildon, *The Life of Mr. Thomas Betterton, the Late Eminent Tragedian* (London, 1710), pp. 5–10.

5 *Biographical Dictionary of Actors*, II, 73–96.

6 *The Tatler*, 3 vols., ed. Donald F. Bond (Oxford: Clarendon Press, 1987), II, 422.

7 See Harold Weber, "Carolinean Sexuality and the Restoration Stage: Reconstructing the Royal Phallus in *Sodom*," in J. Douglas Canfield and Deborah C. Payne, eds., *Cultural Readings of Restoration and Eighteenth-Century English Theater* (Athens: University of Georgia Press, 1995), pp. 67–88.

8 Allan S. Jackson, "The Frontispiece to Eccles's *Theater Musick* 1699," *TN* 19 (Winter 1964/65), 47–49.

9 Anthony Aston, *A Brief Supplement to Colley Cibber*, in *An Apology for the Life of Mr. Colley Cibber*, ed. Robert W. Lowe, 2 vols. (London: John C. Nimmo, 1889), II, 300.

10 *An Apology for the Life of Mr. Colley Cibber*, II, 85–86.

11 All the passages above are quoted in *Thesaurus Dramaticus*, 2 vols. (London, 1724), I, 199–224.

12 *The Laureate* cited in *An Apology for the Life of Mr. Colley Cibber*, II, 335.

13 In 1698 the House of Lords felt constrained to intervene in the scandal of an actor drawing on a gentleman: see documents 1580, 1581, and 1583 in Hume and Milhous, *Register*, vol. I.

14 John Downes, *Roscius Anglicanus; or, An Historical Review of the Stage* (1706), ed. Judith Milhous and Robert D. Hume (London: Society for Theatre Research, 1987), p. 41.

15 "Killigrew's Patent, 25 April 1662," cited in *Restoration and Georgian England*, p. 18.

16 H. Wilson, *All the King's Ladies: Actresses of the Restoration* (University of Chicago Press, 1958), p. 73. For more current accounts of the roles of actresses, see Elizabeth Howe, *The First English Actresses: Women and Drama, 1660–1700* (Cambridge University Press, 1992) and Deborah Payne, "Reified Object or Emergent Professional? Retheorizing the Restoration Actress," in *Cultural Readings of Restoration and Eighteenth-Century Theater*, pp. 13–38.

17 John Dennis, *Reflections Critical and Satyrical*, cited in Emmett L. Avery and Arthur H. Scouten, *The London Stage 1660–1700: A Critical Introduction* (Carbondale: Southern Illinois University Press, 1968), p. cvii.

18 *The Diary of Samuel Pepys*, ed. R. Latham and W. Matthews, 11 vols. (Berkeley: University of California Press, 1970–83), II, 161 and IV, 162.

19 [Thomas Betterton], *The History of the English Stage from the Restoration to the Present Time* (London, 1741), pp. 15–16.

20 Judith Milhous, "An Annotated Census of Thomas Betterton's Roles, 1659–1710," *TN* 29 (1975), 33–45 (part 1); 85–94 (part 2).

3

MICHAEL DOBSON

Adaptations and revivals

Seven years before Charles II was returned to power, eleven after the Puritan régime had brought all legitimate theatrical activity in London to an abrupt halt, Aston Cokaine, writing a dedicatory poem to Richard Brome's belatedly published *Five New Plays* (1653), was already looking forward to the day when the playhouses would reopen. Presciently, he imagined a restored theatre which would be first and foremost a place for the revival of England's native dramatic classics, and only secondarily a venue where living playwrights might resume their interrupted careers:

> Then shall learn'd Jonson reassume his seat,
> Revive the Phoenix by a second heat,
> Create the Globe anew, and people it
> By those that flock to surfeit on his wit.
> Judicious Beaumont, and th'ingenious soul
> Of Fletcher too may move without control,
> Shakespeare (most rich in humors) entertain
> The crowded theatres with his happy vein.
> Davenant and Massinger, and Shirley, then
> Shall be cried up again for famous men.[1]

As Cokaine's poem in part suggests (apparently remembering Elizabethan and Jacobean playwrights among the glories of the lost Caroline stage), the repertories of the pre-Civil War playhouses had always included a substantial percentage of revived plays, some of them half a century old by the time the theatres were closed in 1642. It is worth remembering, too, that such plays had often been retouched to fit them to the needs and styles of their current performers: one thinks here, for example, of Thomas Middleton's contributions to the script of Shakespeare's *Macbeth*, or the additions made by Ben Jonson in 1601 and 1602 to Thomas Kyd's *The Spanish Tragedy*, a play whose continuing ability to compete with newer dramas Jonson himself had gone on to regret in the induction to *Bartholomew Fair* in 1614. But the previous history of the English commercial stage provided no precedent for the far heavier extent to which the revived theatre, much as Cokaine's wistful and nostalgic prophecy envisioned it, would indeed rely on old plays – albeit sometimes revived in such a manner that one of the contemporaries this poem names, Sir William Davenant, is now more often "cried up" (or down) as a Restoration adaptor of earlier scripts than as a dramatist in his own right.

When public theatre did resume in 1659–60, ending a two-decade hiatus during which there had been no working playwrights, it was of course inevitable that the first shows on offer should be productions of plays now already at least a generation old. It was not inevitable, however, that the new playwrights of the Restoration should make such a comparatively small impact on this all-revival repertory over the next forty years. Two years into the new era, in the 1661–62 theatrical season, records show only 4 new plays being performed, as opposed to 54 written before the Interregnum, and though the proportion of new plays had greatly increased by 1667–68 – when there were 12 recorded premières alongside revivals of 20 plays written since 1660 and 33 written before 1640 – there was little significant change thereafter (for 1674–75, for example, the numbers are much the same, with 13 new plays acted alongside 16 written since 1660 and 25 written before 1640). Although these figures are neither exhaustive nor definitive (the distinction between an adaptation and a new play can be very blurred, as we shall see, and a count of titles alone can't take account of how many times each was acted), they are accurate in their suggestion that Restoration theatre companies usually spent only about half of their time performing strictly Restoration drama. Any consideration of what the theatres were doing between 1660 and 1700, consequently, needs to pay serious attention to the question of what they made of the pre-war dramatic corpus, and whether the extensive uses to which it continued to be put are symptoms of cultural conservatism (as some commentators, such as Nancy Maguire, have argued),[2] or of an active transformation and renewal of the theatrical past, or of an increasingly uneasy combination of the two.

The most familiar answer to this question hitherto has been that the Restoration made a great deal, or a great mess, of the plays it inherited, trampling on its dramatic heritage in a misguided and arrogant spirit of innovation; for views of the later seventeenth century's treatment of older scripts have been dominated by outrage over the period's notorious adaptations of Shakespeare. Looking at the more famous, or infamous – Davenant's *Macbeth* (1663), with its rhyming couplets and singing, flying witches, Davenant and John Dryden's *The Tempest, or the Enchanted Island* (1667), in which Caliban and Miranda both have sisters and Prospero's extended family further includes a male ward who has never seen a woman, or Nahum Tate's *The History of King Lear* (1681), with its happy ending in which Edgar marries Cordelia while Lear and Gloucester look forward to a peaceful retirement – commentators have been tempted to regard the theatre managers of the Restoration as ignorant vandals, uncomprehendingly vulgarizing the masterpieces of the previous era in quest of novel but crassly simple dramatic effects and the easy popularity they might earn.

There is something to be said for this view, of course – whatever else the adaptors of the Restoration may have done for some of Shakespeare's plays, they rarely made them more sophisticated – but it greatly over-estimates both the importance of adaptation within the period's Shake-spearean repertory and the centrality of Shakespeare to the Restoration's larger archive of pre-war drama. In fact, a small but perennial cluster of Shakespeare plays – *Othello, The Merry Wives of Windsor, 1 Henry IV, Julius Caesar,* and *Hamlet,* all of them still on the boards when the theatres had closed in 1642 – were at once among the most conservatively treated and the most frequently revived of all pre-war plays, together with a similar knot of favorites by Ben Jonson and a rather larger group from the Beaumont and Fletcher canon: had the Restoration companies confined themselves to this group of scripts when in search of older material, England might conceivably have developed a tradition of theatrical revival as reverent as that of the Comédie Française. Outside this stable of unrevised classics, it was by no means only Shakespearean plays which were substantially rewritten for Restoration production: although Jonson escaped entirely (excepting the collaborative *Eastward Ho*), seventeen works from the Beaumont and Fletcher canon were rewritten at different times, along with countless other pre-war plays, from Marlowe's *Dr. Faustus* to Middleton's *No Wit, No Help Like a Woman's.* In effect, a line was drawn during the 1660s (and rarely redrawn thereafter) between those old plays which would merely be revived and imitated and those which would be treated more freely as available raw material by Restoration playwrights, and the placing of that line was in part determined by the relative circumstances of the two patent companies at their inception.

By 1660, the Commonwealth's necessary recourse to reading plays in print instead of seeing them performed had already done much to exagge-rate the preeminence among the old dramatists of those whose work had achieved the prestige (and sheer physical durability) guaranteed by publica-tion in folio, namely Jonson, Shakespeare, and the younger and more fashionable Beaumont and Fletcher, singled out for special praise by Cokaine in a manner which was already a critical commonplace in 1653. When two companies of players began to perform in London from late

1659 onward, one of survivors from the old King's Men and one of younger players, both had repertories, in keeping with the closet-drama tradition which Moseley and his ilk had kept alive, which were dominated by Beaumont and Fletcher plays, supplemented by some Shakespeare and Jonson and a number of other old favorites preserved only in quarto. Unfortunately for the members of the younger troupe, Jonson, Shakespeare, and Fletcher had something else in common beyond folio publication: they had all been closely associated with the old King's Men. When the veteran actors were reorganized under Thomas Killigrew in 1660 as the King's Company, seen as the King's Men's lawful heirs, they used this fact to try to lay claim to exclusive performance rights to the works of all three; and in the complex negotiations which followed between Killigrew and the rival Duke's Company under Sir William Davenant (who had recruited the members of the younger troupe), it is clear that Killigrew got a decisive upper hand.[3] The King's Company were able not only to ratify a monopoly on the only Jonson plays the Restoration would ever revive (principally *Epicoene*, *Bartholomew Fair*, *Volpone*, *The Alchemist* and *Catiline*), but to secure much of the Shakespeare canon, including those plays which had already re-established themselves at the Red Bull (*Othello*, *1 Henry IV* and *Merry Wives*). Perhaps more advantageously still, they were able to appropriate most of the safest bets in the Fletcher canon, notably *The Humorous Lieutenant*, *The Maid's Tragedy*, *A King and No King*, *Rollo*, *The Scornful Lady*, *The Elder Brother*, *The Chances*, *Philaster*, and *The Tamer Tamed*.[4] (This last play had been revived by both pre-patentee companies, but was now definitively given to the elder actors: even *Rule a Wife and Have a Wife*, which had been performed by the younger troupe alone, was only grudgingly conceded to Davenant for a short period, reverting thereafter to Killigrew.[5])

This manifestly unfair division of the dramatic heritage contributed significantly to the recognizably different approaches adopted by the two companies to the materials at their disposal. Innovation, in the treatment of old plays as in much else, became the hallmark of the Duke's Company, conservatism of the King's: of those "Old Stock Plays" which would remain in the repertory in comparatively unaltered form down to 1700 and beyond (long after the two patent companies had merged and then splintered again), the vast majority were plays which had been the preserve of the King's Company in the 1660s and 1670s. When in August 1661 the Duke's Company mounted their first Shakespearean revival, it was, predictably, a production of the only pre-war favorite from the Shakespeare folio which they had been permitted, *Hamlet*, and although Davenant cut the script so as to fit it for the display of his new changeable scenery and slightly modernized some of its diction, his acting version is far from being a full-scale adaptation.[6] (Davenant, indeed, teaching the young Thomas Betterton to play the Prince just as he had seen Joseph Taylor of the old King's Men play him before the civil wars, seems here to have been consciously competing with the King's Company on their own ground, the revival of pre-war traditions of performance.[7]) But the other Shakespeare plays he had been allotted, unperformed for generations, required more drastic treatment, their apparently unpromising and archaic dramatic materials stimulating Davenant to grow ever more inventive in suiting them to the new possibilities of the Restoration playhouse and the changing tastes of the Restoration audience. The patents granted to both companies had specified, in a token bid to placate anti-theatrical opinion, that any old plays should be "reformed and made fit" before being revived, and from 1662 onward Davenant seems to have taken this injunction to heart, albeit in a spirit of aesthetic rather than moral reformation. He transplanted Beatrice and Benedick from *Much Ado* into a sanitized *Measure for Measure* to produce a fashionable love-and-honor play, largely in couplets, called *The Law Against Lovers*, acted in February 1662; in 1663 he further showed off his theatre's capacity for grand scenic effects with a lavishly decorated *Henry VIII*; in 1664 he staged his equally spectacular, and far more heavily rewritten, *Macbeth*; and in 1667 appeared his last Shakespearean adaptation, co-written with Dryden, *The Tempest; or, The Enchanted Island*. A 1674 prologue to one of countless productions of this play (the most frequently revived of the entire period), scoffing at the King's Company, makes it clear that it was precisely the raw deal given the Duke's Company in the sharing of the pre-war repertory which had helped to motivate their emphasis on new stage effects and new writing:

> Without the good old plays we did advance,
> And all the stage's ornament enhance.
> Too much of the old wit they have, 'tis true:
> But they must look for little of the new.[8]

The King's Company may have established themselves as the rightful custodians of the pre-war theatrical tradition, but according to this prologue their productions were in danger of merely curating the "good old plays" they had been granted when compared to the new ornaments and new writing displayed by their competitors, features no less of their revivals than of their premières.

While it is true that the practice of full-scale adaptation thus begins with Davenant's Shakespearean experiments in the 1660s, and can be related to the fact that Killigrew had secured most of the old plays which a contemporary audience was likely to wish to see in their original forms, the distinction between "adaptation" and "revival" in the Restoration is more blurred than the above may suggest. For one thing, there were certain crucial respects in which it was simply no longer possible for any company to perform pre-war plays without radically altering them, whether or not such alterations extended to their texts. On becoming the King's Company in 1660, the veteran players had forever abandoned the Red Bull, the last survivor of the unroofed playhouses for which most of the older repertory had been written, and once Killigrew had followed Davenant's lead thereafter in adopting changeable scenery, both companies were performing their pre-Commonwealth plays on stages (and now sets) quite unlike those envisaged by their playwrights. As any playgoer accustomed to late twentieth-century revivals of Renaissance drama knows, a play can be transformed almost as thoroughly by the provision of unfamiliar décor and stage design as it can by the actual rewriting of its text, whether or not the former in practice mandates the latter. Even Jonson's critically revered comedies must have looked quite different after 1660, although their neoclassical respect for the unity of place saved them from some of the omissions and transpositions of scenes which the new playhouses required of most other pre-war plays.

The other factor which transformed the pre-war corpus, equally affecting the unadapted repertory no less than the adaptations which it often stimulated, was the advent of the female player. Within a few seasons of the Restoration, none of the female roles which had been written for boys were still in male custody: confusingly, even the boy who passes himself off as the Silent Woman in Jonson's *Epicoene* was played by an actress from 1663 onward, perhaps the most extreme example of the 1660s' interest in transforming the cross-dressed boy heroines of the early 1600s into opportunities for the display of actresses' legs in tight-fitting breeches. Even plays which didn't have new female roles written into their scripts in the manner of Davenant's *Tempest* were liable to have their existing ones enlarged, if only by the provision of interpolated songs and dances. The combined effects of the arrival of onstage women and the discrepancy between pre-war and Restoration playhouses are vividly exemplified by a revival attended by Samuel Pepys in August 1667. In a bid to emulate the success of the Duke's Company's Tudor spectacular *Henry VIII*, the King's Company had exhumed two of the most popular plays of the entire pre-war period, Thomas Heywood's chronicle of the youthful sufferings and triumphant reign of Elizabeth I, *If You Know Not Me, You Know Nobody*, parts 1 and 2 (1605, 1606).[9] Pepys, however, despite his compassionate lifelong interest in Gloriana, was only intermittently impressed:

[August 17 1667] to the King's playhouse, where the house extraordinary full; and there was the King and the Duke of York to see the new play, *Queen Elizabeth's Troubles, and the History of Eighty-Eight.* I confess I have sucked in so much of the sad story of Queen Elizabeth from my cradle, that I was ready to weep for her sometimes. But the play is the most ridiculous that sure ever came upon stage, and indeed is merely a show; only, shows the true garb of the queens in those days, just as we see Queen Mary and Queen Elizabeth painted – but the play is merely a puppet-play, acted by living puppets. Neither the design nor the language better; and one stands by and tells us the meaning of things.

For Pepys, Heywood's popular drama, written sixty years earlier for the Red Bull, seems hopelessly vulgar in the presence of real royalty at the King's Playhouse, its dumb shows and chorus performing expository work which nowadays ought to be performed by more psychologized dialogue and representational scenery. Furthermore, its principal female roles are clearly inadequate, reducing their players to mere clothes-horses: historically interesting as their dresses remain, they fail to compensate Pepys for what he has learned to expect from actresses, the display of a female interiority identified with the female body itself. Characteristically, the actress in the cast to whom Pepys does respond positively is the one wearing the minimum of costume:

Only, I was pleased to see Knepp dance among the milkmaids, and to hear her sing a song to Queen Elizabeth – and to see her come out in her night-gown, with no locks on, but her bare face and hair only tied up in a knot behind; which is the comeliest dress that ever I saw her in to her advantage.[10]

Neither dancing milkmaids nor any song by the Queen's confidante feature in the original *If You Know Not Me* plays, so that although the text used on this occasion doesn't survive (as Pepys' comments might lead us to expect, the show was not sufficiently popular to send any bookseller rushing into print with the script) it is clear that there had been some additions made along with the major abridgment required to compress two plays into a single entertainment, much of it to the benefit of Mrs. Knepp. By 1667, clearly, the King's Company had begun to emulate Davenant's habit of adapting lesser-known plays: in the same year they also performed John Lacy's *Sauny the Scot,* an updated version of *The Taming of the Shrew* designed to make it a better companion piece to Fletcher's Anglicized sequel *The Tamer Tamed,* and in 1669 they would even mount an anonymous adaptation of one of their cherished Fletcher plays, *The Island Princess.*

What is perhaps more interesting than this evidence of minor adaptation, however, is the way in which Pepys refers to the show (under its altered title) simply as "the new play," without reference to any author, whether Thomas Heywood or the choreographer of the interpolated milkmaids. He may be thinking of it as an old play newly revived, remaining unconscious of how its script has been altered, or he may genuinely believe that it is a wholly new play, but in either case its authorship is of little interest. For the Restoration, vintage plays belonged to theatre companies much more securely than they belonged to their dead authors, and beyond the most famous masterpieces of Jonson, Shakespeare, and Fletcher (writers granted authorial personae by the preliminary materials of their respective folios), old plays were generally regarded as fair game for any writer prepared to carry out the work of making them worth performing.[11]

This is an attitude which began to change over the course of the period. Aphra Behn, for example, had trouble with Thomas Killigrew's publisher after transforming his closet drama *Thomaso* (1664) into her own *The Rover* (1677). As a result, she published two subsequent adaptations of pre-war plays, *The Debauchee* (1677, from Brome's *A Mad Couple Well Matched*) and *The Revenge* (1680, from Marston's *The Dutch Courtesan*), anonymously. For most playgoers, though, adaptations of unknown old plays were simply new plays, and whether we now categorize a Restoration adaptation as such or as a Restoration play in its own right tends simply to reflect our own sense of the relative importance of the two writers involved. If by some freak of literary history Thomas Durfey had achieved the status of a major playwright while Shakespeare and Fletcher had faded into obscurity, we would now be reading his *Trick for Trick, or the Debauched Hypocrite* (1678) and *The Injured Princess* (1682) as a Restoration intrigue comedy and an unusual heroic tragicomedy, rather than as adaptations of Fletcher's *Monsieur Thomas* and Shakespeare's *Cymbeline* respectively. Even those members of Durfey's audience familiar with these two source-plays are unlikely to have regarded his efforts to update them as innately reprehensible (though they might have expected Durfey to make more acknowledgment of his debts to Fletcher and Shakespeare than in either case he did): to contemporary criticism, a play's "fable" and "sentiments" mattered far more than mere verbal details, so an adaptation, preserving both while stripping what had become obscuringly obsolete superficies of idiom, might more genuinely "revive" an old play than what we would now call a revival.[12]

Hence even that expert in the various shades of dramatic rewriting, Gerard Langbaine, author of *Momus Triumphans: or the Plagiaries of the English Stage* (1688), could use the verb "revive" either in the sense it retains now ("[Brome's *The Northern Lass*] was revived by the players.") or as a synonym for "adapt" ("[*Eastward Ho*] ... hath lately appeared on the present stage, being revived by Mr Tate under the title of *Cuckold's*

Haven").[13] When dealing with better-known plays than these examples, more self-consciously literary writers might produce what were in effect "closet" adaptations, designed less for performance than for leisurely comparison with their well-known originals (such as Rochester's version of Fletcher's *Valentinian*, and Waller's of *The Maid's Tragedy*, both published posthumously, in 1685 and 1690 respectively). Similarly, the authors of acknowledged stage adaptations might discuss the grounds on which they had made alterations in the prefatory materials to their printed editions (the best-known examples being the simultaneously exasperated and reverential engagement with Shakespeare visible in Dryden's prefaces and prologues to *The Tempest, or the Enchanted Island*, 1667, *All for Love*, 1678, and *Troilus and Cressida, or, Truth Found Too Late*, 1679). But in either case there was no stigma attached to adaptation, quite the contrary: the title-page of the 1678 stage version of *Timon of Athens* actively boasts that it has been "Made into a PLAY ... by Thomas Shadwell", and when Colley Cibber published his enduringly popular version of *Richard III* in 1700 with inverted commas in the margins to indicate which lines he had left unaltered, it was as much to allow his readers to savour his redactive talents – and to counter the allegation that he had rewritten the play for political motives – as to clear himself of any accusation of either plagiarism or misguided literary zeal. In general our sense of a difference in kind between revivals, adaptations, and new plays based on old is largely anachronistic: as we have seen, all Restoration revivals were to a greater or lesser degree adaptations, as were a great many new plays (even Dryden's *The Wild Gallant*, supposedly a definitively early Restoration comedy, may have been based on a now lost play by Brome), and it is often more useful to consider the different purposes to which the Restoration put the older corpus in general than to devote undue attention to matters of authorship and copyright which were only beginning to take their modern shape.

For the pre-war dramatic heritage was the laboratory of the Restoration stage, and it is perhaps most useful to examine the period's revivals and adaptations alike as experiments in negotiating the political position of the restored theatres, and attempts to find new genres which might flourish within them. Publicly reviving pre-war drama at all, and with it by implication the Royalist culture of the Caroline court, made a conspicuous statement about the defeat of the Commonwealth in 1660, and Pepys cannot have been alone in seeing a political "use" behind the early King's Company's repeated performances of such specifically anti-Puritan plays as Jonson's *Bartholomew Fair*.[14] (Other early Restoration favorites, clearly rendered topically loyal to the new monarchy by recent events, included *1 Henry IV*, a play about the successful defeat of a rebellion, and Fletcher's *A*

King And No King, a play about the miraculous restoration of the legitimate heir.) The full-scale adaptations of the 1660s often similarly display an agenda as much political as literary, supplying resolutions designed to replay the most favorable version possible of the Restoration itself: Davenant's Macbeth is an Oliver Cromwell doomed to exemplary punishment ("Farewell vain world, and what's most vain in it, Ambition," he gasps before his onstage death), and his Duke Vincentio and Prospero are both righteous Charles IIs, happily restored to power after the aberrations of Angelo's Puritan régime and Antonio's usurpation. As the political situation grew more troubled through the constitutional crises of the late 1670s and 1680s, the usually blurred distinction between adaptations and revivals – between what had been added to a play, and what had been in its script all along – made the rewriting of lesser-known old plays an even more attractive medium for covert political comment by playwrights who would have been wary of making such observations in scripts which would be regarded as all their own work. Hence the suspicion which attached to Cibber's *Richard III*, accused of Jacobitism when first performed in 1699: by the turn of the century the censors had seen a good many old history plays mined for instructive parallels with contemporary politics. These included Tate's *Lear* (1681) – whose bastard Edmund, his evil enhanced by a rape attempt against Cordelia, was clearly intended to remind the audience of the aspiring illegitimate Duke of Monmouth – and John Crowne's *Henry the Sixth, the First Part* (1681), banned for its interpolated satire against Catholics at a time when the heir to the throne, the future James II, was himself a member of the old faith. Even the respectably classical *Julius Caesar* had been slightly rewritten after the Glorious Revolution in order to make it more unambiguously sympathetic to the constitutional libertarian Brutus.

Such examples of local topicality in the deployment of the older drama, however, are probably less interesting than instances where we can see Restoration playwrights, in their various attempts to render the miscellaneous old plays they had inherited theatrically useful, actually discovering the genres they would make their own. Thus while the broad influence of Jonson and Fletcher on the development of early Restoration comedy is clear, it is particularly illuminating to see Davenant contributing the "gay couple" tradition of repartee to the form by adding Shakespeare's Beatrice and Benedick to the cast of *The Law Against Lovers* (1662). Likewise the emergence of semi-opera as a form in the 1660s owes much to Davenant's particular sense of how the new scenic and musical resources of the indoor playhouses might be called into play by Shakespeare's scenes of magic and the supernatural in *Macbeth* (1663) and *The Tempest, or the Enchanted*

Island (1667, a musical whose score was extended still further in 1674). The renaissance of semi-opera in the unsettled and experimental 1690s similarly took shape around such lavish revivals and adaptations, with some of Henry Purcell's best music accompanying Thomas Betterton's versions of Fletcher's *The Prophetess* (in 1690) and Shakespeare's *A Midsummer Night's Dream* (heavily and ingeniously rewritten, probably by Betterton, as *The Fairy Queen*, 1692). In an odder experiment still in combining the appeals of opera and drama, Purcell and Tate's *Dido and Aeneas* found itself transplanted in installments into Charles Gildon's version of *Measure for Measure* (1700). Perhaps the most striking instance, though, of the contribution of remodeled old plays to a new form is the emergence of affective tragedy in the late 1670s and early 1680s, which coincided with the stage's discovery – at a time when crises in the monarchy were making Restoration heroic tragedy look ideologically obsolete – of several tragedies of Shakespeare, often rewritten with an emphasis on private pathos, most signally in Thomas Otway's ancient Roman version of *Romeo and Juliet, The History and Fall of Caius Marius* (1679).

It is perhaps in cases such as these – of adaptations visibly metamorphosing into contemporary plays of wholly new kinds – that the Restoration's characteristically divided response to its theatrical heritage is most intriguingly visible. Nominally revered old plays might be "revived" by judicious rewriting, as if in a bid to prove that the cultural gap between the pre-Commonwealth and post-Restoration worlds could be effortlessly bridged, and yet the scope of the alterations they required often demonstrated the complete impossibility of this project – the attempt at cultural nostalgia actually produces cultural innovation. Perhaps the restoration of the monarchy was itself just such an exercise in "revival, with alterations." Just as the gradual dwindling in the proportion of the repertory devoted to unaltered revivals of Jonson and Fletcher from the 1700s onward appears to suggest in the theatre, eventually the element of alteration would become more obvious than the element of revival.

NOTES

1 Richard Brome, *Five New Playes* (London, 1653), A2.
2 See Nancy Klein Maguire, *Regicide and Restoration: English Tragicomedy, 1660–1671* (Cambridge University Press, 1992), esp. chs. 1–2; also Nicholas José, *Ideas of the Restoration in English Literature, 1660–1671* (Cambridge, Mass.: Harvard University Press, 1984), ch. 7.
3 On the complicated matter of how the repertory was divided, see especially Gunnar Sorelius, "The Rights of the Restoration Theatre Companies in the Older Drama," *SN* 37 (1965), 174–89; Robert D. Hume, "Securing a Repertory: Plays on the London Stage, 1660–5," in Antony Coleman and Anthony

Hammond, eds., *Poetry and Drama, 1500–1700: Essays in Honour of Harold F. Brooks* (London: Methuen, 1981), pp. 156–72; Judith Milhous, *Thomas Betterton and the Management of Lincoln's Inn Fields, 1695–1708* (Carbondale: Southern Illinois University Press, 1979), esp. pp. 15–19; and John Freehafer, "The Formation of the London Patent Companies in 1660," *TN* 20 (1965), 6–30.

4 The popularity of these plays can be gauged from their frequent appearances on such records we have of which plays were being revived both just before the Commonwealth and just after the Restoration: see, for example, the overlaps between the lists of "Plays acted before the King and Queen" for 1636 and 1638, and "Plays acted by the Red Bull actors," provided by the disgruntled Master of the Revels displaced by Davenant and Killigrew's patents, Sir Henry Herbert. Joseph Quincy Adams, ed., *The Dramatic Records of Sir Henry Herbert, Master of the Revels, 1623– 1673* (New Haven: Yale University Press, 1917), pp. 75–76, 82. See also John Downes, *Roscius Anglicanus* (London, 1708), pp. 18–19, on the Fletcher-dominated repertoire of the younger troupe before the establishment of the patent companies.

5 This arrangement whereby companies held sole performing rights to particular old plays broke down with the secession of Betterton's troupe from the United Company in 1695: from then onward, the two licensed companies might offer rival productions of the same old play at the same time, a situation exploited most famously by the notorious "War of the Romeos" in 1748, when both Drury Lane and Covent Garden presented competing productions of *Romeo and Juliet* for twelve successive performances.

6 It was published, without Davenant's name, as *The tragedy of Hamlet, Prince of Denmark: as it is now acted at his Highness the Duke of York's Theatre* (London, 1676).

7 See Downes, *Roscius Anglicanus*, p. 21.

8 Printed in W. J. Lawrence, *The Elizabethan Playhouse and Other Studies* (Stratford-upon- Avon: Shakespeare Head Press, 1912), pp. 200–01.

9 The pre-war popularity of these plays can be gauged by their publishing history: before the closing of the theatres, part 1 had gone through eight editions and part 2 through four.

10 Samuel Pepys, *The Diary of Samuel Pepys*, ed. Robert Latham and William Matthews, 11 vols. (London: Bell and Hyman, 1970–83), VIII, 388–89.

11 On authorship, performing rights and literary property in this period, see Laura J. Rosenthal, *Playwrights and Plagiarists in Early Modern England* (Ithaca: Cornell University Press, 1996), esp. ch. 1.

12 On adaptation and Restoration criticism, see especially Jean Marsden, *The Re-Imagined Text: Shakespeare, Adaptation and Eighteenth-Century Literary Theory* (Lexington: University Press of Kentucky, 1995), pp. 1–71.

13 Gerard Langbaine, *An Account of the English Dramatick Poets* (London, 1691), pp. 37, 66. On Langbaine's sense of the distinction between adaptation and plagiarism see Paulina Kewes, "Gerard Langbaine's 'View of *Plagiaries*': the Rhetoric of Dramatic Appropriation in the Restoration," *RES* 48 (1997), 2–18.

14 See Pepys, *Diary*, IX, 298–99.

4

BRIAN CORMAN

Comedy

What is Restoration comedy? The first temptation is to define the comedy of the fifty years following the restoration of Charles II in the terms used by the playwrights themselves. But it does not require much reading of seventeenth-century comic theory to realize that playwrights and critics shared few assumptions about comedy and fewer conclusions. Most agreed that comedy should meet the Horatian requirements for all literature – that it please and instruct. Most, though not all, privileged instruction over pleasure, since most maintained that the end of comedy was moral. But when the playwrights and critics turned to how that moral end was to be recognized, not to mention realized, they quickly reached the limits of their small consensus.[1]

The best-known exchange of views about comedy in the period took place in the 1660s between two of the most important playwrights, John Dryden and Thomas Shadwell, early in their careers as comic writers. In *An Essay of Dramatick Poesie* (1668), Dryden had argued that although Ben Jonson is "the most learned and judicious Writer which any Theater ever had," his "genius" in comedy was limited to the representation of humors. His best comic characters are "Mechanick People." In Restoration London, a society more refined than Jonson's, Dryden observes the desire for more "gayety" in the audience, and for comedies in which "making Love" is central to the action. Since Jonson's "genius was too sullen and saturnine to do it gracefully," the Restoration audience preferred the more gracious and witty John Fletcher among the earlier playwrights.[2] Dryden makes this case in part to authorize his own practice, a practice more in line with Fletcher than Jonson, but performance records support his contention that Fletcher was the most popular pre-Restoration writer of comedy on the stage.

Shadwell's preference, in theory and practice, was for the tradition of Jonson. In the preface to his first play, *The Sullen Lovers* (1668), he took exception to Dryden's version of the history of comedy, with its evolutionary movement from Jonsonian humors to Flecherian wit:

> Though I have known some of late so Insolent to say that *Ben Johnson* wrote his best *Playes* without Wit, – imagining that all the Wit in Playes consisted in bringing two persons upon the Stage to break Jests, and to bob one another, which they call Repartie, not considering that there is more wit and invention requir'd in finding out good Humor, and Matter proper fit for it, then in all their smart reparties.

Wit versus humor remains central to the debate about comedy throughout the period, a debate with strong moral implications as Shadwell makes clear when he argues that not only is wit comedy trivial, but also immoral with its "two chief persons ... most commonly a Swearing, Drinking, Whoring Ruffian for a Lover, and an impudent, ill-bred *tomrig* for a Mistress, and these the fine people of the *Play*."[3]

The debate continued for at least another round between Dryden and Shadwell, and it set the terms for the rest of the period. True to his Jonsonian roots, Shadwell affirms the predominant theory of comedy since the Renaissance that it should achieve its moral end by rendering "Figures of *Vice* and *Folly* so ugly and detestable" that the audience will learn to "hate and despise them." Dryden counters that the moral function of comedy depends on the audience first being moved to pleasure and then analyzing the source of that pleasure. To cause laughter at folly is to instruct by appealing to the lowest of human emotions. Wit comedy, by contrast, provides the pleasure of listening to "the conversation of Gentlemen" and observing the behavior of high society. Wit comedy, in other words, teaches by positive example and is thus to be preferred over humours comedy with its negative examples.[4]

Such debates continue throughout the period and make clear how little ground is shared by seventeenth-century comic theorists. Nor do the theorists practice with any rigor what they preach. For example, *The Sullen Lovers*, one of Shadwell's most successful plays, is indeed full of humours characters with names like Sir Positive At-all, Ninny, Woodcock, Huffe, and Lady Vaine, but the plot centers on the courtships of two sisters, Emilia and Carolina, by two young men of fashion, Stanford and Lovel. In addition, although comic theorists almost universally condemned personal ridicule in favor of a more general satire of types, one of the causes for the initial success of *The Sullen Lovers* was that two of the humours characters, Sir Positive At-all and Poet Ninny, were readily recognizable portraits of the playwrights (and Dryden's brothers-in-law) Sir Robert and Edward Howard. And though Dryden's *An Evening's Love* (also 1668) centers on three courtships, its action revolves around the duping of a humourous father and rival lover. The father, Don Alonzo, is a fervent astrologer, and one of the young lovers, Bellamy, wins his daughter by pretending to share

Don Alonzo's passion for the stars. Both plays end happily with marriages secured and the folly of the humours characters exposed. Both plays borrow heavily from French sources, including Molière. The most accurate descriptions of the comic practice of Restoration playwrights recognize its theoretical impurity. Dryden's claim that "I approve most the mixt way of Comedy; that which is neither all wit, nor all humour, but the result of both"[5] accurately reflects the pragmatic approach of playwrights more concerned with artistic and commercial success than with meeting the requirements prescribed by a theory.

It is not surprising that the comedy of wit and the comedy of humours, personified in the work of Fletcher and Jonson respectively, dominated conceptions of comedy for years after the Restoration. When the theatres reopened after an eighteen-year hiatus, they no longer had a resident supply of playwrights. The managers had no choice but to turn to earlier plays to provide work for their companies. By far the most popular of the earlier comic playwrights was Fletcher; Jonson had the respect of the critics but not the love of the audiences. Shakespeare's comedies placed a distant third. The theatres were small repertory houses with devoted but modest audiences. Most plays did not run a full week in their initial run; popular plays were, however, regularly revived as part of the repertory of the company. To survive, the companies needed a body of crowd-pleasing plays that could be mounted with very short notice. Plays like Fletcher's *Rule a Wife and Have a Wife*, *Beggar's Bush*, *The Scornful Lady*, and *Wit Without Money* (the last two written with Francis Beaumont) and Jonson's *Volpone*, *The Alchemist*, *Epicoene*, and *Bartholomew Fair* provided the theatres with reliable repertory pieces until enough new plays had been written to free them from dependence on pre-Commonwealth plays. And the most popular of these old plays remained in the repertory through most of the eighteenth century.

Fletcher and Jonson can also be seen as setting the terms for post-Restoration comedy, a comedy that tends to work between the poles represented by Dryden's binary opposition of wit and humour, or similar alternative binaries such as the exemplary and the satiric or the sympathetic and the punitive.[6] Very few plays indeed fail to draw on either of these two traditions; most follow Dryden's "mixt way" and draw on both. Nor were the new playwrights of the Restoration content to be clones of the old masters. Instead, they incorporated the comic tradition they inherited into new variations that allowed them to address the needs and desires of their own audiences. The managers were content to recycle the old plays that continued to please, but even here the old plays were brought up to date in the performances of new actors – and actresses (appearing in roles originally written for boys). And if the old plays no longer pleased, they were often rewritten by Restoration playwrights. Among the most successful of these adaptations in the comic repertory were John Lacy's *Sauny the Scot* (1667) from Shakespeare's *The Taming of the Shrew*, Dryden and Davenant's version of Shakespeare's *The Tempest* (1667) and Shadwell's operatic revision of their *Tempest* (1674), the Duke of Buckingham's version of Fletcher's *The Chances* (1667), Aphra Behn's *The Rover*, part 1 (1677) from Thomas Killigrew's *Thomaso*, and George Granville's *The Jew of Venice* (1700) from Shakespeare's *The Merchant of Venice*. In many cases, the adaptations are genuine improvements on the originals (for example, from this brief list, *The Chances* and *The Rover*), but regardless of their value for twentieth-century readers and audiences, if they pleased Restoration audiences, they were the versions to enter the repertory.

The comedies of the Restoration were influenced most by the practice of Fletcher, Jonson, and other pre-Restoration English playwrights. But not to the exclusion of other influences, most notably those of continental playwrights. Few continental plays were performed unchanged on the Restoration stage. The English preference for multiple plots and rejection of the unities of time, place, and action as prescribed by French critical theorists meant that few continental plays had sufficient plot material to satisfy English audiences. And continental treatments of such fundamental social issues as gender and class required a more than literal translation to make them relevant to the very different conditions and concerns of English society. Restoration playwrights nevertheless continued to find in French and Spanish source plays a fertile field for pillaging.[7] No playwright provided more raw material for adaptation than Molière, whose texts were routinely ransacked and incorporated into countless English plays. Some particularly successful examples are John Caryll's *Sir Salomon* (1669), Thomas Betterton's *The Amorous Widow* (1670), John Crowne's *The Countrey Wit* (1675), Thomas Otway's *The Cheats of Scapin* (1676), and Dryden's *Amphitryon* (1690).

Before Molière, the first new important influence on Restoration comedy was the Spanish *comedia*, most notably the comedies of Calderón. The impact of the *comedia* was early and strong, established by the enormous success of Sir Samuel Tuke's *The Adventures of Five Hours* (1663), a play that treats many of the same issues of love and honor that figure so prominently in the heroic play, while limiting them to the domestic sphere and emphasizing their comic potential most effectively through the use of distinctly unheroic servants. *The Adventures of Five Hours* started a vogue for cape and sword plays that lasted for several years, a vogue for plays with action-filled plots, exemplary characters, and a high-toned purity that did not survive the decade. Instead, Spanish comedies were more heavily adapted for English audiences, so that by the time Dryden borrowed two of Calderón's plots for *An Evening's Love*, the result, despite its Spanish origin and setting, could not be mistaken for a Spanish play any more than the many adaptations from Molière and his contemporaries could be mistaken for their French originals. The Spanish influence continued throughout the period, contributing elements to many plays including such highly successful pieces as William Wycherley's *Love in a Wood* (1671) and Crowne's *Sir Courtly Nice* (1685).

The comedy of the Restoration, then, inherited and absorbed a number of comic traditions to produce a highly flexible and highly diverse repertory that could incorporate new elements without strain, all in a highly conventional form that required only minor adjustments. A limited number of familiar character types (young lovers, blocking parents, witty servants, fools, gulls, bullies, cast mistresses, whores, cuckolds, unhappy wives) in search of a limited number of goals (courtship, seduction, cuckolding, gulling) in a theatre that expected considerable variety in all its entertainments produced a comedy at once conservative in its adherence to its traditions yet ever-changing in response to the concerns of the society that produced and supported it. Although tragedy was the most prestigious dramatic form for playwrights and critics alike throughout the period, performance records demonstrate that comedy was by far the preferred theatrical genre with audiences. The likelihood of longer runs (and the resulting financial rewards) encouraged the best playwrights of the period to try their hands at comedy.

The comedy under discussion was performed over a fifty-year period, a period of considerable and occasionally turbulent political and social change. As an especially popular form of entertainment, available to anyone with the price of admission, comedy could be expected to address the concerns of its audiences. Why else would they come? And just as social issues do not remain stable, comedy continued to change in response to those issues, both proactively and reactively. Comic writers were able to continue to please their audiences, in other words, through a series of formal and thematic changes, changes that usually took place so gradually and smoothly that later critics have tended to see the comedy of the entire period as a seamless, static monolith. Such conclusions are as understandable as they are inaccurate. There was a wide range of comedy on stage at all times, and that range changed – slowly – from season to season throughout the period.

Most recent critics have insisted upon the need to divide the playwrights of the period into at least two groups, chronologically. Since there is a noticeable change in comedy after the death of Charles II, the mid-1680s is the favored place to mark the divide. The plays of the earlier period are often called Carolean; no equivalent adjective yet exists for the plays of the reigns of James II, William and Mary, and Anne. The playwrights of the earlier period were born before the Restoration; they include Behn, Buckingham, Crowne, Dryden, Durfey, Etherege, Howard, Otway, Shadwell, and Wycherley. They flourished in the 1660s and 1670s. The second group, born after the Restoration, includes Centlivre, Cibber, Congreve, Farquhar, Manley, Pix, Southerne, Steele, and Vanbrugh; they flourished after the Glorious Revolution. (Some, of course, are active on both sides of this artificial divide.) The best comedies of the period cluster around the mid-1670s, and, again, in the mid-1690s. But good comedies are written throughout the period, and the repertory continues to welcome plays from virtually every season; short-lived successes and a considerable number of outright failures, plays that never enter the repertory, are also scattered throughout the period. While there are a few plays that failed in their original productions but are now held in high regard (for example, Lee's *The Princess of Cleves* [1680] and Southerne's *The Wives' Excuse* [1692]), in most cases, the best plays are the ones that entered the repertory.

Restoration comedy is known today for its wit, its urbanity, its sophistication. But it did not begin that way. The fad in the early 1660s for Spanish *comedia* generated by the enormous success of *The Adventures of Five Hours* produced a series of plays with heightened sentiments, especially about love and honor. Yet despite Tuke's heightened sentiments, and despite the novelty (in 1663) of drawing on a Spanish source and of following the three unities (always unusual in English comedy), Tuke's plot is the familiar one of two pairs of lovers, Porcia and Octavio and Camilla and Antonia, whose marriages are opposed by blocking parents (here represented by the brothers of the young women, Carlos and Henrique). The brothers' objections result in part from confusion based on misinformation, confusion that can be readily resolved in the end. And the noble sentiments of the exemplary lovers are set off by the behavior of Octavio's cowardly servant, Diego, a character who would seem more at home in a low comedy. His forced marriage to Porcia's maid, Flora, provides closure parallel to that of the high plot, demonstrating the effective mix of high and low exploited by most successful comic playwrights. Tuke's comedy is long on artifice, but wanting in wit. The story of young lovers who must overcome a series of misunderstandings and obstacles puts a standard comic plot in Spanish dress; high moral principles, exemplary behavior, and great emphasis on love and honor are leavened by comical servants, a knowing self-consciousness, and extravagant sentiments. But its foreign setting, lack of obvious domestic application, purity of manners, and shortage of negative examples distinguish it from the better-known comedies of the 1670s.

The Adventures of Five Hours is so elevated a comedy that Tuke described it (neither helpfully nor accurately) as a tragicomedy. If the other great hit of the early 1660s, Sir Robert Howard's *The Committee* (1662), were to be mistaken for anything but comedy, it could be only for farce. Originally written as an attack on the recently subdued Puritans for the immediate gratification of the victorious Royalists, *The Committee* is structured around a far more domestic tale of love and honor. The Cavalier colonels Blunt and Careless come to Cromwellian London to secure their estates from the Committee of Sequestration. The same coach that carries Blunt also carries Arbella, an heiress who has fallen into the clutches of Mr. and Mrs. Day, the Chairman of the Committee and his domineering, ambitious wife. Mrs. Day has brought Arbella to London after the death of her parents to marry the Days' son Abel, and thus to gain permanent control of her large estate. The Days also have a daughter, Ruth, who has recently learned that they are not her real parents, but rather that they won control of her at age two after the death of her father, the Cavalier Sir Basil Thorowgood. The love plot quickly falls into place: Ruth and Arbella wish to escape the Days to marry Careless and Blunt.

But most of the energy of the play comes not from removing the obstacles to the marriages (as in *The Adventures of Five Hours*), but from defeating the schemes of the social climbing, hypocritical Puritans (Mrs. Day had been Careless's father's kitchen maid). Also essential to the success of the play was Careless's servant, Teague, a poor, innocent, bungling, but honest and lovable Irishman, played to perfection in the original production by the great John Lacy, and a favorite of the best low comic actors for well over a hundred years. The plot is simple, with few surprises; the satire is effective, but entirely predictable. Yet with the addition of Teague, at best marginal to the plot, and with a full dose of trickery including considerable physical comedy, *The Committee* was almost as successful as *The Adventures of Five Hours* in its initial run, and remained in the repertory much longer and to greater acclaim. Its topicality proved no problem, while Tuke's play dated quickly.

Neither *The Adventures of Five Hours* nor *The Committee* fits the traditional model for Restoration comedy, a model based on the plays of the 1670s. But both employ the inherited, traditional elements that would remain the building blocks of comedy throughout the period, and well beyond. They also represent the two poles of the comedy of the period, Tuke's play the Fletcherian, Howard's the Jonsonian. Like most plays, neither is a pure example of its form: Tuke exploits punitive, physical comedy in his treatment of Diego, Howard sympathetic, exemplary comedy in his love plots. In other words, the dynamic, productive tension between the two recognized forms of comedy was in place well before Dryden and Shadwell crystallized the debate.

The best-known, most representative Carolean comedies, those of the mid-1670s, have fully assimilated the conventions of English comedy to meet the needs and expectations of post-Restoration audiences. Courtship remains central to the plot lines involving the sympathetic characters, but the lovers are more worldly and sophisticated, and their oft-praised exchanges of wit, exchanges again treasured by audiences today, are central to their courtships. The gulls in the punitive actions lack wit; when older men, especially former Cromwellians, they are relieved of their wives by cuckolding and of their daughters by marriage to town wits; when they are country bumpkins, they are similarly relieved of their intendeds and/or their money by town wits and/or sharpers. The lines between town and city are used to redraw those that separate the gentry from the upwardly mobile bourgeois, and the plays invariably, if imperceptibly, reinforce the values of the town: loyalty to the monarchy, the established church, and a reworked cavalier code of ethics; urbanity, sophistication, classical education; a self-reflexive interest in and commitment to a small, close-knit, privileged, ruling class, firmly based in London.

But the traditional nature of Carolean comedy does not mean that the plays are all of a piece. Four of the best of the plays from a two-year period should provide some sense of the impressive variety achieved by the playwrights of the period within the constraints of a highly conventional dramatic form. William Wycherley's *The Country Wife* (1675) offers an especially interesting example. Most twentieth-century discussions of "Restoration comedy" focus on a "comedy of manners" or "comedy of wit" represented by the plays of Etherege, Wycherley, and Congreve. Wycherley's name always appears on short lists of "wits" of the period, yet despite the sharpness and effectiveness of his wit, he produced a comedy more punitive than sympathetic, more satiric than exemplary, and, arguably, more of humour than of wit.

The plot is tightly structured around three comic intrigues ("love triangles" would suggest a level of emotional commitment not to be found in *The Country Wife*), each consisting of two men and a woman: Sir Jaspar–Lady Fidget–Horner, Pinchwife–Margery–Horner, and Sparkish–Alithea–Harcourt. Each follows the Jonsonian pattern of clever rogues gulling deserving victims, though the objects of the rogues' attention here are exclusively women; money is more often the central object in Jonsonian comedy. Horner's scheme to pass himself off as impotent as a result of botched medical treatment for venereal disease in France in order to gain free access to women of "reputation" who "love the sport" is as Jonsonian a premise for comic action as any after the Restoration. His gulling of Sir Jaspar and consequent sexual relations with Lady Fidget and her circle evoke an audience response analogous to that of Volpone and Mosca taking in Corbaccio, Corvino, and Voltore, or of Doll, Face, and Subtle sporting with Dapper, Drugger, and Sir Epicure Mammon. The duping of self-centered, greedy, or hypocritical characters, each morally inferior to the none-too-perfect rogues, points to the common elements between punitive comedy and farce.

It is the other two triangles, however, which clearly distinguish *The Country Wife* from farce. For like Jonson, Wycherley is not content merely with gulling the deserving in a plot dominated by physical comedy and sight gags – though *The Country Wife* is long on both, and some directors choose not to look beyond them. Horner's intrigue with the title-character, Margery Pinchwife, is different in kind from his intrigues with Lady Fidget and her self-styled "virtuous gang." She is not a bored, worldly-wise city wife looking for adulterous amusement. Pinchwife married her because she was country-bred, "silly and innocent." Horner's scheme was designed to target the Lady Fidgets of his world; Margery falls in love with him as a result of the inept tuition of her husband. Pinchwife's attempts to keep Margery to himself while they are in London for his sister's wedding backfire, and it is Pinchwife who is responsible for the subsequent affair, including conveying Margery to Horner's lodgings. (Horner is so ill-prepared, so taken by surprise, that he nearly reveals the identity of the disguised Margery to her husband, who believes she is his sister Alithea.)

Margery is so delighted by her brief fling with Horner that she tries to exchange Pinchwife for him as her husband. By the end of the play, she has learned that changing husbands is not an option, and that she must return to the country with Pinchwife. Unlike the Horner/"virtuous gang" plot, in which the characters remain unchanged, free to continue their affairs without consequence or punishment, the Horner/Pinchwife plot is unsettling in its providing Margery with a window of opportunity for a happier life before slamming that window shut. She will never again be the silly innocent we first met.

The third intrigue, the courtship of Alithea by Harcourt who must undermine her engagement to Sparkish in order to win her, also results in permanent change. Harcourt begins the play as a traditional rake; Alithea begins the play committed to a loveless marriage to the foolish, but apparently loyal and trusting, would-be wit Sparkish. Harcourt tries a number of ploys to trick Sparkish and Alithea out of their wedding. Each fails. It is only when Sparkish believes Pinchwife's erroneous allegation that Alithea is having an affair with Horner, revealing his hitherto unrecognized jealousy, that Alithea feels justified in extricating herself from marriage to a fool in favor of marriage to a traditional comic hero. Despite the (mainly unsuccessful) attempts at gulling, this plot is nearly a textbook example of a sympathetic comic plot, the gulls serving as traditional blocking figures.

The Country Wife, then, leavens the punitive with the sympathetic to produce a mixed comedy that utilizes the full range of comic devices and conventions. What distinguishes it from most earlier – and later – comedies, that is, what makes it a typical if unusually brilliant comedy of the 1670s, is that Wycherley raises a number of difficult and complex moral issues about private life and especially love and marriage among the middle classes and gentry without offering comfortable solutions or resolutions, and without a dose of conventional morality to cover over the exposed problems. Horner is not punished for his randy behavior: he is free to remain a sexual predator among willing victims. The innocent Margery cannot escape her miserable marriage. And Alithea, the only genuinely virtuous character in the play, has learned that she cannot trust her own judgment in evaluating potential husbands. These are all standard dilemmas in comedy, but most playwrights offer more satisfying, though perhaps more facile, resolutions. Wycherley's comic vision is darker and less compromising than most; no easy closure here. His plays were too unsettling for most audiences by the early eighteenth century, and they remained unplayable until well into the twentieth.

Sir George Etherege's *The Man of Mode* (1676) reverses the balance between the punitive and the sympathetic. *The Man of Mode* is constructed around two courtship plots that culminate in marriage or the promise of marriage. The archetypal rake, Dorimant, courts the beautiful and witty heiress, Harriet, to the point that he is prepared to follow her into the country as a sign of the sincerity of his interest. Meanwhile, his friend, Young Bellair, marries his beloved, Emilia, overcoming the objections of his widower father, who also proves to be his rival. This subplot reveals especially clearly the persistence of traditional, Fletcherian comedy after the Restoration while pointing to its origins in Greek new comedy (via Plautus and Terence).[8] Bellair and Emilia quietly manipulate the ineffective blocking father with the assistance of virtually all the other characters. Their commitment to each other is secure and beyond doubt. There is minimal dramatic tension about the outcome, and most of its interest comes from the comical machinations of Old Bellair.

The main plot is far more clearly a product of the 1670s. Dorimant not only pursues Harriet, but, during the course of the play, he is in the final stages of an affair with Loveit and approaching the triumphant climax of his seduction of Bellinda. Much of the action concerns his guarding of his reputation as chief rake about town, a position that precludes commitment to any single woman. Earlier comedy abounds in sexually active young men uninterested in limiting their attentions to one woman only (Fletcher's Mirabel in *The Wild-Goose Chase* and Jonson's Truewit in *Epicoene* are two well-known examples). Most often these plays conclude with the promise of marriage, signaling the end of the wild-oats stage of the young man's life. What distinguishes *The Man of Mode* is Dorimant's almost ruthless pursuit of power over women, his dedication to a life of libertine pleasure, and Etherege's apparent sympathy for his protagonist. Dorimant does undergo some mild comic punishment when he is laughed at by his social inferiors, but he manages to recover and solidify his position while simultaneously winning the witty young virgin. The fact that the play does not challenge the social values that support Dorimant with more transcendent moral values helped insure its place by the early eighteenth century as a model for all that was reprehensible about the Carolean theatre.

While *The Man of Mode* is largely a sympathetic, Fletcherian play, it is not without Jonsonian elements, most notably Sir Fopling Flutter, the most famous Carolean stage fop. Like Teague, Sir Fopling has little to do with the action of the play – he is a pawn in the power struggle between Dorimant and Loveit – but, like Jonson's fops, he frequently displays an unselfconscious folly that amuses the other characters and, perhaps, improves the audience. And again like Jonson's humours characters, he helps define the values of the play, most significantly those represented by Dorimant. Etherege emphasized Sir Fopling's importance as a measuring stick by naming the play *The Man of Mode; or, Sir Fopling Flutter.* The ambiguities suggested by that title continue to fascinate critics.

Thomas Shadwell's *The Virtuoso* (1676) tilts the balance back toward the Jonsonian, particularly with Shadwell's determination to create "entirely new" humors characters in each new play. But even the committed Jonsonian Shadwell structures his play around a sympathetic love plot. Bruce and Longvil are in love with Clarinda and Miranda. In order to gain access to them, they must enter the circle of their intendeds' guardian, the virtuoso Sir Nicholas Gimcrack. The wits, like Dryden's Wildblood and Bellamy in *An Evening's Love*, pass themselves off as sharing the blocking character's obsession, a ploy that succeeds with minimal difficulty.

The greatest obstacles to the lovers come from two other sources, one internal, one external. The internal obstacles come from Bruce and Longvil fixing their attentions on the wrong women, an obstacle overcome when

Clarinda and Miranda persuade them to exchange intendeds. They quickly come to terms with the ladies' proposal, and all is well. The external obstacles come from Lady Gimcrack, who wishes to have the young men for herself, and from Sir Formal Trifle and Sir Samuel Hearty, Bruce and Longvil's declared rivals and the most successful humours characters in the play. Lady Gimcrack is a formidable opponent; the humours characters are not since the ladies hold them in contempt. But even Lady Gimcrack is unable to put the resolution in serious doubt, and the lovers are happily united at the end of the play.

The sympathetic plot of *The Virtuoso*, however, reflects neither its energy nor its power. The lovers are not among the most memorable in Carolean comedy. But the punitive elements in the play are of a higher order. The title-character, who sacrifices his estate to worthless, pseudoscientific experiments; the rival lovers; Sir Formal, a pedant who prides himself on his false learning and thinks himself a great orator; Sir Samuel, an energetic fool who thinks himself a great wit; and Sir Nicholas's uncle, old Snarl, a misanthrope who believes that civilization has declined hopelessly since the days of his youth and takes consolation by being whipped by his whore – all of these provide most of the play's action. Shadwell includes more physical comedy than Wycherley (trap doors, mistaken identities, bedroom farce complete with overheard conversations), also in aid of well-constructed satiric ends. And he is much truer to Jonson in restoring traditional moral values at the end of the play. The love plot is clearly subordinate to the satire, but the Fletcherian elements are fully integrated in a play that unites both traditions effectively.

In my final example from the 1670s, Aphra Behn's *The Rover*, part 1 (1677), the balance shifts once more back to the sympathetic. Behn's play is set in Spanish Naples during the 1650s. It focuses on the courtship of Florinda by the English cavalier, Colonel Belvile, who fell in love with her in Spain and followed her back to Naples. Their marriage is opposed by her brother, Pedro, the main blocking character, who intends her for the Viceroy's son, Don Antonio. Her father, conveniently absent, is said to intend her for "rich old Don Vincentio." The love interest of Florinda and Belvile drives much of the action, including the parallel courtship of their friends Valeria and Frederick, and a considerable amount of the fast-paced intrigue, trickery, and disguise so important to the success of the play. There is also a third courtship, somewhat independent of the others and far more lively and engaging, between Florinda's sister Hellena, intended by her family for a nunnery, and Willmore, the title-character and friend of the other "banished cavaliers." Willmore proves to be a rover in several senses: a pirate, a wanderer, and a philanderer. Hellena, desperate for a husband to save her from the veil, pins her hopes on Willmore and shows enormous wit, initiative, and energy in winning him for a husband. The balance between the serious, high-toned lovers, Florinda and Belvile, and the wilder, wittier Hellena and Willmore best exemplify a standard structural unit in the comedy of the period, one that would become still more popular by the end of the century.

The Rover is, if anything, action-filled; the two remaining plot lines show the range and variety of elements Behn draws upon to keep up the pace. The more important focuses on Angellica Bianca, a renowned courtesan, who has come to Naples after the death of her former keeper to sell herself for a thousand crowns a month. Both Antonio and Pedro seek to possess her, as does the penniless Willmore. Rivalry for Angellica produces extensive cape and sword action. And unexpected, additional complications occur when Angellica falls in love – for the first time – with the inconstant, rakish Willmore, and like Etherege's Loveit and Bellinda, must pay a heavy price for her passionate indiscretion. The resulting pathos is represented so powerfully that it nearly undermines the impact of the marriage of Willmore and Hellena. The final plot line, its most Jonsonian and farcical, consists of the gulling of the English country gentleman, Ned Blunt, another friend of the cavaliers, by the play's other courtesan, Lucetta. Blunt is flattered into believing that Lucetta is a woman of quality who has fallen in love with him, lured to her house, stripped of his clothes and money, and, as he gropes his way to her bed in the dark, dropped through a trap door that leads through an underground passage to the street. Spanish *comedia* is here modified by the presence of English characters, English politics, and a low-comic gulling action. Love and honor are balanced by sex and farce. Behn makes full use of her Neapolitan setting, complete with its Carnival, to create still another version of the mixed comedy so favored by playwrights and audiences.

By the time *The Rover* appeared, Carolean comedy had reached its maturity, adding to the pre-Restoration repertory a body of comedies among the finest in the history of English drama. The second generation of playwrights was able to maintain that quality while imposing modifications necessary to meet the demands of post-Carolean audiences, demands that remained for the most part stable in the eighteenth century. The most popular playwrights of the first decades after the Glorious Revolution, Cibber, Farquhar, Vanbrugh, Congreve, and Steele, remained the most popular writers of comedy for the next hundred years.[9] By the early eighteenth century most plays by Wycherley, Etherege, Shadwell, and Behn were no longer performed. The growing demands to reform the theatre, in reaction to the perceived excesses of Carolean society and its comedy, encouraged a number of changes, though many would probably have occurred in any event. The prevailing change was one away from the social values that inform so much of Carolean comedy in favor of moral values of a more traditional and timeless sort, values shared in common by many pre-Restoration and post-Carolean comedies. The major casualty is the rake. Rakish behavior does not instantly vanish, but its prominence is reduced, and more talked about – often in the past tense – than represented. Rakes reform; the rake unreformed by the end of the play is marginalized as an antisocial being.

The decline of the rake is accompanied by the decline of wit as the quality that distinguishes superior characters. Moral qualities become more important, though not at the expense of all social distinctions. Rather, moral and social values are reunited in the modified behavior of a new generation of sympathetic characters. Such changes required adjustments to comic conventions that altered both the Fletcherian and Jonsonian approaches to comedy. Libertine values are replaced by a new set of social virtues that emphasize the importance of honesty, decency, amiability, and integrity. Good nature and benevolence increasingly mark the worthy characters, with conversion to these new values frequently central to the plot. The characters may be duller as a result, but they are also more human and more real, that is, more like their audience.[10] The new exemplary figures also make an impact on the Jonsonian elements, most notably by rejecting the cruel satire and malicious laughter that was a hallmark of Jonson's own theatre. Benevolent people laugh with, not at, their inferiors, an attitude that changes humors characters, gradually, from negative examples to valued sources of harmless amusement.[11]

These changes in the comedy represent trends, not overnight revolutions. A brief examination of four of the best-known, most successful plays from the end of the period should provide a sense of the kinds of changes taking place, and of the pace of those changes. All four share in the increased post-1688 interest in what happens to couples after they marry, that is, in the marital discord that afflicts so many couples in these plays.[12] Sir John Vanbrugh's *The Provok'd Wife* (1697) centers on the troubled relationship between Sir John and Lady Brute two years after their marriage. Physical attraction has worn off; Sir John prefers to spend his time drinking and carousing with his friend, Lord Rake, while Lady Brute prefers the company of her gallant, Constant. In Carolean comedy, this would be a formula for cuckolding, but Vanbrugh chooses to look more thoughtfully at the problems of dysfunctional marriages. He refuses the easy solutions in favor of the more realistic recognition that both parties are at fault and must suffer the consequences. Punishing Sir John solves nothing, merely diverting attention from the real problems. Lady Brute is, of course, understandably tempted by Constant, but fear of exposure helps firm up her moral principles as she toys with the possibility of consummation.

The second plot is a more conventional, sympathetic courtship plot. Lady Brute's niece, Bellinda, converts the previously confirmed bachelor-misogynist, Heartfree, into a sincere, smitten lover. The blocking figure, Lady Fancyfull, a vain and affected woman Heartfree had tried unsuccessfully to reason out of her folly, is determined to prevent him from transferring his interest to another. Her attempts fail, and she must suffer appropriate comic ridicule. Even this plot has a difference that demonstrates Vanbrugh's reworking of Carolean comedy. Heartfree is a younger brother without a significant fortune; Bellinda is an heiress who deliberately chooses him over a wealthier alternative who would be less likely to make her happy. The Brutes clearly provide the negative example she intends to avoid.

My discussion thus far suggests a play more earnest than it is. Constant's pursuit of Lady Brute is full of lively, clever dialogue. Bellinda and Heartfree's tentative movements toward matrimony are similarly comic in tone. Lady Fancyfull is a humours character who is ridiculed and punished for her folly. Several scenes are devoted to Sir John in his cups, beating the watch and swearing and lying to a Justice of the Peace. Lady Fancyfull's French maid and Sir John's servant offer additional low comedy. Fletcherian and Jonsonian elements, in other words, continue to structure *The Provok'd Wife*, providing a comedy full of the range and variety demanded by English audiences but brought up to date for the late 1690s.

The same can be said for William Congreve's *The Way of the World* (1700), though in Congreve's play the humours characters are incorporated into a more purely Fletcherian plot. Virtually the entire action is subordinated to the courtship of Mirabell and Millamant, but since the obstacles to their marriage involve most of the other characters, an apparently simple story becomes unusually complicated. Mirabell tries to trick the principal blocking character, Millamant's aunt, Lady Wishfort, into granting her permission in order not to lose half of Millamant's fortune. He must also contend with three rival suitors. None poses a serious threat, but each further complicates the action. He must also deal with the consequences of his earlier affair with Lady Wishfort's daughter, Arabella, now Mrs. Fainall after a hasty marriage to a man of low moral standards occasioned by Arabella's fear that she was pregnant. Fainall wishes to prevent Millamant from inheriting the money controlled by Lady Wishfort so that he can win control of it for himself. And his mistress, Marwood, seeks to prevent the marriage to revenge her sense of having been slighted by Mirabell.

The Jonsonian elements are again limited to the minor characters, Lady

Wishfort and the rival suitors, Witwoud, Petulant, and Sir Wilfull Witwoud. The Jonsonian action, the attempted deceit of Lady Wishfort through a mock-marriage to Mirabell's servant, Waitwell, is a failure, an example of a growing separation between comic heroes and rogues or sharpers. Moreover, Mirabell's intended victims, from Lady Wishfort to Sir Wilfull, are more complex than their predecessors. Similar characters in Carolean comedy tend to be merely gulls or victims; Congreve's richer, more well-rounded characters receive a more humane treatment than earlier, simpler comic types. Also more complex are Congreve's villains, Fainall and Marwood. Fainall is Mirabell's equal in wit; they are distinguished on moral, not social, grounds. Marwood, similarly, has a complexity beyond that of most rejected mistresses, one that also includes unexpected moral depth. The result is a moral seriousness analogous to that of the best punitive comedy translated into the idiom of a traditional sympathetic plot. Mirabell and Millamant's ultimate triumph over the folly and malice that are so much a part of their world gains a special significance from Congreve's emphasis on the difficulty and rarity of such a triumph.

Far more conventional is the treatment Colley Cibber applies to similar material in *The Careless Husband* (1704). Sir Charles and Lady Easy are another couple married long enough for problems to emerge. Sir Charles is bored with marriage and with his wife. He is a philanderer, but he is no more passionate about his mistresses than his wife. Cibber subscribes more fully than Vanbrugh or Congreve to the new humane values. As a result, Sir Charles is at heart an amiable man, but one who has never taken the trouble to look beneath the surface of the world around him. His wife, a thoroughly virtuous woman who loves him, determines that the best way to win him over to a more thoughtful, virtuous life is through patience and trust. Her strategy proves the correct one when this plot line reaches its climax in the famous "steinkirk scene." Lady Easy discovers her husband asleep with her maid in his bedroom. Though shocked and upset, her response is to cover his bare head with her neckcloth (steinkirk). When Sir Charles awakens and discovers the steinkirk, he is shamed into reform, proclaiming himself a convert to a more self-reflective and virtuous life.

The other plot is a sympathetic, courtship plot. Lord Morelove has been courting Lady Betty Modish for several years with singleminded devotion. The reward for his earnest, open behavior has been rejection and ridicule. Lady Betty enjoys her power over him so much that she is unwilling to give it up for a more serious relationship. And he is so much the benevolent man of sense (and so little the rakish man of wit) that he has been unable to find an effective response. Lord Morelove turns to his friend, Sir Charles, for help, and they are eventually able to bring the courtship to fruition. In the end, two fundamentally good couples are happily (re)united. The Jonsonian elements in the play are again reduced to the redefined humours characters, that is, characters no longer merely negative moral examples. Sir Charles and Lady Betty, the characters whose reform is required for the happy ending, are as much humours as Sir Charles's mistress, Lady Graveairs, and Lord Morelove's rival for Lady Betty's attention, Lord Foppington. And though the latter two characters are the losers, they are not subjected to punishment beyond their losses.

Humours characters also receive a kinder treatment in my final example, George Farquhar's *The Beaux' Stratagem* (1707), though it incorporates a larger number of conventions from Jonsonian comedy. The plot's premise, that Aimwell and Archer, two younger brothers who have squandered their limited resources, are heading into the country to trick a wealthy heiress into marriage, is very much in the spirit of punitive comedy. And their scheme works. Dorinda falls in love with Aimwell, who is masquerading as his elder brother, Viscount Aimwell. But Aimwell proves too benevolent to marry her under false pretenses. Instead, he confesses the truth, only to be loved the more for his honesty and to be rewarded with the identity he had falsely appropriated when news arrives of the death of his brother. This is the new Jonsonian comedy, stripped of its punitive origins in response to the rejection of the satiric principles that had been its underpinning. Not only is punishment of the humours reduced to the gentlest of reminders of Jonson's own practice, but the notion that audiences should laugh at the humours in order to learn from their examples how not to behave – and not to be laughed at – has similarly been reduced to a faint echo with the rejection of malicious laughter.

The second plot anatomizes the Sullens and their dysfunctional marriage. Sullen married to get an heir for his estate; his wife married to enjoy the pleasures of society. Neither partner's expectations have been fulfilled. Mrs. Sullen has been amusing herself with the attention of Count Bellair, a French prisoner being held at Lichfield, before the arrival of Aimwell and Archer. Now she falls for Archer, disguised as Aimwell's servant. Like Lady Brute, she is seriously tempted, but unlike Lady Brute, she is offered a resolution to her problem that allows her to escape from her husband, reputation intact. Her brother effects the divorce that shares the closing, celebratory spotlight with the marriage of Aimwell and Dorinda. Squire Sullen is an unattractive figure, but he is not blamed disproportionately for the failure of the marriage, and he is not cuckolded.

Farquhar does not do away with laughter, but he shows how well and effectively it can be manipulated without malice. His characters, even the wicked ones like the innkeeper, Boniface, the head of a gang of high-waymen, are treated gently and as sympathetically as possible. Farquhar's comic world provided a model for generations of comic playwrights, embodying the new, humane values without sacrificing laughter, humours characters, physical comedy, love or sex. The long lasting success of his generation of playwrights insured that English stage comedy of the eighteenth century would remain the conservative, slowly changing mix of Fletcherian and Jonsonian elements that had formed so effective and resilient a partnership throughout the seventeenth century.

NOTES

1 Robert D. Hume, *The Development of English Drama in the Late Seventeenth Century* (Oxford: Clarendon Press, 1976), pp. 32–62.

2 John Dryden, *An Essay of Dramatick Poesie*, in *The Works of John Dryden*, ed. H. T. Swedenberg Jr., *et al.*, 20 vols., in progress (Berkeley: University of California Press, 1956–), XVII, 57. Hereafter, Dryden references are to this edition.

3 Thomas Shadwell, "Preface to *The Sullen Lovers*," in J. E. Spingarn, ed., *Critical Essays of the Seventeenth Century*, 3 vols. (1908–09; rpt. Bloomington: Indiana University Press, 1957), III, 150.

4 Thomas Shadwell, "Preface to *The Humorists*," in Spingarn, ed., *Critical Essays*, II, 154; John Dryden, preface to *An Evening's Love*," in *The Works of John Dryden*, X, 205–07.

5 Ibid., p. 206.

6 See Hume, *English Drama*, pp. 45–48, and Brian Corman, *Genre and Generic Change in English Comedy 1660–1710* (University of Toronto Press, 1993), pp. 9–11.

7 See John Wilcox, *The Relation of Molière to Restoration Comedy* (New York: Columbia University Press, 1938); Norman Suckling, "Molière and English Restoration Comedy," in John Russell Brown and Bernard Harris, eds., *Restoration Theatre* (London: Edward Arnold, 1965), pp. 92–107; John Loftis, *The Spanish Plays of Neoclassical England* (New Haven: Yale University Press, 1973).

8 Northrop Frye, "The Anatomy of Comedy," in *English Institute Essays 1948* (New York: Columbia University Press, 1949), pp. 58–73.

9 Shirley Strum Kenny, "Perennial Favorites: Congreve, Vanbrugh, Cibber, Farquhar, and Steele," *MP* 73 (1976), S4–S11.

10 Shirley Strum Kenny, "Humane Comedy," *MP* 75 (1977), 29–43; Hume, *English Drama*, pp. 381–96.

11 Stuart M. Tave, *The Amiable Humorist: a Study in the Comic Theory and Criticism of the Eighteenth and Early Nineteenth Centuries* (University of Chicago Press, 1960), pp. 43–87.

12 Robert D. Hume, "Marital Discord in English Comedy from Dryden to Fielding," in *The Rakish Stage: Studies in English Drama, 1660–1800* (Carbondale: Southern Illinois University Press, 1983), pp. 176–213.

5

CHRISTOPHER J. WHEATLEY

Tragedy

While Restoration playwrights were influenced by Shakespeare and earlier English tragedians, the years that Charles II and his court had spent in France during the Interregnum (1642–60) made them acquainted with French playwrights and theorists who exercised an important (albeit unfortunate) critical authority concerning tragedy that created a thematic and stylistic disjunction between the major serious dramatists of the Restoration and earlier English playwrights.

French influence on Restoration drama can be overstated. French critics, for instance, thought they could derive from Aristotle a set of rules called "the unities." The unity of action meant that there should be a single, serious action of magnitude to the play; i.e., not merely the elimination of subplots, but assuredly the absence of comic interludes (such as the grave-digger scene in *Hamlet*). The unity of place stipulated a single setting. The unity of time limited the play to a representation of at most twenty-four hours. While some Restoration plays do fulfill the unities – notably Dryden's *All for Love* (1677) – many simply ignore them. Even unity of action, the only unity actually Aristotelian, was frequently disregarded, most radically in plays such as Thomas Southerne's *Oroonoko* (1695), an adaptation of Aphra Behn's novel. In this play, the tragic story of an enslaved African chief is paired with a comic subplot about husband-hunting young women. Still, French ideas of character do shape English drama. A French prince would not trade quips and equivocations with a gravedigger; this would be a violation of "decorum," behavior appropriate to social rank and role. By the Restoration, the princes of the English stage are stiff, noble figures, like the princes of French tragedy, and unlike Shakespeare's protean Prince Hal; a "general idealization of character" replaces the range of characterizations possible in earlier English tragedy.[1]

The differences between Restoration drama and Elizabethan and Jacobean drama can also be overstated. The Restoration audience included servants, apprentices, tradesmen, and merchants, as had Shakespeare's, even though the overall composition of the audience was more élite. In *An Essay of Dramatic Poesy* (1667), John Dryden, one of the most important of the English tragic playwrights of the Restoration (along with Nathaniel Lee, Thomas Otway, John Banks, and John Crowne), expressed his admiration for his English predecessors over both French and classical authors. Aquilina's description of her client Antonio, in Thomas Otway's *Venice Preserv'd* (1681) shows the continuity between the Jacobean and Restoration stages:

> The worst thing an old Man can be's a Lover,
> A meer *Memento Mori* to poor woman.
> I never lay by his decrepit side,
> But all that night I ponder'd on my Grave.[2]

The combination of sex and death through morbid wit recalls the atmosphere of decay that pervades Jacobean drama.

Nevertheless, the modern reader – some of the plays held the stage until the nineteenth century but are rarely performed now – may well wonder exactly why some of these plays were called tragedies. Robert Hume, in his influential *The Development of English Drama in the Late Seventeenth Century*, deliberately avoids discussing "Theories of Tragedy" in favor of "Theories of Serious Drama" because of the diversity of Restoration drama.[3] Plays identified as tragedies by their titles sometimes have happy endings. Tragic heroes are sometimes entirely innocent of any moral offense. The motivations of characters can appear simplistic or profoundly psychotic. The language of tragedy varies between overly emotional rant and simple, even pedestrian dialogue, while almost always eschewing the dense metaphors of earlier English drama. Whatever the weaknesses of Restoration tragedy, the problem was not a limited range of options. J. Douglas Canfield divides the possibilities into heroic romance, romantic tragedy, political tragedy, personal tragedy, and tragical satire.[4] Without resorting to such a taxonomy, some generalizations about Restoration tragedy can be derived from the critical debates of the period. These debates largely center on the proper purpose of tragedy and the means of achieving that purpose.

Thomas Rymer was the English critic most influenced by French interpretations of the classical heritage. In *The Tragedies of the Last Age Consider'd and Examin'd* (1678) he states with admirable clarity that

1. I believe the end of all Poetry is to *please*.
2. Some sorts of Poetry please without profiting.
3. I am confident whoever writes a Tragedy cannot please but must also profit; 'tis the physic of the mind that he makes palatable.[5]

Yet this apparently simple series of propositions conceals a complex synthesis of two different emphases in dramatic construction, based on the Roman poet Horace, and the Greek philosopher Aristotle.

Poetry, according to Horace, should be *utile et dulce*, both instructive and delightful. Rymer believed that in Restoration tragedy, the "fable" of the play should be constructed in such a way that the audience learned a moral lesson. Alternately, tragedy, argued Aristotle, through the tragic emotions of pity and fear, allowed *catharsis* (in Greek, the word means "purgation" or "purification"). On the one hand, this is also instructive as we pity the tragic hero who is superior to us, and learn prudence, inspired by fear, from seeing his errors. But catharsis may also mean that, by watching a play, potentially dangerous emotions are released harmlessly, much to the benefit of the audience and the state. An added complication of Aristotle's *Poetics*, however, is the philosopher's recognition that the audience finds the experience of pity and fear pleasurable in itself. In short, while Horatian and Aristotelian theories of tragedy overlap, the former is largely concerned with the didactic or instructive capacity of tragedy through poetic justice, while the latter is interested in the emotional response of an audience to tragedy.[6]

Some Restoration tragedies inculcate moral lessons through the catastrophe so unequivocally that the modern reader is left uncomfortable. In Nathaniel Lee's *Lucius Junius Brutus* (1680), the title-character, founder of the Roman Republic, must execute his own sons for monarchical sympathies. Though played for broad pathos, we are clearly supposed to admire Brutus when he says "Of the immortal gods it is decreed / There must be patterns drawn of fiercest virtue, / Brutus submits to the eternal doom." To emphasize Brutus' virtue, Valerius, his friend, immediately asks "May I believe there can be such perfection. / Such a resolve in man?"[7] Lee's fierce defense of the Whig position in the Exclusion Crisis (see chapter 10, p. 170) does not allow for moral ambiguity in the choice between private and public virtue.

If Brutus is a type of the perfectly virtuous tragic hero, Aphra Behn's *Abdelazer, Or the Moor's Revenge* (1676) reveals the vicious protagonist who richly earns his death. Although recalling Jacobean revenge tragedies, Abdelazer's unambiguous and unashamedly evil desires separate Behn's work from the murky moral atmosphere of Middleton or Ford. Abdelazer schemes to become king of Spain: "Now all that's brave and Villain seize my soul, / Reform each faculty that is not Ill, / And make it fit for Vengeance." The adulterous Queen is his willing accomplice and match in depravity: "No rigid Virtue shall my soul possess, / Let Gown-men preach against the wickedness; / Pleasures were made by Gods!"[8] There is an echo here of the philosopher Thomas Hobbes, author of *Leviathan*, who argued that what we desire we call good, and the Queen and Abdelezar perhaps also have something in common with the skeptical libertinism of the "merry Band," the court wits of the Restoration: Charles Sedley, John Wilmot, Earl of Rochester, the Duke of Buckingham, and others. But even if the energy of the villains is perversely appealing, their deaths mark the restoration of moral order and the rightful blood line.

Restoration tragedy is not, however, two-dimensional, divided between heroes and villains. Just as Macbeth is both a man of great virtues and crimes, Lee's Alexander in *The Rival Queens* (1677) is a passionate lover and a great commander, while at the same time he is the protagonist doomed by his own mistakes (the Greek word is *hamartia*, a term from archery meaning "to miss the mark"). In a fit of rage, Alexander kills his best adviser, Clytus, who has chided him for his vanity: "The poor, the honest Clytus thou hast slain! / Are these the laws of hospitality? / Thy friends will shun thee now[.]" This is the recognition scene of classical tragedy (*anagnorisis*) where the protagonist sees his errors but cannot mend them. Alexander is also a classical tragic figure in that his central weakness is hubris, or overweening pride. As his Queen Statira dies, Alexander tells her to wait for his messages:

> Tell the gods I'm coming
> To give 'em an account of life and death,
> And many other hundred thousand policies
> That much concern the government of heav'n.[9]

In Restoration tragedy, then, the range of characters for possible protagonists include the perfectly virtuous, completely criminal, and classically flawed.

At the core of Rymer's didactic program was poetic justice, or as Oscar Wilde's Miss Prism would put it two hundred years later describing her novel, "The good ended happily, and the bad unhappily. That is what fiction means." Rymer was particularly annoyed about Desdemona's death in *Othello* because she was innocent of any sin. Yet Rymer's conflation of the cathartic emotions of pity and terror with moral instruction allows Dryden to sidestep poetic justice by claiming that pity is more easily evoked through the suffering of the innocent. Thus Dryden splits the tragic emotions between two characters or sets of characters:

> And chiefly we have to say (what I hinted on Pity and Terror in the last Paragraph save one) that the Punishment of Vice, and Reward of Virtue, are the most Adequate ends of Tragedy, because most conducting to good Example of Life; now Pity is not so easily rais'd for a Criminal (as the Ancient

> Tragedy always Represents its chief Person such) as it is for an Innocent Man
> and the Suffering of Innocence and Punishment of the Offender, is of the
> Nature of English Tragedy.[10]

The villain is still punished in Dryden's emendation, but since the tragic
emotions take pride of place over the moral utility of tragedy, innocent
victims are frequent in Restoration tragedy.

Roger Boyle, first Earl of Orrery, provides a clear example of the tragic
hero as innocent victim. In *The Tragedy of Mustapha* (1665), the title-
character is framed by corrupt ministers as desiring his father Solyman's
throne, so Solyman orders his execution, which Mustapha willingly
accepts:

> That Chearfulness with which to Death I go,
> Some Proof, Sir, of my Innocence does show.
> And since by Death I would your Hate remove,
> What would I not have done to gain your Love?[11]

Implicitly Boyle warns of the danger of ambition, especially in a state
where a ruler's absolute power inspires political paranoia. The audience
sees the consequences of court corruption for a character who combines the
roles of loyal son, loving brother, gallant lover, and brave soldier. In short,
pity inspires fear because even the best are not safe in a tragic universe.

The difference between earlier English tragedy and Restoration tragedy
is one of degree in the extent to which the protagonist is responsible for his
catastrophe. King Lear should not divide his kingdom between his older
daughters, but he does not deserve what happens to him. By the Restoration, some characters are entirely blameless. In plays where the tragic hero
is innocent of crime, responsibility shifts to villains, and all the virtuous
hero can do is refuse to compromise. In John Crowne's *Darius, King of
Persia* (1688), traitors first arrest the title-character hoping to gain advantage with Alexander the Great when he invades, and then attempt to return
the king to the throne. Darius refuses their aid:

> I favor treason? I assume your guilt?
> I'll rather bravely die than basely reign.
> Indeed my children are most dear to me,
> But, for that cause, I will not taint their blood,
> And make the children of a King become
> The children of a traitor to a king.[12]

The political implications here are obvious. Crowne was an unrepentant
Tory, and Darius represents James II, a rightful monarch being "robbed" of
his throne. In this political context, Darius' refusal to compromise preserves
his heirs' right of succession (as James II, from safety in France, continued

to claim the right of James III to be king of England). Despite this rigidity, Darius is absolved from any responsibility for his own downfall. His unwillingness to compromise earns the audience's respect, reaffirms his fundamental innocence, and, presumably, establishes his right to our pity. As we shall see below, the absence of personal responsibility and the increasing importance of emotional expression as the reason for tragedy leads to a shift in the sphere and topics of tragedy from the public to the private. Affairs of state are replaced by affairs of the heart.

While one strand of Restoration tragedy followed Horatian criteria in emphasizing a morally instructive plot, another emphasized the affective nature of tragedy, implicit in Aristotle's observations about an audience's emotional response to tragedy. This created two related types of drama. Characters whom the audience admired or at whom the audience marveled could aid the didactic program through emotional identification. On the other hand, if the experience of emotion was pleasurable in itself, then characters should experience as many powerful emotions as possible in a play, so that the audience could vicariously experience them as well, and moral instruction becomes irrelevant.

In the overlap between "heroic" drama (serious plays written in rhyming couplets, popular between 1663 and 1676) and tragedy, Dryden presents protagonists who may be either virtuous or vicious, but who inspire "admiration" because of their irregular greatness.[13] These characters are sometimes purely magnificent, modeled after the epic heroes of Homer and Virgil. In Dryden's two-part *The Conquest of Granada* (1670–71), Abdalla describes the hero Almanzor as a moorish Achilles (Almanzor turns out ultimately to be Spanish):

> Vast is his Courage; boundless is his mind,
> Rough as a storm, and humorous as wind;
> Honour's the onely Idol of his Eyes:
> The charms of Beauty like a pest he flies:
> And rais'd by Valour, from a birth unknown,
> Acknowledges no pow'r above his own.   (XI, 31)

The "humorous"ness of Almanzor is apparent through his sudden changes of allegiance throughout the play, both political and emotional as he falls in love with Almahide at first sight, despite the fact that she is betrothed to Boabdelin, the king of Granada.

Not just modern readers, but Restoration commentators savaged the heroic protagonist. The Duke of Buckingham in *The Rehearsal* (1671) satirized Almanzor as Drawcansir, "a fierce hero that frights his mistress, snubs up kings, baffles armies, and does what he will, without regard to numbers, good manners or justice." The sacrifice of the carefully designed and morally instructive fable to character and language also drew fire, as Bayes, the play's caricature of Dryden, defends the introduction of dialogue that is irrelevant to the action: "why, what a devil is the plot good for but to bring in fine things?"[14] These criticisms make sense from the Horatian perspective, since there is little to be learned from Almanzor, even though he does learn self-control and necessary subordination to authority when he discovers his Christian heritage. His character is divorced by its greatness and wilfulness from the common sense of the audience, but his "grandeur of soul" is supposed to stand in opposition to meanness and pusillanimity.[15]

The tragical-epic hero – one cannot avoid sounding like Polonius when looking at some of the hybrid forms of the Restoration – can neatly embody the moral instruction of tragedy. In Dryden's *Aureng-Zebe* (1675), Morat, the younger brother of the title-character, desires to usurp both his father's throne and his brother's beloved. Indamora (the beloved) links his qualities to his destructive desires:

> Yours is a Soul irregularly great,
> Which wanting temper, yet abounds with heat:
> So strong, yet so unequal pulses beat.
> A Sun which does, through vapours dimnly shine:
> What pity 'tis you are not all Divine!   (XII, 230)

Morat's restless energy cannot be bound by the conventions of patrilineage and he is destroyed because of it. But although Morat shows that heroic drama could incorporate the moral instruction of French tragedy, ultimately Dryden does not feel any need for moral instruction at all.

In the introduction to his play *The Indian Emperour* (1665), Dryden defends his use of rhyme against the attacks of his brother-in-law Sir Robert Howard:

> for delight is the chief, if not the only end of Poesie; instruction can be admitted but in the second place, for Poesie only instructs as it delights. 'Tis true that to imitate well is a Poets work; but to affect the Soul, and excite the Passions, and above all to move admiration (which is the delight of serious Plays) a bare imitation will not serve.   (IX, 5–6)

Here rhyme is praised for its representation of nature heightened, and Dryden will heighten the passions of his characters also for the sake of delight rather than moral instruction. The French critic René Rapin agreed with Aristotle's observation that members of an audience enjoy tragedy because of the experience of emotion, and supported it with the seventeenth-century philosophy of the passions that Descartes had promulgated.

The agitation of the soul by the passions became an end in itself, and the greater the agitation, the better.[16]

Consequently Dryden frequently constructs scenes whose sole purpose is to create an emotional response in the audience. Thus in *All for Love*, various Romans attempt to lure Mark Antony from Cleopatra and back to Rome. In one scene his wife, Octavia, has his children hang on his legs while a fellow soldier and young friend also plead with him:

> [*Here the Children go to him*, &c.]
> *Ventidius* Was ever sight so moving! Emperor!
> *Dollabella* Friend!
> *Octavia* Husband!
> *Both Children* Father!
> *Antony* I am vanquish'd: take me, Octavia; take me Children; share me all. (XIII, 67)

Whatever thematic implications the scene possesses, they are secondary to the pathos generated by the tableaux. This overt emotionalism represents perhaps the greatest difficulty of Restoration tragedy. Again, as Oscar Wilde said about the death of Little Nell in Dickens's *The Old Curiosity Shop*, one needs a heart of stone to read this scene without laughing.

The ability to feel appropriate emotions, both in the characters, and by extension in the audience, does have ethical implications. In *All for Love*, the recurring charge against Augustus Caesar is his lack of passion: "O, 'tis the coolest youth upon a Charge, / The most deliberate fighter!" (XIII, 43). The contrast between the calculating Augustus and the impulsive Antony goes back to Plutarch, and Shakespeare exploits it to great effect. In Dryden's version, Antony is a noble gentleman and lover, and the unseen Augustus unworthy of his position precisely because he is never distracted by the appeal of sex or honor. Even the cultural polarity between Egypt (love and hedonism) and Rome (stoicism and self-denial) that Richard W. Bevis points out ultimately does not affect our judgment of Antony, as all his choices have been made long before the play begins.[17]

At its best however, Restoration tragedy powerfully depicts the emotional distress of an individual whose choices do not make any difference. Thomas Otway's *Venice Preserv'd* (1681), provided three great leading roles, Jaffeir, Pierre, and Belvidera, for more than a century, because of the anguish of conflicting loyalties. Jaffeir in particular is caught between his obligations to his friend Pierre, a conspirator trying to overthrow the Venetian Senate, and love for his wife, Belvidera, the daughter of a senator. Worse, the senators are corrupt and perverse (in particular Antonio, who likes his prostitute, Aquilina, to beat him like a dog and spit on him), while the conspirators promise to make the streets run with blood. By the time the play begins, there are no good choices available for Jaffeir, and his despair at his lost honor and love is movingly portrayed.

Affective tragedy combines with the innocence of the protagonist to create "private" tragedy. Tragedy had traditionally concerned itself with "affairs of state." That is, the destruction of the protagonist had widespread social and political consequences (with a few notable exceptions, such as *Romeo and Juliet*). Over the course of the Restoration, even the tragedies of princes and queens became mostly personal, with the social effects largely passed over in the dramatization. Ultimately, social problems that affected private individuals, such as marriages of economic convenience, became legitimate topics for tragic treatment.

The first step is the emphasis on important social figures as individuals. John Banks's *Virtue Betray'd* (1682) treats Anna Bullen as a political football, kicked around between Cardinal Wolsey and the Duke of Northumberland, and ultimately as a Protestant martyr. Nevertheless, the private sorrow of Anna and Piercy (son of Northumberland), who love each other, is as important thematically as any political agendas in the play, and Henry VIII's tyranny is shown by the intended forced marriage of Piercy and Diana. Piercy says, "What would the Tyrant be a God? / To take upon him to dispose of Hearts!"[18] Henry's hubris is shown by his intrusion on the newly private realm of affection. Interestingly, as Frances Kavenik observes, the distinction between male and female is collapsed in order to elevate the personal; many of the speeches of Anna and Piercy could equally well be spoken by the other.[19]

Dryden's *Don Sebastian* (1689) in its published form was fairly openly Jacobite (i.e., supportive of the deposed James II). But as a play, the political is subordinate to the private. Don Sebastian, victorious over his enemies the Moors, beloved by his subjects, is ready in the fifth act to live happily ever after with Almeyda, when they discover they are half brother and sister. They separate mournfully, and he imposes private exile on himself as penance. The consequences of this for Sebastian's Portuguese subjects are not developed. The closing lines of the play attempt to provide a moral lesson:

> And let *Sebastian* and *Almeyda*'s Fate,
> This dreadful sentence to the World relate,
> That unrepented Crimes of Parents dead,
> Are justly punish'd on their Children's head.   (xv, 217)

However, it is doubtful that those who engage in fornication and adultery are likely to be dissuaded by the fear that this may ultimately involve, through a series of nasty coincidences, their children in incest. Sebastian as prince is heroic and successful; he only becomes tragic because of private reverses.

Catherine Trotter's *The Fatal Friendship* (1698) represents the completed movement to private tragedy. Gramont, secretly married to Felicia for two years, marries the widow Lamira as well in order to protect his wife and child from poverty and his friend Castalio from imprisonment. Bigamy destroys not merely Gramont but Castalio, and Lamira retires from the world to a life of prayer. Gramont's father is forced to recognize that his refusal to allow the marriage of Gramont and Felicia has partially contributed to the disaster, and he promises to raise his grandson. The social system of marriage, where affection is secondary to advantage, is the underlying cause of the tragedy. Even Lamira in her first marriage was a victim and seeks to marry for love the second time around: "You've reason now, delivered from the tyrant / Your parents forced upon your tender years, / To let your heart direct your second choice."[20] Still, while the problem is social, the tragic mistakes of the characters affect only themselves, just as Willie Loman's suicide in *Death of a Salesman* is unnoticed by the rest of society.

Mechanistic theories of consciousness increasingly emphasized a common denominator of humanity. Isabella in Thomas Southerne's *The Fatal Marriage* (1694), thinking her first husband dead (because her brother-in-law has concealed his knowledge of her husband's survival), marries a worthy man who loves her, only to have her first husband return; she goes mad and dies. Aside from the fact that unwitting bigamy looks more like a comic than a tragic plot to the twentieth-century reader, the purely personal nature of the disaster relies on the assumption that this would be a tragedy for anyone, and that social rank is irrelevant. Isabella reflects that

> The Beggar and the King
> With equal steps, tread, forward to their end:
> Tho' they appear of different Natures now;
> Not of the same work of Providence;
> They meet at last: the reconciling Grave
> Swallows Distinction first, that made us Foes,
> The all alike lie down in peace together.[21]

Shakespeare's Richard II insists that he is just like other men, when he hears news of the success of the rebellion, but the point of that scene is that he is wrong, needs to summon his courage, and start acting like a king. Isabella and Don Sebastian to a much greater extent affirm that there is no fundamental difference between the griefs of a prince and a private citizen.

To this point, I have implied that most of the characteristics of Restoration tragedy can be understood through the theoretical debates of the mid- and late seventeenth century. This is misleading as the stagecraft of the period shapes the drama at least as much as literary theory. Shakespeare's theatre made do with boys playing women's roles. This did not eliminate significant women's parts. In John Webster's *The Duchess of Malfi*, the title-character would have been played by perhaps a fourteen year old who had been acting professionally for nine years. However, in the Restoration theatre, playwrights had the advantage of experienced and talented women actresses who simply had a greater range than any adolescent male could match (whatever the apologists of Renaissance drama may say).

John Banks's *The Island Queens: Or, the Death of Mary, Queen of Scotland*, though suppressed shortly after its premiere (1684) succeeds as a vehicle designed with plenty of star turns for leading actresses. Queen Elizabeth is a wonderful-scenery chewing part:

> Ha! am I dar'd! brav'd by a Slave! a Snake!
> Crawl'd from the frozen Corner of my Land,
> But warm grown by my Beams of Majesty,
> To hiss me to my Face! Malicious Rebel!—
> Quick, take him, bind him, gag him, bore him through
> The tongue, this haughty *Scot!—*

A fourteen-year-old boy would sound shrill here; a Restoration star like Elizabeth Barry undoubtedly carried scenes like this on the strength of her technique and personality. Queen Mary shares several scenes with Elizabeth, but she is also allowed individual scenes where the audience is invited to bring out their handkerchiefs, such as when she addresses the executioner:

> Hear me Friend,
> Thou with the Vizour; if thou'rt Death be not
> Asham'd to shew thy Face, for I can dare thee.
> How long hast thou been practis'd in thy Art?
> And how many brave Heads hast thou cut off?
> Why dost not speak?[22]

The actress here must show courage, fear, pride, entreaty, and anger simultaneously. These parts may be melodramatic, but it is far from easy either to write or perform effective melodrama.

The development of great stage effects in the Restoration also led to the exotic settings and miraculous events that distinguish Restoration tragedy from Elizabethan and Jacobean drama, just as the special effects of *Star Wars* ignited a science fiction boom in the 1970s. Anyone who attends the opera is familiar with the "ahh" followed by applause that attends the opening of the curtain on an impressive set. Something similar probably happened at the première of Elkanah Settle's *The Empress of Morocco* (1673) when

> *The Scene opened, is represented the Prospect of a large River, with a glorious Fleet of Ships, supposed to be the Navy of* Muly Hamet, *after the Sound of Trumpets and the Discharging of Guns.*

The painted scenes alone must have been impressive enough to an audience unused to them, but the staging was not merely static and picturesque. Later in the play,

> *The Scene open'd, is represented a Prospect of a Clouded Sky, with a Rainbow. After a shower of Hail, enter from within the Scenes* Muly Hamet, *and Abdelcador.*[23]

The tongue-in-groove sliding scene system allowed for multiple impressive sets, and the large, enclosed backstage area made possible surprising effects like hail.

John Crowne's *Destruction of Jerusalem* (1677) multiplies sound effects for suspense. First a "*Noise is heard like an earthquake*" to startle audience and characters alike. Then "*A Small voice is heard*" under an altar for contrast, followed shortly thereafter by "*A great voice is heard from under the stage like a tube.*" The climax comes when "*The Veil flies open, and shews the Sancta Sanctorum*" – the progression of sound effects sets up the visual, just as the sound of footsteps and crashing furniture in a horror film introduces the slasher wearing a hockey mask – and "*An Angel descends over the altar, and speaks.*"[24] Shakespeare's characters describe the marvelous, while the Restoration playwright frequently found it possible to show it; the modern reader simply needs to be attentive to "hear" Shakespeare's stage effects, but a much greater act of theatrical imagination is required of the modern reader to recreate the Restoration theatrical experience because of its visual nature.

In one area, however, no amount of sympathetic historical imagination will bridge the gap between the late twentieth century and the Restoration theatre: the language of tragedy. Shakespeare is so much a part of our living language, indeed so much determines what we regard as acceptable English, that it is with a sense of shock that we read Dryden's pronouncement about the poetry of earlier seventeenth-century tragedy in his defense of the Epilogue to the second part of *The Conquest of Granada*: "But malice and partiality set apart, let any man who understands English, read diligently the works of Shakspeare and Fletcher, and I dare undertake that he will find in every page either some solecism of speech, or some notorious flaw in sense; and yet these men are reverenced, when we are not forgiven."[25] Shakespeare's language was both unclear and ungrammatical. Restoration tragedy aspired to be both elegantly and "correctly" written, while at the same time clear and emotionally powerful.

Sometimes this led to the use of rhetorical effects such as initial repetition with variation as in these lines from *Mustapha* where Solyman describes his hardships:

> Did I in Winter Camps spend Forty Years;
> Out-wear the Weather, and out-face the Sun,
> When the wild Herds did to their Coverts run;
> Out-watch the Jealous, and the Lunatic;
> Out-fast the Penitential, and the Sick;
> Out-wait long Patience, and out-suffer Fear;
> Out-march the Pilgrim, and the Wanderer?
>
> (*Five Heroic Plays*, pp. 24–25)

The common view in the Restoration was also that rapid, short utterances showed emotion, and this led to much more use of *stichomythia* (rapid exchanges in verse), than was common in earlier English drama, as in this example from Dryden's *Oedipus* (1679):

> *Oedipus* 'Tis plain, the Priest's suborn'd to free the Pris'ner.
> *Creon* And turn the guilt on you.
> *Oedipus* O, honest *Creon*, how hast thou been bely'd!
> *Eurydice* Hear me.
> *Creon* She's brib'd to save her Lover's life.
> *Adrastus* If, *Oedipus*, thou think'st—
> *Creon* Hear him not speak.
> *Adrastus* Then hear these holy men.
> *Creon* Priests, Priests, all brib'd, all Priests.
>
> (XIII, 171)

Emotion is indicated both by the rapid exchanges in meter, and even more by the breakdown of the iambic pentameter into sharp utterances.

At its worst, the desire for linguistic transparency frequently turned dialogue into an extended debate over the relative merits of love and honor. Sadly, the desire for emotion combined with clarity created the sometimes painful "rants" of Restoration tragedy. The most egregious perpetrator of rant was the talented Nathaniel Lee. In *Sophonisba* (1675) King Massanissa's refusal to give up the title-character at the request of his ally and mentor Scipio is unconvincing precisely because of the speech's histrionic excess:

> *Massanissa* Have I for this, in thy accursed Cause,
>   Starv'd Life, by lavishing her precious Food,

My Spirits lost, emptied my dearest Blood,
Fought till I Rampiers made of Bodies round;
So mark'd with Fate, that I appear'd one Wound,
Yet rais'd thy bleeding Eagles from the Ground?
Scipio Think no more on't; her Memory forget.
Massanissa Cut me to Atoms, tear my Soul out; yet
In every smallest Particle of me
You shall the form of *Sophonisba* see:
All like my Soul, and all in ev'ry Part;
Bath'd in my Eyes, and bleeding in my Heart.   (*Five Heroic Plays*, p. 311)

Lee was a widely admired playwright in the Restoration for his luxuriant language and evocation of passion. This, perhaps more than anything else, shows the gap between the late seventeenth-century theatre audience and the late twentieth-century reader, who is likely to regard this cascade of hyperbole as more characteristic of a childish temper tantrum than a disappointed lover and warrior.

But the desire to avoid obscurity and the rise of private tragedy also led to Thomas Durfey's daring *The Famous History of the Rise and Fall of Massaniello* (1700), a tragedy about a fisherman who rises against oppression and is destroyed. The originality of a peasant as hero of a tragedy is reflected in the dialogue. Blank verse appears in the play as well, but Massaniello expresses himself in blunt and earthy prose. And at its best, the language of Restoration tragedy combined simplicity with pathos in scenes that remain effective today. The dying Monimia in Thomas Otway's *The Orphan* (1680) fades wistfully despite the fact that she did not know she was committing adultery with her husband's brother. Her restrained language mirrors her inability to assert any kind of control over the tragic world that destroyed her:

Speak well of me, and if thou find ill tongues
Too busie with my fame, do'nt hear me wrong'd;
'Twill be a noble Justice to the memory
Of a poor wretch, once honour'd with thy Love.
How my head swims! Tis very dark. Good night. [*Dyes*.[26]

Otway deserved his reputation for being "next to Shakespeare" as a writer of tragedies. The simplicity of this language recalls Cordelia's response to Lear, "No cause, no cause"; the words are almost entirely from Anglo-Saxon roots, and the succession of single syllables (there are only three two-syllable words in the five lines) captures more of Monimia's essentially childlike innocence than any elaborate speech could.

The hyperbolic language and characters of Restoration tragedy have disappeared from the stage, but the theatricality which it celebrated and star system it developed linger on. Its greatest legacy was an expansion of the subject matter of tragedy. No longer would the affairs of kingdoms be the only permissible subject for tragic treatment. Instead, the heartbreak of private life, the individual torn apart by larger forces, was established as a dramatic subject. If Arthur Miller and Tennessee Williams dramatize the subject rather more convincingly, they owe the Restoration dramatists thanks for the three hundred years of experimentation they initiated.

NOTES

1 Gunnar Sorelius, *"The Giant Race Before the Flood": Pre-Restoration Drama on the Stage and in the Criticism of the Restoration* (Uppsala: Almquist & Wiksells, 1966), pp. 138–39.
2 *The Works of Thomas Otway*, ed. J. C. Ghosh (Oxford: Clarendon Press, 1968), II, 217.
3 (Oxford: The Clarendon Press, 1976), p. 149.
4 *Heroes and States: on the Ideology of Restoration Tragedy*, précis of book in progress with same title, 1997.
5 (New York: Garland, 1974), p. 140.
6 Eric Rothstein describes these approaches as the "fabulist" and "affective" in *Restoration Tragedy: Form and the Process of Change* (Madison: University of Wisconsin Press, 1967), pp. 3–23.
7 Ed. John Loftis (Lincoln: University of Nebraska Press, 1967), p. 71.
8 *The Works of Aphra Behn*, vol. v, ed. Janet Todd (Columbus: Ohio State University Press, 1996), pp. 252, 264.
9 Ed. P. F. Vernon (Lincoln: University of Nebraska Press, 1970), pp. 83, 92.
10 *Heads of an Answer to Rymer*, in *The Works of John Dryden*, ed. H. T. Swedenberg, Jr., *et al.*, 20 vols., in progress (Berkeley: University of California Press, 1956–), XVII, 191. Hereafter, Dryden references are to this edition.
11 In *Five Heroic Plays*, ed. Bonamy Dobrée (London: Oxford University Press, 1960), p. 78.
12 *The Dramatic Works of John Crowne* (1874; New York: Benjamin Blom, 1967), III, 450.
13 H. Scouten, "Tragedy" in *The Revels History of Drama in English*, vol. v, 1660–1750 (London: Methuen, 1976), pp. 256–60.
14 *British Dramatists from Dryden to Sheridan*, ed. George H. Nettleton *et al.* (Carbondale: Southern Illinois University Press, 1969), pp. 59, 53.
15 Eugene M. Waith, *Ideas of Greatness: Heroic Drama in England* (New York: Barnes & Noble, 1971), pp. 186–87.
16 *The Continental Model: Selected French Critical Essays of the Seventeenth Century, in English Translation*, rev. edn. Scott Elledge and Donald Schier (Ithaca: Cornell University Press, 1970), p. 300.
17 *English Drama: Restoration and Eighteenth Century, 1660–1789* (New York: Longman, 1988), p. 60.
18 The Augustan Reprint Society, nos. 205–06, intro. Diane Dreher (Los Angeles: Clark Memorial Library, 1981), pp. 41–42.

19 *British Drama, 1660–1779. A Critical History* (New York: Twayne, 1995), p. 59.
20 In *The Female Wits: Women Playwrights of the Restoration*, ed. Fidelis Morgan (London: Virago, 1981), p. 152–53.
21 *The Works of Thomas Southerne*, ed. Robert Jordan and Harold Love (Oxford: Clarendon Press, 1988), II, 82–83.
22 The Augustan Reprint Society, nos. 265–66, intro. Jayne Elizabeth Lewis (New York: AMS Press, 1995), pp. 8, 57.
23 In *Five Heroic Plays*, pp. 114, 141.
24 *The Dramatic Works of John Crowne*, II, 270–73.
25 *Dramatic Essays* (London: J. M. Dent, n. d.), p. 98.
26 *The Works of Thomas Otway*, II, 84.

6

NANCY KLEIN MAGUIRE

Tragicomedy

*our best poets have differed from other Nations (though not so happily) in
usually mingling and interweaving Mirth and Sadness through the whole
Course of their Plays, Ben. Johnson only excepted.*
　　　　　Sir Robert Howard, *Four New Playes* (1665)

This Oleo of a Play; this unnatural mixture of Comedy and Tragedy
　　　　　John Dryden, *An Essay of Dramatick Poesie* (1668)

Sometime at the end of the seventeenth century, George Villiers, the second
Duke of Buckingham, wrote a play which he called *The Restauration: Or,
Right will take Place. A Tragicomedy* (February 1683)[1]. Since the
beheading of the English monarch Charles I in 1649, the idea of "Restoration" had obsessed English playwrights – the theme permeates Restoration
drama. Not coincidentally, Buckingham's title includes the designation "A
Tragicomedy." To an experienced reader of seventeenth-century drama, the
plot of *The Restauration* sounds very familiar. A usurping king harasses a
dispossessed prince, Philander, whose countrymen are waiting to take arms
in his defense. A foreign prince has just arrived to marry the princess and
thus becomes heir to the throne. The true prince, who loves the princess,
assigns his page to her. An evil harlot wrongfully accuses the princess and
the page of an illicit love affair: death threatens the righteous, everything is
moving toward a tragic ending, when, *alors*, the page turns out to be a
love-sick woman disguised as a boy – creating a familiar sexual tremolo.
And, of course, the dispossessed prince is restored.

　　John Fletcher (with his early collaborator Francis Beaumont) wrote the
original of this tragicomedy, *Philaster, Or, Love Lies a Bleeding*, in 1609.
Over half a century later, a Restoration poet and playwright, Edmund
Waller, still promoted Fletcher, claiming that "Of all our elder Plays,"
Philaster had "the lowest fame."[2] In *An Essay Of Dramatick Poesie*
(1668), John Dryden stated that "The first Play that brought Fletcher and

him in esteem was their *Philaster*."[3] Fletcher's first box-office success kept on succeeding, appearing eleven times on the London stage between 1660 and 1700 with three new printed editions. Indeed, Restoration playwrights endlessly copied *Philaster*. After the theatres reopened in 1660, Roger Boyle, the Earl of Orrery, imitated *Philaster* in the first rhymed heroic play (1661).[4] In *Marriage A-la-Mode* (1671), John Dryden used Fletcher's usurper and restored heir for his major male characters. Playwrights relentlessly copied the play's usurpation-restoration plot as well as imitating *Philaster's* impetuous hero, faithful heroine, and self-sacrificing page-lover. In *The English Princess; or the Death of Richard the III. A Tragedy* (1667), John Caryll copied *Philaster's* pattern so closely as to suggest outright plagiarism. *Philaster* epitomizes Fletcher's alloy of tragedy and comedy and, above everything, the Restoration audience wanted tragicomedy.

Most readers of this chapter will have some idea of what comedy and tragedy are, but very few, if any, will have a clue about tragicomedy. What is tragicomedy? This essay cannot answer the question definitively. Tragicomedy is a large generic field, and the form is so slippery that critics fear being lost forever if they venture into definition. Few have even had the courage to grapple with the problem of setting limits to this elusive and controversial dramatic form. At best, we can create working definitions. One of the finest playwrights of the early Restoration, Sir Robert Howard, recognized that "in the difference of Tragedy and Comedy, and of Fars it self, there can be no determination but by the taste."[5] To a great extent, he is right, and this judgment also applies to tragicomedy.

Tragicomedy: reception, genesis, and definition

Tragicomedy was such an important Restoration phenomenon that even the secluded and retired Milton entered the critical conversation, bemoaning the infamy "happning through the Poets error of intermixing comic stuff with tragic sadness and gravity; or introducing trivial and vulgar persons."[6] Escaping its critical confines, tragicomedy spread everywhere. Commonplace use of "tragicomedy" points to its popular acceptance – even in religious texts. John Donne used the term in a 1629 sermon: "The book of *Iob* is a representation of God, in a Tragique-Comedy, lamentable beginnings comfortably ended."[7] In 1653, a Presbyterian minister named John Rowe published a pamphlet which described the collapse of a makeshift theatre during a theatrical performance; he entitled the pamphlet *Tragi-Comaedia*. In 1658, the theologian and historian Peter Heylyn concluded "the *Trage Comedy* of the *two Harlots* in the first of *Kings*, may seem to have been acted over again on the Stage of *England*."[8]

Continental influence, especially that of the French, spurred interest in tragicomedy. Charles I's wife, Henrietta Maria, was a French princess with strong dramatic interests. Many of the Restoration playwrights had been with Charles II during his exile and spent many years in France. They acquired French tastes, and among those tastes was a taste for tragicomedy. The tragicomic tradition had dominated French dramaturgy from the last part of the sixteenth century. Between 1630 and 1639, eighty French tragicomedies were produced (in contrast to thirty-eight tragedies). For the next twenty years, when the exiled Stuart court was in France, French playwrights wrote nearly an equal number of tragedies and tragicomedies. After 1660, tragicomedy rapidly declined in France. The most influential work on dramatic theory *Art poétique* (1674) does not mention tragicomedy, and, by 1679, French playwrights had completely discarded the word "tragicomedy." Even though disenfranchized by the fashionable French, tragicomedy flourished in England amidst vigorous critical debate.

The Restoration playwrights grew up with tragicomedy. Around 1554, tragicomedy took center stage in Italy. By the early seventeenth century, *literati* in England and the Continent had read – or heard about – Giovanni Battista Guarini's seminal play *Il Pastor Fido* (1590) which started the tragicomic fad. *Il Pastor Fido* was so popular that, by 1602, the play went into a twentieth edition. Five years later, a character from Ben Jonson's *Volpone*, Lady Politic Would-be (who carries a copy of *Il Pastor Fido* with her), predicted that all English authors "Will deign to steal out of this author." She explains to Volpone, "He has so modern, and facile a vein, / Fitting the time, and catching the court-ear."[9] A few years later, *circa* 1609, Fletcher adapted Guarini to suit the English popular audience. Forty years later, clearly understanding the connection between "restoration" and tragicomedy, Sir Richard Fanshawe translated Guarini's play into English and dedicated it to the usurped Prince Charles, later the restored Charles II.[10] During the Restoration, playwrights wrote at least three translations/ adaptations of *Il Pastor Fido*.

Even though tragicomedy did not become popular until the seventeenth century, the concept goes back very far, and Restoration playwrights, especially those who were educated at Oxford or Cambridge, were certainly familiar with its origins. Alluding to the idea of tragicomedy, Socrates noted "how people enjoy weeping at tragedies" and commented on "the condition of the soul at comedies, how there also we have a mixture of pain and pleasure."[11] Plautus, however, first used the word "tragicomedy" in his *Amphitryon*, translated by Dryden and often cited by Restoration playwrights. In the play, Mercury asks:

Frowning because I said this was to be a tragedy? I am a god: I'll transform it. I'll convert this same play from tragedy to comedy, if you like, and never change a line ... I understand your feelings in the matter perfectly. I shall mix things up: let it be tragicomedy.[12]

The next use of "tragicomedy" appears in 1493/94 when Carolus and Marcellenus Verardus labeled *Fernandus Servatus* a tragicomedy. In the next century, the authors of the "Christian Terence" plays (sixteenth-century academic drama written for moral and religious instruction) frequently designated their plays tragicomedies. Lodovicus Crucius (fl.1570), for example, called three of his plays *tragicocomoediae* and cited Plautus' *Amphitryon* to justify his use of the generic designation.[13] Petrus Philicinus labeled *Magdalena Evangelica* (1546) a *Comoedia Tragica*: "because I am doubtful that it will seem tragic, I have been disposed to call it a tragic comedy, since the title fits the content."[14] Often echoing the "Christian Terence" dramatists, Giraldi Cinthio introduced Aristotle into the debate, clearly legislating that *tragedie miste* comprised tragedies with happy endings. Cinthio never recognized "tragicomedy" as a legitimate term, but he led the way in its development.

Thus far, "tragicomedy" meant tragedy with a happy ending. But, in the dedicatory epistle of *Christus Redivivus* (1543), a "sacred tragi-comedy," an Oxford student, Nicholas Grimald, presented a different concept of tragicomedy: "as far as the treatment of this tragicomedy is concerned ... great things had been interwoven with the small, joyous with sad, obscure with manifest, incredible with probable." For Grimald, tragicomedy depicted a movement from sadness to happiness:

the first act yields to tragic sorrow ... so the fifth and last adapts itself to delight and joy; likewise, in order that variety may be opposed to satiety, in all the other intermediate acts sad and cheerful incidents are inserted in turn.

Like Crucius, Grimald justifies his work by citing another play by Plautus – in this case, the *Captivi*.[15] For the first time, instead of identifying tragicomedy as tragedy with a happy ending, Grimald intersperses the sad and cheerful elements of comedy and tragedy throughout the play. Thus started the critical struggle which obsessed the Restoration playwrights, especially Dryden – the nature of tragicomedy.

Tragicomedy implies more than a "happy ending," yet the easiest tragicomedies to define are plays which start out looking like tragedies then, at the very end, do a turnabout and become comedies. The author of *The Merry Devill of Edmonton* (1602) comments on the type: "The Commick end of our sad tragique show."[16] Restoration playwrights frequently forced classical tragedy into this kind of tragicomedy. Although entitling her translation/adaptation of Corneille's *Pompey. A Tragedy* (1663), Katherine Philips intersperses the *"Tragedy"* with cheerful songs and dances between the acts and ends with: "a Grand Masque is Danc'd before Cesar and Cleopatra."[17] Philips also ended her translation of Corneille's *Horace. A Tragedy* (1668) with a celebratory dance. In Sir Robert Staplyton's *The Tragedie of Hero and Leander* (1668), only five lines after the announcement of Hero's death, Hero's sister asks: "*Celena*, Will you please to be his Bride?" The audience forgets the drowning of Hero and Leander as a double marriage takes place.[18] This turnaround involves tremendous suspension of credibility, reversals, bizarre coincidences, and a slightly macabre taste.

Guarini defines tragicomedy in his *Compendio Della Poesia Tragicomica*, the first and only carefully formulated Renaissance theory of tragicomedy. In the late 1580s and early 1590s Guarini wrote this detailed defense in the midst of an extended critical quarrel with Giasone Di Nores. The Italian edition appeared in England in 1591, followed by an English translation in 1602. Guarini insists that tragicomedy is a separate, independent genre:

> he who makes a tragicomedy does not intend to compose separately either a tragedy or a comedy, but from the two a third thing that will be perfect of its kind and may take from the others the parts that with most verisimilitude can stand together.[19]

Sir Philip Sidney dismissed the "mungrell Tragy-comedie" with great scorn in *An Apologie for Poetrie* (1595),[20] but *circa* 1609[21] Fletcher snatched English tragicomedy from dismissive oblivion by repeating Guarini's practice and restating his theory in the text and preface to *The Faithful Shepherdess*. Yet Fletcher's slight and often misused definition gives us only a limited sense of what he himself meant by "tragicomedy":

> A tragie-comedie is not so called in respect of mirth and killing, but in respect it wants deaths, which is inough to make it no tragedie, yet brings some neere it, which is inough to make it no comedie; which must be a presentation of familiar people, with such kinde of trouble as no life be questiond, so that a God is as lawfull in this as in a tragedie, and meane people as in a comedie.[22]

If we go beyond this elementary and somewhat confusing theory to Fletcher's practice, we might say that Fletcher's theatrical and artificial tragicomedy provides distance from the murkiness and muddle of ordinary life. Fletcher insists on clear-cut dichotomies between good and evil; in *Philaster*, for example, the good page opposes the "lascivious" whore. Fletcher engineers the surprising dénouement through his own language rather than through the decisions of his irresponsible characters. Informed by a social code rather than a moral law, Fletcher's characters have a sense of individual helplessness, and an awareness of diffuse but impending disaster broods over the action.

Clearly, Grimald's comments, Guarini's definition, and Fletcher's practice do not limit tragicomedy to tragedy with a happy ending – but rather, in tragicomedy, "sad and cheerful incidents are inserted in turn." The frontispiece to Ben Jonson's folio (1616) encouraged this broader generic interpretation. The illustrator shows tragicomedy supported between comic and tragic columns, with tragicomedy arched above both columns. At either end of the spectrum, tragedy and comedy separate life into orderly structures; they have restraining borders; they are arranged. In contrast, the mood of tragicomedy is open; the playwright does not attempt to order life into neat segments. Life and tragicomedy happen. In the words of a French critic, François Ogier, in 1628:

> To say that it is indecorous to mix in the same piece people discussing serious, important, and tragic affairs, and then forthwith, to discuss common, vain and comic things, that is to ignore the human condition, in which days and hours are very often intersected with laughter and tears, with contentment and affliction, as people are driven by good or bad fortune.[23]

An essentially intuitive perception of reality, tragicomedy imitates the human condition and, above all, keeps overwhelming emotions out of play. As George Bernard Shaw later remarked, "Life does not cease to be funny when people die anymore than it ceases to be serious when people laugh."[24]

In tragicomedy, two views of reality struggle for ascendency. In the "happy ending" concept, the views of reality are serial – comedy follows tragedy in the fifth act. The more common form of tragicomedy in England – especially in Restoration England – alternates the opposing views, mixing the elements of tragedy and comedy in every scene. Instead of following each other, the two views struggle for supremacy throughout the play. A new kind of tragicomedy flourished during the English Restoration, an "olio," in which the two views of reality are split and run parallel to each other in independent plots. The playwrights found patterns for this form in Fletcher's independent and separate plots, such as in *The Loyal Subject* (1618). The controlling emphasis on plot, episodic plot at that, wreaks havoc with character development. Superficial characterization, expedient motivation, and constant turns and reversals characterize these plays. Only serious in form, this tragicomedy, or any tragicomedy, does not attempt to involve the audience emotionally or to purge it of pity and fear. Instead of provoking a catharsis, tragicomedy distracts, entertains, or works at changing political reality.

The Restoration critics

The playwrights, who were also the critics, normally defended their own dramatic works rather than theorizing about the nature of drama. Thomas Shadwell, in fact, frankly says, "whatever I have said of it, was intended not in Justification, but Excuse of it."[25] Dramatists were extremely self-conscious about what they were doing. At the outset of the Restoration, playwrights published their meager dramatic criticism in dedications, prefaces, prologues and epilogues. But, in 1665, Sir Robert Howard started a prolonged critical argument in print with his young kinsman, the neophyte playwright John Dryden. This imbroglio and Dryden's *An Essay of Dramatick Poesie* three years later initiated an abrupt rise in dramatic criticism. The resulting texts either argued about the nature of comedy and tragedy or debated the merits of tragicomedy *ad nauseum*. Although the discussion does help to explain some of the hard choices playwrights had to make, these texts do not make it easy to draw any conclusions about tragicomedy. The playwrights argue constantly and show either ambivalence or an honest attempt to see both sides. Dryden's comments in *Of Dramatick Poesie*, of course, are most familiar. Since Dryden dominated tragicomedy both in critical theory and practice, his comments are also the most useful.

Sir Robert Howard initiated the tragicomic debate in the preface to *Four New Playes* (1665). Echoing Grimald, Howard describes plays in which two views of reality run a parallel course rather than following one another. Howard distinguishes English tragicomedy from French tragedy with a happy ending, described by his French contemporary Samuel Chappuzeau: "Tragicomedy presents us with the noble adventures of Illustrious people menaced with some terrible misfortune, which is followed by a happy ending."[26] Commenting on the English tragicomic pattern, Howard regrets that "our best Poets have differed from other Nations (though not so happily) in usually mingling and interweaving Mirth and Sadness through the whole Course of their Plays, Ben Johnson only excepted." He concludes "I am now convinc'd in my own Judgement, That it is most proper to keep the Audience in one entire disposition."[27] (Like Dryden, however, Howard failed to make his practice match his theory.) In contrast, Sir Robert's playwright brother Edward Howard speaks for the "mixt" plays of the native English tradition. Defending his predecessors, he realizes that earlier playwrights found that the "mixt Plays were very suitable to the English stage." He strongly defends English tragicomedy: "nor do I believe that it is less natural (as some have thought) to form a Play, that shall have this variety of Genius."[28]

No one suffered more than Dryden over the issue of tragicomedy. He agonized over classical precedents, yet he continued to write irregular tragicomedies. A neophyte in 1660, Dryden still ranked below Sir Robert Howard in the mid-1660s both in popularity and in critical reputation, and he needed full houses. Yet he curiously presented both sides of the controversy in *Of Dramatick Poesie*. Representing Sir Robert's position, Dryden's Lisideius complains that

> many Scenes of our Tragicomedies carry on a design that is nothing of kinne to the main Plot; and that we see two distinct webbs in a Play; like those in ill wrought stuffs; and two actions, that is, two Plays carried on together to the confounding of the Audience. (XVII, 34)

Lisideius maintains with obvious disgust: "There is no Theater in the world has any thing so absurd as the *English* Tragicomedies." He disparages even Ben Jonson himself, who "has given us this Oleo of a Play; this unnatural mixture of Comedy and Tragedy" (XVII, 35, 37). Dryden's own struggle with tragicomedy clearly emerges. In contrast to Lisideius, Dryden's spokesman Neander concludes that "A Scene of mirth mix'd with Tragedy has the same effect upon us which our musick has betwixt the Acts, which we find a relief to us from the best Plots and language of the Stage, if the discourses have been long" (XVII, 46). Neander turns the Anglo-French paradigm on its head and claims that the French playwrights of late "have been imitating afar off the quick turns and graces of the *English* stage. They have mix'd their serious Playes with mirth, like our Tragicomedies." Yet, "for their new way of mingling mirth with serious Plot I do not with *Lidiseuis* condemn the thing, though I cannot approve their manner of doing it" (XVII, 45, 46). Neander concludes: "we have invented, increas'd and perfected a more pleasant way of writing for the Stage then was ever known to the Ancients or Moderns of any Nation, which is Tragicomedie" (XVII, 34, 46). Throughout his professional life, Dryden teetered on this seesaw, alternating between the personae of Lisideius and Neander.

Dryden attended Westminster School where the famous Dr. Busby trained his students in the classics, so, not surprisingly, Dryden veered toward classical drama. Yet, part of Dryden's problem with tragicomedy is the rigidity of French neo-classicism. After the 1638 quarrel over Pierre Corneille's *Le Cid* (1637), the French Academy decided in favor of the unities, forcing Corneille to change his designation of *Le Cid* from "tragicomedy" to "tragedy." By 1660, the French showed little patience with the concept of tragicomedy and even less with the term. In *The Whole Art of the Stage*, Monsieur Hédelin, abbot of Aubignac, devotes an entire dismissive chapter to tragicomedy. Although not translated into English until 1684, the Francophile court certainly read the 1657 French original. Referring to the prevailing French concept of tragedy with a happy ending, Aubignac says,

> This New Word which seems to have been introduc'd to signifie some new sort of Drammatick Poem, obliges me to explain it more clearly, and at length, then any of our Modern Authors have done, and to that end I must shew all that in our Plays is different from, or conformable to the Works of the Ancients.[29]

He complains "for we have taken away the name of Tragedy from all the Plays where the Catastrophe is happy, and without blood, though both the Subject and Persons are heroick, and have given them the name of tragicomedys" (sig. s4v). Aubignac not only strenuously objects to the genre, he also objects to the very word since "when once the word Tragicomedy is prefix'd, the catastrophe is presently known" (sig. T1r).

The Francophile Dryden, of course, was well aware of the unfashionableness of tragicomedy. Yet, while complaining bitterly, Dryden kept writing tragicomedies. He defended the genre because the English audience required tragicomedy, they needed it. Restoration playwrights have a unique, almost obsessive concern with audience – Dryden, in particular, recognizes the need of meeting audience expectations. In *Of Dramatick Poesie*, Neander acknowledges that "we, who are a more sullen people, come to be diverted at our Playes" (XVII, 48). Yet, Dryden apologizes for his acquiescence: "but I confess I have given too much to the people in it, and am asham'd for them as well as for my self, that I have pleas'd them at so cheap a rate" (X, 204). Other playwrights who preferred classical models shared his concern; William Joyner, for example, confesses that "For satisfaction of the English Stage, which delights in variety, I have sought to entertain the Audience with the divertisement of new accidents."[30]

How did Restoration playwrights survive the tragicomic debate? They struggled with box-office reality. Theoretically, they admired the clear-cut generic distinctions of Ben Jonson, but their audiences, and perhaps they themselves, demanded Fletcherian tragicomedy. No matter how much they claimed to admire Shakespeare and Ben Jonson, the Restoration playwrights copied Fletcher. Waller candidly admits:

> *Fletcher*, to thee we do not only owe
> All our good Plays, but all those other [*sic*] too,
> Thy Wit repeated, does support the Stage
> Credits the last, and entertains this Age.[31]

Dryden points out that Fletcher's "Plays are now the most pleasant and frequent entertainments of the Stage; two of theirs being acted through the year for one of *Shakespeare's* or *Johnsons*" (XVII, 57). Of the 105 plays revived in the first decade of Restoration, Fletcher wrote 28, and these plays had more than 100 performances. *The London Stage* (a daily calendar of theatrical performances) records more than 70 additional performances between 1670 and 1700. Dryden suggests the reason for this popularity: "there is a certain gayety in their Comedies, and Pathos in their more serious Playes which suits generally with all mens humors" (XVII, 57).

Tragicomedy and Restoration

The playwrights clearly had theoretical troubles with tragicomedy. They also had practical problems. Although the new playwrights knew the tragicomic tradition and were brought up in a culture which popularized the genre, they had no experience in writing plays. Joyner grumbled that "there is nothing more difficult; or which requires a more elevated wit, richer fancy, or subtiler judgement" than the art of playwriting.[32] Another new playwright, Edward Howard, complained that tragicomedy was the most difficult kind of play to write "because it is not easie to give humor and mirth a natural rise and generous correspondency with the grandeur of the other . . . it being as it were two Plays in one."[33]

The new playwrights clearly considered tragedy the superior genre. Thomas Porter, for example, carefully designates *The Villain. A Tragedy*, as does John Caryll *The English Princess, or the Death of Richard the III. A Tragedy*, or Elkanah Settle *Cambyses King of Persia: A Tragedy*. But this means nothing, no more than generic designation meant to the French who changed their labels erratically. In French drama, there are "occasional inconsistencies in labeling a play's genre within the same original edition . . . and embarrassed admissions by certain authors that, although the play is really a tragedy, they are calling it a tragicomedy in order to conform to the taste of the time."[34] Sir William Killigrew outdid the French; to please his audience, he actually changed *Pandora, or The Converts* (1665) from a tragedy to a comedy. In the hands of the new playwrights, tragedy, at best, became tragedy with a happy ending – or tragicomedy. The generic blend is rough; there is nothing subtle about these tragicomedies. Although the plays frequently end with the stage strewn with dead bodies, three marriages take place amidst the gore. Using the simplest definition of tragedy as a play which ends unhappily, only five of these plays have what could be considered unhappy endings. Critics might consider Porter's *The Villain* and the tragic version of Sir Robert Howard's *The Vestal Virgin* as conveying a sense of tragedy, but Howard, imitating French practice, undercuts this tragic sense by writing an alternate happy ending. The only genuine tragedy of the decade, if it is of the decade, is Milton's *Samson Agonistes*.

The "serious" plays of this era are all variations of tragicomedy. The Restoration playwrights needed tragicomedy to prop up the Restoration. The reopening of the theatres reverberated as an unmitigated victory yell for the Royalists, and the playwrights embedded the uneasy monarchical myth into the very structure of the new tragicomedies. During the first decade, two evanescent forms of tragicomedy developed, flourished, and disappeared. Both forms are split with parallel, independent plots. The first, divided tragicomedy, splits abruptly and distinctly into upper and lower plots. In these equally dominant plots, the characters from one plot seldom if ever communicate with those in the other plot. Besides achieving unique theatrical effects, the dichotomized plots also made a subtle psychological and political comment. In the heroic plot, the playwrights recalled the troubled days of 1640–60 at the same time that they distanced them by the reassuring low plot which mimicked the everyday life of Charles II's court. The new form culminated in Dryden's *Marriage A-la-Mode*. In contrast to the abrupt structural split of divided tragicomedy, the second form of tragicomedy, the formal, masque-like rhymed heroic play, divides more subtly. Although having only one idealized plot, the play-wrights created an ambivalence of mood, a hesitation about heroics. This hesitation separates the heroic fantasy from the reality of everyday life, allowing the audience (or reader) an almost suppressed snicker at the absurdity of the heroic hero. Besides imitating the masque's loftiness of tone and general heroic attitude, the rhymed heroic play imitates its political orientation. In contrast to divided tragicomedy, a political theme always organizes the rhymed heroic play, which is best represented by Dryden's *The Conquest of Granada*.

Like a Rorschach test, early Restoration drama tells us much about the emotional history of the Civil War and Interregnum years. Tragicomedy lies at the center of Restoration consciousness. Historians know little of what the survivors of civil war, regicide, and restoration felt and thought, but if we examine these tragicomedies, we clarify much of what has remained mysterious about the mental and emotional habits of Restoration Eng-lishmen. The new playwrights remembered the time, in the words of Hédelin's 1684 translator: "when we were Embroiled in civilWars [*sic*] here in England ... the Whole Kingdom was become the Stage of real Trage-dies."[35] Their mentality contained one major story: in a frenzy of malice, the villainous Oliver Cromwell murdered the holy martyr Charles I, but Providence intervened to bring back his son. No matter how tragic the days after 1642 and 1649, in the end the King came into his own again. This tragicomic lesson is at the base of Restoration tragicomedy – and except for formal comedies, all Restoration plays are tragicomedies.

The very nature of tragicomedy made the genre suitable for marketing a restored king with a decapitated father. The playwrights used tragicomedy as a political tool for reinstating the Stuarts. Tragicomedy prevailed in part as a compliment to the king, reassuring him that all the world rejoiced in his return. Teetering between tragedy and comedy, Restoration England was never secure about the happy ending. The playwrights rewrote tragedies into tragicomedies, always in a tremor of suspense, wondering if the happy ending would continue, hoping that the king would stay on his throne. Their primary organizing principle was the need for a happy ending, no matter what the cost to the art form. The playwrights assured the king of unfeigned devotion to the new régime – the new ending to regicide is restoration, tragedy becomes tragicomedy. The very structure of the plays allowed them to be readily used for political propaganda. Playwrights deliberately set up a state of anxiety whose resolution reinforced the established régime and confirmed the divine right of the Stuarts.

Tragicomedy was the only viable serious genre after 1660 for reasons intrinsic to the genre. The playwrights could use the genre to portray the movement from the threatened environment of regicide to the hoped-for stability of restoration. If we look at tragicomedy in more complex terms, we find that the emotional ambivalence of tragicomedy was even more useful to the playwrights. The potential for depicting two opposing views of reality made tragicomedy a natural tool for politicizing. The playwrights created forms of tragicomedy which depicted interchangeable ideal (tragic) and pragmatic (comic) worlds: the ideal world compatible with how they wished they had lived and the practical world compatible with how they wished to live under Charles II. In order to construct a world which dramatized the post-Restoration regicide/restoration myth, they readily appropriated tragicomedy's movement from a threatened environment to a stable one. The alternate-ending plays which were popular during the 1663–65 season encouraged the fantasy of reversal and may have contributed to this myth.

All the plays are political, sometimes very topically so. A very early play, Cosmo Manche's *The Banished Shepherdess* (early 1660?), for instance, refers to the act of regicide with thinly veiled allegory and reenacts exile and restoration. The unaltered *Hamlet* of 1661 shows life after regicide. In the first Shakespearean adaptation, *The Law Against Lovers* (1662), Sir William Davenant rewrote Shakespeare's dark *Measure for Measure* into Fletcherian tragicomedy, showing how peaceful succession could be achieved. The revised *Tempest* (1667) shows the problematical nature of succession. The playwrights often commented on contemporary events. When Charles ousted his old tutor, the Duke of Clarendon, Sir Robert Howard, one of the prime movers for Clarendon's impeachment and the King's crony, wrote a play which detailed the story. *The Duke of Lerma* (1668), one of the finest plays of the decade, shows what happens to those who interfere with the true king; Howard emphasizes mercy – the trait most associated with Charles II.

The *tour de force* of this decade, and the culmination of the rhymed heroic play, is Dryden's *The Conquest of Granada By the Spaniards* (part 1 1670; part 2:1671). By this time, Dryden had captured the titles of poet laureate and historiographer royal. In his own words, he now began "a greater task." Although Englishmen already suspected Charles's brother James, the heir apparent, of being a Catholic, Dryden boldly dedicated the play to him. In his dedicatory letter, Dryden claims to "restore to you those Ideas, which, in the more perfect part of my characters, I have taken from you" (XI, 3). Considering the problem of "transmitting" James "to Posterity," Dryden hopes to "draw to all the world, a true resemblance of your worth and vertues; at least as farr as they are capable of being copied" (XI, 6, 7). Restoration playwrights created super-human heroes, and Dryden's depiction of James has the tone and temper of the Restoration superman. Claiming that James's "whole life has been a continu'd Series of Heroique Actions" (XI, 3), Dryden mythologizes him in the warrior lover Almanzor who is a retooled Philaster or, more closely, an Arbaces from Fletcher's *A King and No King* (1613). As in both Fletcher plays, a civil war theme again connects the two plots, and revenge and/or lust motivate the constantly changing political reversals. Sex clearly has more power than usurpation, and women have increasingly greater power – Almanzor flips governments around to please his mistress Almahide. In this tragicomedy, Dryden celebrates political expediency and *de facto* monarchy; in the early 1670s, he clearly believed that power makes kings: "He is a king, who does a Crown possess" (XI, 83).

After Dryden's intense ten-act analysis of kingship, playwrights became less preoccupied with issues of kingship and civil war. Plays became increasingly spectacular. In 1673, for instance, Elkanah Settle used a complete Orpheus and Euridice masque and sensational, audience-drawing, torture scenes in his blockbuster *The Empress of Morocco*. Yet obsession with the regicide/restoration myth and tragicomedy revived with a vengeance when the Whigs attempted to exclude James from succeeding to the throne in the late 1670s. The Exclusion Crisis was, of course, another crisis over Restoration. Memories of regicide and hope of peaceful succession again flood the theatre. Restoration playwrights had used

Fletcher's tragicomedies to shore up the restoration of Charles II; they again used Fletcher to ensure that restoration continued in the succession of James. Of the ninety-eight Fletcher plays performed between 1660 and 1700, twenty-five were performed between 1685 and 1688, the years of James's reign. All the revivals and/or adaptations, of course, are more or less subtle ways of taking a position in regard to the succession of James.

Playwrights used Fletcher's prototypical tragicomedy *A King and No King* to comment on the monarchical situation. Fletcher's tragicomedy encapsulated the major conflict of the time – the nature of kingship – and became almost a political catchword. In 1662, Sir Roger L'Estrange had cited the play's title: "we are now upon the very *Crisis*, of *King* or *No King.*"[36] *The London Stage* lists twelve performances of *A King and No King* between 1660 and 1700, but five performances date from the early years of Charles's restoration, and another five cluster between 1685 and 1687. Even the Members of Parliament lapsed into Fletcher's play. The exclusionist lawyer Sir Francis Winnington, for example, concluded in 1681: "if he be King, and have no power to govern, he is King and no King."[37] The House of Commons carried on a protracted argument over whether James should retain the name of King. Sir William Jones argued: "should the Duke of *York* come to the Crown, he should retain the name only of King" (sig. x8v). Three years later, Tate called his adaptation of Aston Cokayne's *Trappolin Creduto Principe* (1657) *A Duke and No Duke* (1684). In the play, Tate emphasizes the difficulties of having two rulers – one sombre and one fantastical – perhaps reflecting James and Charles. The rightful duke pleads "Restore my state, and right an injur'd Prince."[38] In 1685, after James's accession, a spinster supposedly said, "He is noe King but an Elective King, and if there were warrs as I believe there will be, I will put on breeches myself to fight."[39] The spinster, of course, threatens to cross-dress, to imitate the familiar Fletcherian female in breeches.

The House of Commons introduced the first Exclusion Bill on 15 May 1679, and on 11 November 1680, the Commons passed the second Exclusion Bill. Charles II effectively destroyed Parliamentary exclusion by dissolving the Oxford Parliament in March of 1681, yet the dissolution did not stop the fear of a Catholic king. Throughout the Summer of 1683, a non-Parliamentary exclusion movement persisted, and playwrights continued to shore up the succession of James.

Probably in February of 1683, the Duke of Buckingham wrote *The Restauration: Or, Right will take Place. A Tragicomedy*, a close adaptation of Fletcher's *Philaster*. Mary and William had been singled out for succession during the Crisis, and Buckingham glances at this possibility. In the play, a usurper is forcing the English princess to marry a foreign prince who is prince only in name, and Buckingham goes to pains to make him appear an oaf. Philander, the rightful heir whose father's throne has been usurped, still has friends, but, like James, he is wronged, broken in fortune, and overcome by grief. The play resonates with the divisions of the Exclusion Crisis. Always a believer in the divine right of Kings and in awe of his martyred father, James did not compromise on the principle of divine-right kingship, and Philander speaks for him:

> Yes, with my Father's Spirit. 'Tis here O King!
> A dangerous Spirit, now he tells me King
> I was a King's Heir, bids me be a King,
> And whispers to me these are all my Subjects.   (sig. B6v)

The subtitle to the play strongly states the case: "Right will take Place." A supporter of Philander says, "but the King must know, / It is in vain for Kings to war with Heav'n" (sig. E7v). His countrymen describe Philander as "A Man that is the Bravery of his Age ... prest down from his Royal Right" (sig. C6v). To the frustration of James's supporters, Charles frequently sent James out of the country during the Crisis. Even James's critics noticed his patience in the face of exile and adversity, and they might well have said: "*Philander* [James] is too backward in't himself" (sig. C6v). Yet, Buckingham may also be glancing at James's notorious philandering. The *Oxford English Dictionary* defines "Philander" as "loving, fond of men," but in 1682, the word also meant "one given to making love."

Dryden and tragicomedy

Dryden is the natural terminus of an essay on Restoration tragicomedy. Like his sixteenth-century predecessors, Dryden could not stop talking about his love-hate relationship with tragicomedy. The first of the new breed of professional writers, Dryden's dedications and prefaces became essays in dramatic criticism. For his entire professional life, he struggled between a love of classical drama and the commercial need for tragicomedy – and perhaps his own liking for tragicomedy. In 1693, a year before his last play was performed, Dryden comments of his "Irregular way, of Tragicomedies," claiming:

> I will never defend that practice: for I know it distracts the Hearers. But I know, withall, that it has hitherto pleasd them, for the sake of variety; & for the particular tast, which they have to low Comedy.[40]

Dryden had judged correctly in the past. The English preference for tragicomedy goes back to Grimald, and, unlike Corneille, Dryden had no French Academy to legislate the genre out of existence. His highly honed critical skills chaffed under the need to write in an irregular way, but he realized early that his audience and his income required tragicomedy.

In his dedicatory letter to *Love Triumphant; Or, Nature will Prevail. A Tragi-Comedy* (1694), Dryden emphasizes that this poem is "the last which I intend for the Theatre" (sig. a1v). In a letter dated 12 December 1693, Dryden offers an alternative title to the play: "Neither Side to blame: which is very proper, to the two chief Characters of the Heroe & Heroine: who notwithstanding the Extravange [*sic*] of their passion, are neither of them faulty, either in duty, or in Honour."[41] Either title evokes the mood of tragicomedy which eschews formal rules. Still complaining and still struggling, and again comparing his work to that of Corneille, Dryden once more defends himself for breaking the rules:

> so long as the Audience will not be pleas'd without it, the Poet is oblig'd to humor them. On condition they were cur'd of this publick Vice, I cou'd be content to change my Method, and gladly give them a more reasonable Pleasure.   (sig. A4r)

He grumpily concludes, "So now, this Poet, who forsakes the Stage, / Intends to gratifie the present Age" (sig. a1v).

Throughout his career, Dryden defended the Stuart succession, and in *Love Triumphant*, as in *The Conquest of Granada*, Dryden boldly declared his loyalty to James, now in exile for six years. Dryden explains how he "voluntarily reduc'd my self: and of which I have no reason to be asham'd" (sig. A3r). After a lifetime of trimming, Dryden became a Catholic after James's succession. When William ousted James, Dryden became an impoverished old man, losing his positions as poet laureate and historiographer royal. He frequently refers to himself as an "old man," and, at this time of his life, he refused to compromise with the new régime. He dedicated *Love Triumphant* to a target of William's government, James Cecil, fourth Earl of Salisbury, also a convert to Catholicism during James's reign and a relative of Dryden's wife. Although Dryden claimed that he would not satirize William's régime, satire was in his blood and criticism of William appears in this essentially Jacobite play. Dryden insists that no foreigner should inherit the throne of England. The false king Veramond/William attempts unsuccessfully to give his crown and his eldest daughter to the foreign mercenary Don Garcia. Jacobites had accused William of sacrificing England to foreigners; indeed, three-quarters of William's commanders in the Irish campaign against James in 1690 were foreign. The children of both true kings assist in their deposition: Veramond overcomes Ramirez, his former best friend and kinsman, through his supposed son Alphonso; William overcame James II, his father-in-law, through James's daughter Mary.

Dryden wrote his valedictory play in a very old-fashioned form of tragicomedy. The play harkens back to his own early tragicomedies, certainly, but it also harkens back to Fletcher. Although "Coin'd from our own Old Poet's Addle-pate" (sig. A4v), Dryden had clearly internalized the Fletcherian tradition of tragicomedy. We again see a brother–sister incest plot straight out of Fletcher's *A King and No King*, and a more sophisticated and developed Philaster reappears. Yet the hero and heroine are eons from Fletcher's lifeless characters. The upper plot carries strongly. The scenes between Alphonso and his "sister" Victoria are powerful enough to make the reader skip all the intervening low-plot material – which is, as one critic notes, "beer" to the upper plot's "chocolate eclairs."

Alphonso clearly represents James, who instinctively prefers the English people to his own glory. In contrast to William who kept 5,000 foreign guards in London, Alphonso mourns for the suffering of his people and eschews an army:

> What have the people done? The Sheep of Princes,
> That they shou'd perish for the Shepherd's Fault?
> They bring their yearly Wool, to cloath their owners,
> And yet when bare themselves, are cull'd for Slaughter
> Shou'd I do this, what cou'd the Wolf do more,
> Than the Master did? (sig. I1v)

William paid the Dutch army 600,000 pounds sterling in 1689, but Dryden's true king goes to his false father without weapons or army, surely a justification of James's flight from London during the Glorious Revolution. Alphonso, like James, is "Proud of my Exile, with erected Face, / I leave your court, your Town, and your Dominions" (sig. G1v).

Dryden knits up the themes of his earlier plays, emphasizing natural, instinctive bonds. *Love Triumphant* echoes *The Conquest of Granada*. The natural king Alphonso is as impetuous and rash as Dryden's Almanzor or his predecessors Philaster and Arbaces. Alphonso again has "That inborn Fierceness of your boyling Mind" (sig. B2r). Like Almanzor, Alphonso made the army, and he knows the value of a kingdom "because I won a Kingdom" (sig. B3r). Veramond, the supposed father of Alphonso, disinherits him as the English people disinherited James, but Veramond recognizes that: "He's Popular, and I am ill-Belov'd" (sig. G1v). Dryden thinks of James, but he also thinks of tragicomedy. As the old man knits up his life, he comments on the turns and reversals of his own tragicomedy. From neophyte playwright, in less than a decade, Dryden had become poet laureate and historiographer royal. After this triumph, in the hostile environment of William's England, Dryden sold subscriptions to his translations to earn his keep and to provide for his sons. In *Love Triumphant*, Alphonso (and Dryden) says to his false father (William):

> Think on the slippery State of Humane Things,
> The strange vicissitudes, and suddain turns
> Of War, and Fate recoiling on the Proud,
> To crush a Merciless and Cruel Victor.
> Think there are bounds of Fortune, set above;
> Periods of Time, and progress of Success,
> Which none can stop before th' appointed limits,
> And none can push beyond.   (sig. B2v)

Dryden reiterates the theme of restoration, personal and political, again and again. Alphonso's true father – the defeated Ramirez – insists: "And 'tis that only Sword that can restore me. / It must, and ought: you owe it to your Duty" (sig. I2r). Alphonso urges him "Restore your self" (sig. I2r). In *The Conquest of Granada*, Dryden had insisted that power made kings. In 1694, after the deposition of the true king, James, Dryden denies the Veramond/William conquest theory in the defeat of Veramond who claims his kingship from "The Right of Conquest" (sig. B3v). William's ingratitude to his father-in-law is mirrored in Veramond. After Alphonso won a war for him, Veramond forgives him for telling the truth and niggardly says, "Your Battel now is paid at the full price" (sig. B3r).

As an astute observer of theatre tastes, Dryden must have realized that the play would not suit the audience of 1693/94. But, at this time, he either chose to write what he wanted to write or, not likely, badly misjudged his audience. In *Love Triumphant*, Dryden chides his countrymen for failing to remain loyal to the rightful king, and, not surprisingly, his last play failed miserably.

A year later, Dryden obsessively returned to the topic of tragicomedy. In *A Parallel betwixt Painting and Poetry*, Dryden condemns the "Gothique" manner in painting, comparing it with "an ill order'd Play."

> For example, our *English* Tragicomedy must be confess'd to be wholly *Gothic*, notwithstanding the Success which it has found upon our Theatre, and in the *Pastor Fido* of *Guarini*; even though *Corisca* and the Satyr contribute somewhat to the main Action. Neither can I defend my *Spanish Fryar*, as fond as otherwise I am of it, from this Imputation: for though the comical parts are diverting, and the serious moving, yet they are of an unnatural mingle. For Mirth and Gravity destroy each other, and are no more to be allow'd for decent, than a gay Widow laughing in a mourning Habit.
>
> (xx, 70–71)

After more than thirty years of writing plays, Dryden still has not come to terms with tragicomedy. It is not, then, surprising, that in spite of these strictures from the most eminent literary man of the half century, Settle wrote yet another adaptation of *Philaster* the next year.

Tragicomedy presents frustrating problems for critics. The genre has rarely had a good press, as witnessed by Sir Philip Sidney's comment about "mungrell Tragy-comedie." The critical issue became much less intense by 1700. Sir John Vanbrugh evades what had apparently become a tiresome topic, "I shan't here enter into the Contest, whether it be right to have two distinct Designs in one Play," and William Congreve, who made "Feasts for Friends, and not for Cooks," simply ignores the problem.[42] But Addison in 1711 tosses off a reference to tragicomedy as a "motley piece of mirth and sorrow." A year earlier, an irate critic had complained,

> Grief and Laughter are so very incompatible, that to join these two Copies of Nature together, wou'd be monstrous and shocking to any judicious Eye ... And yet this Absurdity is what is done so commonly among us in our *Tragi-Comedies*; this is what our *Shakespear* himself has frequently been guilty of.

In 1759, a critic deplores "the ill success of that odd composition *Tragic Comedy*, a monster wholly unknown to antiquity," which "sufficiently shews the danger of novelty in attempts like these".[43] Samuel Johnson, the last pre-modern defender of the form, goes against the tide and receives "tragicomedy to his protection, whom, however greatly condemned, her own laurels have hitherto shaded from the fulminations of criticism."[44] And then critical discussion disappeared. Tragicomic discussion and practice revived with a vengeance in the late twentieth century. Scholars examined tragicomedy as political statement, and playwrights such as Samuel Beckett, Bertolt Brecht, Henrik Ibsen, Eugène Ionesco, Federico García Lorca, and Harold Pinter, created another kind of tragicomedy.

NOTES

1 *The Restauration: Or, Right will take Place. A Tragicomedy*, "Written by George Villiers, late Duke of Buckingham, from the original copy, never before printed" (London, 1714). The epilogue's allusion to Shaftesbury who died in Holland in January 1682/83 is the only means of dating this play.

2 Edmund Waller, *The Maid's Tragedy Altered. With some other Pieces* (London, 1690), sig. B2r; misprinted F2r. Wing W502. Waller includes *The Maid's Tragedy* in his comment.

3 John Dryden, *The Works of John Dryden*, ed. H. T. Swedenberg, Jr., et al., 20 vols., in progress (Berkeley: University of California Press, 1956–), XVII, 56. Hereafter, Dryden references are to this series.

4 Orrery imitated even the names of *Philaster's* characters as well as the Sicilian civil-war setting in *The Generall*.

5 Sir Robert Howard, *The Great Favourite, or The Duke of Lerma*, in *Dryden & Howard 1664–1668*, ed. A. A. Arundell (Cambridge University Press, 1929), pp. 212–81.

6 *The Complete English Poetry of John Milton*, ed. John T. Shawcross (New York University Press, 1963), p. 150.

7 *The Sermons of John Donne*, ed. E[velyn] M. Simpson and G[eorge] R. Potter, 10 vols. (Berkeley: University of California Press, 1953–62), IX, 132.

8 Peter Heylyn, *King Charles: a Short View of the Life and Reign of King Charles* (London, 1658), sig. E9r.

9 Ben Jonson, *Volpone*, ed. Philip Brockbank (London: Ernest Benn, Ltd, 1968), 3.4.89, 3.4.91–92.

10 *A Critical Edition of Sir Richard Fanshawe's 1647 Translation of Giovanni Battista Guarini's Il Pastor Fido*, ed. Walter F. Staton, Fr., and William E. Simeone (Oxford: Clarendon Press, 1964), p. 5.

11 Plato, *Philebus*, ed. and trans. Harold N. Fowler, in *Plato*, The Loeb Classical Library, gen. eds. E. Capps, T. E. Page, and W. H. D. Rouse (New York: G. P. Putnam's Sons, 1925), III, 331.

12 Titus Maccius Plautus, *Amphitryon*, trans. Paul Nixon, 5 vols. (London: William Heinemann, 1937), I, 9–10.

13 Marvin Herrick discusses these plays in *Tragicomedy: Its Origin and Development in Italy, France, and England*, Illinois Studies in Language and Literature 39 (Urbana: University of Illinois Press, 1955), pp. 29–30. Herrick considers "The Contribution of the Christian Terence" at chapter length.

14 "Et auia nescio auid tragicum spirare videtur, libuit tragic ... appellare Comoediam, vt nomen, rei conueniat" in *Comœdia Tragica, Qvae inscribitor Magdalena Euangelica, Autore Petro Philicino* (Anwterp: 1546), sig. A2r. English translation from Herrick, *Tragicomedy*, p. 27.

15 *The Life and Poems of Nicholas Grimald*, ed. L. R. Merrill (New Haven: Yale University Press, 1925), p. 109, 110.

16 Anon., *The Merry Devill of Edmonton* (London, 1608), sig. A3v.

17 Katherine Philips, *Pompey. A Tragoedy* (London, 1663), sig. MM3v. Wing C6317.

18 Sir Robert Stapylton, *The Tragedie of Hero and Leander* (London, 1669), sig. G1r. Wing S5262

19 Giovanni Battista Guarini, *Compendio della poesia tragicomica* in Allan H. Gilbert, *Literary Criticism: Plato to Dryden* (New York: American Book Company, 1940), p. 507.

20 Sir Phillip Sidney, *An Apologie for Poetrie* (London: Printed for Henry Olny, 1595), sig. K2r.

21 The first quarto of *The Faithful Shepherdess* is undated. The partnership of the publishers Richard Bonn and Henry Walley sets the limits for the date of publication – December of 1608 to January of 1610. Judging from the paucity of work published by Bonian and Walley in 1608 and 1610, the most likely date for publication is 1609.

22 John Fletcher, "Preface," *The Faithful Shepherdess, The Dramatic Works in the Beaumont and Fletcher Canon*, gen. ed. Fredson Bowers, 6 vols. (Cambridge University Press, 1966–85), III, 497.

23 "Car de dire qu'il est mal seant de faire paroistre en une mesme piece les mesmes personnes traittant tantost d'affaires serieuses, importantes et Tragiques, et incontinent apres de choses communes, vaines et Comiques, c'est ignorer la condition de la vie des hommes, de qui les jours et les heures sont bien souvent entrecoupées de ris et de larmes, de contentement et d'affliction, selon qu'ils sont

agitez de la bonne ou de la mauvaise fortune." F[rançois] O[gier], "Preface au Lecteur," Jean de Schélandre, *Tyr et Sidon: Tragicomédie Divisée en deux journées* in 1975 edition by Joseph W. Barker (Paris: Librairie A.-G. Nizet), p. 159.

24 Bernard Shaw, *The Doctor's Dilemna: a Tragedy* (Baltimore: Penguin Books, 1974), p. 185.

25 Thomas Shadwell, "Preface," *The Sullen Lovers* (1668) in *The Complete Works of Thomas Shadwell*, ed. Montague Summers, 5 vols. (London: The Fortune Press, 1927), I, [12].

26 "La *Tragi-comedie* nous met deuant les yeux de nobles auantures entre d'Illustres personnes menacées de quelque grande infortune, qui se trouue suiuie d'vn heureux euenement." Samuel Chappuzeau, *Le Théatre François*, ed. Georges Monval (Paris: Jules Bonnassies, 1875), p. 25.

27 Sir Robert Howard, "Preface," *Four New Plays* (London, 1665), p. 4.

28 Edward Howard, "Preface," *The Womens Conquest: a Tragicomedy* (London, 1671), sig. A3v. Wing H2976.

29 Monsieur Hédelin [François Hédelin], Abbot of Aubignac, *The Whole Art of the Stage* (London, 1684), sigs. A2r–v.

30 William Joyner, *The Roman Empress. A Tragedy* (London, 1671), sig. A3r. Wing J1159.

31 Edmund Waller, *Poems, &c. Written upon several Occasions, And to several Persons*, 5th edn. (London, 1686), sig. L6v. Wing W517.

32 Joyner, *The Roman Empress*, sig. A1v.

33 Edward Howard, "Preface," *The Womens Conquest*, sig. A4r.

34 Perry Gethner, "Jean de Mairet and Poetic Justice: a Definition of Tragi-comedy?," in Douglas Cole, ed., *Renaissance Drama* (Evanston: Northwestern University Press, 1980), pp. 171–72.

35 Monsieur Hédelin [François Hédelin], Abbot of Aubignac, *The Whole Art of the Stage* (London, 1684), sigs. s2v.

36 Sir Roger L'Estrange, *A Memento: Directed To all Those that Truly Reverence the Memory of King Charles the Martyr* (London, 1662), sig. ii2r.

37 Anchitell Grey, *Debates of the House of Commons, From the Year 1667 to the Year 1694*, 10 vols. (London, 1763), vol. VIII,, sig. Y3r–v.

38 Nahum Tate, *A Duke and No Duke. A Farce* (London, 1685), sig. F4v.

39 *Middlesex County Records*, ed. John Cordy Jeaffreson, for Middlesex County Records Society (London: Chapman & Hall, 1892), IV, 285.

40 *The Letters of John Dryden*, collected and edited by Charles E. Ward (Durham, N. C.: Duke University Press, 1942), p. 62.

41 Ward, *Letters*, p. 62.

42 Sir John Vanbrugh, "A Short Vindication of the Relapse and Provok'd Wife," *The Complete Works of Sir John Vanbrugh*, ed. Bonamy Dobree and George Webb (Bloomsbury [London]: The Nonesuch Press, 1927), I, 210; William Congreve, epilogue to Thomas Southerne's *Oroonoko: a Tragedy* (London, 1696), sig. M3r.

43 "A Dissertation Upon the Greek Comedy," *The Spectator*, no. 40 (16 April 1711); *Remarks on the Plays of Shakespear: an Essay on the Art, Rise, and Progress of the Stage, in Greece, Rome and England*, attributed to Charles Gildon ([London] 1710), p. ix; *The Greek Theatre of Father Brumoy*, 3 vols., trans. Mrs. Charlotte Lennox (London, 1759), III, 153.

44 Samuel Johnson, *The Rambler*, no. 156.

7

Farce

The problem of farce

If one believes the column in *Annals of English Drama* which defines the "Type" of each play listed, Thomas Otway's *The Cheats of Scapin* (1677) ought to be the first English farce.[1] Whatever else may be distinctive about Otway's play, it seems inherently improbable that it could claim that honor. But perhaps it is no honor: the naming of a work as a tragedy is construed as a label of dignity, an attempt to lay claim to an elevated cultural position and a network of weighty cultural resonances within which the work demands to be deemed worthy of a place; the naming of a work as a farce is more likely to be accompanied by an apology. When Leo Hughes and A. H. Scouten edited a collection of ten Restoration and eighteenth-century farces, their preface immediately set out to answer any accusation that they thought the plays good: "We have no illusions about the intrinsic merit of these little pieces. There is no great literary merit to be found in any one of them. In fact, their significance lies not so much in their merit as in their popularity."[2] Restoration playwrights would have had no difficulty understanding their point of view. Again and again, throughout the Restoration and long before the appearance of *The Cheats of Scapin*, Restoration dramatists sought carefully to define their own work as not being farce, a scrupulous resistance to the triviality that they too assumed to be inherent in the form, a resistance as necessary in the 1660s as in the 1940s.

In addition to worrying about low aesthetic value, Restoration playwrights fretted about the popularity of farce. In the preface to his tragedy *Cleomenes* (1692),[3] John Dryden wrote of his surprise at the success of his play "at a time when the World is running mad after *Farce*, the Extremitie of bad Poetry, or rather the Judgment that is fallen upon Dramatique Writing,"[4] just as, twenty years earlier, in the preface to *An Evening's Love* (1668), he had been fulminating against "those Farces, which are now the most frequent entertainments of the Stage."[5] Dryden's fulminations sit uncomfortably coming from the author of *Sir Martin Mar-All* (1667), a hugely successful and influential farce and the first major adaptation of a Molière farce for the Restoration stage.

There is nothing unusual in Dryden's ambivalence, his ability both to attack farces and to write them. This horror of anything popular and of farce in particular, common in many other Restoration playwrights, places farce in a peculiarly vulnerable position: few dramatists were prepared to defend writing farces. The practice of farce-writing had its own financial rewards but attempts to claim "great literary merit" were as infrequent in the Restoration as now. Nahum Tate's substantial defense of farce, in the preface to the second edition of his farce *A Duke and No Duke* (published 1693), is an unusual and remarkable document. The opponents of farce could not deny its popularity. It held a prominent place in the theatrical repertory, even more so after 1700 when, in the guise of the after-piece, it occupied a significant position in daily performances and in the economics of the company.

"Farces, what be those?"

Restoration farces are not difficult plays. They do not deal directly with the ambiguities of desire, the social problems of relationships, the tense difficulties of status and power which characterize Restoration comic drama. Their characters are straightforward, stereotypical, often bland, always keeping their thoughts and emotions subordinate to the action. As Richard Flecknoe wrote, "A *Farce*, is but a *merry Play*, affords / You *Mimick Gesture*, to your *Comick words*."[6] That emphasis on physical action, on disguise and trickery, on – most often – the servants aiding their young masters to win the women they desire (an aim in which, in farce, the young men are always successful), results in a prolonged emphasis on the servants themselves and other lower-class figures, often transformed socially through their choice of disguise or, occasionally, through magic.

Restoration farces are unashamedly conventional but they also deny many of the premises of the supposedly higher forms of comedy. Unembarrassed in their celebration of action, of the processes by which the servants engineer their employers' success, farces enjoy the mechanics of plot. Their methods make no claim to the kinds of realism in the representation of social activity that critics have repeatedly found in the best-known Restoration comedies, for in farce the conventions inevitably lead to an unambiguous restoration of social hierarchies. When, for instance, in Thomas Jevon's *The Devil of a Wife* (1686), Nell, "a simple innocent Girl," the wife of Jobson, "a Psalm-singing Cobler," magically changes places with Lady

Lovemore, "A Proud Phanatick, always canting and brawling, a Perpetual Vixen and a Shrew" (sig. a2v), Lady Lovemore learns temperate behavior, Jobson earns £500 from Sir Richard Lovemore and both men carefully check that they have not been cuckolded in the meantime. There is no doubt on anyone's side about what has happened in the experience of the farce – nothing stays hidden – and there has been no social transgression or immoral activity. Order is unambiguously reasserted and the play's dalliance with social upheaval and magically induced upward mobility is a fantasy that the play both opens and rigorously closes down.

If servants become princes (e.g., Tate's *A Duke and No Duke*) or uneducated men can play at being doctors (e.g., John Lacy's *The Dumb Lady* [1669]), the transformation suggests the performability of social behavior, but it is a suggestion whose logic the plays refuse to pursue. In the Restoration, as later, farce is a fundamentally conservative form. But the freedom it allows servants is also an unnerving denial of their normal place.

But the theatre of farce is also actors' theatre, a dramatic form that depends on and relishes the actors' skills. It is a physical theatre, as the attacks on farce repeatedly identify and complain. Its physicality often mocks the intellectualism and verbal wit of higher forms of comedy and, in so doing, it opens up the restrictions of those forms, allowing the audience to focus on the actors' bodies, not as sexual objects but as metamorphic realities that can transform their worlds.

Restoration farces share little with the future form represented by, say, Feydeau. Consequently, accounts of farce that overlook the specificity of the historical moment tend to elide these generic differences.[7] But, in any case, the word itself was shifting meaning in the period, taking on a specific theatrical sense that it had not had before.[8] At the opening of Sir William Davenant's *The Playhouse to be Let* (1663), a play made up of a medley of five separate acts, employees of an unoccupied theatre are confronted by a Frenchman who wants to rent the playhouse to perform there with his troupe:

Monsieur Me vil make Presentation of de Farce.
Tirewoman Farces, what be those? New *French* Bobs for Ladies?
Player Pray peace; I understand the Gentleman.
　　　Your Farces are a kind of Mungril Plays.[9]

The Tirewoman's ignorance of the word is revealing. While the word "farce" had been in use in English from the earliest moments of the language, it had been restricted to a meaning closer to its root in the Latin verb *farcire*, to fill or stuff. Hence a cookbook of 1430 instructed "broach thine pig, then farce him" and Chaucer could write of "words farsed with plesaunce" in *The Legend of Good Women* (line 1373). The type of play which in the Restoration would become known as farce was, prior to the Renaissance, usually identified as an "interlude."

What the Monsieur was offering to put on in Davenant's play was a type of performance which could be most easily identified by its French name. It is not surprising that one of the few pre-Restoration examples of the use of "farce" specifically to describe a type of play should be linked to the visit of a French company: the Revels documents of Sir Henry Herbert for 4 November 1629 record a fee paid "For the allowinge of a French company to play a farse at Blackfryers."[10]

To an extent never true of English medieval drama, farce was a central part of French medieval theatre and more than 150 survive. Though attacked for their failure to observe classical style and morality from the 1550s onward, farces continued to be performed in popular theatre venues like provincial fairs. In the mid-seventeenth century, with the increasing success of the Italian companies in France, French or bilingual French-Italian farce appeared with greater and greater success. Molière, the greatest French writer of farce in the century and the strongest single influence on the specific forms of Restoration farce, was the inheritor of a twin tradition of farce, combining both the native French tradition and an Italian import, the work of the Comédie Italienne in Paris.[11]

The English reluctance to approve of farce was also to be found in France. The word "farce" itself was often avoided as being unfashionable, replaced by "petit divertissement" or "petite comédie"; hence, for example, Molière's triumphant success in performing in front of the king in 1658 was with a farce, *Le Docteur amoureux*, but he sought permission to play it as "un de ces petits divertissements" which had won him a reputation in the provinces.[12] Molière's playwriting, throughout his career, negotiated with the possibilities of farce: while he "continued to write ... true farces[,] he also wrote short comedies in one act like *Les Précieuses ridicules* or *Sganarelle* which follow the line of the genre of farce."[13]

The dialogue in Davenant's *The Playhouse to be Let* goes on to consider the appropriateness of French farce to English tastes:

> *Player*   But, Sir, I believe all *French* Farces are
> Prohibited Commodities, and will
> Not pass current in *England*.
> *Monsieur* Sir, pardon me; de *Engelis* be more
> Fantastick den de *Fransh*. De Farce
> Bi also very fantastick, and vil passe ...
> De vise Nation bi for tings heroique,
> And de fantastique, vor de Farce!

The tirewoman's response to this voiced a xenophobic distrust that would be central to the consideration of farce thereafter: "I like not that these *French* pardonne-moys / Should make so bold with old *England*" (p. 68). Though English dramatists clearly understood the theatrical brilliance of Molière's work, they could do nothing to overcome a nationalistic dislike of anything that came from across the Channel.

"Farce" stretched its range of usage well beyond the theatre. It came to be used in the period to describe anything ridiculous: an individual could be mocked as a "mere farce"[14] and so too could a government, albeit in a prologue which argued that the Interregnum suppression of the stage made the government theatrical: "[They] silence't us that they alone might *act*; / ... Ours were the *Moral Lectures, theirs the Farse*."[15] But "farce" also quickly took on the sense of defining a particular type of stage action or segment of a play (usually involving physical stage business, practical jokes, or the gulling of the gullible) as well as a specific genre of theatrical practice, without the word's ever losing something of that association with France and the fear of being taken over by French fashions. Dryden's complaint in 1671 that "most of those Comedies, which have been lately written, have been ally'd too much to Farce" is immediately followed by a recommendation of how to stop this decline: "and this must of necessity fall out till we forbear the translation of *French Plays*: for their Poets wanting judgement to make, or to maintain true characters, strive to cover their defects with ridiculous Figures and Grimaces" (x, 204).

The Playhouse to be Let is referring to a new form of theatre: no pre-Restoration play was published with the word "farce" on the title-page. In the course of the Restoration the word starts to appear as a precise label; hence, for instance, Aphra Behn's *The False Count* was published with two different title-pages, one of which puts the genre first, *A Farce Call'd The False Count* (published 1682). If the label was now precise it was also inclusive: farces included burlesques and travesties so that Buckingham's burlesque of heroic tragedies, *The Rehearsal* (1671) was often described as a farce and the title-page of Thomas Duffett's brilliant mockery of Elkanah Settle's tragedy *The Empress of Morocco* for the rival theatre company (published in 1674) identifies his burlesque as "A Farce."

In his diary Pepys demonstrates his command of this comparatively new usage as a theatrical term for genre, strikingly again in connection with a visit of a French company which he saw on 30 August 1661 where "there being nothing pleasant but the foolery of the Farce, we went home." But when he saw Thomas Shadwell's play *The Sullen Lovers* on 2 May 1668 he described how "a little boy, for a farce, doth dance Polichinelli," using the word to mean something that filled out or was stuffed into a play as an extra entertainment, as "farce" had commonly been used earlier. After seeing a tragedy on 19 January 1669 which had had dances added to it, Pepys wrote that "Lacy hath made a farce of several dances, between each act, one. But his words are but silly, and invention not extraordinary as to the dances."

John Lacy, who had made the farce of dances, wrote a number of plays in the 1660s which can unarguably be defined as farces. At a performance of one of them, *The Old Troop*, on 31 July 1668, Pepys saw the "King and Court all there, and mighty merry: a Farce" but, going back to see the play again the next day, 1 August, he found that "[I] do like the play better now then before; and endeed there is a great deal of true wit in it – more then in the common sort of plays."

The play modulates on second viewing, Pepys no longer feeling obliged to dub it a farce but instead to approve of its wit, offering "wit" and "farce" as effectively opposing values. The same contradictory impulses had been in play when he saw a performance of Dryden's *Sir Martin Mar-All* on 16 August 1667: "It is the most entire piece of Mirth, a complete Farce from one end to the other, that certainly was ever writ. I never laughed so in all my life; I laughed till my head ached all the evening and night with my laughing, and at very good wit therein, not fooling." Pepys seeks to reassure himself that his laughter was not wasted on mere "fooling" but justified by the "very good wit." The play may have been "a complete Farce" but that need not be pejorative for Pepys provided there was "wit." If "farce" necessarily denotes a type of play in which the audience is encouraged to laugh frequently, lengthily, and noisily to mark their response to the stage action, the quality of the laughter may need, for audience members like Pepys or critical judges like Dryden, to be carefully monitored and evaluated. Though the word had become part of the vocabulary of theatrical forms, it did not thereby gain acceptability.

Pepys enjoys farces but is reluctant to admit it. He doubts whether he ought to enjoy farce, not only because of his obsessive anxiety over whether he ever ought to be enjoying himself but also because a delight in farce is in tension with the canons of dramatic value which he knows he ought to accept. For a frequent theatre-goer like Pepys, as for Dryden and other playwrights, farces are worrying precisely because he cannot help himself liking them and laughing uproariously. Farce becomes for Pepys the source of an unnerving and uncontrollable breakdown in the boundaries of socially approved behavior, for which even the laughter of the king and the court is not enough sufficient sanction. Such laughter made his head ache in more ways than one.

The sources of farces

Farces moved into the mainstream of professional London theatre from performances rooted in popular – rather than aristocratic – culture. In 1673 Francis Kirkman published his second collection of brief plays, most of which had been performed during the closure of the theatres, in fairs, closed-down playhouses, and similar venues by small traveling troupes: *The Wits, or Sport upon Sport. Being a Curious collection of several Drols and Farces*. Each of the playlets is prefaced by an argument providing a summary of its plot except, for example, in "The Humour of Simple" or in "The Humour of Bumpkin" where, Kirkman announces, "Argument needless, It being a Thorow Farce, and very well known."[16] "Simple" and "Bumpkin" are unusual in *The Wits* for having no known source, though they are plainly versions of earlier plays, but at least 24 of the 38 drolls and farces that are included in the two volumes of *The Wits* are abridged from identifiable pre-Restoration English plays, usually simply excerpting the comic scenes (Elson, *The Wits*, p. 19). So "The Bouncing Knight" weaves together snatches of five scenes from Shakespeare's *Henry IV Part 1* to create a Falstaff farce while, at an even less sophisticated level of narrative, "The Grave-makers" uses Hamlet's encounter with the gravedigger to provide a tiny snatch of drama.

Robert Cox, identified by Kirkman as "not only the principal Actor, but also the Contriver and Author of most of these Farces" (Elson, *The Wits*, p. 268), clearly led a company of six or eight actors who could perform these pieces surreptitiously, often "under pretence of Rope-dancing, or the like." These farces are perhaps less plays than popular entertainments, short and cheap substitutes now that the theatres had been closed, or pieces to be played in towns which did not have theatres usually available. Though they may have been excerpted from major and popular Renaissance plays, they do not reflect these origins so much as they define their kinship with the kinds of commercial entertainment that lay outside the physical structures of the London public theatres.

A few of the farces in *The Wits* necessitated a larger cast and may not have been within the range of Cox's company. *The Wits*, for instance, included one farce, significantly longer than the norm of the collection, taken from Shakespeare's *A Midsummer Night's Dream*, which was also published separately in 1661 as *The Merry Conceited Humours of Bottom the Weaver*, announcing on its title-page that the farce had been "lately, privately presented, by several apprentices for their harmless recreation." A private amateur production, this farce was offered as having been a form of entertainment about which no one need be anxious, the beginnings of a justification for drama in the transitional return to professional theatre practice after the Restoration. Unlike tragedy, which was far more likely to come under suspicion for its possibly oppositional politics, farce could appear safe, a "harmless" form of pleasure which did not need the weight of state censorship.

Robert Cox carved out his texts efficiently to provide a fragmentary form of drama, quarried from larger texts just well enough to stand alone. The remains of the five-act comedy or tragicomedy became a farce, denied a larger structure within which to be seen. The association of farce with brevity, even if not usually as extreme as in the cases of many of the drolls and farces of *The Wits*, would potently remain in Restoration practice.

The form of writing and performance of farce which Cox's work defines was not restricted to the Interregnum. A company of a similar size and working in a similar way was touring East Anglia under the control of Robert Parker in the late 1670s.[17] In 1680 the company received its highest accolade, performing, or so they claimed, no fewer than "Three Farces ... before the King and Court at New-Market," probably all on the same evening. Published as *The Muse of Newmarket* in 1680, these three plays are again adaptations from pre-Restoration plays like Thomas Nabbes's *Tottenham Court* (published 1638) or Philip Massinger's *The Guardian* (published 1655), with, in each case, a substantial emphasis on a clown role (perhaps a role for Parker himself) and on anything that could easily become obscene. In each of the plays, justice is finally done, wantonness (on the rare occasions that the intention turns into the deed) punished, and a moral proclaimed.

The Wits and *The Muse of Newmarket* represent the margins of known Restoration and Interregnum drama, examples of an area of dramatic activity that is rarely considered or even glimpsed. These plays are an efficient response to a popular demand for short farces, confining the originality of creativity to the ability of the abridger and the skillfulness of the performers. One of the characteristics of Restoration farce lies in its close reliance on the performers' abilities and these plays too represent a theatrical culture in which plays are generated to suit particular small companies, usually working in difficult conditions and needing to keep an audience amused for long enough to be paid. Farce is the only kind of drama that could be guaranteed to meet such economic circumstances.

The reliance here on English drama as the source for these playlets is largely uncharacteristic of farce in the main London theatres. There were isolated examples: John Lacy abbreviated *The Taming of the Shrew* into a short farce *Sauny the Scot* (1667); Nahum Tate turned to the Jonson-Chapman-Marston play *Eastward Ho* for his *Cuckolds-Haven* (1685);

Thomas Doggett adapted his own full-length comedy *The Country Wake* (1696) into a one-act farce *Hob* in 1711. But most Restoration farces rely on French and Italian models. Even Nahum Tate, in basing *A Duke and No Duke* on Sir Aston Cokayne's *Trappolin Creduto Principe or Trappolin Suppos'd a Prince* (published 1658), deliberately chose a play which, as its Italian title suggests, was itself based on an extremely common scenario for performances by *commedia* troupes and was written as a result of Cokayne's direct experience of seeing *commedia dell'arte* companies in Italy in the 1630s.[18]

But, after the Restoration, *commedia dell'arte* companies visited England, usually playing at court. While the performance of farce in the London theatres derives from the English traditions of popular theatre represented by Cox and Parker, the sources for the plots of most Restoration farces do not come from an equivalent vernacular resource of professional performance at the margins of theatrical activity. Restoration farce is a dramatic form that links together the popular and the aristocratic in uneasy harmony. The most important of the visits by *commedia* companies were those by Tiberio Fiorilli's company who first performed at court in 1673, so successfully that the King ordered the provision of a chain and medal of gold for six members of the company and a large piece of plate for Fiorilli himself.[19] Coming soon after the successful visit of a French company, the triumph of Fiorilli as Scaramuccio infuriated Dryden who attacked them in an epilogue for a theatre performance in Oxford in 1673:

> Th'*Italian* Merry-Andrews took their place,
> And quite Debauch'd the Stage with lewd Grimace;
> Instead of Wit, and Humours, your Delight
> Was there to see two Hobby-horses Fight,
> Stout *Scaramoucha* with Rush Lance rode in,
> And ran a Tilt at Centaure *Arlequin* . . .
> Nature was out of Countenance, and each Day
> Some new born Monster shewn you for a Play.   (1, 147–8)

Even more successful was the return of Fiorilli's company in 1675 when they were given unprecedented permission to charge members of the court admission, even though they were acting at the Hall Theatre in Whitehall, effectively within a royal palace. John Evelyn found this "very scandalous," though "having seen him act before in Italy . . . I was not averse from seeing the most excellent of that kind of folly."[20]

In the aftermath of the success of these visits – and the transition of their performances from private court theatricals to such a direct challenge to the finances of the professional London theatres – new English farces including Scaramouch and other characters from *commedia scenarii* began to be written. Edward Ravenscroft's *Scaramouch a Philosopher, Harlequin a School-Boy, Bravo, Merchant, and Magician* appeared in 1677, announcing itself as "a comedy after the Italian manner." In *The Second Part of the Rover* (1681) Aphra Behn incorporated a Harlequin as Willmore's servant, making him speak in what Behn defines as Italian (but printing a translation of some of his lines) on the rare occasions that he speaks at all and giving him a freedom over physical business onstage that suggests a performing style as unscripted and improvisatory as *commedia* styles; at one point the text simply announces Harlequin meets another character "in the dark and plays tricks with him" (p. 77).

Behn wrote extensive scenes for Harlequin and Scaramouch in her three-act farce *The Emperor of the Moon* (1687) and her Harlequin, Thomas Jevon, and her Scaramouch, Anthony Leigh, had by then already played the same roles in William Mountfort's transformation of Marlowe's *Dr. Faustus* into what was finally published in 1697 as *The Life and Death of Doctor Faustus made into a Farce … with the Humours of Harlequin and Scaramouche.*

Though this sequence would suggest a substantial and direct debt to the Italian companies, almost all the material is actually filtered through a French mediator. Behn may claim that her Harlequin in *The Second Part of the Rover* speaks Italian but his lines are a mixture of French and Italian (e.g., "No, Seignior, un vieule Femme," p. 73). The principal source for *The Emperor of the Moon* is *Arlequin empereur dans la lune*, a typical *commedia* play performed by the Italian comedians in Paris, with its scenes in French written by Fatouville and its Italian scenes improvised. Precisely because *commedia dell'arte* dramas were improvised, adaptations could only borrow a situation, never the language. Hence its dependence on the actors' brilliance is enormous and Mountfort's farce proudly announces the humors of Harlequin and Scaramouche "As they were several times Acted by Mr Lee and Mr Jevon." The physicality of the performance of farce is the essence of its translatability. What the court admired in the visiting foreign companies and what the professional theatre built upon were precisely the same skills as the fairground performers like Robert Cox had needed. Ravenscroft's play, which so stridently proclaims its Italian source, disingenuously claims in its prologue to be experimental in its reliance on actors:

> The Poet does a dang'rous trial make,
> And all the common Roads of Plays forsake.
> Upon the Actors it depends too much,
> And who can hope ever to see two such
> As the Fam'd *Harlequin* & *Scaramouch*.   (sig.A2r)

Ravenscroft also claims that, while his play was delayed by the actors, Otway's *The Cheats of Scapin* was performed at Dorset Garden, the rival theatre, and "The City House comes out with half our Play." While claims of priority are impossible to determine, there are substantial sections of the two plays that are direct and close translations of the same source. The source for both, however, is not Italian at all but Molière's *Les Fourberies de Scapin* and Ravenscroft, like Otway, predictably includes the scene with one of the most famous repeated lines in all French drama, "Que le diable allait-il faire dans cette galère?", as well as taking other scenes from Molière's *Le Mariage forcé*.

Even at its most apparently Italian, then, Restoration farce can prove the attacks of the Francophobe opponents of farce to be true. Again and again the principal source for a farce can be identified as French: Ravenscroft's successful farce *The Anatomist* (1697), for instance, is based closely on Hauteroche's popular *Crispin médecin*, performed in the 1670s, except toward the end where Ravenscroft saw the comic potential of repeating a scene in a different form, giving the servant Crispin, who had been terrified by having to hide by lying on a dissecting-table and listening to a detailed account of what the doctor is about to do to the "corpse," a chance to turn the tables by threatening to dissect the *senex* of the play, Old Gerard.[21] Such plays do little to hide their French origins. In adapting Molière's play for *The Cheats of Scapin*, Otway created a mixture of comic names in which Octavian and Leander, the young men of the play, co-exist with Scapin while the fathers are re-named Thrifty and Gripe and the action notionally removed to England through transient references to place: "My Father is this Day arriv'd at *Dover* with old Mr. *Gripe*, with a resolution to Marry me." Such gestures toward Anglicization do nothing to hide the true origins.

French companies visited London even more frequently than Italian ones throughout the period and, while some only performed opera, others found that linguistic barriers could be best crossed by comedy. Dryden, infuriated by the success of one company in 1673, mocked the audience's reactions:

> We dare not on your Priviledge intrench,
> Or ask you why you like 'em? They are *French*.
> Therefore some go with Courtesie exceeding,
> Neither to Hear nor See, but show their Breeding,
> Each Lady striving to out-laugh the rest,
> To make it seem they understood the Jest.   (1, 145)

But even without such visits, the success of Molière's company in Paris and the new wave of publication of a wide range of French farce in the 1660s must have suggested a fruitful source for popular drama. As Dryden put it, "*French* farce worn out at home, is sent abroad;/ And, patch'd up here, is made our *English* mode,"[22] though it was Dryden's own success with *Sir Martin Mar-All* that gave a particular impetus to the cross-channel traffic. John Lacy's *The Dumb Lady*, for instance, combines Molière's *L'Amour médecin* and his *Le Médecin malgré lui*; Behn's *The False Count* derives from Molière's *Les Précieuses ridicules*. Ravenscroft, in particular, turned to Molière frequently: *The Citizen Turned Gentleman or Mamamouchi* (1672) is an adaptation of *Le Bourgeois Gentilhomme* and *The Careless Lovers* (1673) takes material from *M. de Porceaugnac*. Ravenscroft's use of Molière is consistently angled toward a skillful representation of the most farcical scenes without a significant concern for any other aspects of Molière's achievement. While critics like Allardyce Nicoll abuse Ravenscroft for "reducing [Molière's] comedies to the meagre limits of the farcical show" or "working towards the reduction of the Molière comedy to mere farce,"[23] contemporaries like Dryden attacked Ravenscroft precisely for pleasing the audience:

> Th'unnatural strain'd Buffoon is onely taking:
> No Fop can please you now of Gods own making ...
> You must have *Mamamouchi* such a Fop
> As would appear a Monster in a Shop.   (XI, 324)

Robert Hume argues, in a benign account of the play, "Ravenscroft cheerfully caters to audience taste ... [He] has excellent theatrical sense, and however crude his artistry, his results are very good fun" but he also identifies the frequent segments of "Plain farce": "numerous laughable episodes have no more necessary connection to the plot than does a custard-pie episode in an old silent film."[24]

Dryden attacks the play for the monstrosity of its characters; Hume finds the play's form a loose and baggy monster. Ravenscroft's play exemplifies Restoration farce's toying with notions of the grotesque and the unnatural. Apparently blithely unconcerned that its design is so inorganic and un-Aristotelian, the play pursues its revelation of extremes of behavior, for such farce is proud that it can drive beyond the limits of naturalism. In defining its claim to that territory which Dryden so distrusted and which orthodox Restoration aesthetics disparaged, farce has its own logic, derived from its very conventionality, refuting the demands of contemporary theories with their high valuing of the "natural," of the necessity of mimetic accuracy.

If Molière's strongest influence on the development of comedy in the Restoration was through an exploration of the possibilities of farce, of a form of physical comedy of disguise and trickery, of stage business and repeated gags, of an actor-dominated drama (and hence quite commonly an actor-written drama), it also suggests that farce is the crucial area in the Restoration theatre for the exploration of the inheritance of classical Roman comedy as a drama of witty servants outwitting dull masters. The servants of Restoration comedy are essentially marginalized but Scaramouch and Harlequin are servants encouraged to occupy center-stage. Farce is recurrently concerned with sequences in which, in the interests of their young masters, servants extract money or permission to marry from their old masters or simply fool them and delay them through tricks played while disguised. The witty servant of Roman comedy is allowed a greater presence in farce than in any other area of Restoration drama. The outstanding translations of Plautus and Terence by Laurence Echard (*Plautus's Comedies Made English* and *Terence's Comedies Made English*, both published in 1694) make Roman comedies into Restoration ones but they also show how much Plautine comedy is present in the forms of Restoration farce. Underlying the disparagement of farce may be an anxiety about the centrality it allows servants, revealing the work of a class which makes the machine of society move but which is, for its social superiors, supposed to be effectively invisible.

"Which makes 'em too much degenerate into Farce"

Echard's praise of Plautus is tempered by an anxiety about some of his characters:

> Plautus ... made it his principal Aim to please and tickle the Common People; and...the better to humor them, he was ... frequently extravagant ... in his *Characters* ..., and drew Men often more Vicious, more Covetous, more Foolish, &c. than generally they were ... With these sort of *Characters* many of our modern *Comedies* abound, which makes 'em too much degenerate into *Farce*, which seldom fail of pleasing the Mob.[25]

The recurrent complaint levied against Restoration farce is that, under the excuse of crowd-pleasing, it breaks realism and represents impossible characters.[26] As Dryden put it in his epilogue to Etherege's *The Man of Mode* (1676),

> Most Modern Wits, such monstrous Fools have shown,
> They seem'd not of heav'ns making but their own.
> Those Nauseous Harlequins in Farce may pass,
> But there goes more to a substantial Ass! (1, 154)

This objection conceals an implicit claim that "true comedy" can adequately be seen as a representation of the real. When Edward Howard, one of farce's fiercest critics in the late 1660s and 1670s, accuses farce of being "rather an entertainment of Mimikry, than a Play in any kind" or of being "Mimikry and other ridiculous Gestures mingled together,"[27] he is creating the same exclusion of farce from comedy that Thomas Shadwell defined in attacking "impossible unnatural farce Fools, which some intend for Comical"[28] or which William Burnaby argued for in 1701: "In *Comedy*, you will not be satisfied with the unnatural Farce of some Poets, which looks like sick Men's Dreams, compos'd of Parts that no Man can reduce to one Body, and run out of Nature to make you laugh."[29]

The recurrent accusation against farce is its deliberate distortion of normality, particularly visible in what is assumed to be the characteristic look of the face of the actor in farce: the grimace. Hence Nicholas Brady in the prologue to his play *The Rape* (1692) could contrast a previous age with the present: "True Nature then and solid Sence took place, / Now ackward Farce prevails; with dull *Grimace*" (sig. [A]3v). Even writers of farce needed to assert, if they could not prove, that their plays were not assemblies of unnatural behavior. Aphra Behn's dedication to *The Emperor of the Moon* (1687) distinguishes between those foolish fops whom "the Word Farce might have offended ... [who] wou'd ... have damn'd it ... as too debas'd and vulgar to entertain a Man of Quality" and the Marquess of Worcester, the dedicatee, "whose refin'd Sence, and Delicacy of Judgment, will, thro' all the humble Actions and trivialness of Business, find Nature there, and that Diversion which was not meant for the Numbers, who comprehend nothing beyond the Show and Buffoonry" (sig. A2v). Farce's appeal is, for Behn, troublingly broad. Its very popularity creates the problem and the nature of the response of such a wide audience might obscure the worth of her play.[30] As Dryden put it in his preface to his son's comedy *The Husband his own Cuckold* (1696), 'There is scarce a Man or Woman of God's making in all their Farces: yet they raise an unnatural sort of laughter, the common effect of Buffoonry; and the Rabble which takes this for Wit, will endure no better, because 'tis above their Understanding." (sig. A4r) In the prologue to *The Old Troop* (published 1672), John Lacy ironically appealed for help from that rabble, the lower-class members of the audience who sat in the upper gallery of the theatre:

> To you that Judges are i'th' publick street,
> Of Ballads without sence, or even feet;
> To you that laugh aloud with wide mouth'd grace,
> To see *Jack* Puddings Custard thrown in's face,
> To you I do address; for you I write,
> From you I hope protection here tonight.
> Defend me, O friends, of th'upper Region,
> From the hard censure of this lower Legion.   (sig. A4r)

By being unnatural, by being derived from foreign sources, by appealing for a non-intellectual response from the intelligent and unintelligent parts of the audience alike, by asking for laughter without thought and entertainment without instruction, farce defined by inversion all those characteristics which proper comedy necessarily wished to achieve. All those oppositions can be heard in Dryden's most extensive definition of the distinction between comedy and farce in his preface to *An Evening's Love* (published 1671):

> Comedy consists, though of low persons, yet of natural actions, and characters; I mean such humors, adventures, and designes, as are to be found and met with in the world. Farce, on the other side, consists of forc'd humors, and unnatural events. Comedy presents us with the imperfections of humane nature: Farce entertains us with what is monstrous and chimerical. The one causes laughter in those who can judge of men and manners, by the lively representation of their folly and corruption; the other produces the same effect in those who can judge of neither, and that only by its extravagances.
>
> (X, 203)

It is from such a position of superior discriminating judgment that John Dennis can show how his play *A Plot and No Plot* (1697) changed genre: "The following Play was at first design'd a Farce: But when I consider'd that the design of it, was both just and important, ... I alter'd my intention, and resolv'd to make it a low Comedy" (sig. [A]3v).

More often, writers of farce defined the modesty of their ambition apologetically. The epilogue to Jevon's *The Devil of a Wife* suggests that farce is not worth critics' attacks, "But who upon a Droll e're spent his wit; / Or criticiz'd an Merry *Andrew* yet?", while also modestly defining Jevon's muse's lack of ambition which 'ne're attempts to fly, / Up to the lofty pitch of Comedy: / Farce is her aim, the persons low and mean, / Humble the language, homely is the scene" (pp. 55–56). But at the same time such humility stakes an implicit claim for the independence of a social territory, that of "persons low and mean," which comedy and its defenders could not abandon. Farce's popularity, not only in its success but also in the social class of the people which it was concerned to represent, could not be left unanswered.

It was not until 1693 that a full-scale attempt to rebut the continual antagonism to farce was offered – at least in the form of a critical essay (though in another sense, of course, the success of farces was its own answer). Nahum Tate had written a brief preface when his farce *A Duke and No Duke* was published in 1685. His main claim at this stage was that the unnaturalness for which farce was attacked was quite properly its concern and that the successful achievement of that aim was hard:

Tragedy, Comedy, and Pastoral it self subsist upon Nature: So that whosoever has a Genius to Copy Her, is assur'd of success, and all the World affords him Subject: Whereas the Business of *Farce* is to exceed Nature and Probability. But then there are so few Improbabilities that will appear Pleasant, and so much nicety requir'd in the management, that the Performance will be found extreamly Difficult.   (sig. a1r–v)

For the new issue of the play in 1693, Tate, newly appointed Poet Laureate, used his new authority to write a lengthy new preface, a response, I suspect, to the wave of attacks on the success of farce in the early 1690s. When even William Mountfort, who had written farces, could moan that "we can see the Town throng to a *Farce*, and *Hamlet* not bring Charges,"[31] Tate's response would have been timely. Tate's preface is largely a translation of an essay by an Italian writer, Agesilao Mariscotti.[32] To Mariscotti's learned disquisition on the presence of farce in ancient drama, Tate adds a particular English slant, arguing forcefully, for instance, that Jonson's *The Alchemist* is "Farce from the opening of the First Scene to the end of the Intreigue" (Holland, "Tate's Defence," p. 109) but also concerned to show that a number of segments of plays by Dryden, the arch-opponent of farce, are truly defined as farce "or near akin to it" (Ibid., p. 110).

In the aftermath of Tate's defense it became possible for farce-writers to be more vocal in their defense. Ravenscroft even included a defense in a prelude in dialogue between a poet and a critic prefixed to his tragedy *The Italian Husband* (published 1698), ending with the statement that "A Farce is like a *Dutch* piece of Painting, or a Grotesque Figure, extravagant and pleasant," as extravagant in its analogy as the claim it makes for farce.

Farce in the Restoration theatre

Tate's defense of farce defines the form as a literary dramatic genre, as a species of writing. But the practice of farce was essentially one which placed its emphasis on performance. Above all, farce was seen as depending more on the brilliance of particular actors than the skill of the playwright and it is striking how many farces were written by actors turned play-wrights (for example Lacy, Jevon, Doggett, and Mountfort). Robert Gould's "The Playhouse, A Satire" attacked Thomas Jevon but could not help offering two-edged praise of him as a natural actor for farce:

> His Face for *Farce* nature at first design'd,
> And matcht it too with as Burlesque a mind,
> Made him pert, vain, a Maggot, vile, ill-bred,
> And gave him *heels of Cork*, and *brains of lead*. [33]

Earlier actors like Edward Angel, James Nokes, and Cave Underhill embodied the brilliance of performance that farce required. All three are brought on stage in the prologue to Edward Howard's *The Womens Conquest* (1670) where their conversation in praise of their own skills and the merits of English farce (as opposed to "the Scaramuchos") is abruptly halted by the appearance of the ghost of Ben Jonson (the embodiment here of true comic writing), as Angel cries "Fly, fly, Associates, there's no being on the Stage longer, for us of the Farce party" (sig. c3r).

By 1701, John Corey could have a character in his comedy *A Cure for Jealousie* complain about players' earnings now that "Farce, Song, and Dance have got the Sovereign Sway. Farce writers and Songsters are now the most fam'd for Wit, and *Jack Puddings* for Acting. A Capering *Monsieur* shall get more in a Month than a good Player can in a Year" (p. 21). Those who attack the writers of farce could argue that a play's success owed nothing to the writing so that, as Brady suggested, "Thus little Poets cheaply get a Name, / Whilst *Nokes* and *Leigh* insure the Author's fame" (sig. [A]3v). Some playwrights were quite prepared to admit that this was true: Nahum Tate explained that *Cuckolds-Haven* (1685) failed because "The Principal Part (on which the Diversion depended) was, by Accident, disappointed of Mr. *Nokes's* Performance, for whom it was design'd, and only proper" (sig. A1r). Nokes had earned the nickname "Nurse" from his performance in the role in *Romeo and Juliet* but he was also outstanding in the title-role of Ravenscroft's *The Citizen Turned Gentleman* and as Gripe in Otway's *The Cheats of Scapin*. His name was often linked with Anthony Leigh as a brilliant farce double-act, for instance as rustic brothers in Durfey's *Madam Fickle* (1676).[34]

Actors may have built their fame on their performances in farce but farce found it difficult to establish its place in the organization of Restoration theatre bills in the structure of theatre entertainment. The drolls that Kirkman printed in *The Wits* were playlets often played to a changing fairground audience. In France short farces had taken a firm place alongside full-length plays in the evening's entertainment: by 1681 the playwright Hauteroche could write to his cousin "you know that putting on a serious play without a one-act farce is guaranteed to empty the theatre."[35] But the professional theatres in London during the Restoration performed a single play as the entire show, though often accompanied by entr'acte performances of songs and dances. The theatres did not acquire the French habit of main play and afterpiece until after 1700. Hence, for example, Otway's *The Cheats of Scapin* was written to accompany his translation of Racine's *Bérénice*, the farce existing solely to fill out the three-act tragedy to sufficient length to provide a full evening's performance. Farces tended to be short and, though Mr Peregrine, in the prelude to Ravenscroft's *The Italian Husband*, could state categorically that "a Farce may be two, three, or five Acts; as you have seen upon our Stage already," he was responding to the Critic's assumption that "If [a play] has but three Acts it must be a Farce" because "did you ever see it otherwise?" (sig. A2r).

Farces, therefore, were often assumed to be in need of accompaniment or were to provide support for another part of the show. Ravenscroft's popular farce *The Anatomist* (1697) was performed initially with Peter Motteux's musical extravaganza *The Loves of Mars and Venus*, which "was written to be inserted into a very short Farce"[36] and whose action is cued by delays in the plot of the farce: "My Master, Madam, has sent word, he can't be at home till dinner-time, but would have you go on with the Musick" (*The Anatomist*, p. 12).

In the period of fierce competition between the theatres after the secession of Betterton and the other senior actors in 1695 – and particularly in the period after 1702 – the additional songs and dances, the added entertainments, became more and more extravagant: an advertisement for a performance on 5 July 1700 promised a little boy dancing, Mrs Elford's new entry, Miss Evan's jig and Irish dance, new comical dances performed by Monsieur l'Sac, a pastoral dialogue by Mr George and Mrs Haynes "and a variety of other Singing."[37] By December 1702 the Lincoln's Inn Fields company were offering a masque-opera after the main tragedy; by April 1703 Dorset Garden was offering two farces plus singing and dancing as the evening's show. In the next few years the format of main show and farcical afterpiece began to become established,[38] finally becoming normative only after the success of afterpieces in John Rich's first season as manager of Lincoln's Inn Fields Theatre in 1714–15. Only by then had farce established its place in the theatre, a position that at last seemed to exempt it from criticism.

Theatrically awkward in its dramatic form and length, damned for coming from France, socially disturbing for its interest in servants, aesthetically unacceptable for its fascination with the body, farce succeeded nonetheless in being popular. Slightly regarded then, little read and never performed now, Restoration farce can be popular theatre at its funniest and most enjoyable. Its lack of pretensions should not hide its greatest strengths: its delight in the power of laughter and its celebration of the arts of the theatre.

NOTES

1 Alfred Harbage, *Annals of English Drama 975–1700*, rev. S. Schoenbaum, 3rd edn., revised Sylvia Stoler Wagonheim (London: Routledge, 1989) p. 181.

2 Leo Hughes and A. H. Scouten, eds., *Ten English Farces* (Austin: University of Texas Press, 1948), p. vi.

3 Dates for plays are the year of first performance unless otherwise indicated.

4 John Dryden, *Cleomenes* (1692), sig. A4r; compare Thomas Shadwell's comment in the dedication to *The Squire of Alsatia* (1688) on the success of the play "as was above my expectation (in this Age which has run mad after Farces) no Comedy, for these many years, having fill'd the Theatre so long together" (sig. [A]2r).

5 *The Works of John Dryden*, ed. H. T. Swedenberg, Jr., *et al.*, 20 vols., in progress (Berkeley: University of California Press, 1956–), x, 203. Hereafter, all Dryden references are to this edition.

6 Richard Flecknoe, "Of Farces" in *Epigrams of All Sorts* (1671), p. 52.

7 See, for example, the brave attempt by Jessica Milner Davis, *Farce* (London: Methuen, 1978).

8 See Leo Hughes, "The Early Career of *Farce* in the Theatrical Vocabulary," *SE* (University of Texas) (1940), pp. 82–95.

9 Sir William Davenant, *Works* (1673), p. 68.

10 N. W. Bawcutt, ed., *The Control and Censorship of Caroline Drama: the Records of Sir Henry Herbert, Master of the Revels 1623–73* (Oxford: Clarendon Press, 1996), p. 169.

11 On Italian comedy in Paris see Virginia Scott, *The Commedia dell'arte in Paris, 1644–1697* (Charlottesville: University Press of Virginia, 1990).

12 Quoted by Leo Hughes, *A Century of Farce* (Princeton University Press, 1956), p. 65.

13 Charles Mazouer, ed., *Farces du grand siècle* (Paris: Librairie générale français, 1992) p. 16 (my translation). Mazouer's collection represents the range of French farce in the period. See also H. C. Lancaster, ed., *Five French Farces 1655–1694* (Baltimore: Johns Hopkins Press, 1937). On Molière and farce see also Bernadette Rey-Flaud, *Molière et la farce* (Geneva: Droz, 1996).

14 Hughes, "The Early Career," pp. 86–87, quoting Ravenscroft's *The Careless Lovers* (1673).

15 In the prologue to Ben Jonson's *The Silent Woman* when performed at court 19 November 1660, in Pierre Danchin, *The Prologues and Epilogues of the Restoration 1660–1700*, part 1, vol. 1 (Nancy: Publications Université Nancy II, 1981), p. 49.

16 J. J. Elson, ed., *The Wits or Sport Upon Sport* (Ithaca: Cornell University Press, 1932), pp. 165, 175.

17 See Sybil Rosenfeld, *Strolling Players and Drama in the Provinces 1660–1765* (Cambridge University Press, 1939), pp. 39–40.

18 See Kathleen M. Lea, "Sir Aston Cokayne and the 'commedia dell'arte," *MLR* 23 (1928), 47–51.

19 See Eleanor Boswell, *The Restoration Court Stage 1660–1702* (Cambridge, Mass.: Harvard University Press, 1932), p. 119. For a listing of visits see also Sybil Rosenfeld, *Foreign Theatrical Companies in Great Britain in the 17th and 18th Centuries* (Society for Theatre Research Pamphlet Series, No. 4, London, 1955).

20 Quoted in Boswell, *The Restoration Court Stage*, p. 121.

21 See Raymond E. Parshall, "The Source of Ravenscroft's *The Anatomist*," *RES* 12 (1936), 328–33.

22 *Works*, XI, 20; little substantial has been written on the influence of Molière since John Wilcox, *The Relation of Molière to Restoration Comedy* (New York: Columbia University Press, 1938).

23 Allardyce Nicoll, *A History of English Drama 1660–1900*, vol. I, *Restoration Drama 1660–1700* (4th edn., revised., Cambridge University Press, 1955), p. 254.

24 Robert D. Hume, *The Development of English Drama in the Late Seventeenth Century* (Oxford: Clarendon Press, 1976), p. 123.

25 L. Echard, preface to *Plautus's Comedies Made English* (1694) sigs. a2v–a3r. See also Laurence Echard, *Prefaces to Terence's Comedies and Plautus's Comedies (1694)*, intro. by John Barnard (Augustan Reprint Society publication 129, Los Angeles: William Andrews Clark Memorial Library, 1968).

26 On attitudes to farce in the period see Sarup Singh, *The Theory of Drama in the Restoration Period* (Bombay: Orient Longmans, 1963), pp. 264–79 and Leo Hughes, "Attitudes of Some Restoration Dramtists towards Farce," *PQ* 19 (1940), 268–87.

27 Edward Howard, preface to *The Womens Conquest* (1671), sigs. b2v and b3v.

28 Thomas Shadwell, *The Virtuoso* (1676), sig. A2v.

29 William Burnaby, letter 5 in *Letters of Wit, Politicks and Morality* (1701) in *The Dramatic Works of William Burnaby*, ed. F. E. Budd (London: Scholartis Press, 1931), pp. 458–59.

30 See her comment in the preface to *The Dutch Lover* (1673) on character "dwindl[ing] into Farce, and so become too mean an entertainment for those persons who are us'd to think" (sig. a1v).

31 William Mountfort, *Greenwich Park* (1691), sig. A2v.

32 The source was identified by A. H. Scouten in "An Italian Source for Nahum Tate's Defence of Farce," *Italica* 27 (1950), 238–40. The preface is discussed by S. A. Golden, "An Early Defense of Farce" in A. Dayle Wallace and Woodburn O. Ross, eds., *Studies in Honor of John Wilcox* (Detroit: Wayne State University Press, 1958), pp. 61–70. It is reprinted in Peter Holland, ed., "Nahum Tate's defence of farce," *Themes in Drama 10: Farce* (Cambridge University Press, 1988), pp. 99–113.

33 Robert Gould, *Poems* (1689), p. 184.

34 On Restoration actors in farce see Hughes, *A Century of Farce*, pp. 153–86 and the entries for individual actors in Philip H. Highfill, Jr., *et al.*, eds., *A Biographical Dictionary of Actors ... in London 1660–1800* (Carbondale: Southern Illinois University Press, 1973–93).

35 Quoted by Hughes, *A Century of Farce*, p. 66, (my translation): "Vous scavez que de représenter une pièce sérieuse sans une petite pièce, c'est absolument chasser le peuple."

36 Peter Motteux, *The Loves of Mars and Venus* (1697), sig. B1r.

37 See *The London Stage*, I, 531.

38 On this transition see Leo Hughes, "Afterpieces: Or, That's Entertainment" in George Winchester Stone, Jr., ed., *The Stage and the Page: London's "Whole Show" in the Eighteenth-Century Theatre* (Berkeley: University of California Press, 1981), pp. 55–70; Hughes, *A Century of Farce*, pp. 60–93; Richard W. Bevis, ed., *Eighteenth Century Drama: Afterpieces* (London: Oxford University Press, 1970), pp. vii–xi.

8

DEREK HUGHES

Restoration and settlement:
1660 and 1688

Little more than a year after Oliver Cromwell's death in September 1658, the English revolutionary régime had collapsed as a result of inner dissension and popular hostility. Early in 1660, General George Monck marched his troops from Scotland to London, reinstated to the Rump Parliament the members whose exclusion in 1648 earned it its name, commanded new elections, and quickly decided to restore the monarchy. These events, up to the calling of a free parliament, were promptly celebrated in the first Restoration comedy, John Tatham's *The Rump* (1660), which satirizes the selfish ambition of the Puritan grandees, and the lechery and parvenu pretentiousness of their wives. (Political insurgency was at this time commonly paired with female insubordination.) But, with the intervention of Monck, hierarchy is restored to a distracted society, many of the upstarts are demoted to street vendors, and a world turned upside is set to rights.

The Rump had many successors; for one of the principal subjects of early Restoration drama was the Restoration itself.[1] For example, the first Restoration heroic play, the Earl of Orrery's *The Generall* (written in 1661),[2] transparently reworks recent events, portraying a general (Clorimun) who turns against a usurper in order to restore a rightful king. Just as topical is Dryden's first heroic play, *The Indian Queen* (1664), written in collaboration with his brother-in-law Sir Robert Howard: here, in an entirely fictional plot, Montezuma is restored to the throne of Mexico. Dramatic representations of monarchy restored were common until the early 1670s, and fascination with the theme also influenced the tailoring of pre-Restoration plays for the contemporary stage. For example, of the four Shakespeare plays which Sir William Davenant adapted, he chose three which depict the suspension and reinstatement of legitimate authority: *Measure for Measure*, *Macbeth*, and (in conjunction with Dryden) *The Tempest*.

In pure comedy, politics were less overwhelmingly dominant, but were still important. The first new comedy to receive professional performance by one of the major Restoration companies, Abraham Cowley's adaptation of his pre-Civil War play *The Guardian* (1641) as *Cutter of Coleman-Street* (1661), gives a strikingly unidealized portrait of a Royalist coping with his deprivation under the Interregnum. In the original play, a guardian attempts to defraud his ward in order to make up for squandering his own estate, though he relents once he has married the Puritan widow who now holds his property. In Cowley's revision, the wastrel becomes a dispossessed Royalist, Colonel Jolly – a martyr rather than a reprobate – but his dishonourable practices remain the same, and the result is an exceptional failure to glamorize the Royalist past, which is paralleled only in John Lacy's more innocently farcical *The Old Troop* (1664), which portrays the plundering and double-dealing of both parliamentarian and Royalist troops during the Civil War. Straightforward glamorization occurs in Sir Robert Howard's *The Committee* (1662), set in the late Interregnum, wherein two exemplary Royalist couples recover their estates from crooked Puritans (one an upstart dairy-maid) as a result of resourcefulness and loyalty. The reliance of the dim Irish servant Teague on their benign, paternalistic protection reveals the beneficial nature of hierarchy, contrasts with the insubordination of the Puritan parvenus, and aids in their defeat. Conversely, the domineering conduct of the former dairy-maid exemplifies the commonplace parallel between insubordinate subjects and insubordinate women. (Davenant's Lady Macbeth wishes that her husband had governed her "by the Charter of [his] sex."[3])

The plight of Cowley's Colonel Jolly was a familiar one, for Royalists had been subject to heavy financial penalties during the Interregnum, and many had sold estates in order to pay them. Equally, however, many who ingratiatingly celebrated the king's return had suffered little in his absence. The Earl of Orrery (then Lord Broghil) had administrated in Scotland and Ireland, been a close advisor of Cromwell, and had even urged him to assume the crown. Davenant and Cowley had also, less spectacularly, reconciled themselves to the *de facto* régime, and Dryden, who came from a Puritan gentry family, had held a secretarial post in Cromwell's administration. For Orrery in particular, the writing of propagandist drama was a form of self-reinvention,[4] and he combined continuing importance as a politician with some years of success as a dramatist, his favorite theme being restoration of rightful authority. The linkage between the king's restoration and its stage celebrations was never stronger than in Orrery's *The History of Henry the Fifth* (1664), which portrays the restoration of English power in France, and which uses actual robes from Charles II's coronation, including the king's own. Orrery does, in apology for his own past, portray situations in which decent men feel ties of loyalty to a usurper, but he specializes in rational social beings whose perfect control over their passions mirrors the rational order of a well governed society. Clorimun, who restores order in the kingdom by reinstating its proper ruler, also masters his own inner life, conquering his love for the heroine and uniting her with her true love. Indeed, in several Orrery plays, the heroic characters so thoroughly subordinate personal love to social obligation that friends actually help each other's courtship when both love the same woman. By contrast, the usurper in *The Generall* is tempted to rape the heroine, his proposed sexual violence paralleling the violence by which he has already gained the kingdom.

In associating the triumph of monarchy over rebellion with that of reason over sexual passion, Orrery gave a rather unrealistic assessment of Charles II's virtues. By contrast, Sir George Etherege's first comedy, *The Comical Revenge* (1664), celebrated the frivolity of the new order. Like *The Committee* (and *Cutter of Coleman-Street*) it is set in the late Interregnum, but it portrays the emergence of a new culture rather than a reinstatement of the world of Charles I. There is a rhymed heroic plot, in which Royalist gentry and soldiers exhibit inflexibly ideal principles similar to those of Orrery's characters, but here the principles are stultifying and even ludicrous: when the men fight an irrational duel because the heroine loves one and not the other, the enthusiasm for bloodshed is clearly absurd; and, when characters virtuously sacrifice their love to a higher principle, they have to change their minds and put love first. The key figure in this play is the easy-going hedonist, Sir Frederick Frollick, who rejects the rigid principles both of the Puritans and the old cavaliers. It is he, for example, who stops the duel from becoming a bloodbath.

But, although the Restoration continued to be an important dramatic subject for eleven years, neither history nor dramatic fashion stood still. There was widespread disappointment – merited and otherwise – with the king. His promiscuity and extravagance offended many of his own supporters, and, more creditably, he desired greater tolerance for dissenters than a parliament of vengeful Royalists was prepared to grant. Royalists did not always gain their expected rewards or redresses. Charles's marriage to Catherine of Braganza was unpopular and, it gradually became clear, childless. The natural disasters of the plague (1665) and the Great Fire of London (1666), in which some saw divine punishment for royal sins, were aggravated by a purely man-made disaster: mismanagement and humiliation in a war against the Dutch. Growing factionalism culminated in 1668 in the impeachment and exile of the Earl of Clarendon, the Chancellor, and the father-in-law of the king's brother, the Duke of York.

By the mid-1660s, there is also a more seriously admonitory approach to the king's lifestyle, with loyal dramatists cautiously reproving their amorous monarch. Montezuma, the restored hero-king of Dryden and Howard's *The Indian Queen*, is a vigorous warrior. In Dryden's sequel, *The Indian Emperour* (1665), he is a man of reason and principle, but he is also enfeebled by unwise love. Orrery's *Mustapha* (1665) and *The Black Prince* (1667) optimistically show noble monarchs triumphing over an enervating love. And, with the assault on Clarendon, criticism of the court becomes overt: in Sir Robert Howard's anti-Clarendon play *The Great Favourite* (1668), a benign but initially weak king, easily subject to political and sexual manipulation, is eventually induced to rid himself of a pernicious counsellor. In *The Committee* and *The Indian Queen* Howard had celebrated the Restoration; he was now anxious to reform what had been restored.

But changes in the social values recorded in drama are not simply direct barometric responses to the reputation of Charles and his court. There were innovations in political philosophy that did not touch the running of the state but which clearly affected the outlook of younger dramatists, who also took a more critical view of Orrery's moral idealism. For Dryden in particular, honor was far more problematic than it was for Orrery: its demands were ambiguous, and morally doubtful. In *The Indian Emperour*, for example, Montezuma's virtuous son Guyomar inadvertently contributes to the destruction of his kingdom with his fierce sense of personal honor, and the play ends with the very situation that the plays of restoration had reversed and exorcised: the killing of the king and the exile of the prince.

Like many other dramatists of his generation, Dryden had a keen, if critical, interest in the materialistic philosophy of Thomas Hobbes. For Hobbes, the fundamental principle of existence was the movement of material particles: man was matter in motion, driven by bodily appetites and aversions, his reason a tool of his desires. Because of man's appetitive nature, his natural relationship to his fellows, in a state prior to society, is that of war. In such a state, there are no laws or moral restraints, because there is no institutional authority with any power to enforce them: all have right to all. In forming political societies, humanity erects defences against the horror of its own aggressive and antisocial nature, surrendering the natural rights exercised in the primal state of war in return for the protection of an absolute political authority.

In contrast to Orrery's rational and sociable heroes, the characters of Dryden's early plays are driven by their passions and isolated within their sensations: according to Almanzor, the hero of the two-part heroic play *The Conquest of Granada* (1670–71), man is "a Pris'ner of the Mind."[5] For this reason, he is not a naturally and innately civilized being. Montezuma, the exiled and finally restored king of *The Indian Queen*, has grown up outside civilization, dwelling in a cave (albeit with a benevolent foster-father). His own desires are at first his only criterion of value, and he has to learn the restraints of civilization, so that the rightful king enters his kingdom as a noble savage, unfamiliar with the complexity of political society and its curbs upon the individual. A far more disturbing portrayal of the restored king as primal savage occurs in Aphra Behn's *The Young King*, not performed until 1679, but by her own account her first play, and therefore perhaps dating from the mid-1660s. Part of the plot is a condensed version of the Spanish dramatist Calderón's *La vida es sueño* (*Life is a Dream*), in which a prince has been imprisoned from birth by his father because of an oracle that he would be a tyrant. He is permitted to rule for a day, acts brutally, and is returned to prison, persuaded that his day of power was a dream. But the oracle is now fulfilled, and will have no bearing on the prince's real reign. Though more violent than Montezuma in *The Indian Queen*, Calderón's prince has much in common with him, having been similarly brought up in the wilds, and thinking his own desires the measure of everything. Behn alters Calderón by deriving the prince's initial behavior from his innately male sexual aggressiveness, and concentrating on issues of sexual difference: the prince has been imprisoned by his mother, not his father (who nowhere appears), and his place in the succession is taken by his Amazonian sister. And, in his initial state, he is a creature of violent and indiscriminate sexual appetites, attempting to rape an unknown woman who is put in the same prison, and even wanting sex with his (equally unknown) mother. He is stabilized by love, and the play concludes with his restoration, the mob preferring male to female rule. But a restoration involving the reform of a priapic king is a rather reserved celebration of the restoration of Charles II.

There is also a lukewarm celebration of restoration in the radical alteration of *The Tempest* produced by Dryden and Davenant in 1667. Shakespeare's play portrays a natural cycle of rebirth and reconciliation, as the old enemies Prospero and Alonso are reconciled through the marriage of their children, Ferdinand and Miranda, and Prospero is restored to the dukedom from which he was once deposed. Much remains immune to the influence of civilization, but social instincts – of which the chief is compassion – triumph in its noblest characters. The best-known, and most ridiculed, alteration of the revisers is their symmetrical duplication of many of Shakespeare's characters. The monster Caliban is given a sister, as is Miranda; and the two female *ingenues* who have never seen a young man are counterbalanced by a male *ingenu*, Hippolito, who has been kept on another part of the island, and who has never seen a woman. But these complications are not merely decorative. By providing an extra monster, and two extra characters to whom the opposite sex is alien and unknown, the revisers emphasize the condition of alienness. The fundamental human relationship is that of stranger to stranger, just as it was in the Hobbesian state of nature. Social conduct is not innate, but precariously acquired, or coercively imposed, and compassion is rarely glimpsed. Ferdinand, in Shakespeare a noble and self-disciplined character, comes close to killing Hippolito, his sexual rival, in a duel, and is sentenced to death by a fiercely vengeful Prospero, only being spared because the spirit Ariel manages to revive Hippolito. At the point where, in Shakespeare's play, the compassionate Prospero gives Alonso the healing vision of Ferdinand and Miranda playing chess, Dryden and Davenant's Prospero is gloatingly offering a sight of a very different kind: the imminent spectacle of Ferdinand's execution. Significantly, and shockingly, the official appointed to wield the "the Sword / Of Justice"[6] is the monster Caliban. The character who in Shakespeare is most hostile to society here becomes the indispensable agent of its workings, and it is noteworthy that, whereas the human characters are repeatedly strange to each other, the revisers' Caliban – unlike Shakespeare's – never has the adjective *strange* applied to him. He is not an outsider. Rather, he is an incarnation of the violence which lurks within society, and by which it is controlled.

Two of Dryden's most important plays of 1670–71 also deal with restored power. The two-part *The Conquest of Granada* portrays the re-establishment of Spanish rule over the Moorish kingdom of Granada. What is notable is the ruthless *realpolitik* with which the restoration is achieved. King Ferdinand cynically exploits the divisions of his foes and even, after the restoration of Christian rule, enthrones as his client ruler the evil (and non-Christian) Lyndaraxa, the most fearsome incarnation of the Hobbesian power drive. As when Prospero appoints Caliban as the executioner of justice, authority includes and depends on the blind violence that it nominally supersedes, and for this reason Dryden again emphasizes the interdependence of civilization and the savage, for the outcome of the power struggle is largely determined by the shifting allegiances of the noble savage Almanzor, who, like the Young Montezuma, has been brought up in the wilds, and who turns out to be Ferdinand's nephew.

Dryden's next play, *Marriage A-la-Mode* (1671), juxtaposes a comic plot of frustrated adultery with a heroic plot featuring a more direct version of the restoration theme, in that it portrays the deposition of a usurper (the Sicilian tyrant Polydamas) and the return to power of the rightful king, Leonidas. But there are nevertheless teasing complications, since the identity of the rightful ruler is both practically and philosophically problematic. Leonidas has been brought up as a fisherman's son, and since childhood has loved the peasant girl Palmyra. His first taste of royal identity comes when, mistakenly, he is identified as Polydamas' long-lost heir, and is commanded by his new-found father to renounce Palmyra. But then Palmyra turns out to be the missing heir, and Leonidas returns to peasanthood. Then, however, he discovers that he is the son of the long-dead rightful king, and he is therefore condemned to death, but is rescued from the scaffold by a popular uprising. In the course of five acts he is thus peasant, usurping prince, peasant once more, and rightful king. He does try to retain a consistent identity amidst his mutations of role, but the parallel experiences of other characters show how difficult this can be. Palmyra's character and emotional allegiances change with startling suddenness when she is promoted from rustic to princess, and her comic counterpart, the social climber Melantha, admits to having a totally different identity in the country and the court (her migration from one to the other parallels Palmyra's social transformation). In Leonidas' case, it is not entirely clear how far he is king in his essential character and how far he is made so by the role which is suddenly and unforeseeably thrust upon him: do we witness the restoration of a king, or the creation of one? Certainly, the public enthusiasm which rescues Leonidas from execution and restores him to power is a mere automatic and unreflective response to the word *king*, for Leonidas is a completely unknown quantity. The only subject with a cogent explanation of her instantaneous enthusiasm is the giddy Melantha, who freely admits that Leonidas had been imposing and handsome during his first stint of royalty, had ceased to be so when returned to peasanthood, but had regained his august presence on regaining his regal status. The public reverence for Leonidas is a subjective and shallow response to the role which has been thrust upon him. With this deeply skeptical view of the nature of restoration, the drama of restored authority came to an end.

The prologue to *Marriage A-la-Mode* notes that war has emptied the theatre of young men. It thereby alludes to a one of a number of factors which were quickly to cause political tension, and materially to change the theatrical representation of royalty. In alliance with France, Britain embarked on another war against the Dutch, and there was a widespread feeling that, in combining with an absolutist Catholic régime against a Protestant country, it had picked the wrong ally and the wrong enemy. Fears of royal policy were increased when the Catholicism of James, Duke of York, heir to the crown in the absence of legitimate royal issue, became public knowledge in 1673. In serious drama of the early 1670s there is a sudden shift from the final celebrations of restoration to a repeated concentration on problems of succession, and there is a marked change in the portrayal of kings, who are now often tyrannical and lustful. Rape, formerly confined to usurpers, is now perpetrated by rightful kings. Mistrust of James's religion, and of his autocratic character, led to the crisis which began in late 1678, when Titus Oates produced fictitious but widely believed details of a planned Catholic uprising. There were sustained parliamentary attempts to exclude James from the succession, finally defeated when Charles dissolved the Oxford Parliament in March 1681, ruling without parliament (and with subsidies from Louis XIV) for the rest of his reign. The drama of this period is covered by Sue Owen in chapter 10, below. But it is worth here observing that the Tories – the supporters of James – did try to revive the spirit of 1660, accusing their Whig opponents of inciting another civil war, and resuscitating the cult of restoration. In Dryden's *The Spanish Fryar* (1680) an apparently martyred king is discovered to have survived, Aphra Behn reworked *The Rump* as *The Roundheads* (1681), and *The Committee* exercised a clear influence on Thomas Durfey's *The Royalist* (1682). At the end of his poem *Absalom and Achitophel* (1681), written when the exclusion movement was clearly defeated, Dryden declares that the king has been "Once more ... Restor'd,"[7] and the point was more laboriously made in his opera *Albion and Albanius* (1685), which portrays, and explores parallels between, Charles's original restoration and his victory over the Whigs. Since Charles died while the opera was in rehearsal, it had to be revised so as to conclude with his apotheosis and the transfer of power to James. Thus, however accidentally, James's accession to power was celebrated with the iconography of 1660.

But, little more than three years later, he was deposed. His confrontational approach to extending the powers of the crown, and to the advancement of his fellow-Catholics, alienated a critical number of his natural supporters. His consequent attempts to woo dissenters and the bourgeois classes made matters worse, as did aborted preparations for rigged elections in 1688; and the birth of a male heir, raising the prospect of a perpetual Catholic dynasty, prompted seven members of the nobility to invite William of Orange to intervene to protect the religion, liberty, and property of the nation. William invaded on 5 November; rendered powerless by mass defections from his own forces, James fled to France the following month.

One of the most pressing necessities after the event was that of interpreting it. Elections were held in January 1689, and the Convention Parliament (a parliament called without royal summons) met to settle the basis of the new régime, to prevent recurrence of the abuses practiced by the old one, and to justify the terms of James's deposition. The Commons declared that James had broken the contract between king and people, but a contractual theory of monarchy was unacceptable to the Lords, and parliament adopted the fiction that James had vacated the throne through abdication. A Bill of Rights was passed, designed to prevent repetition of the arbitrary policies of Charles and James: for example, the ability of the king to bypass parliament was curtailed, and freedom of speech within parliament was guaranteed. There remained disagreement as to the basis of William's authority, the Whigs regarding him as ruling *de jure*, while many Tories accepted him only as a *de facto* monarch. Later, in 1694, despite William's unwillingness, an act was passed stipulating that parliaments should meet at least once every three years, and should last no more than three years. Charles II had kept the same parliament from 1661 to 1679; during the Exclusion Crisis he had dissolved parliaments at will; and, from 1681 until his death, he had ruled without any parliament at all. Such subordination of parliament to the monarch's interests was now impossible. Nevertheless, the Revolution was conceived as an ending of abuses, a recovery of ancient liberties, rather than the forging of a new order.

Yet its aftermath produced considerable tension and disillusionment. The British had looked to William as a benevolent liberator, and had not expected their country to be used as a base for an expensive war against Louis XIV, which caused an unprecedented level of taxation, and which brought little success for some years after 1692. There is coded criticism of the new régime in the Jacobite Dryden's last plays, which repeatedly dwell on the figure of the exile (implicitly, James), and which criticize imperialistic militarism, but aggressively anti-Williamite drama is scarcely to be expected: Dryden's *Cleomenes* (1692), concerned with an exiled ruler languishing in a foreign court, was initially banned on the orders of Queen Mary; and, when Colley Cibber adapted Shakespeare's *Richard III* (1700), and included the murder of Henry VI from *Henry VI*, part 3, all references to the unfortunate king were nervously censored for fear of arousing sympathy for James II. Yet, however unrealistic it might be to expect a spate of counter-revolutionary drama, one can notice a dip in theatrical enthusiasm for William between mid-1692 and the spring of 1696: that is, between the French defeat at La Hogue in May 1692, which ended the immediate threat of invasion by the French, and the disclosure early in 1696 of a Jacobite plot to assassinate the king as prelude to a French invasion. This boosted William's popularity, as did hopes of a successful end to the war against France, which were initially dashed, but eventually gratified by the treaty of Ryswick in the autumn of 1697. Between these limits, one finds Williamite songs and sentiments in plays, and some

Williamite plays, but nothing like the surge of celebration that followed the Revolution and the events of 1696–97.

With whatever frequency they occur, however, theatrical reactions to the Revolution are predominantly favorable: dramatists overwhelmingly support the war, and the grievances of the heavily taxed are acknowledged only in satire of their short-sighted avarice. In tragedy, the most obvious consequence of the Revolution was a sudden readiness to sanction the deposition of tyrants, even when legitimate rulers. Predominantly (though with some notable exceptions), pre-Revolution drama had only approved the deposition of usurpers (as in *The Generall*). Even after the Revolution, the willingness to depose legitimate rulers takes a little time to appear. One of the earliest reactions to the Revolution, George Powell's *Alphonso King of Naples* (1690), retains the fiction that James had abdicated. *King Edward the Third* (1690), possibly by John Bancroft, creates a detailed parallel between the three-year tyranny of Roger Mortimer after the deposition of Edward II and the three year tyranny of James II. But there is an obvious difference between the two situations: Mortimer, unlike James, was a usurper; Edward III, unlike William, was direct lineal heir to his father's throne. *King Edward the Third* is, in fact, a play of restoration; for so dominant is the idea that the Revolution reinstated ancestral rights that Bancroft can justify it in a historical parallel that could have been equally appropriate in 1660.[8] More radical, and unusually reflective of the actual malaise in the years after the Revolution, is John Crowne's *Regulus* (1692), which portrays a Carthage (Britain) that, in the midst of its war against Rome (France and James II), is self-destructively beset by faction and corruption. Hereditary monarchy is mocked – the villain, Asdrubal, claims lineal descent from Dido – and the gentry support the rights of kings in order to justify their own right to oppress their social inferiors. Asdrubal is counterbalanced by Xantippus, a Spartan fighting on the Carthaginian side: a foreign savior who clearly alludes to William III. The Spartan constitution which Xantippus represents and praises is explicitly a republican one, so that the play endorses a very extreme interpretation of the Revolution, with an analogy that could not possibly have been used in 1660. But, ominously, it ends with the nation rejecting its savior, and with his transformation into an enemy.

Only after the Assassination Plot, however, do tragedies justifying the essential event of 1688 – the deposition of a legitimate, hereditary monarch – start to appear in any quantity: plays such as Mary Pix's *Ibrahim, the Thirteenth Emperour of the Turks* (1696), Charles Gildon's *The Roman Bride's Revenge* (1696), and Cibber's *Xerxes* (1699). Like many deposition plays, these resemble Orrery's *The Generall* in associating tyranny with rape: an association that is partly due to political symbolism and partly to the fashion for seeing Anne Bracegirdle and Jane Rogers, actresses who specialized in vulnerable beauty, titillatingly ruffled. In so far as the rapes are politically significant, however, there has been a clear change since the time of Orrery. In *The Generall*, the would-be rapist is not a rightful ruler, and his wrongful desire to possess the heroine's body parallels his wrongful possession of the throne. But the rape is prevented, and the political disorder is cured. Even during the reign of Charles II, the politicized dramatization of rape changes. Rape succeeds, and royalty, not a usurper, performs it, thereby showing how ruthless absolutism assaults private rights. But, although the corrupt régimes collapse, it is difficult to feel enthusiasm for their successors. In the plays of the late 1690s, however, although the rape victim herself never survives her dishonor, the assault on private rights is answered by decisive and beneficial social change.

The revolution of 1688 has often been described as a bourgeois revolution. This it was not, for James fell because he had alienated a critical number of the nobility and gentry. But the need to fund William III's long and expensive war against Louis XIV did create new scope for the financier, bringing to the fore types of wealth that seemed both intangible and arbitrarily acquired. Trade in stocks flourished (and was satirized in two little-known plays, Shadwell's *The Volunteers* [1692] and Durfey's *The Richmond Heiress* [1693]); David Ogg has written that "For the first time in English history it is possible to express in commercial figures and stock-exchange quotations the severity of a national crisis."[9] In 1694 the Bank of England was founded, in order to borrow money for the war, covering the gap between assets and liabilities by paying investors in paper currency. State lotteries were run, and inspired a number of private imitations (lottery fever was satirized in a very minor play, Joseph Harris's *Love's a Lottery* [1699]).

Like the wealth which is made and lost on the computers of the modern stock market, that of the late seventeenth-century investor could seem a puzzling abstraction, deeply suspected by those for whom wealth was inseparable from the solid possession of ancestral land. The rise of new forms and conceptions of wealth is ingeniously reflected in the comedies of George Farquhar, which portray mathematically organized societies, in which power is numerically measured, whether in the listing of women seduced, the enumeration of wealth, or the meticulous measurement and control of time and space.[10] In long-established social terminology, which preserved the values and influence of the feudal hierarchy, *place* had an almost theological dimension, defining a person's position in a divinely ordained ladder of privilege and responsibility. Now it loses its symbolism, and becomes a neutral space to be numerically measured.

The shift from ancient, feudally derived values is recorded in two of the most successful tragedies of the 1690s: *The Fatal Marriage* (1694) and *Oroonoko* (1695), both by Thomas Southerne, who had supported James II in the immediate aftermath of the Revolution, but had gradually, if rather ambivalently, reconciled himself to the new order. *Oroonoko* is the tragedy of an African prince who is sold into slavery, having been tricked and captured by an English captain through the violation of two traditional aristocratic virtues, fidelity to one's word and hospitality (Oroonoko is overpowered at a banquet). With the turning of the prince into a helpless commodity, royalty is very literally destroyed by commercial forces, and the dominance of commerce in social relations is emphasized in the comic subplot, which shows women rebelling against a marriage market in which they are as much objects of sale as the Negro slaves. The power of money is also paramount in *The Fatal Marriage*, whose heroine has for almost seven years remained faithful to the memory of her apparently dead husband, but is eventually forced by poverty into a second marriage. Her first husband promptly returns, and she is destroyed by overwhelming guilt at her broken vows. Like *Oroonoko*, if less obtrusively, this play portrays a shift from one order to another: from the order of the word to the order of the purse. *Oroonoko* was based on Aphra Behn's novella of the same name (1688), whose doomed and self-destructive hero may reflect the author's sense of the dangers which were gathering around James II.[11] It is unlikely that Southerne intended so precise an analogy in either play; but they certainly express a shift in values, a triumph of economic forces over older and more sacred bonds, of which the Revolution and its aftermath are a prime and archetypal example.

Treatments of the Revolution in comedy were predominantly celebratory, a favorite procedure being to portray the reconstitution of disrupted families and households: the reordering of the home parallels the reconstruction of the state, and emphasizes that the value of a political order depends on its protection of private rights. The best-known comedies of this kind are Congreve's two masterpieces, *Love for Love* (1695) and *The Way of the World* (1700), which (as has often been recognized) implicitly support a contractual theory of government: in both, the power of a capricious and tyrannical parent, whose authority comes by mere biological transmission, is eventually superseded by the authority of legal contract. Both also portray heroines who choose husbands after prolonged testing – a distinctive theme of post-Revolution drama, implying that husbands, like kings, derive their authority from consent. But what if, after marriage, the husband turned out to be a domestic James II? There was some debate as to whether the subject's right to rebel against an unsatisfactory king did not by analogy imply the wife's right to rebel against an unsatisfactory husband (see Staves, *Players' Scepters*, pp. 111–89): tempted to adultery, the mistreated Lady Brute in Vanbrugh's *The Provok'd Wife* (1697) muses that "The argument's good between the king and the people, why not between the husband and the wife?"[12] The validity and limits of the analogy were problematic, but the Revolution did cause dramatists to change their representation of relations between men and women. The early Restoration equation between political authority and male authority had quickly succeeded to a more sympathetic treatment of female aspirations, but only occasionally (as in Shadwell's Whig play *The Woman-Captain* [1679]) are these linked to wider calls for political liberty. After the Revolution, the linkage is commonplace.

The seminal study of contractual authority in a familial setting had, in fact, appeared in the last months of James's reign: *The Squire of Alsatia* (May 1688), by Thomas Shadwell, the most talented (and consistent in principle) of the writers who had supported the Whig cause during the Exclusion Crisis. Like two earlier Restoration comedies, Sir Charles Sedley's *The Mulberry Garden* (1668) and Aphra Behn's *The City-Heiress* (1682), this provides a politically weighted reworking of elements from *Adelphi* (*The Brothers*) by the Roman dramatist Terence, which contrasts a father's repressive upbringing of one of his sons with an uncle's more understanding upbringing of the other son. The two earlier plays had been Royalist propaganda: the climax and conclusion of Sedley's is the king's restoration, and Behn attacks the leader of the exclusion movement, the Earl of Shaftesbury; in both, predictably, the repressive and indulgent figures of authority had represented Puritan harshness and Stuart lenity. But Shadwell reverses the application: the tyrannical father, trusting blindly in the rights conveyed by biological generation, presents an analogue to Stuart absolutism, whereas the kind step-father, who realizes that authority must be earned, not merely inherited, represents an authority that is conditional, potentially contractual.

The four comedies that Shadwell wrote after the Revolution develop, but change, the imagery of *The Squire of Alsatia*. All feature step-parents or guardians (generally female), but these are now mostly tyrannical, and three of the plays show the purging of the household by expulsion of the interloper or escape from her power. In a total reversal of *The Squire of Alsatia*, James, the hereditary ruler, is now figured as an intrusive step-parent, and William acquires all the authority of the natural father. In *Bury-Fair* (1689), for example, Oldwit, a clownish but kindly lover of Shakespeare and Jonson, has taken as his second wife the affected, Francophile Lady Fantast, who brings into the household her equally affected and

Francophile daughter. One of his natural daughters mysteriously disappears (to avoid an unwanted marriage). In a ruse inspired from Molière's comedy *Les Précieuses ridicules*, the poseurs are taken in by a false aristocrat: a barber masquerading as a French count, who (to their delight) praises the militarism and social exclusiveness of Louis XIV's régime. Their folly is thus not merely snobbery, but admiration for an alien, oppressive, and destructive tyranny. When the imposture is exposed, their embarrassed flight leaves the household free for Oldwit and his love of English culture, and his vanished daughter returns into the reconstituted family. The shift from *The Squire of Alsatia* – from James as genetic father-king to James as an alien step-parent – is in keeping with the view of the Revolution as a reinstatement of ancestral rights. *Bury-Fair* is, in its way, a play of restoration, but the restoration is not of the person of a monarch but of the values of a people: the culture, traditions, and liberties of the English nation. In two of his plays written during the Exclusion Crisis, *The Woman-Captain* (1679) and *The Lancashire Witches* (1681), Shadwell had portrayed the traditions of Shakespeare and Good Queen Bess as being under threat from alien forms of tyranny: French authoritarianism and Irish Catholicism (as an anti-Catholic paragon, Elizabeth I had been a Whig heroine). *Bury-Fair* celebrates the defeat of these threats. Perhaps significantly, Bury St. Edmunds had associations with Shadwell's childhood, for he had spent a year of his schooldays there. In portraying the deliverance of native values, he also portrays the safeguarding of his own past and origins.

It is perhaps confidence in the security of the individual that most marks the positive and celebratory reactions to the Revolution. If Southerne portrays social and familial bonds being pulverized by economic forces, dramatists such as Shadwell and Congreve portray individuals who can manage their lives in a social framework that is favorable to them. By contrast, pre-Revolution drama had often portrayed the relationship between the individual and the state as being one of unresolvable tension or crisis. Many Carolean plays – *The Country-Wife*, for example – envisage no stable accommodation between the demands of social existence and of the sexual drive, and the increasingly pessimistic political tragedies of the 1670s rarely see a remedy to oppressive power, finding any violent cure far worse than the disease. After the Revolution, the problems of egocentric instinct and egocentric power are more readily subject to solution, and the shifting outlook is shown in one small but significant detail. After the early years of the Restoration, Carolean drama shows very little interest in the threat of the literal stranger: of the simple economic or cultural outsider, such as Shylock. As in the revised *Tempest*, attention is focused on the stranger within; on the alien, intractable forces inside the community. After the Revolution, intrusive or menacing foreigners become common again. In part, dramatists are dutifully satirizing the French enemy; but they are also (as in *Bury-Fair*) expressing a new faith in the political order, confidently measuring Britain against inferior foreign régimes. When one reads the history of William III's reign, one reads of corruption, faction, disillusionment, high taxes, bad harvests, and corn riots. Like the loyal dramatists of the early Restoration, those of the 1690s were myth-makers of selective vision. But their selective vision does include a major a shift in outlook, suggesting that we have passed into a new age: in post-Revolution drama, the power of the state over individual lives is restricted and conditional in a fashion that pre-Revolution dramatists could only dream of, or strenuously oppose.

NOTES

1 The fullest study of theatrical representations of the Restoration is Nancy Klein Maguire, *Regicide and Restoration: English Tragicomedy, 1660–1671* (Cambridge University Press, 1992). See also Nicholas Jose, *Ideas of the Restoration In English Literature, 1660–71* (London and Basingstoke: Macmillan, 1984).

2 It was performed in Dublin in 1662 under the title of *Altemera*. Its first London performance was in 1664.

3 Christopher Spencer, ed., *Davenant's "Macbeth" from the Yale Manuscript: an Edition, with a Discussion of the Relation of Davenant's Text to Shakespeare's* (New Haven: Yale University Press, 1961), 4.4.63.

4 Susan Staves, *Players' Scepters: Fictions of Authority in the Restoration* (Lincoln, Neb., and London, 1979), p. 52.

5 Part 2, 4.3.148 in *The Works of John Dryden*, ed. H. T. Swedenberg, Jr., *et al.*, 20 vols., in progress (Berkeley: University of California Press, 1956–), vol. XI. Hereafter, all Dryden references are to this edition.

6 5.1.28–29, in *The Works of John Dryden*, vol. X.

7 1030 in *The Works of John Dryden*, vol. II.

8 This play is well discussed in Staves, *Players' Scepters*, pp. 101–04, and Richard Braverman, *Plots and Counterplots: Sexual Politics and the Body Politic in English Literature, 1660–1730* (Cambridge University Press, 1993), pp. 186–92. Staves points out that "usurpation" in this play means usurpation of a people's rights, not of a royal throne (p. 102).

9 *England in the Reigns of James II and William III*, rev. edn. (Oxford: Clarendon Press, 1963), p. 435.

10 Derek Hughes, "Who Counts in Farquhar?", in Luis Gámez, ed., *A Subtler Music: Essays on the Drama and Opera of Enlightenment Europe* (Stamford: Paul Watkins, 1997), pp. 7–27.

11 Janet Todd, *The Secret Life of Aphra Behn* (London: André Deutsch, 1996), pp. 417–21.

12 1.1.65–67, in *Sir John Vanbrugh: Four Comedies*, ed. Michael Cordner (London: Penguin, 1989).

9

Change, skepticism, and uncertainty

Panegyrics hailing the arrival of Charles II in England in 1660 celebrated the return of an old order – a restoration of former ways and prior certainties.[1] The previous two decades of political experiment and religious innovation were to be firmly canceled by the restoration of the monarchy and the Church of England, bringing with them political stability and settled order. In his *Defense of the Epilogue* appended to the second part of *The Conquest of Granada* (1669), John Dryden refers to the king and court's exile "in the most polish'd Courts of *Europe*" and argues that this experience "waken'd the dull and heavy spirits of the English" so that "insensibly our way of living became more free."[2] Another way of putting this brilliant apologia for changes in cultural habit is that the Restoration could not, in fact, restore the previous structures of authority. Politically and culturally, despite efforts to turn back the clock, the Restoration was a period of change, dynastic uncertainty, and intellectual inquiry. Although tied by both law and patronage to the fortunes and policies of the court élite, the Restoration theatres performed plays which reflected national unease and social alteration.

R. D. Hume has stressed that plays were written and produced to entertain London audiences and make profits for theatres and not to dramatize philosophies.[3] Indeed, the amount of philosophy behind the aggressive sexual behaviors of the young males depicted on stage can be exaggerated. Behn's hero Willmore in *The Rover* (1677), for instance, has a great deal of sexual energy but very little philosophy. Nevertheless, the targets, topics, and themes of the dramas, both tragic and comic, are inescapably informed by the fact that authors and audiences alike were living through a period which, as Richard W. Kroll has said, "experienced a transformation in the ways the culture imagined and represented itself."[4] Fundamental to transformed modes of representation were new ways of thinking about man, nature, language, and God, intertwined concepts since tradition posited that God created nature, and placed man, a language-bearing creature, in it as his supreme creation.

Long established habits of analogical thought had formed an integral part of the seventeenth-century discourse of man, state, and religion, inscribing a signifying chain of correspondences between the natural world and the social and political world. This analogical, semi-magical habit of thought, however, was breaking down; in part, due to the self-evident failure of the traditional modes of government, and in part due to a new confidence in the potential of scientific forms of explanation. Dryden's *Annus Mirabilis* (1666), for instance, celebrates English navigation and foresees a time when not only "The Ebbs of Tydes and their mysterious flow, / We, as art's elements, shall understand," but when man will survey the skies with equal accuracy "And on the Lunar world securely pry" (1, 645–46; 656). New modes of thought and social organization tend, however, to produce anxiety as well as optimism. As the men and women of the Restoration sailed into what were, in fact, uncharted waters, one may observe mixed – indeed often mingled – responses: reassertions of traditional authority alongside progressive theories of change, and skeptical doubt over the validity of either or both approaches.

The traditional view of man, both in the domestic and national realm, was reasserted by the publication in 1680, a period of intense political crisis, of Sir Robert Filmer's *Patriarcha*. This work, written in 1642, stated in a very literal form the role of the monarch as father of his people and hence head of his state, indicating that rebellion – in the home or the state – is not only treasonable but unnatural and, since God created in Adam the first father and ruler, irreligious. As Michael McKeon points out, however, this publication "marks not the triumphant ascendancy of patriarchal thought, but its demise as tacit knowledge, the fact that is in crisis."[5] Indeed, the serious dramas of the 1660s onward had problematized the political trope of the family as a microcosm or emblem of the state and the state as an emblem of the family. In serious dramas from the 1670s onward, royal families are frequently portrayed as dysfunctional – the kings and queens adulterous, incestuous, and murderous, the sons rebellious. The political and social forces working against the unquestioning acceptance of authority are articulated in the many plays that depict rulers as weak, tyrannical, lustful, and, on occasion, entirely insane. The Emperor Maximin in Dryden's *Tyrannick Love* (1669), for instance, Nero in Nathaniel Lee's play of that name (1674), or King Philip in Thomas Otway's *Don Carlos* (1676) are all insane from the start or by the conclusion.

Comedies also registered the weakening of the patriarchal trope. It had long been traditional for strict fathers to function as blocking devices as they sought to prevent their children from marrying the partner of their choice. What now emerge are portraits of fathers and elders who are incompetent, sometimes perverse, and whose authority needs more than correction: it needs to be overturned. Few dramatists portrayed such unsavory fathers as did Otway, but other writers also dismiss or severely qualify paternal authority. In William Wycherley's *The Gentleman Dancing-Master* (1672), the heroine concludes the play by announcing "When Children marry, Parents shou'd obey, / Since Love claims more Obedience far than they"; and, in a more decorous spirit, the virtuous Benzayda in Dryden's *The Conquest of Granada*, part 1 (1670) argues that "When parents their commands unjustly lay, / Children are privileged to disobey" (4.2.289–90).[6] The rebellion of daughters against marriage partners can be seen as a way in which a political language of rights and liberties could be safely deployed and also as an indication that Puritan doctrines glorifying "married chastity" and emphasizing the need to allow daughters the right of refusal had gained ground.[7]

Parents continued to select marriage partners for their children, and children, by and large, continued to obey. There are, however, signs that the aristocratic/wealthy family as a unit was in transition. The new legal instruments that evolved, such as the strict settlement marriage contract with provisions for younger children and widows, enhanced patriarchal control while also undermining some of its traditional ability to consolidate power and wealth.[8] Sir George Etherege's Widow Rich in *The Comical Revenge* (1664) or Wycherley's Widow Blackacre in *The Plain-Dealer* (1676) provide comic characterizations of widows empowered over men by the provisions of their marriage contracts. The new concern over marriage contracts and the position of women in marriage is also reflected in the many "proviso" scenes in Restoration courtship and marriage comedies where the young couple work out their own personal agreement over the distribution of power in the relationship.

Where there had been a tacit consensus that females are subordinate, there was now an increasing awareness that such subordination was a social rather than natural or inevitable inequality. In her poem, "The Introduction," Anne Finch, Countess of Winchelsea, refers to women as education's rather than "Nature's Fools," and Aphra Behn claimed that Thomas Creech's translation of Lucretius' *De Rerum Natura*, "Equals us to Man!" by redeeming women (who generally could not read Latin) "from the State of Ignorance."[9] The idea that intellectually, at least, women could be equal or even superior to men was widespread. Wycherley, certainly no feminist, depicts Alithea in *The Country Wife* (1675) as effortlessly more intelligent than her fiancé Sparkish; Etherege's Harriet in *The Man of Mode* (1676) displays a wit and determination equal to that of Dorimant's, and

Hillaria in Edward Ravenscroft's *The Careless Lovers* (1673) argues "Have not we Rational Souls as well as Men; what made Women Mopes in former Ages, but being ruled by a company of old Men and Women?" (3, p. "33"[25]).

Cross-dressed roles allow heroines to reverse the usual flow of power. In Thomas Shadwell's *The Woman-Captain* (1679), for instance, the beleaguered woman of the title assumes military costume and puts a group of volunteers through rigorous exercises. Such roles often merely offered the opportunity for a display of female legs and sexy roguishness, but they could also indicate that it is custom, not ability or intrinsic modesty, that keeps women covered and quiet.[10] The cross-dressed heroine of Thomas Southerne's *Sir Anthony Love* (1690) overtly questions a fundamental gender distinction: "'tis only the Fashion of the World, that gives your Sex a better Title than we have – to the wearing of a Sword" (1.1.17–18).[11] Female claims to equality in drama, however, are usually only temporary and partially endorsed. In tragedies the female who challenges male power is generally a villainess; in comedy she is a butt for humor. On the whole, the heroine's liberty of choice is confined to marriage with the man of her choice since, like Millamant in William Congreve's *The Way of the World* (1700), she will eventually "dwindle into a wife" (4.1.177).[12]

Nevertheless, masculine supremacy is clearly no longer axiomatic; anxiety on this front is articulated in the genre of "Imperfect Enjoyment" poems, as well as in dramatic references to masculine impotence. Indeed, sexually unsatisfied wives are standard fare in Restoration drama. Giles Slade has suggested that "the centrality of impotence to Restoration discourse of all types, derives ... from the upheavals following the Civil War which challenged cavalier gender ideology and led to a pervasive insecurity about what masculinity was" and that such insecurity produced the nightmare figure of the eunuch and the compensatory figure of the rake.[13] The example of the king, famed for his many mistresses, equated sexual potency with political power. Authority was reinscribed as sexual acts – rapes in tragedies and seductions in comedies – turning female bodies into a territory, often implicitly an England, to be possessed and controlled. As a corollary, too great a love for a woman, which transfers power to her, brings with it a deeply misogynistic discourse.[14] In comedies and tragedies alike, the onset of love is frequently greeted as both a curtailment of male freedom and a diminution of masculinity. In *The Conquest of Granada*, Almanzor, assailed by the power of Almahide's eyes, feels "pained" as well as "pleased" and discovers that "Honour burns in me not so fiercely bright" (part 1, 3.1.361, 365). More wretchedly, Castalio in Otway's *The Orphan* (1680) describes himself as "'Fast bound in chains to be chastis'd at will' and turned into a 'creeping slave ... tractable and dull'" (II, 309, 389) by his love for Monimia.[15] In Sir Charles Sedley's *Antony and Cleopatra* (1677), Antony's infatuation with Cleopatra is characterized not merely as a diminution of rulership and masculinity, but also as a violation of the laws of nature – "What Horse the Mare, what Bull obeys the Cow?" (3.1, p. 21).

The Earl of Rochester's song beginning "Love a woman? You're an ass" depicts heterosexual intercourse as a type of degrading labor, "Things designed for dirty slaves" who "Drudge... / To get supplies for age and graves" (lines 6–8), and Richard Braverman has suggested that an apprehension of a new economic power challenging traditional landed aristocratic hegemony could produce anxiety over the nature of aristocratic male sexuality.[16] This was a deeply aristocratic era with power – land and office – accumulated in the hands of an élite few; nevertheless, there was a sense that social categories were becoming unfixed. Michael McKeon notes that actions of *scandalum magnatum*, legal action that could be taken by peers of the realm to defend their honor against social inferiors, peaked during the reign of Charles II and suggests that these actions "registered an increasingly defensive awareness that social hierarchy was under assault."[17] Like J. G. A. Pocock, McKeon argues that this period sees a transvaluation of the terms that traditionally elevated, justified and characterized the nobility: "'Honor' now fails to unite internals and externals. Progressive ideology requires that it resolves itself into virtue on the one hand and aristocratic rank on the other, a discrimination that repudiates the automatic aristocratic signification of internals by externals."[18] For women, honor had always narrowly referred to chastity, but the elaborate chivalric male code of honor could be characterized by Richard Allstree in 1660 as merely referring to "one that can start and maintain a Quarrel" with "such a multitude of Punctilio's, that the next Age will be in danger of receiving the Fable of *Don Quixot* for Authentick History."[19] Terms like "virtue" and "fortune" are narrowing in compass during this period, increasingly limited to material meaning and losing their ethical dimensions.

Chivalric behavior, ambiguously upheld in tragedies, is often treated in the comedies as hypocritical and/or as a mark of a stuffy formality practiced by the older generation. In *The Man of Mode*, for instance, Dorimant gains access to Harriet's home by pretending to be "Mr. Courtage," flattering her mother, and hypocritically criticizing the freedom of modern manners: "Forms and ceremonies, the only things that uphold quality / and greatness, are now shamefully laid aside and neglected" (4.1.11–12).[20] Mannerly behavior can be characterized as dishonest, a social mask assumed to cover the anti-social impulses shared by all. In *The Princess of Cleves* (1680), Lee's lecherous "hero," the Duke of Nemours, defends his "way" – "Obscenity" – as both open and gentlemanly claiming that it is

> ... the way of ye all, only you sneak with
> it under your Cloaks like Taylors and Barbers; and I, as a Gentleman
> shou'd do, walk with it in my hand.   (2.3.34–36)[21]

However, if "Obscenity" is the sign of a gentleman and "Forms and ceremonies" no longer underpin an ideology validating social hierarchies, what constitutes social superiority is open to question.

Anxiety over the blurring of social distinctions and definitions is frequently articulated in Restoration drama. Dorimant's shoemaker is warned that his "whoring and swearing are vices too genteel for a shoemaker" (1.251–52), and city wives, like Mrs. Saleware in Behn's *The Debauchee* (1677), dress themselves like ladies in "fine Clothes, and Tours, and Points and Knots" (2.1.20–03). The desire to reassert the significance of "birth" can be seen in Wycherley's *The Gentleman Dancing-Master* when the comical Don Diego, whose manners are a good example of "Punctilio," is revealed to have had a great-grandfather who was "a feltmaker, his son a wine-cooper, your father a vintner, and so you came to be a Canary merchant" (5.1.464). In an angrier vein, Otway's penniless and disbanded soldier heroes in *The Souldiers Fortune* (1680) express a horror of status instability as they describe passers by, an ex-footman, a "Retailer of Ale," and a one time vagabond, all of whom now count as gentlemen (2.363–98). The energy and success with which the noble rakes of the mid-1670s and early 1680s cuckolding comedies seduce merchants' wives can be read as demonstrations of aristocratic male power and also as assertions of that power in the face of City and Whig political ascendancy. Concern over the instability of social categories is less evident in tragedies, usually set in courts, than in comedies set in contemporary London, although Otway's tragedy *Caius Marius* (1680) depicts jealous patrician contempt for Caius Marius' plebeian origins.

If man's – and woman's – place in the social hierarchy seemed to observers to be undergoing alteration, this alteration almost inevitably affected ways of looking at nature, traditionally regarded as a kind of divine book inscribing patterns of order and hierarchy. For centuries the pastoral mode had served various functions in European literature – as nostalgic representations of the Golden Age when humans lived in harmony, ease, peace, and equality and also as justifications for hierarchy as instanced by the state of nature. For the conservative Sir William Temple following nature was still "the great rule in this, and perhaps everything else, as far as the conduct not only of our lives, but our governments."[22] In either its pastoral or more realistic guises, however, nature was increasingly ceasing to offer soothing analogies or plausible models. The models nature offered could seem irrelevant to human organization, especially as nature became the subject of scientific study and commercial exploitation. Indeed, to cite Dryden's *Annus Mirabilis* again, the navigation of the globe could be imagined as precisely uniting science and trade, "Instructed ships shall sail to quick Commerce / ... Where some may gain, and all may be supplied" (1, 649; 652).

Restoration writers continued to use pastoral names, sometimes seriously, but often with an ironic dimension. Pastoral poems by "Orinda," Katherine Philips, operate inside the Caroline traditions of delicacy and order, but the Earl of Rochester sets "Fair Chloris" in a pigsty where, visited by erotic dreams, she eases "Nature" and "frigs." An example of the way the pastoral was ceasing to work in Caroline terms as an emblem of the ideal civil polity is Dryden's *Marriage A-la-Mode* (1672). This is a dual-plot play, the versified "high" plot dealing with problems of state and love for the pastorally named Leonidas and Palmira, alongside the prose "low" plot dealing with the adulterous inclinations of the no less pastorally named but much less pastorally inclined Dorinda, Melanthia, Rhodophil, and Palamede. The relationship between the two plots has been much debated with some critics arguing that they are entirely distinct. Recent criticism, however, has tended to stress their interconnections, noting that both plots deal with issues of legitimacy – in marriage and in the state – and depict the need for rational agreements to achieve social stability in either realm.[23] The military intervention of the low-plot characters, Rhodophil and Palamede, who are without romantic or heroic illusions, helps to restore the rightful heir, Leonidas, suggesting that their practicality is a remedy. The pastoral realm is not self-sufficient: it cannot signify of itself order and control.

In Wycherley's *The Country Wife*, for instance, country innocence is redefined as rural ignorance. The anti-hero, Horner, points out that he has known "a clap gotten in Wales" (1.1.360), while the country-bred wife, Margery Pinchwife, demonstrates an appetite for sex uninhibited by morality. In comedies the country is a site of exile and rural tedium: when Ariana in Etherege's *She Wou'd if She Cou'd* (1668) regrets leaving "the benefits of the fresh air, and the delights of wandering in the pleasant groves," her livelier sister Gatty roundly takes her to task (1.2.110–11). In tragedies, if nature retains some pastoral overtones, it also gains implications of savagery and, as a model for human action, can be used to justify the enactment of violent desires.

Thomas Hobbes's political works provided the major (but not the sole) source for variant readings of nature. Hobbes depicts man as the victim of his own passions which, without external pressure establishing sovereignty over actions, desires, and meanings, prevents the establishment of community. In *Leviathan* (1658), he envisages life in the condition of the "State of Nature" as one of constant warfare, with human beings governed by strong primal drives of desire and fear:

> there is no place for Industry; because the fruit thereof is uncertain: and consequently no Culture of the Earth; no Navigation, nor use of the commodities that may be imported by Sea; no commodious Building; no Instruments of moving, and removing, such things as require much force; no Knowledge of the face of the Earth; no account of the Time; no Arts; no Letters; no Society; and which is worst of all, continuall feare, and danger of violent death; and the life of man, solitary, poore, nasty, brutish, and short.[24]

Hobbes lays stress not on a ruler's morality, or hereditary legitimacy, but on the ability of the ruler as a "Leviathan" (a figure of total power) to subdue man's natural inclination toward warfare and impose agreement – a "covenant." It is on the basis of this covenant, by which subjects abrogate personal desires to the will of Leviathan, that social and political stability is imposed. And it is this imposition of a covenant that erases warfare and disorder and allows civilization to flourish. The natural condition of man in Hobbes's thinking is thus anti-social and violent, and civil society, which opposes it, is a man-made construction – rather than divinely ordained – based on the subjugation and exploitation of man's basic natural instincts. A "paradox," Susan Staves notes, "the Restoration was quick to appreciate: nature and law are first understood as opposed to each other."[25]

On stage Hobbes's political philosophy underwent a sea-change. Hobbesian concepts of vicious nature intermingle with classical concepts of the lawless ease of the Golden Age when humans, gods and nature lived in harmony. It becomes ambiguous whether in following nature the characters are reverting to savagery or reacting against modern man's depravity which has necessitated the rule of law. In Dryden's *Conquest of Granada*, the hero Almanzor declares "I alone am king of me. / ... free as nature first made man / Ere the base laws of servitude began" (IX, 1.1.90–92). In a similar vein, in Otway's *Don Carlos* Don John, who if not a hero is no villain, defines "Law" as "an Innovation" subsequent to the fall of man, "When Fools began to love Obedience, / And call'd their slavery Safety and defense" (2.1.1–8).

Rakes in comedies frequently express their drive to fulfill personal desires as justified by the appetitive nature that Hobbes abhorred. Ramble in John

Crowne's *The Country Wit* (1674/75?) states that "the order of Nature is to follow my appetite," and a character in Sir Francis Fane's *Love in the Dark* (1675) asks, "Why should Mankind live by Rule and Measure / Since all his Virtue rises from his Pleasure?" (p. 77).[26] In Shadwell's *The Libertine* (1675), a retelling of the Don Juan legend, Don John and his libertine disciples provide an absurdist extension of the doctrine of appetite, debating, for instance, whether in pursuing pleasure they are following sense, reason, or nature:

> *Don John*: My business is my pleasure, that end I will always compass, without scrupling the means; there is no right or wrong but what conduces to, or hinders pleasure . . .
> *Don Antonio*: We live in the life of Sense, which no fantastick thing, called Reason, shall controul.
> *Don Lopez*: My reason tells me, I must please my Sense.
> *Don John*: My appetites are all I am sure I have from Heav'n, since they are Natural, and them I always will obey. (I, 28)[27]

Characters like Horner, Dorimant, the Duke of Nemours, or Shadwell's libertine trio are dangerous because they use and abuse social conventions, skeptically aware of them as instruments of a social control from which they cynically exempt themselves. In effect, they resurrect a savage state of nature inside the drawing-rooms and bedrooms of a settled polity.

The comedies' rake-heroes and the heroes of serious dramas have frequently been seen as diametrically opposed figures, but they are better understood as differently nuanced versions of figures who pit their drives – for sex, for glory – against civil or religious authority. However, while libertine skepticism with regard to the binding power of oaths, the sanctity of marriage, or the personal relevance of morality or social control, may, as in Shadwell's *The Libertine*, be allowed full expression, it is not endorsed. In comedies, the last act generally sees the rake who has reformed engaged to the virtuous heroine or, if unrepentant, discomforted and mocked. In tragedies, the villains or heroes who have followed nature and personal inclination are defeated or subdued. Nevertheless, in either mode it is the liberating energy of those who question or defy authority that has driven the plot. The conventionally moral endings given to plays are sometimes satisfying, but are more frequently ambiguous or inconclusive.

Expressions of libertine appetite often take the form of admiring the sexual freedom of the animal world. Pharnaces in Lee's *Mithridates* (1678) waxes eloquent on the happiness of the "generous Horse" with

> all his cheerful Mistresses about him,
> The white, the brown, the black, the shining bay,

And every dappled Female of the Field;
Now by the Gods, for ought we know, as Man
Thinks him a Beast, Man seems a Beast to him.   (2.1.47–51)[28]

Polydore in Otway's *The Orphan* (1680) echoes this speech, admiring not only the way "The lusty Bull ranges through all the Field," to take his choice of the herd, but the fact that he "Enjoyes her, and abandons her at Will" (1.362–68).

These sentiments owe more to Michel de Montaigne than to Hobbes, and to the traditions of admiration for the "happy beast" whose instinctual life is seen, as in Rochester's "Satyr against Mankind," as superior to that of the imperfectly rational creature man.[29] In *The Orphan*, Otway, who briefly enjoyed the Earl's patronage, explores the conflict between human beings' animal and rational qualities that underwrites much Restoration drama. This is a traditional distinction, but where tradition pointed to the supremacy of reason, which enables man to transcend his physical being, Otway presents man as entrapped, not ennobled, by his power of rationality. For Castalio, man is a "Monster" whose rationality merely ensures that unlike the animals, who seasonally "taste of love," "the Beast of Reason is its Slave / And in that Folly drudges all the year" (5.17.26–28).[30] Regarded as vicious or "golden," nature has ceased to offer coherent models for human actions: man is seen as uneasily situated in relation to nature, part of it, but severed from either instinctual life or patterns of harmony. In place of certainty about man's role in nature and society, there is skepticism over the moral validity, or divine organization, of either nature or society, and a corresponding uncertainty about the nature of man.

Tragically and comically, plays depict human life as irreconcilably divided between private appetitive nature, which is anarchic, and the public demands of "Forms and ceremonies" which are confining and/or false. *Mise-en-scène* frequently reflects these divisions, moving in tragedies from private apartments to public spaces, and in comedies from parks and piazzas to inside locations. Dramatists utilized stage spaces, which could be rapidly transformed by innovations in scenic design and machinery, to establish and also to unsettle assumptions as to what is the domain of the private and what is public. The rake, for instance, may be at ease in the park and discomforted in the bedroom, or conversely may be lost in "nature" but at ease prowling the boudoir. Either way, what is dramatized is man as a divided creature living in worlds that cannot accommodate all his needs or desires. The structure of authority that would demarcate firm boundaries, and establish what was owed to self, society, and God, or that could satisfactorily define self, was often longed for as much as rejected, but had been weakened.

The sense of the limits of human rationality, and therefore, supremacy over the animal kingdom, extends to skepticism over man's capacity for speech, the characteristic that was seen to distinguish man most clearly from the beasts and relate him to God. Language, traditionally regarded as "Adamic" – that is, having its meanings divinely established – becomes severed from the sacred and, as a purely human instrument of communication, is understood to be that which makes societies cohere and also that which instigates disagreement and breeds confusion. In *De Cive* (1642), for instance, Hobbes writes that

> Good and Evil are names given to things to signify the inclination of aversion of them by whom they are given. But the inclinations of men are diverse, according to their diverse constitutions, customs, opinions; as we may see in those things we apprehend by sense . . . but much more in those that pertain to the common actions of life, where this man commends the other undervalues . . . Whilst thus they do, necessary it is that there should be discord and strife. There are therefore so long in the state of war, as by reason of the diversity of the present appetites, they mete Good and Evil by diverse measures.[31]

The apprehension that language is arbitrary and meaning subjective, which in part can be traced back to the works of Francis Bacon, underwrites the attempts by Royal Society members – such as John Wilkins who wrote *An Essay Towards a Real Character, And A Philosophical Language* (1668) – to produce universal language. As James Thompson has noted, "where to Milton eloquence is virtuous, to Pepys eloquence is dangerous."[32] If words are not subject to an external and divine linguistic law then, indeed, as we find in many Restoration serious dramas, oaths may be given and taken without sincerity.[33]

Otway's *The Orphan* is plotted around insincerity in oath taking and, in a lighter vein, Courtall in *She Wou'd if She Cou'd*, informs the woman he is courting that "the keeping of one's word is a thing below the honour of a gentleman" (2.2.201–02). Indeed, in *The Country Wife* Lady Fidget and her friends treat insincerity as normal – the way of the world in a world where all appearances, words, and oaths intimate their reversal:

> Why should you not think, that we women make use of our Reputation, as you men of yours, only to deceive the world with less suspicion; our virtue is like the Statesman's Religion, the Quaker's Word, the Gamester's Oath, and the Great Man's Honour, but to cheat those that trust us.   (5.4.89–93)

Reference to the failure of language to establish singular and unambiguous meanings does not necessarily indicate an endorsement of anarchic solipsism – contingent and subjective. Thompson, for instance, argues that Wycherley had a "vested interest in maintaining aristocratic privilege" and that "however corrupt and immoral contemporary society and speech may be made to appear, standards for right speech remain."[34] Nevertheless, Peter Hynes comments that although Wycherley's world "is a stable enough place ... each field of knowledge ... has its interesting ragged edge, a zone of doubt which hints at a failure to be absolutely valid, absolutely true."[35] Above all, it is in the works of those dramatists outside the charmed circles of power and patronage, such as Settle, Lee, Otway, and Behn, that one finds most instances of anarchically subjective worlds in which language does not produce agreed upon or verifiable meanings.

The skepticism that questioned the divine underpinning of political and linguistic authority was more cautiously extended to religion itself. Thorough-going atheism, as opposed to Deism, was rare in the late seventeenth century: Hobbes was frequently denounced as an atheist, may have been one, but certainly never declared himself one. In works such as *Great is Diana of the Ephesians: or, The Origin of Idolatry* (1680), Charles Blount, an atheist who briefly corresponded with the Earl of Rochester, followed Hobbes's mode of religious relativism by describing the beliefs of pagans in such a way as to make them indistinguishable from those of Christians. However, for many theologians, such as John Tillotson, doubt over the certainty of knowledge, the way that "we do not know things in their realities, but as they appear and are represented to us with all their masks and disguises" was an argument for the necessity of faith.[36] Similarly, for Robert Boyle in his essay *Some Considerations About the Reconcileableness of Reason and Religion* (1675), man's inability to perceive accurately or to think without prejudice, must in the end be an argument for his submission to God:

> Yet really our intellectual weaknesses, or prejudice, or prepossessions by custom, education &c, our interests, passions, vices, and I know not how many other things, have so great and swaying an influence on them that there are very few conclusions that we make, or opinions, that we espouse, that are the pure results of our reason, that no personal disability, prejudice or fault has any interest in them ... the very body of mankind may be imbued with prejudices, and errors, that from childhood, and some also even from their birth, by which means they continue undiscerned, and consequently unreformed.[37]

It is something of a paradox to argue rationally for the limits of rationality and therefore the need to subordinate reason to faith. Such willed belief in the unbelievable may be sincere, but it can also lack conviction. The miracles that an earlier age could accept unblinkingly and which consolidated faith were now an impediment – or decoration.

In drama, especially during the 1670s when stage spectacle was in vogue, supernatural events and appearances were commonplace; however, as Derek Hughes points out, technological advances in stage presentation made "elaborate visible spectacle ... available at the very point at which the visual was losing much of its traditional weight."[38] In the works of Lee and Otway in particular, the signs and portents of divine intervention are open to diverse, often perverse, interpretation. Even when superhuman signs appear to be seriously intended, they may be undercut by cynical comments or misapplied. The Emperor Titus in Crowne's *Destruction of Jerusalem*, part 2 (1677), for instance, is portrayed sympathetically, but he mistakenly, if in the circumstances reasonably, assumes that Jewish portents regarding a Messiah refer to himself. At the least, there is a running theme treating religious activity as a means to cheat and delude; in Etherege's *She Wou'd if She Cou'd*, Sir Oliver is conventional in describing marriage as a "trick that the clergy might have a feeling in the cause" (1.1.134).[39] Satirical attacks on what was seen as Puritan religious hypocrisy on the one hand or Roman Catholic tyranny on the other are not, of course, necessarily attacks on religion *per se*, but they are an indication of a distaste for "enthusiasm" and a desire in some élite quarters, at least, to treat religious persuasion as a private issue. Clerics lamented from the pulpit and in polemics that the age was ungodly, which it clearly was not; however, if few dramatists have characters express their religious beliefs with quite the weary negligence of Beaugard in Otway's *The Atheist* (1.94–98), neither can one find many whose works express very sincere or fervent religious views. For Sir Edward Hartford in Shadwell's *The Lancashire Witches* (1681), for instance, the role of the household clergyman is strictly limited for reasons as much social as religious:

> Your Father is my Taylor, you are my Servant.
> And do you think a Cassock and a Girdle
> Can alter you so much, as to enable
> You (who were before but a Coxcomb, Sir)
> To teach me. (4.1.)

During this time, men and women still died for their religious beliefs. The stage, though, catered to the worldly attitudes of an élite minority familiar, at least in passing, with the skeptical and libertine literature of their era. Indeed, the sophisticated and baroque mixture of mockery and martyrdom in Dryden's *Tyrannick Love* is hardly an exception. The irreligiosity of Restoration drama earned it opprobrium in the last years of the seventeenth century and it was strongly denounced in Jeremy Collier's *A Short View of the Immorality and Profaneness of the English Stage* (1698).

Skeptical attitudes with regard to religion, politics, and society can be equally found in conservatives anxious to maintain the status quo – since they cannot imagine anything would be better – and in radical libertarians advocating change. In Restoration drama progressive and regressive skepticism – doubt as to the validity of traditional authority and doubt over the possibility of positive change – are articulated, sometimes in the same play. Skepticism expresses a fashionable iconoclasm that was, in part, a reaction to Puritan dogmatism; however, it also articulates an ideological crisis within the patriarchal monarchism of an aristocratic culture. Both in practice and in theory, the certainties underpinning the relationships of monarch, peoples and parliaments, church and state, had failed to cohere following the restoration of the monarchy. Doubt was produced by, and then reinforced, an apprehension of fractures, uncertainties, and alterations in the nature of authority at a time of accelerating change.

After 1688, dramas reflected the new political consensus that emerged: rakes reform, ranting heroes become the standby of burlesque, merchants become patriots, not parasites, adultery is treated seriously, religion and the clergy receive respect, and gender definitions, if not resolved, are codified. At the moments of change, however, themes and ideas of uncertainty and skepticism energized Restoration dramas. Their skeptical energy retains the ability to shock as they question, doubt, rethink and rearrange social relations, sexual identities, political authority, and moral criteria.

NOTES

I should like to thank Dan Doll, Sally Mooney, and Penny Richards for their suggestions and corrections.

1 See Nicolas Jose, *Ideas of the Restoration in English Literature 1660–71* (Cambridge, Mass.: Harvard University Press, 1984).

2 *The Works of John Dryden*, ed. H. T. Swedenberg, Jr., *et al.*, 20 vols., in progress (Berkeley: University of California Press, 1956–), vol. 1. Hereafter, all Dryden references are to this edition.

3 R. D. Hume, *The Development of English Drama in the Late Seventeenth Century* (Oxford: Clarendon Press, 1976), pp. 30–31.

4 Richard W. F. Kroll, *The Material Word: Literate Culture in the Restoration and Early Eighteenth Century* (Baltimore: Johns Hopkins University Press, 1991), p. 8.

5 Michael McKeon, "Historicizing Patriarchy: the Emergence of Gender Difference in England, 1660–1760," *ECS* 28 (1995), 296.

6 *The Plays of William Wycherley*, ed. Peter Holland (Cambridge University Press, 1981). All Wycherley references are to this edition.

7 See Jean Marsden, "Ideology, Sex, and Satire: the Case of Thomas Shadwell," *Cutting Edges: Postmodern Critical Essays on Eighteenth-Century Satire* Gill (Knoxville: The University of Tennessee Press, 1995), p. 48.

8 See Lloyd Bonfield, *Marriage Settlements 1601–1740: the Adoption of the Strict Settlement* (Cambridge University Press, 1983) and McKeon, cited above.

9 Anne Finch in *Eighteenth-Century Women Poets*, ed. Roger Lonsdale (Oxford University Press, 1990); Aphra Behn, *The Works of Aphra Behn*, ed. Janet Todd, 7 vols (Columbus: Ohio State University Press, 1992), vol. I, *Poetry*. All Behn references are to this edition.

10 See Pat Rogers, "The Breeches Part," *Sexuality in Eighteenth-Century Britain*, ed. Paul- Gabriel Boucé (New Jersey: Manchester University Press, 1982).

11 *The Works of Thomas Southerne*, ed. Robert Jordan and Harold Love (Oxford: Clarendon Press, 1988).

12 *The Comedies of William Congreve*, ed. Eric. S. Rump (Middlesex: Penguin, 1985).

13 Giles Slade, "The Two Backed Beast: Eunuchs and Priapus in *The Country Wife*," *RECTR*, 2nd series, 7.1 (1992), 23.

14 See Felicity Nussbaum, *The Brink of All We Hate: English Satires of Women 1600–1740* (Kentucky: University of Kentucky Press, 1984).

15 *The Works of Thomas Otway, Plays, Poems, and Love-Letters*, 2 vols., ed. J. C. Ghosh (Oxford: Clarendon Press, 1932; reprt. 1968). All Otway references are to this edition.

16 John Wilmot, Earl of Rochester, *The Complete Works*, ed. Frank H. Ellis (London: Penguin, 1994); Richard Braverman, "Economic 'Art' in Restoration Verse: Etherege's 'Cease Anxious World,'" *PQ*, 69.3 (Summer 1990), 383–88.

17 Michael McKeon, *The Origins of the English Novel, 1600–1745* (Baltimore: Johns Hopkins University Press, 1987), pp. 151.

18 See J. G. A. Pocock, *Virtue, Commerce, and History: Essays on Political Thought and History, Chiefly in the Eighteenth Century* (Cambridge University Press, 1985); McKeon, *Origins of the English Novel*, p. 155.

19 Richard Allestree, *The Gentleman's Calling* (London, 1660), p. 123–34.

20 *The Man of Mode*, ed. W. B. Carnochan (Lincoln, Nebr.: University of Nebraska Press, 1966).

21 *The Princess of Cleve*, in *Four Restoration Marriage Plays*, ed. Michael Cordner (Oxford University Press, 1995).

22 *Five Miscellaneous Essays by Sir William Temple*, ed. Samuel Holt Monk (Ann Arbor: University of Michigan Press, 1963), p. 28.

23 See Laura Brown, "The Divided Plot: Tragicomic Form in the Restoration," *ELH* 47 (1980), 67–79; Derek Hughes, "The Unity of Dryden's *Marriage a la Mode*," *PQ* 61 (1982), 125–41; Michael McKeon, "Marxist Criticism and *Marriage a la Mode*," *ECent*, 24 (1983), 225–29.

24 Hobbes, *Leviathan*, ed. C. B. Macpherson (London: Penguin 1968), p. 186.

25 Susan Staves, *Players' Scepters: Fictions of Authority in the Restoration* (Lincoln: University of Nebraska Press, 1979), p. 254.

26 *The Dramatic Works of John Crowne*. ed. James Maidment and W. H. Logan, 4 vols. (Edinburgh; London, 1872–74), II, 44.

27 *The Complete Works of Thomas Shadwell*, ed. Montague Summers, 5 vols. (London: Fortune Press, 1927), vol. III.

28 *The Complete Works of Nathaniel Lee*, ed. Thomas B. Stroup and Arthur L. Cooke, 2 vols. (Metuchen, New Jersey: Scarecrow Press, 1954–55), vol. I.

29 See George Boas, *The Happy Beast in French Thought on the Seventeenth Century* (Baltimore: John Hopkins University Press, 1933); see also Keith Thomas, *Man and the Natural World: Changing Attitudes in England 1500–1800* (London: Allen Lane, 1983).

30 For a discussion of this play, see my book, *Restoration Drama and Politics: the Plays of Thomas Otway 1675–83* (New Jersey: University of Delaware Press, 1995).

31 *De Cive*, in *The Philosophical Rudiments Concerning Government*, ed. Howard Warrender, 5 vols. (Oxford: Clarendon Press, 1983), III, 31.

32 James Thompson, *Language in Wycherely's Plays: Seventeenth-Century Language Theory and Drama* (Mobile: University of Alabama Press, 1984), p. 15.

33 See J. Douglas Canfield, *Word as Bond in English Literature from the Middle Ages to the Restoration* (Philadelphia: University of Pennsylvania Press, 1989).

34 Thompson, *Language in Wycherley's Plays*, pp. 3–4.

35 Peter Hynes, "Against Theory? Knowledge and Action in Wycherley's Plays," *MP* 94 (1996), 187.

36 *The Works of the Most Reverend Dr. John Tillotson. Late Lord Archbishop of Canterbury*, edited by Ralph Baker, 9 vols. (London, 1728), II, 538.

37 Cited in Henry G. Van Leeuwen's *The Problem of Certainty in English Thought, 1630–1690* (The Hague: Martinus Nijhoff, 1965), p. 97.

38 Hughes, *English Drama 1660–1700* (Oxford: Clarendon Press, 1996) p. 5.

39 *Restoration Comedies*, ed. Dennis Davison (Oxford University Press, 1970).

10

SUSAN J. OWEN

Drama and political crisis

In the late 1670s, political crisis in the nation had a profound effect upon the theatres. Intense political engagement in the drama radically transformed dramatic form and content. The relationship between politics and culture is complex. It is certainly not a simple case of (political) cause and (dramatic) effect. Yet it can scarcely be a coincidence that the crisis coincided with three important dramatic shifts: a change in comedy, the development of tragedy, and the rise of the sentimental.

The mid-Restoration crisis is often called the Exclusion Crisis, due to the Whigs' desire to exclude Charles II's Catholic brother and heir, James Stuart, from the succession. Yet the term hardly seems strong enough for what many thought would become another civil war. It is hardly surprising that there should have been a marked effect on the drama at this time when political divisions became deep enough to give rise to rival parties, Whigs and Tories, and to the beginnings of party politics. Whigs feared the growth of Catholicism (or "popery") and "arbitrary government" in high places, as in France. These fears were exacerbated by the so-called Popish Plot scare of 1678. Tories feared renewed rebellion of the sort which had led to the English civil wars and the execution of Charles I in 1649.

The onset of deep crisis is usually dated to the autumn of 1678, when Titus Oates's allegations of a "popish" plot to assassinate the king and introduce Catholicism caused a furor which the murder of Sir Edmund Bury Godfrey, the magistrate who had taken Oates's deposition, intensified to fever pitch.[1] At the same time Montagu, the former ambassador to Paris, revealed secret dealings between the Danby administration (acting for Charles II) and the French monarchy, at a time when the ministry had been asking Parliament for money, ostensibly for war with France. It was feared that Charles, like his father before him, wanted the money for a standing army to use against his own people. Soon afterwards treasonable secret correspondence between James's secretary Coleman and the French came to light. Fears of "Popery and Arbitrary Government," as Andrew Marvell put it in his book-length pamphlet, *An Account of the Growth of Popery and Arbitrary Government in England* (1677), now led to the fall of Danby and the end of the cavalier parliament which had been sitting since 1661. The opposition, soon to be called Whigs, won the new elections decisively, and many, including the Duchess of Portsmouth who was the king's mistress, and the French ambassador, thought they would be successful in their campaign to exclude James from the succession. Many feared renewed civil war. "Forty-one is come again" was the cry. However, after four years of turbulence, Charles managed to obtain French funds to enable him to rule without Parliament; and the opposition to popery and arbitrary government went into abeyance until 1688.

The Crisis affected the theatres badly. People were more interested in the political arena, or what was called the theatre of news, than in attending plays. "The Devil take this cursed plotting age," wrote Aphra Behn, " 'T has ruin'd all our Plots upon the Stage."[2] Partly for this reason, and partly due to mismanagement at the King's Company in Drury Lane, the two theatre companies had to merge in 1682 to form a single United Company. The drama was also subjected to censorship during the Crisis, more than at any time since the theatres reopened in 1660. Plays banned included Lee's *The Massacre of Paris* and *Lucius Junius Brutus*, Tate's *Richard the Second* and Crowne's *Henry the Sixth*. Dryden's and Lee's *The Duke of Guise* and Crowne's *City Politiques* were banned in summer 1682. Banks had *Cyrus the Great* banned in 1681, *The Innocent Usurper* in 1683 and *The Island Queens* in 1684.

However, it is interesting to note that most of these plays were initially licensed without any problem. *The Massacre of Paris* was banned at the request of the French Ambassador.[3] *Lucius Junius Brutus*, *Richard the Second* and *Henry the Sixth* were banned after a few days' performance, following complaints to the Lord Chamberlain from powerful courtiers in the audience.[4] Shadwell's *The Lancashire Witches*, initially licensed with few alterations, was cut after similar complaints, as he notes in his "Preface to the Reader." The two Tory plays, *The Duke of Guise* and *City Politiques*, were simply held up for a few months, almost certainly to avoid making a political provocation at a sensitive time when the government was trying to engineer a Tory victory in the City of London. The plays were put on in the autumn after the elections were past.

Moreover, while censorship may have worked to some extent to limit criticisms of the authorities in performance, it did not stop publication. Even during the Exclusion Crisis play texts appeared in print uncensored. It made no difference if the play had been banned from performance. Control of printed material was never very effective, and was virtually non-existent between the expiration of the Printing Act in 1679 and 1681 when, following the Oxford Parliament, steps were finally taken to control the press.[5] Even so, play publication was unaffected. Shadwell published *The Lancashire Witches* in 1682 at the height of the Tory Reaction period, with the passages which the Master of the Revels had deleted from the performance given extra prominence by being printed in italics.

The conclusion to be drawn from this is that the effect of the Exclusion Crisis on the theatres was not quite as bad as may have appeared at first. When we come to the drama which was performed in the theatres, we can go further, and say that the effect of the Crisis was actually beneficial. I stated at the beginning of this essay that the Crisis coincided with three dramatic developments: a change in comedy, the development of tragedy, and the rise of the sentimental. It is time now to look at these developments in more detail.

In comedy there is a sharp break in 1678/9. Earlier in the decade sex comedy was in fashion, including those plays most remembered today, such as William Wycherley's *The Country Wife* and George Etherege's *The Man of Mode*.[6] As the political crisis intensified in the months prior to the Popish Plot scare, sex comedy went into eclipse. Spring 1678 saw the astonishing failure of a series of sex comedies by major writers.[7] Then, as deep crisis gripped the nation, there was a virtual cessation of comedies: only one in the 1678/9 season. That one, *The Feign'd Curtizans* (1679) by Aphra Behn, looked both forward and backward.[8] It was a sign of what was to come, and a reminder of the past; for what was to come was a revival of the comic themes of the early 1660s.[9] Behn's play sets the tone for a new wave of political comedies which employ methods and modes reminiscent of 1660s comedy to attack the Whigs. Of Behn in the early 1670s, Robert Hume notes, "As a versatile professional catering to popular taste, she stands almost as a paradigm for the pattern of development we will see in surveying this decade."[10] Behn, as much as Dryden, has her finger on the political-dramatic pulse. She is the first to enunciate what Arthur Miller calls "not-yet-popular ideas which are already in the air."[11] *The Feign'd Curtizans* offers satire of upstarts and Puritans, coupled with a celebration of upper class good taste across national boundaries. Behn suggests in her prologue that the Popish Plot scare is dishonest. She sets her play in Rome, but thwarts any expectation of plotting papists. Italian and English gentlemen share common codes of civility. Satire is reserved for the boorish Sir Signall Buffoon and his Puritan tutor, Tickletext. The latter is crudely anti-papist, stupidly patriotic, but hypocritically glad to exploit Roman custom to get a whore, a procedure which he justifies by a legalistic quibble. He is a philistine, condemning Roman church architecture for reasons of bigotry and himself writing in a style which combines Puritan plainness with bathos and credulity about portents. He is self-seeking and mercenary, forcing his pupil to trade in gloves, stockings, and pins on his grand tour. Behn thus associates Whiggish anti-popery and patriotism with Puritan sexual hypocrisy, folly, pretension, philistinism, and low-class money-grubbing.

The following season sees two new anti-Whig city comedies: *The Revenge* (1680), probably by Behn, and Thomas Otway's *The Souldier's Fortune* (1680). The Whigs' strength in the city of London offered an ideal opportunity to graft royalism onto city comedy. In *The Revenge*, an adaptation of Marston's *The Dutch Courtesan*, anti-Whig satire takes the form of a revenge plot against a cheating wine seller who is ridiculously Puritan and patriotic, and credulously anti-popish. In *The Souldier's Fortune* it takes the form of "cuckolding the Whig." The Tory Reaction period of 1681–82 sees a boom in city comedies which satirize Puritans and Whigs: the anonymous humors comedy *Mr. Turbulent*, Thomas D'Urfey's *Sir Barnaby Whigg*, Edward Ravenscroft's *The London Cuckolds* (all 1681), Aphra Behn's *The City Heiress* (1682), and John Crowne's *City Politiques* (1683). Other comedies attack the Whigs by direct reference to their Interregnum predecessors. Again, Behn is in the forefront with *The Round-Heads* (1681), an adaptation of Tatham's *The Rump*. Behn adds to her source play a hypocritical Puritan, Ananias Gogle, and Royalist heroes, Loveless and Freeman who are referred to as Tories. She also adds Corporal Right, a Cromwellian officer whose sympathies are secretly cavalier. Corporal Right illustrates a groundswell of hidden, "natural" royalism, as do the wives of parliamentarians Lambert and Desboro, who have an affinity for the sexy cavaliers. D'Urfey's *The Royalist* (1682), also set in the Interregnum, invokes a mythologized memory of republican villainy and Royalist heroism through the adventures of its suggestively named hero, Sir Charles Kinglove. The play ends with the Restoration, in the fashion of plays of the 1660s.

Tragicomedy is rarer in the Exclusion Crisis than in the early Restoration, but there are some notable examples of Royalist tragicomedy, all of which end with the restoration of a monarch on the 1660s model. In *The Young King* Behn develops topical themes which she had explored in *Abdelazar* (1676): a divided royal family and the dangers of tampering with the succession because of religious or superstitious scruples. John Dryden's *The Spanish Fryar* offers a moderate royalism. The play harks back to the 1660s. It ends on a note of reconciliation, as the old king is miraculously restored and the true prince is united in marriage with the usurper's daughter.[12] William Whitaker's *The Conspiracy* (1680) also recalls the values of the 1660s. Whitaker revives the defunct form of the Royalist heroic play in rhyming couplets and the 1660s tragicomic model of regicide followed by restoration. Whitaker's play is possibly the most fervent and wholehearted Royalist play of the Exclusion Crisis. The play offers a spectacle of an exemplary royal couple resembling the idealized Charles I and Henrietta Maria, beset by demonic regicides and rebels. The rebels are guilty of rabble-rousing, arrogance, arbitrariness, hypocrisy, religious zeal and atheism together, lying, lust, presumption, and fanatical cruelty. The rebels succeed in killing the Sultan, but are routed in their turn by exemplary Royalist heroes who manage to restore the royal couple's son to the throne.

Royalist comedies are quite well known, but Whig comedy is perhaps less familiar. Whig comedy reserves for Catholics the satire which Tory comedy directs at Puritans. *Rome's Follies; or, the Amorous Fryars*, performed at a private house in autumn 1681, and published with a dedication to the Whig leader Shaftesbury, reverses the paradigm of Tory comedies by associating hypocritical rampant sexuality with Catholic friars rather than Puritans. The friars cuckold deluded parishioners and absolve a man who has had sex with a goat. *Rome's Follies* is an odd play which both satirizes and revels in the friars' libertine ingenuity. The aim is presumably to demonstrate that Whig anti-papists are not whey-faced Puritans (contrary to Tory assertions), but can be part of the aristocracy of taste which appreciated *The Country Wife*. Thomas Shadwell's *The Lancashire Witches* (1680) reverses the model of Tory comedy in a different way. Shadwell associates with the Catholic priest Tegue the qualities which Tory dramatists associated with Puritans: self-interest, changeability and flexibility of conscience. More controversial is the character of Smerk, a popish Anglican priest whose fanatical anti-Puritanism mirrors the anti-popery which is satirized in Tory comedies. Smerk is also a low-born upstart who presumptuously censures the follies of the Whig gentleman who employs him. The Whig gentry are moderate, cultured, and civilized, the wise defenders of English Protestant tradition. In terms of sexual politics, this comedy also reverses the Tory norm: it is the papists and their apologists who are hypocritically lustful. Whiggery is anti-patriarchal, guarantees the liberties of the Protestant Englishwoman, and ensures freedom of choice in marriage. The play ends on a note of harmony based not on the values of 1660, but on the Whig country gentry values of old-fashioned decency, moderation, patriotism, Protestantism, charity, hospitality, and good sense.

Protestant tradition is also celebrated in the anonymous *The Coronation of Queen Elizabeth*, performed at the London fairs in the summer of 1680.

In this anti-Catholic black farce, the Pope compacts with devils, eventually flees to England when the corruption of his church outrages the local population, and is captured by trusty English artisans who thereby secure the safety of the realm while their social superiors are busy fighting the Armada. The positive treatment of the artisans here contrasts with the largely negative depiction of the "lower orders" in Tory plays. Queen Elizabeth is grateful for the artisans' loyalty, a pointed contrast to Charles's different sentiments towards his politically concerned subjects. The use of Elizabethanism as a criticism of Charles was prevalent in Whig propaganda. Elizabeth in the play is humble before God, concerned for the whole "commonwealth" of England, and vigilant in combating Catholicism at home and abroad: a deliberate contrast to Stuart "popery and arbitrary government."

Possibly even more significant than the effect of the Crisis upon comedy is its influence on tragedy. Just as the Exclusion Crisis was foreshadowed by growing social divisions, so the development of political tragedy had slightly earlier antecedents. It was the Crisis, however, which brought the new form to fruition. Henry Neville Payne's *The Siege of Constantinople* (1674) foreshadows the tragedies of the Exclusion Crisis in its use of blank verse, its political topicality, and its peculiar combination of royalism with scepticism and pessimism. The wicked, plotting Chancellor, modeled on opposition noblemen such as Shaftesbury, was a model for subsequent villains of Tory tragedy; but Payne's play also evinces what was to become typical unease about the problems caused by unruly royal desire and caprice. The tension between the ruler's desires and political necessity is also central in two adaptations of Shakespeare's *Antony and Cleopatra*, Charles Sedley's *Antony and Cleopatra* and Dryden's *All For Love*; and in Nathaniel Lee's *The Rival Queens* (all 1677). Sedley's treatment of the issue prefigures Whig tragedy. His Antony is a critical portrait of Charles II, blind to the way in which his foreign mistress manipulates him, and inappropriately merciful and severe at the wrong times.[13] The battle of Actium is a critical depiction of Charles's unpopular Third Dutch War. As in later Whig drama, the Roman Republic is viewed with nostalgia, while the common people are treated kindly, and Antony is glad to be set right by them. Poet Laureate Dryden's *All For Love*, as might be expected, treats the ruler's unruly passion for an unpopular foreigner more sympathetically. The proto-Whiggish values of Roman civic virtue and respect for law are treated correspondingly more negatively. Meanwhile, Alexander in Lee's *The Rival Queens* is an ambiguous figure, somewhere in between the hero and tyrant, the tragic lover and the libertine.

As tragedy develops, and polarization in the nation deepens, it is possible to discern rival Tory and Whig dramatic perspectives. This is not to say that the dramatists found it easy to take sides, but that it is possible to identify a difference between Whig and Tory tragedies in outlook and in the treatment of particular themes. Tory tragedies tend to idealize heroic absolute loyalty, to place a high value on "quietism," and to demonize rebellion.[14] Whig factiousness, legalism, and patriotism are satirized. In place of the positive value Whigs place on the nation, liberty and law, Tory plays privilege class values. In comedy this takes the form of satire of the Whiggish citizen-merchant class. In tragedy rebels (or Whigs) are depicted as dangerous rabble-rousers who incite an unruly mob which they cannot then control. The king and (loyal) nobility possess an inherent social superiority, and there may be a privileging of aristocratic bonds across national boundaries, as against national bonds. Whig anti-popery may also be satirized as credulity and superstition, and the satiric focus is shifted to Puritans and Dissenters, who may be likened to papists. Tory tragedies can make powerful use of family themes, drawing upon the political association of absolute monarchy and patriarchal authority: the violation of the family by rebels and ambitious plotters mirrors subversion in the state. Rebellion may be associated with lust, rape, sexual hypocrisy, and female unruliness. There is often a strong emphasis on the need for unity against the paramount threat of disorder and potential civil war emanating from ambitious noblemen, factious malcontents, or rebellious plebeians. However, evidence of difficulty is found in the fact that Tory tragedies, following Payne's *Siege of Constantinople*, often seem rather fraught, offering a somewhat hollow royalism, shot through with contradictions. Examples are: Crowne's *The Ambitious Statesman; or, the Loyal Favourite* (1679); Nahum Tate's *The Loyal General* (1679); Otway's *The Orphan* (1680) and *Venice Preserv'd* (1682); Dryden's and Lee's *Oedipus* (1678); and Dryden's *Troilus and Cressida* (1679).[15]

A major contradiction arises from the inherent difficulty in dramatizing Tory quietism convincingly. However much moral and political force the idea of absolute loyalty is felt to have, there is something unconvincing about the spectacle of "quiet" heroes. The heroes of avowedly Royalist or Tory plays are often masochistic, passive, and paralyzed by a sense of the difficulty of right action. A second contradiction arises from the fact that, if absolute loyalty is to be heroic, it must be tested and found true even in the face of vitiated kingship. Yet there is something troubling from a Royalist point of view about the spectacle in play after play of royal faults which correspond with the faults of the Stuart brothers as even the most tolerant contemporaries perceived them. Thus we find royal lies, ineptitude, passivity, misrule, "effeminacy," and excessive mercy towards the kingdom's enemies, which are all failings for which Charles was criticized; arbitrariness, rage, and self-centeredness, considered to be faults in James; and lust and (quasi-) Catholicism, perceived faults of both. There are times when the assertion that the monarch will rule well if the people will be quiet and courtiers constant rings distinctly hollow. If the radical alternative was unthinkable for loyal playwrights, conformity is a bleak prospect too, especially for Otway, whose plays offer little more reassurance than that misfortune might possibly be endured. Loyalty without hope of reward is a stifling ideal when loyal heroes must annihilate themselves in conformity with the ideal of absolute obedience to kings who do not deserve or value it.

Even family values, a powerful Tory ideological counter, can give rise to problems and contradictions. For example, the spectacle of bad fatherhood in the microcosm, even if intended to dramatize the evils of republicanism, as in Otway's *Caius Marius* and *Venice Preserv'd*, can resonate uncomfortably for Royalists. The Exclusion Crisis was a crisis of fatherhood: Charles had no legitimate son, was considered to have scattered his seed irresponsibly throughout the land and to be over-indulgent towards his illegitimate son, Monmouth, who was now in league with the Whigs. Problems were posed for the Stuarts by the disparity between patriarchalist ideology and the perceived reality: Charles I was virtuous but impotent, so unable to be a good father to the nation, and Charles II was unable to be a good father literally in terms of securing the succession with a legitimate son, or figuratively in his conduct as leader of the nation. Tory tragedies often seem to depict a bleak world in which both family and state are vitiated by corruption; there is nothing to hold on to except an ideal of loyalty without hope of reward, and there are no heroic alternatives.

Let me illustrate these remarks with a famous example: Otway's *Venice Preserv'd*.[16] This play was proclaimed as a Tory play in various prologues and epilogues which Otway and Dryden wrote for different performances, including special performances for James and his wife. Set in the Venetian republic, the play problematizes rebellion, in keeping with Tory advocacy of non-resistance even to corrupt authority, and also problematizes republicanism in power. Both the Venetian senators and those who rebel against them are despicable. Senator Antonio is a sexual sado-masochist whose theft of Pierre's mistress has driven the latter to rebellion. Senator Priuli is a bad father whose cruelty prompts his son-in-law Jaffeir to join the rebels. The rebels have misplaced idealism, but their leader Renault is no better than the Senators, as Jaffeir finds when his wife Belvidera is almost raped by Renault. By setting his play in a republic, Otway avoids some of the problems and contradictions in plays such as *The Ambitious Statesman* and

The Loyal General which attempt to dramatize heroic loyalty to vitiated kingship. However, the universal nastiness of the world of the play, and the absence of heroic possibilities, pose their own problems. Belvidera attempts to assert the political importance of her near-rape. To her, it shows the horror of rebellion, and the importance of loyalty to the established order and non-resistance. Jaffeir, however, is more doubtful. He betrays the conspiracy, but then regrets deserting his friends "in fond compassion to a woman's tears."[17] He goes off to die with Pierre on the scaffold, leaving the abandoned Belvidera to sink into madness. This makes for interesting theatre, but not for wholehearted loyalism.

Bad fatherhood is a central theme in *Venice Preserv'd*, contributing to the problematizing of republicanism in power: Priuli's failure to protect his loyal daughter, or to show gratitude to the son-in-law who has saved his daughter's life, parallels the dishonorable conduct of the republican govern- ment in failing to reward loyalty, show mercy, or keep its word. The play ends with Priuli's regret, and the warning: "bid all cruel father's dread my fate" (5.4.37). There is an implicit contrast with the generous and indulgent "fatherhood" of Charles II. As Dryden put it in his prologue to the April 1682 performance: "A Tyrant's Pow'r in rigour is exprest:/The Father yearns in the True Prince's Breast." Yet the moral, that bad fatherhood should be avoided, is the wrong one from the Tory point of view. Toryism puts the burden of political responsibility upon the son/subject, not the father/king. Moreover, there is no monarchist alternative in the Venetian state. This makes it harder to demonize republicanism by specific reference to the form of government than it is in plays set in the English Interregnum: there is no glorious, counter-revolutionary future. It is also a paradox that the republican setting makes it impossible to engage convincingly in the moralizing against rebellion on which other Tory plays rely for their effect. Otway has eliminated one set of contradictions, only to find himself confronted with another.

Loyalty to corrupt authority produces pessimism and masochistic self- destructiveness. It is common in Otway's tragedies for the young characters to try to moralize themselves into "correct" attitudes, to struggle with contradictory desires and obligations, and to end by longing for pain and death. Jaffeir likens himself to a sacrificial lamb, who "hardly bleats, such pleasure's in the pain" (4.1.94). To win Pierre's forgiveness he will "Lie at thy feet and kiss 'em though they spurn me" (4.2.235). When Pierre is on the scaffold, Jaffeir asserts, "stripes [from a whip] are fitter for me than embraces" (5.3.34). Sado-masochism and self-loathing shade into suicidal despair, expressed in Jaffeir's demented curse: "Final destruction seize on all the world!" (5.2.93). The atmosphere of pessimism here parallels the "hard-boiled" cynicism of some cavalier comedies. The outlook is too close to nihilism to be compatible with fervent Toryism.

Otway participated in another important dramatic trend at this time. This was a vogue for politicized adaptations of Shakespeare's tragedies and history plays. Otway adapted *Romeo and Juliet* in a Roman setting as *The History and Fall of Caius Marius* (1679). Sedley and Dryden, as we have seen, adapted *Antony and Cleopatra*, and Dryden also adapted *Troilus and Cressida* (1679). Crowne's *The Misery of Civil War* (1680) and *Henry VI: the First Part* (1681) were adaptations of the *Henry VI* trilogy. Tate offered *The History of King Richard The Second*, *The History of King Lear* (both late 1680 or early 1681), and *The Ingratitude of a Common-wealth* (1681), an adaptation of *Coriolanus*. These plays foreground the dangers of rebellion, rabble-rousing, mob-rule, faction, ingratitude, and civil war. The dangers of banishment and exclusion may be stressed, with clear application to the fate of James, banished by Charles in response to pressure from the Whig-dominated Parliament which also wished to exclude him from the throne. Tate's Coriolanus, in particular, bears a strong resemblance to James. Various alterations in the plays are aimed at arousing pity and fear for England's royal brothers. In *The Ingratitude of a Common-wealth*, for example, the characters of Virgilia and Volumnia, and their relationships with the hero, are sentimentalized. Both pity and fear (as well as incredulity!) are aroused at the end as horror succeeds horror: Coriolanus cannot die until he has witnessed the wounding and threatened rape of his wife by Aufidius, the torturing of his little son, and the mad ravings of Volumnia who has been driven demented by the boy's sufferings. The appearance on stage of the boy's mangled body and his pathetic dying speech add a further touch. Crowne, in *the Misery of Civil-War*, uses horrors to create a moralized spectacle: in Act 3, scene 2, soldiers are shown robbing and tormenting peasants and raping their daughters. The peasants have only themselves to blame for they have railed seditiously in ale houses instead of living "honestly and quietly." The soldiers repeatedly sneer "How do you like Rebellion?" Then the lesson is driven home as "The Scene is drawn, and there appears Houses and Towns burning, Men and Women hang'd upon Trees, the Children on the tops of Pikes."[18]

Like Royalist tragedies, the Shakespeare adaptations show varying degrees of anxiety about rulers' ineptitude, lust, bad fatherhood, or intransigence. Even when the dramatists are straining every nerve "to Recommend Submission and Adherence to Establisht Lawful Power, which in a word, is *Loyalty*," as Tate puts it in his Dedication to *The Ingratitude*,[19] they do not succeed. Tate works hard to exculpate his hero and to demonize "the busie Faction of our own time ... those Troublers of the

State that out of private Interest or Mallice, seduce the Multitude to ingratitude, against Persons that are not only plac't in Rightful Power above them; but also the Heroes and Defenders of their Country" (sig. A2r–v). Yet his improvement of Coriolanus/James does not really work: nothing can assuage the uncomfortable resonance of a man in league with his country's enemies, Volscian or French, and making war on his own people. There was enough apparent criticism of James in the play for it to be revived as an anti-Stuart piece after the rebellions of 1715 and 1745.

Whig tragedies fall into several types.[20] Some, like Whig comedies, rely for their force on anti-Catholicism. Anti-Catholic plays offer a mirror-image of Tory plays, attributing to "papists" all the qualities which Tories attributed to rebels: ambition, arrogance, arbitrariness, hypocrisy, lying, plotting, secret atheism and secret lust, presumption, fanatical cruelty, and even rabble-rousing. A precursor of Whig anti-Catholic tragedy is Thomas Shipman's anti-Catholic *Henry III of France* (1672). Shipman's depiction of the horrors of counter-Reformation Catholicism, and his unease about royal supineness in the face of it, foreshadow Lee's explicitly Whiggish banned play, *The Massacre of Paris* (1679?). In Lee's play the hero is a Protestant patriot who resorts to arms to defend the true religion in the face of Catholic duplicity and ferocity and royal corruption. With obvious topical application, a weak king called Charles is manipulated by evil Catholics through a manipulative woman (Catherine de Medici). A similar image of female monstrosity is used to demonize Catholicism in Settle's *The Female Prelate* (1680) in which the ambitious, cruel, and lustful Pope Joan typifies the horrors of popery. Lee's *Caesar Borgia* shows popish ambition and tyranny rampant in Rome in a way which reflects the particular anxieties and events of the Popish Plot scare, and concludes with the moral, drawn by Machiavel: "No power is safe, nor no Religion good,/ Whose Principles of growth are laid in Blood."[21]

Atrocities in these plays, arousing pity and terror, rival anything in *The Misery of Civil War* or *The Ingratitude of a Common-wealth*. In *The Massacre of Paris* the hero is literally torn apart by a papist-inspired mob. In *Caesar Borgia*, as in Tate's *The Ingratitude*, there is the "mangling" of a little boy (Borgia's much loved bastard son) and a descent into madness, this time by the protagonist himself, as the demands of popish machiavellian villainy prove too much to execute or endure. *The Female Prelate* offers moralized spectacles. For example in Act 3 the persecuted hero Saxony is taken into a chamber where the scene opening "discovers variety of Hereticks in several Tortures."[22] In Act 4 the imprisoned heretics set the prison on fire and the ghost of the old Duke of Saxony, murdered by Pope Joan in her youth, writes "MURDER" on the wall in "bloudy fire" (4.3,

p. 50); and in Act 5 "The Scene opens, and discovers a Stake and Faggots, with Priests with Lighted Torches to kindle the Fire, and the Rabble hurrying Saxony to the Fire" (5.2, p. 70).

Otway shows rebels as rapists and republicans as perverts. Whig tragedians reverse the application. In *The Massacre of Paris* the Admiral and his wife are an exemplary Protestant couple, in contrast to the decadent sensuality of the Catholic villain Guise and his mistress Marguerite. The exemplary couple also appears in *The Female Prelate,* in contrast to the perverted lusts of the papists, by whom both husband and wife are raped. In *Caesar Borgia* Rome is a center of unnatural relationships: Borgia, at Machiavel's instigation, rejects love and eventually murders both brother and wife; Orsino tyrannizes over his daughter; and the corrupt, bisexual Cardinal Ascanio Sforza violates the family further by his murder of Borgia's son. Even plays which are not explicitly anti-Catholic rely for their effect on quasi-papist atrocities. For example, in Lee's *Lucius Junius Brutus* (1680) the Royalist plotters who try to undermine the fledgling Roman republic are in league with treacherous priests, and most of Act 4 is devoted to atrocities as Royalist conspirators and priests engage in bloodthirsty ranting, and burn, crucify, and consume their victims. Tory dramatists sometimes made concessions to anti-Catholic sentiment. Dryden offers jibes at priests in *Troilus and Cressida* and *The Spanish Fryar,* although he also warns in *Troilus and Cressida* and in *Oedipus* against over-hasty anti-clericalism. Troilus and Oedipus both give vent to outbursts against priests which are unjustified and based on false assumptions. In *The Duke of Guise* (1682) Dryden offers a sustained treatment of a theme common in Tory pamphlets and prologues, that the Whigs are just as bad as the papists they condemn. The attempt to attack the Whigs by analogy with popish malpractice backfired, however, as it involved emphasis of the popish threat which Tories had managed by 1682 largely to deny. Dryden's enemies were quick to point this out.

Not all Whig tragedies work by demonizing Catholicism. The twin evils for the Whigs were, as Marvell put it, popery and arbitrary government, and some plays focus on the latter to celebrate heroic resistance to tyranny, or republican virtue. John Bancroft's Roman play *The Tragedy of Sertorius* (1679) makes a Whiggish distinction between good and bad rebellion. The virtuous Sertorius heroically resists Sulla's tyranny and establishes order, while the ambitious rebel Perpenna resists Sertorius's good government for reasons of personal ambition and brings about chaos. Sertorius stands for godliness, liberty, law, parliamentarian values, and the common good. Perpenna is blasphemous and atheistic, abuses libertarian rhetoric, and seeks only the free play of his own destructive passions. Sertorius and his wife Terentia are the exemplary couple typical in Whig drama; Perpenna's wife Fulvia holds a corrupt court. Another Roman play, Lee's *Lucius Junius Brutus*, dramatizes the expulsion of the Tarquins, kings of ancient Rome, and the founding of the Roman republic. The play was banned after a few days' performance for "Scandalous Expressions & Reflections upon ye Government."[23] The play celebrates parliamentary institutions, the rule of law, and the ability to put political obligations before personal ones. The rape of Lucrece by Tarquin, like the attempted rape of Otway's Belvidera, is a signifier of corruption, but here it is Royalists who are the villains. After the expulsion of the Tarquins, the Royalist counter-revolutionary plotters and their priest-allies engage in a hollow rhetoric of self-justification, while reveling in rape and slaughter. Brutus, in contrast, like the Admiral in *The Massacre of Paris* and Bancroft's Sertorius, is honest, pious, public spirited, self-sacrificing, and courageous. The common people are valued as "the good people" instead of being despised as a rabble.[24] There is also a significant difference in the treatment of the young characters in this play, as compared with the young in Otway's plays who seem buffeted by arbitrary parental caprice and end in self-annihilation. Like Otway's Jaffeir, Brutus' son Titus toys with rebellion, but unlike Jaffeir, Titus progresses to a sense of fixed republican resolve and dies a death of heroic sacrifice. There is a constant temptation to give way to emotion and women's tears and pleadings. Even Brutus falters at the end of Act 4. But Titus raises his grieving father from the ground and persuades him of the necessity for his own death. The glorious cause takes precedence over personal concerns. Titus's dying words are rousing:

> I hope the glorious liberty of Rome,
> Thus watered by the blood of both your sons,
> Will get imperial growth and flourish long   (5.2.168–70)

The contrast with Stuart self-indulgence must have struck an audience largely composed of Members of the second Exclusion Parliament, then sitting. The play's topical resonance was enhanced by the fact that the Stuarts were likened to the Tarquins elsewhere, for example in satirical poems and Whig pamphlets, and in Algernon Sidney's *Discourses Concerning Government*. Not all Whig dramas are as bold as this. Some, such as Lee's *Theodosius* (1680) and Settle's *The Heir of Morocco* (1682), offer more coded discussions of bad kingship and loyal opposition, though still with a Whiggish slant.

The third and final aspect of the dramatic resonance of the Exclusion Crisis is the rise of the sentimental. As we have seen, both Tory and Whig playwrights use sentimentalized, suffering characters to dramatize the horrors of rebellion and republicanism, and tyranny and popery, respectively. The master of the sentimental in this period is John Banks. Whereas Otway uses sentimental effects to offer a Tory message, Banks combines sentimentalism with moderate Whiggery. Banks had three plays banned: *Cyrus the Great* (1681), *The Innocent Usurper* (1683) and *The Island Queens* (1684). His Elizabethan play *The Unhappy Favourite* (1681) at first seems critical of the Whigs in its depiction of Burleigh as an ambitious schemer (like Whig leaders), and possibly in a passing resemblance between the play's Earl of Essex and the rebellious Restoration Duke of Monmouth. Yet there are also more Whiggish aspects, such as strong criticism of royal intemperance, and an emphasis on the need for reconciliation between sovereign and subject. Banks whips up pity both for Elizabeth, the victim of her passions, and for Essex, the victim of royal caprice. As noted above, Elizabethanism was often used to criticize Charles II, for example in Whig pamphlets, and in plays such as *The Coronation of Queen Elizabeth*, and Banks's play is no exception.

Another Whiggish feature is the strong Protestant values which imbue both *The Unhappy Favourite* and Banks's *Vertue Betray'd* (1682). The latter play, published with a fervently Protestant Dedication and a second prologue by the Whig Shadwell, centers upon Anna Bullen (Anne Boleyn). Anna becomes a sentimentalized, suffering heroine who stands for love in opposition to *realpolitik*. She is also a Protestant martyr, undone by the diabolical papist machinations of Wolsey. Like Whig plays and pamphlets, *Vertue Betray'd* has strong patriotic values: it is repeatedly stressed that Anna is an English heroine, concerned about the fate of England, in opposition to Romish villainy. There is a constant mingling of politics and sentiment. Henry is a tyrant in matters of the heart, as well as in matters of state. He has the high-handedness and predatory amorousness of James Stuart, though unlike James he eventually sees through popish villainy. At the end of the play, Anna looks forward to her daughter Elizabeth's triumph over the Pope. The little girl Elizabeth herself appears, shows an instinctive mistrust of Wolsey, and begs her father to save her mother's life in sentimental terms:

> Father, will you not let your *Betty* kiss you?
> Why do you let 'em pull me from you so?
> I ne're did anger you:
> Pray save my Mother, Dear King-Father do;
> And if you hate her, we will promise both,
> That she and I will go a great, huge way,
> And never see you more.[25]

This is typical of Banks's achievement of political effects through sentimental devices.

It used to be the fashion for twentieth-century critics to replicate Behn's view that the effect of the Exclusion Crisis on the drama was a "curse." We have seen that, on the contrary, the politicization of drama in the Exclusion Crisis was energizing and transformative. Engagement with the burning issues of the day gave the drama immediacy, intensity, and vitality. Political involvement stimulated the revival of satirical comedy and the development of political tragedy, and gave rise to a new sentimentality which was to be the hallmark of much eighteenth-century drama and fiction. The Exclusion Crisis was a crux both in the political life of the nation and in the development of Restoration drama.

NOTES

1 For an account of the Exclusion Crisis see my *Restoration Theatre and Crisis* (Oxford: Clarendon Press, 1997), chs. 1 and 2; John Kenyon, *The Popish Plot* (Harmondsworth: Penguin, 1974); Jonathan Scott, *Algernon Sidney and the Restoration Crisis* (Cambridge University Press, 1991); K. H. D. Haley, *The First Earl of Shaftesbury* (Oxford: Clarendon Press, 1968); Tim Harris *et al.*, eds., *The Politics of Religion in Restoration England* (Oxford: Blackwell, 1990), chs. 5 and 6.

2 Prologue to *The Feign'd Curtizans* (1679).

3 John Dryden, *The Vindication of The Duke of Guise* (1683), p. 41.

4 John Loftis, "Introduction," to Nathaniel Lee's *Lucius Junius Brutus* (Lincoln: University of Nebraska Press, 1967), p. 12; Tate, *Epistle Dedicatory to The History of King Richard the Second* (1681), sig. A2v; Crowne, *Dedication to The English Frier* (1690), sig. A3v. For a discussion of the political composition of theatre audiences during the Exclusion Crisis, see my *Restoration Theatre and Crisis*, pp. 13–16.

5 Timothy Crist, "Government Control of the Press After the Expiration of the Printing Act in 1679," *PubHist* 5 (1979).

6 It is important to note, however, that other forms of comedy, such as the intrigue play, the romantic comedy and the "chatty display of manners" were also popular at this time: see Robert D. Hume, *The Development of English Drama in the Late Seventeenth Century* (Oxford: Clarendon Press, 1976), p. 295.

7 See Robert D. Hume, "'The Change in Comedy': Cynical Versus Exemplary Comedy on the London Stage, 1678–1693," *EiT* 1.2 (May 1983), 107–08.

8 For the dating of this play and others discussed see my *Restoration Theatre and Crisis*, Appendix.

9 For a discussion of 1660s comedy see Derek Hughes, *English Drama 1660–1700* (Oxford: Clarendon Press, 1996), and his essay in this volume.

10 Hume, *Development*, p. 284. See also my "Sexual Politics and Party Politics in Behn's Drama, 1678–83" in J. Todd, ed., *Aphra Behn Studies* (Cambridge University Press, 1996).

11 Arthur Miller, *Introduction to Collected Plays* (London: Methuen, 1990), I, 11.

12 For a fuller account and a survey of the debate about the play's politics see my "The Politics of John Dryden's The Spanish Fryar; or, the Double Discovery," *English* 43 (1994).

13 Charles had several foreign mistresses, but the most notorious at this time was Louise de Kéroualle, Duchess of Portsmouth. For the widespread view that Charles was too severe to his friends and merciful to his enemies, see the opening paragraphs of Jessica Munns's essay in this volume.

14 Quietism was both political and religious. In John Nalson's *Project of Peace* (1678), an early document of quietism, dissenters are attacked because they disrupt the God-given unity and peace of the nation. Chapter 14 makes a plea for quiet on the grounds of the difficulty of right knowledge and action, leading to the need to respect existing civic and religious authority, a central theme in Dryden's and Lee's play *Oedipus* (1678). Dryden returns to this theme in *Religio Laici* (1682): "But Common quiet is Mankind's concern" (*The Works of John Dryden*, ed. H. T. Swedenberg, Jr., *et al.*, 20 vols., in progress [Berkeley: University of California Press, 1956–] II, 122).

15 The large question of why Tory tragedies and some comedies are fraught with political and ideological contradiction, whereas Whig drama partakes of the vitality of opposition, is addressed in my *Restoration Theatre and Crisis*, chs. 7 and 8. See also Susan Staves, *Players' Scepters: Fictions of Authority in the Restoration* (Lincoln: University of Nebraska Press, 1979).

16 A full discussion of Tory tragedies can be found in my *Restoration Theatre and Crisis*, ch. 7, and there is an excellent discussion of Otway's plays in Jessica Munns's *Restoration Politics and Drama: the Plays of Thomas Otway, 1675–1683* (Newark: University of Delaware Press, 1995).

17 Thomas Otway, *Venice Preserv'd*, ed. M. Kelsall (Lincoln: University of Nebraska Press, 1969), 4.1.16.

18 First edition (London, 1680), 3.3, p. 36.

19 First edition (London, 1682), sig. A2r.

20 For a full discussion of Whig drama, the existence of which has been denied by some critics, see my *Restoration Theatre and Crisis*, ch. 8.

21 *The Works of Nathaniel Lee*, ed. T. Stroup and A. Cooke (New Brunswick: Scarecrow Press, 1954–55), 5.3.371–72.

22 First edition (London, 1680), p. 40.

23 Public Records Office, LC 5/144, 28. For a full discussion of this play see my "'Partial Tyrants' and 'Freeborn People' in *Lucius Junius Brutus*," *SEL* 31 (1991).

24 Nathaniel Lee, *Lucius Junius Brutus*, ed. J. Loftis (Lincoln: University of Nebraska Press, 1967), 3.2.34.

25 Facsimile reprint of first edition of 1682 with introduction by D. Dreher (Los Angeles: Augustan Reprint Society, 1981), 5, p. 68.

II

JEAN I. MARSDEN

Spectacle, horror, and pathos

Restoration theatre was a visual as well as a verbal medium, complementing its dialogue with a range of sensational effects. Although composing a neat history of the development of spectacle in the later seventeenth century would be reductive, it is possible to construct a rough chronology of its changing role in Restoration drama. Theatrical spectacle, particularly in the form of gruesome killings, had long been characteristic of the English stage; Elizabethan and Jacobean tragedies often featured multiple suicides or homicides, leaving the stage littered with dead bodies. In their fondness for spectacle, especially lurid scenes of rape and murder, English playwrights participated in a dramatic tradition distinctly different from that of their French contemporaries. French neoclassical theory dictated that scenes of violence occur offstage, and some French critics condemned the English stage for its "barbarism." English dramatic practice, however, never adhered to such rules; although many English playwrights, such as John Dryden and later John Dennis, respected the French theorists, most English writers attacked the decorum and orderliness of French drama for its blandness and insipidity.[1] By contrast, English drama, with its battles, violence, and elaborate spectacle, was seen as "manly" and "lively," a testament to the vigor of the nation and its people.

Throughout the later seventeenth century, theatre managers expanded upon this tradition of gore and exploited visual effect in order to draw patrons into their theatres, using effects ranging from graphic horror to the display of actresses in erotic tableaux.[2] Often dependent on the physical capabilities of the theatres in which plays were staged, spectacle can be traced in part to quantifiable developments in staging. Thus some of the most sensational special effects appear only in theatres such as the new theatre at Dorset Garden which could accommodate the machinery needed to make witches fly and fire stream from the firmament.

But specific patterns in theatrical spectacle can be tied to cultural currents as well as to technical facilities. Two especially noteworthy forms of spectacle are largely independent of the sophisticated machinery found in the new theatres: horror and pathos. The cult of horror popular in the late 1670s owes little to theatrical innovation; rather, its prevalence can be clearly tied to the political turmoil sweeping England in the wake of the Popish Plot and the Exclusion Crisis. A more long-lived development can be seen in the growing popularity of the pathetic play in the last decades of the seventeenth century. Using pathos to excite emotion rather than grand vistas or breathtaking special effects, such plays emphasize female suffering and depend on the physical presence of actresses to titillate the audience rather than on heroic landscapes or supernatural visions.

Forms of spectacle

On its most basic level, theatrical spectacle could consist of "low tech" devices such as magnificent processions and exotic settings, but, once the new playhouses were completed in the 1670s, more elaborate special effects were possible. Adaptations of Shakespeare's *Macbeth* (1664) and *The Tempest* (1674),[3] took full advantage of the technical possibilities for staging intricate productions, augmenting Shakespeare's depiction of the supernatural with new scenes of witches flying and spirits descending. Contemporary audiences were intrigued by spectacle and were clearly attracted by the promise of newer and more dazzling wonders. Advertising "puffs" for new plays and even for the revivals of older plays often stressed "with new scenes," meaning that the production was providing new painted backdrops, not merely recycling the scenery from another play. In the case of plays with supernatural components, playbills were even more explicit about the special effects. One such play was Thomas Shadwell's political comedy, *The Lancashire Witches* (1681). Shadwell's play combines a conventional romantic comedy with virulent anti-Catholic satire, setting a group of energetic witches against an idiotic Irish priest and the foolish neighbors who support him. Along with its depiction of courting couples and confused identities, *The Lancashire Witches* includes scenes of witches flying over the stage and even summoning the devil. John Downes underscores the importance of the play's theatrical spectacle in his account of Restoration theatre, describing it as "being a kind of Opera, having several *Machines* of flyings for the Witches, and other Diverting contrivances in't." He reports that because of these elements, "it prov'd past Expectation; very Beneficial to the Poet and *Actors*."[4] Advertisements for later revivals of the play stressed the theatrical spectacle; the advertisement for the 1 July 1707 performance focused on the entertainment value of the witches, assuring viewers that the play would be staged "with all the Risings, Sinkings, and Flyings of the Witches, as they were Originally perform'd."[5]

One of the great Restoration masters of spectacle was Elkanah Settle, a playwright whose bombastic couplets became the object of ridicule but whose instinct for showmanship was unerring. Settle's first play, *Cambyses, King of Persia* (1671), demonstrates the direction which much serious drama was to take in the following decades. Although written and staged before the new theatre at Dorset Garden was completed, *Cambyses* nonetheless provided a spectacular show as well as foreshadowing the cult of horror which would come to dominate drama in the later 1670s and early 1680s. Settle presented his audience not only with the conventional bloodbath, but also included a severed head in a bowl of blood, a dream vision in which spirits descend from a cloud, and a series of heathen rites during which spirits descend and a bloody cloud appears amid flashes of fire. These devices, more than the play itself, made *Cambyses* an immediate success. But it was in his next play, the exceptionally successful *Empress of Morocco* (1673),[6] that Settle brought theatrical spectacle to a peak. With its crowd scenes, special effects, and horrific ending, *The Empress of Morocco* demonstrates the variety of spectacle possible in late seventeenth-century drama. The staging of special effects was so integral to the play – and so popular – that the play was published with the illustrations of some of its most sensational scenes. Through these illustrations we can see not only the nature of the visions Settle designed, but the importance such scenes held in the eyes of the play's original audience.

The Empress of Morocco provided its audiences with a potent mixture of sex, violence, and grandiose scenic effects. Settle's stage directions require the sounds of trumpets and discharging guns in addition to elaborate painted backdrops of dungeons and torture scenes as well as *"the Prospect of a large River, with a glorious Fleet of Ships."*[7] In addition to the magnificent displays of exotic vistas provided by the scenery and musical numbers such as a troop of Moors who bring in an artificial palm tree *"about which they dance to several antick Instruments,"* Settle titillates his audience with scenes of sexual wrong-doing, most notably in the form of a post-coital tableau. The third act begins with a "discovery" scene designed to display immorality in no uncertain terms:

Scene: A Bed-Chamber.
The Scene opens, and discovers Crimalhaz *and Queen Mother sleeping on a Couch, a Table standing by, with* Crimalhaz's *Plume of Feathers, and his Drawn Sword upon it.* (3.1)

Such a scene would have been staged by drawing back the painted flats from the previous scene to reveal ("discover") the tableau. By using such a technique, Settle fixes the audience's attention on the tableau revealed, a scene which is both explicitly erotic and morally coded. The couch provides an indicator of sexual activity as do Crimalhaz's habiliments strewn on the table, particularly the "Drawn Sword." Next, the virtuous Muly Hamet enters and, like the audience, acts the voyeur, spelling out the implications of the scene. The queen's illicit sexuality defines her as both wanton and murderous while Crimalhaz's presence reveals him as a traitor. To prevent the destruction of all their nefarious plans, Crimalhaz stabs his arm and accuses Muly Hamet of attacking him, an act which not only effects the general's imprisonment but which also provides an opportunity for explicit gore: the stage directions stress that after Crimalhaz stabs himself, the arm *"immediately appears bloody"* (p. 19).

Settle saves his most sensational scenes for the final acts of the play. In the early scenes of the fourth act, Muly Hamet escapes from prison, then battles a company of villains to the accompaniment of clashing swords and roaring guns. This stirring scene of bloodshed is followed by an elaborate masque representing Orpheus' trip to the underground in search of Euridice: as staged it included a grand prospect of hell and its fires, as well as music and a dance *"by several infernal Spirits, who ascend from under the Stage"* (p. 49). The climax comes as the evil Empress's plot against her son unfolds. During the masque, the king, disguised as Orpheus, grasps his wife and she, not recognizing him, stabs him to the heart. The final act concludes the bloodbath as the empress stabs the young queen and then herself, while the most gruesome fate is left for the villain Crimalhaz, a punishment vividly depicted in the final illustration published with the play (fig. 9): *"Here the Scene opens, and* Crimalhaz *appears cast down on the Gaunches, being hung on a Wall set with spikes of Iron"* (p. 70). The grotesque depiction of seemingly dismembered bodies is deliberately sensational, a technique Settle uses to drive home the play's moral. In an explicit statement of the efficacy of spectacle, Muly Hamet's friend Abdelcador instructs the remaining cast – and the audience – to view the physical manifestation of Crimalhaz's downfall and "see the reward of Treason."

Horror and politics

Where plays of the early 1670s, such as *Cambyses* and *The Empress of Morocco*, incorporated a variety of visual effects, serious drama of the late 1670s and early 1680s was to focus almost exclusively on horror. Play after play depicts scenes of rape, torture, and bloodshed, rarely lightening the gloom with less gruesome spectacles such as Settle's exotic masques and

Figure 9 Engraving of a scene of prisoners on spikes from Settle's *The Empress of Morocco*

dances. These dark and often disturbing dramas coincide with the current political turmoil of the Popish Plot and the Exclusion Crisis (see chapter 10), and in them horror becomes more than an end in itself; playwrights on all sides of the political spectrum incorporate horrifyingly graphic scenes as the vehicle for political messages. The purpose of such scenes is not only, as in *The Empress of Morocco*, to shock or amaze but to evoke a specific political response within the theatre audience. (A similar link between horror and politics can be seen in the science fiction films of the 1950s which reflect the era's near hysterical fear of communism.) This use of horror for propaganda was not limited to the years of the Exclusion Crisis; John Dryden employs similar methods in *Amboyna* (1672) to vilify the Dutch, with whom the English were at war.[8] Although plays such as *Amboyna* appeared occasionally in the early 1670s, the real glut of stage horror made its appearance after 1678. At this time, England faced social and political instability as factions argued over the succession of the crown and fears of Catholic insurrections haunted the nation. Dramatists brought these tensions into their plays, drawing upon the English fondness for spectacle and large-scale bloodshed to create bleak pictures of corruption and the potential for social disintegration, as in this scene from John Crowne's *The Misery of Civil War* (1680):

> *The Scene is drawn, and there appears Houses and Towns burning, Men and Women hang'd upon Trees, and Children on the tops of Pikes.*
> 1 & 2 *Country Girls*: Oh Heaven! have mercy on us! have mercy on us!
> 1 *Souldier*: Now Rogues, how do you like Rebellion?[9]

Focusing on the terrifying results of rebellion, this apocalyptic scene provides a visual argument in favor of a strong monarchy. The play's political message is hardly subtle, and scenes such as this are designed to startle the audience into recognizing the potential ramifications of topical problems, in this case, of siding with Shaftesbury and Monmouth against Charles II and his brother James, Duke of York.

The true master of politicized horror was Nathaniel Lee, whose virulently anti-Catholic plays were frequently banned for what the Lord Chamberlain termed "very Scandalous Expressions & Reflections vpon ye Government."[10] At his best, Lee matches scenes of bloodshed with an intensity of emotion and language which sometimes spills over into rant. Remarkable for his ability to yoke the techniques of horror to a political agenda, Lee is responsible for some of the bloodiest and most shocking scenes in Restoration drama. *The Massacre of Paris* (written 1679–81, banned until 1689), for example, a catalog of sufferings endured by the Huguenots at the hands of the French, concludes with the staging of a mass execution of Protestants by a firing squad while the Queen Mother of France orders their death. After the soldiers fire, the dismembered body of the noble Admiral of France is displayed as "the Scene draws, and shews the Admiral's body burning."[11] The scene is enhanced by a description of the Admiral's death ("the Common People / Who from the Shoulders tore the mangled Head, / Cut off his Hands, and at Mountfaucon hung him, / Half burning, by one Leg upon the Gallows," 5.5.5–8) while the King of France cries "O horror! horror!" In his next play, the lurid but unsuccessful *Caesar Borgia, Son of Pope Alexander the Sixth* (1679), Lee paints a sensational picture of the corrupt court of Borgia. Once again, tyranny and Catholicism are linked together, most vividly by a series of gruesome murders. By the end of the play, the audience has been subjected to five stranglings, a prolonged death by torture, a stabbing, the appearance of Borgia's son "with his Eyes out, and Face cut"[12] and three poisonings, including that of Borgia himself. In each play, Lee links these excesses of bloodshed and sadism with Catholicism; the perpetrators of the crimes are illegitimate children of the Pope and their victims both innocent and sympathetic. He relentlessly employs horror as a means by which to attack absolutism and, as the censors saw it, the Catholic sympathies of Charles and James.

Perhaps the single most horrific and politically explosive scene in Restoration drama appears in one of Lee's finest plays, *Lucius Junius Brutus* (1680). The play begins in the aftermath of Tarquin's rape of Lucrece, an event which Lee uses to equate Tarquin, ruler of Rome, with tyrannic rule. In vowing to avenge the ravished matron, Brutus argues for a commonwealth; the ties to topical events are clear, and it is not surprising that the play was suppressed as a dangerous attack on the monarchy. Throughout the middle acts, much of the play's violence is spoken, not represented, as when Brutus describes the fate of Rome under Tarquin's rule:

> Or will you stay till Tarquin does return
> To see your wives and children dragged about,
> Your houses burnt, the temples all profaned,
> The city filled with rapes, adulteries,
> The Tiber choked with bodies, all the shores
> And neighboring rocks besmeared with Roman blood?[13]

The final acts fulfill this prediction of atrocities. In a grotesque parody of a mass, Lee vilifies the Catholic theory of transubstantiation in which the wafer and wine become the body and blood of Christ; in this scene, sadistic priests actually consume human flesh and blood. After a series of horrified comments from an observer, the grisly tableau is revealed:

The scene draws, showing the sacrifice: one [man] *burning and another crucified; the* Priests *coming forward with goblets in their hands, filled with human blood.*

First Priest: Now drink the blood

To make the conjuration good.

Vinditius [*from window*]:

O the gods! What, burn a man alive! O cannibals, hell-hounds! Eat one man and drink another! ... What drink a man's blood! Roast him and eat him alive! A whole man roasted! Would not an ox serve the turn! Priests to do this!   (4.102–03, 113–14, 120–25)

Here the Roman setting acts as a thin veil for the scene's anti-Catholic moral. The "priests," with their cannibalistic human sacrifice, become the representatives of a corrupt régime which violates even the most fundamental of human taboos. Horror becomes a means of accentuating the threat of tyranny which Lee suggests those aligned with Catholicism represent – what happens to Rome can happen to England.

Such macabre scenes, with their political subtexts, present the viewer with both a thrill and a moral. They go beyond the bloodbaths which traditionally ended many earlier heroic plays; mere stabbings or poisonings did not provide the effect which playwrights such as Lee strove to achieve. In works such as *Lucius Junius Brutus*, the goal is to shock through an excess of blood and through graphic representations of monstrous events. These plays enacted widespread fears of political instability and corruption. When the emphasis on horror began to die out after 1682, it was not necessarily because the nation's ills had been solved, but because financial problems in the theatres themselves forced the companies to combine and to limit severely the production of new plays. Indeed, Aphra Behn complained that "this cursed plotting Age" had emptied theatres and "ruin'd all our Plots upon the Stage."[14]

Pathos and Female Distress

A new element enters serious drama after 1680, an effect contemporary writers referred to as "distress." This different quality of spectacle, more familiarly known as pathos, got its start in the 1680s, just as the scenes of horror created by Lee and Crowne and others reached their peak. From 1680 onward, the pathetic play dominated the theatres, deriving its power not from its potential to shock, but from its ability to titillate with scenes of suffering innocence. The spectacle in these cases arises not from grisly scenes of blood, torture, or human sacrifice, but from displays of emotional and sometimes physical suffering inflicted upon blameless victims who are almost inevitably female. In contrast to *The Empress of Morocco*, where the climactic scene features the physical suffering of the villain, Crimalhaz, these plays stress the pain of the innocent; the works are not heroic, but intimate. They eschew battle scenes or elaborate spectacles for a focus on the distress of a leading character. Of the plays discussed above, the only one which could be said to have even an element of pathos, however brief, is Lee's *Caesar Borgia* when, near the end of the play, the young son of Borgia is brought on stage dying, blinded, and mutilated.

The role of such innocent suffering would, by the end of the seventeenth century, be taken by female characters; the success of the pathetic play, in fact, can be said to be dependent on the introduction of actresses on the stage. By 1680, actresses were no longer a novelty, however, they were a powerful sexual presence on the stage. The pathetic play, with its scenes of female suffering, incorporated the titillation of sex comedies popular in previous decades but avoided the aggressive sexuality displayed by women in the earlier plays, thus bringing the stage characters closer to popular ideals of feminine behavior. (Conduct books and other moral writings identified women as the "weaker sex" and lauded them for passive virtues such as patience and obedience.) This cult of suffering also provided playwrights with a new way of enacting honor and integrity. As serious drama moved away from the hollow oaths of earlier plays, such as the heroic drama of the 1660s and 1670s, playwrights sought a new means of representing truth, visually rather than verbally. The pathetic play represents a new form of authenticity, demonstrated through a heroine's ability to suffer.

The key to the success of the pathetic play was not simply that its characters felt emotion, but that they were able to provoke it in those who watched. Playwrights who wrote in this vein strove not to shock or horrify their audience but to move them to tears, and the quality of a play was often determined by its ability to arouse pity through the distress of its female characters. In *The Lives and Characters of the English Dramatick Poets*, Charles Gildon, playwright and critic evaluates tragedies specifically on the intensity of distress endured by their female characters, for example praising Mary Pix's tragedy, *Ibrahim, the Thirteenth Emperor of the Turks* (1696) for its "Passions" by which he means specifically its depiction of female suffering, "for the Distress of Morena never fail'd to bring Tears into the Eyes of the Audience; which few Plays, if any since *Otway*'s have done; and yet, which is the true End of Tragedy."[15]

This redefinition of the "true End of Tragedy" was so prevalent that a new form of serious drama developed which focused specifically on the suffering of innocent women. In these "shee tragedies" as they were later termed,[16] women are targets of adversity, appearing frequently as victims of sexual crimes such as rape or unwitting adultery, events which lead inevitably to poignant scenes of suffering and madness. In addition to being the blameless victims of misfortune, these women are helpless in the face of disaster, a studied submissiveness which reflects the cult of passivity already prevalent in the conduct literature of the period. The women in the majority of these plays can do nothing but suffer; they are defenseless in their virtue, and to take a more active role in their fate violates their status as innocents. Instead, their virtue is defined by and dependent on their inability to act. In this sense they literally embody the passive virtue praised in the conduct books of the late seventeenth century where some moralists argue that even acting in self defense is less than feminine. When tears and sighs are touted as a woman's most potent and proper weapons, she becomes incapable of action and submission becomes a virtue. The literary result is a generation of tragic heroines who are constrained to suffer passively, victims of fate seemingly incapable of acting to save themselves from disaster. This systematic passivity goes beyond the relegation of women to their proper domestic realm. Not only is the heroine without political or social power, but she even loses power over her own senses; a favorite literary device in the pathetic play is the madness of the anguished heroine – ultimately even her sanity is out of her control.

The most influential play in this new movement was Thomas Otway's tragedy, *The Orphan* (1680). Otway, touted by his contemporaries as a second Shakespeare, was especially praised for his refined depiction of female characters, a quality many Restoration critics felt that Shakespeare lacked. *The Orphan* was tremendously popular, not only at the time of its first performance, but for decades afterwards. The source of its popularity can be traced to a compelling plot and the exquisite distress of its heroine, Monimia. The play centers around the competition of two brothers, Castalio and Polydore, for the love of their beautiful foster sister Monimia. Monimia favors Castalio, and the two are married secretly. Polydore, not realizing Monimia is now legally his sister, clandestinely takes his brother's place in Monimia's bed on the wedding night, thus causing the innocent Monimia to commit both adultery and incest. Her horror upon discovering the dual sin is extreme (she faints and then for the rest of the play refers to herself as a "pollution" devoid of humanity), but rather than responding with anger, she blames herself. Unable to endure the shame of her sexual stain, she drinks poison in the final act. In a death scene notable for its quiet pathos and absence of rant, she tells Castalio "none can ever love thee like *Monimia*" and begs him to "Speak well of me … 'Twill be a noble Justice to the memory / Of a poor wretch, once honour'd with thy Love."[17]

Her final words poignantly sketch the poison's effect: "How my head swims! Tis very dark: Good night [*Dyes*" (5.470). While both Polydore and Castalio die before the end of the play, it is Monimia's demise, with her mournful and self-deprecating pledge of love which Restoration playgoers found most memorable. Critics praised *The Orphan* for its depiction of female distress, and the play became a model for later playwrights.

Other female-centered plays emulated Otway's use of simple pathos rather than rant, most notably the historical tragedies of John Banks. Banks's plays commonly deal with young women, innocent victims of political schemes, who desire only love and whose executions provide the plays with the requisite duress. While two of these plays, *The Innocent Usurper* (the execution of Lady Jane Grey) and *The Island Queens: Or, the Death of Mary, Queen of Scotland*, were deemed too politically volatile to be staged, Banks's third historical drama, *Vertue Betray'd: Or, Anna Bullen* (1682) became a popular success. In this version of the life of Henry VIII's second wife Anne Boleyn, Anne is the blameless victim of a series of court intrigues. Although she remains faithful to the king, her enemies accuse her of adultery, and the play ends with her execution. The final scene, like that in *The Orphan*, focuses on Anna's emotional suffering. In it, she pays a brave but tearful farewell to her daughter, Princess Elizabeth, and then, robed in innocent white, goes quietly to her execution. As she is called to the block she remarks plaintively, "My Lord, I've but a little Neck; / Therefore I hope he'l [the Heads-man] not repeat his Blow."[18] The "little Neck" she will bare for the executioner epitomizes her defenselessness and the meekness with which she submits to her fate.

In Banks's plays the tragedy not only focuses on a central female character, but makes her distress the play's emotional core, a focus which would become increasingly popular. As the number of new plays grew in the 1690s, a rash of new tragedies appeared, many of them conforming to this pattern of female suffering. One of the finest examples of she-tragedy written during these years is Thomas Southerne's *The Fatal Marriage: Or, The Innocent Adultery* (1694), a play drawn from Aphra Behn's novella *The History of the Nun: or the Fair Vow Breaker* (1689). Behn's novella stresses Isabella's sensational life first as a saintly nun and later as a bigamous murderess; notably, it omits any references to torments of conscience or emotional pain. In contrast, Southerne's tragedy is self-consciously and explicitly a display of female suffering, and its heroine is a helpless victim of chance. The play opens with the widowed Isabella and her young son, destitute, begging her husband's family for aid. Her words evoke the effect the scene should have not only on the audience within the play, her father-in-law and his household, but on the theatre audience as well:

> O my Child!
> Kneel with me, knock at Nature in his Heart.
> Let the resemblance of a once-lov'd Son,
> Speak in this little One, who never wrong'd you,
> And plead the Fatherless, and Widow's Cause.[19]

Isabella's words here express the aim of pathos, to "knock at Nature" in the hearts of the audience, to move them by a demonstration of indigence and humility.

Cast into the street by Biron's family, Isabella's troubles mount as creditors arrive to evict her and seize her few belongings. Significantly, when asked what she will do under these extreme circumstances, Isabella responds, "Do! Nothing, no, for I am born to suffer" (2.2.66). Her passivity under the blows of fortune is characteristic of the she-tragedy heroine; in order to represent virtuous womanhood, no matter how tainted by unwitting sexual transgressions, the heroine must be incapable of acting, masochistically accepting pain and blaming herself rather than reproaching others. Isabella articulates her role within the play, and the role of countless other heroines, as a form of spectacle:

> Am I then the sport,
> The Fame of Fortune, and her laughing Fools?
> The common spectacle, to be expos'd
> From day to day, and baited for the mirth
> Of the lewd Rabble? must I be reserv'd
> For fresh Afflictions?   (2.3.21–26)

She links her afflictions to her position as spectacle, and while Southerne would not wish to compare patrons of the theatre to the "lewd Rabble," Isabella functions in much the same way for both audiences.

Made desperate by her poverty, Isabella agrees to marry for a second time, and thus she, like Monimia, becomes the unwilling perpetrator of a sexual crime. The play's crisis occurs in the fourth act when Biron returns, and she discovers that she has profaned her original marriage vows. By the moral codes of seventeenth-century drama, Isabella cannot live, but one of the triumphs of Southerne's tragedy is that it rises above such simplistic moralism to illustrate her horror at what she has done and to arouse sympathy effectively for a woman who is, as she has said, the victim of fortune. In contrast to Behn's novella, which ends with a calm Isabella executed for the murders of both her husbands, Southerne concludes his play with a display of Isabella's madness and eventual death. In the final scene she enters *distracted, held by her Women, her Hair disheavel'd, her little Son running in before, being afraid of her* (5.4). In her madness, she stabs herself, injuring herself rather than those that have injured her. She regains her sanity long enough to die pathetically, asking only that all her husband's "wrongs" "be buried in my grave" (5.4.299), to the last accepting blame for circumstances beyond her control.

The popular fascination with she-tragedies such as *The Fatal Marriage* continued into eighteenth century and beyond. Almost every author of serious drama wrote at least one such play, and Poet Laureate Nicholas Rowe, whose greatest tragedies were written in the first decades of the eighteenth century, was to compose some of the most celebrated pictures of female pathos to appear on the English stage. While the emphasis on female suffering depicted in the pathetic play clearly conforms to patriarchal power structures in its glorification of female submission, it cannot be labeled a male phenomenon. Although some women playwrights such as Delariviére Manley and Catherine Trotter eschewed female pathos in favor of more heroic or stoic drama, others, most notably Mary Pix, did not. Plays such as Pix's *Queen Catherine: Or, the Ruins of Love* (1698) and *Ibrahim, the Thirteenth Emperor of the Turks* (1696) depend for their emotional appeal on female distress; it was Pix's *Ibrahim* which stirred Gildon to praise distress as the "true end" of tragedy. One particularly egregious case, *The Unnatural Mother* (1697) by an anonymous "Young Lady," surpasses practically all male texts in its misogyny and in the excessive anguish, both physical and emotional, it inflicts upon its female characters.

The most sensational depictions of female suffering were often achieved through the incorporation of a rape into a play's plot, a device so widespread that John Dennis labeled it "the peculiar barbarity of the *English* Stage."[20] Although rape scenes appeared in Restoration drama as early as 1662, they are particularly common after the advent of the pathetic play in the 1680s. Such scenes create an explicitly erotic spectacle as well as furnishing the suffering necessary to move the passions. The visual dynamics of rape offer a distillation of the ingredients of pathos: an innocent woman victimized by the villain's lust, compelled to suffer for a sexual crime she was forced to commit. Her fate, inevitably, is death. In addition to the requisite pathos, rape scenes also allowed playwrights to titillate their audiences with tableaux of distressed women, their torn or disordered clothing revealing breasts and legs to the audience's gaze. The suffering was both explicitly sexual and emphatically visual. Rape became such a common event in Restoration drama that Vanbrugh parodied the cliché in his comedy *The Relapse* (1696); in one scene Loveless carries the willing Berinthia off stage as she protests – "very softly" – in the style of serious drama heroines: "help, help, I'm ravished, ruined, undone."[21]

The rape in Nicholas Brady's aptly titled *The Rape: Or, the Innocent Imposters* (1692) provides a useful model of this popular form of female spectacle. Not only is the rape of an innocent and virtuous heroine the central incident of the play, but the play reiterates the ways in which rape functions as spectacle, both for the characters on stage and for the larger audience within the theatre. The play's main action involves the rape of the virtuous Eurione by the evil Genselarick, a villain whose frequently articulated lust establishes Eurione both as victim and as erotic spectacle. While the rape necessarily occurs offstage, the progress of the villain's attack is relayed to the audience by an extended description of the "shrieks" of Eurione as Genselarick completes his foul deed. Immediately after, "*the Scene draws, and discovers Eurione in an Arbour, gagg'd and bound to a Tree, her hair dishevel'd as newly Ravished, a Dagger lying by her.*"[22] Evidence of ravished womanhood such as disheveled hair, disordered clothing, and phallic dagger is a trademark of Restoration rape scenes, and Brady's emphasis on the details of Eurione's appearance demonstrates that the scene was designed for its visual appeal, creating an overtly sexual display. These details are repeated in numerous plays; one such scene is depicted in an illustration to Dryden's *Amboyna* (fig. 10). In it, the woman's violation is visually represented by her loosened or "ravished" hair, her disordered clothing (note the ungartered stocking and exposed breast), and by her helpless posture. Such set pieces, with their tableaux of the newly raped woman, were deliberately designed as erotic spectacle; the frequency with which they appear suggests that they were both popular and effective.

The impact of a rape could persist far beyond the actual moment of violation. In *The Rape*, Eurione's position as spectacle extends beyond the discovery scene while the very fact of her violation establishes her as erotic curiosity for the remainder of the play. Two scenes later, Eurione's mother presents her daughter to the collective gaze of the Goth aristocracy, as well as the theatre audience, announcing "Behold my Lords, the Ruines of your Princess!" (p. 29). Eurione herself reiterates her specific role as object of all eyes, lamenting "I cannot bear their eyes; already see / All turn and gaze, as if they saw a Monster" (p. 53). Such statements are common; like Eurione and Monimia, the heroine of *Amboyna* describes herself as a monstrous spectacle, insisting: "Look on me as thou wou'dst on some foul Leapor; and do not touch me: I am all polluted."[23] By urging characters to "look on" them and stressing their status as sexually "ruined," the heroines of these plays perpetuate their position as erotic object; through scenes such as these, playwrights encourage the audience to envision the heroine – and the actress who embodied her – as an ongoing sexual spectacle.

Figure 10 Frontispiece engraving to *Amboyna* from John Dryden's
Dramatick Works of . . . 1735

Rapes, pathos, horror, and special effects were some of the means Restoration playwrights used to provide their plays with the visual appeal which could mean the difference between a successful run and dismal failure. Although these devices all aim to thrill the theatre audience, their fate on the eighteenth-century stage was to differ radically. While revivals of spectacle-intensive plays such as Shakespeare's *The Tempest* and Shadwell's *The Lancashire Witches* appeared throughout the eighteenth century, new plays rarely included the grand displays favored by playwrights such as Settle, and soon such special effects were relegated to opera and pantomime. Horror, with its ties to topical events, had a shorter lifespan. When the political memories had faded, the scenes lost their pertinence, and the excess of blood spilled by writers such as Lee offended the taste of later generations of theatre audiences.

The emphasis on pathos which dominated serious drama of the last decades of seventeenth century was to become the most influential of the forms of spectacle described here. Unlike the cult of horror which was concentrated into the span of less than a decade, pathos not only held the stage during the later years of the Restoration but remained popular during the eighteenth and nineteenth centuries. With the introduction of sentimental comedy early in the eighteenth century, pathos, with its emphasis on the sufferings of innocent virtue, appeared in both tragedy and comedy (much to the dismay of dramatists such as Oliver Goldsmith and Richard Brinsley Sheridan). "Knocking at the hearts" of spectators, this stage effect remained emotionally powerful to generations of theatre audiences after large-scale spectacles had faded from view.

NOTES

1 Dryden himself denigrates the French mode of drama in *The Essay of Dramatic Poesy* (1668) and later in his unfinished "Heads of an Answer to Rymer" (1677). The anti-French sentiment became even more widespread after the publication of Rymer's *Short View of Tragedy* (1693). Rymer's condemnation of the English style of drama and his notorious attack on *Othello* inspired writers to vindicate Shakespeare and the English tradition. See Jean I. Marsden, *The Re-Imagined Text: Shakespeare, Adaptation, and Eighteenth-Century Literary Theory* (Lexington: University Press of Kentucky, 1995).

2 See Elizabeth Howe, *The First English Actresses: Women and Drama 1660–1700* (Cambridge University Press, 1992) for a discussion of the use of actresses in drama.

3 Sir William D'Avenant adapted *Macbeth* in 1664 while *The Tempest* was adapted in stages, first by D'Avenant and Dryden in 1667 and again in 1674 by Thomas Shadwell.

4 John Downes, *Roscius Anglicanus*, ed. Montague Summers (London: The Fortune Press, [1928]), pp. 38–89.

5 Variations on this advertisement appeared regularly. *The London Stage 1660–1800: a Calendar of Plays, Entertainments and Afterpieces Together with Casts, Box-receipts and Contemporary Comment Compiled from the Playbills, Newspapers and Theatrical Diaries of the Period*, ed. Emmett L. Avery *et al.* (Carbondale: Southern Illinois University Press, 1962–68).

6 The play was popular enough to spawn a burlesque as well as a debate over the play's extravagant language.

7 Elkanah Settle, *The Empress of Morocco* (1673), 2.1.

8 In this early play, the Dutch are depicted as sub-human barbarians who torture and rape English merchants in the Spice Islands; the mistreatment of the English is represented graphically and repeatedly.

9 John Crowne, *The Misery of Civil War* (1680), p. 36.

10 Quoted in *The Works of Nathaniel Lee*, ed. Thomas B. Stroup and Arthur L. Cooke, 2 vols. (New Brunswick, N.J.: The Scarecrow Press, 1955), II, 317.

11 Nathaniel Lee, *The Massacre of Paris*, in Ibid., 5.5.

12 Nathaniel Lee, *Caesar Borgia; Son of Pope Alexander the Sixth* in Ibid., 5.3.241.

13 Nathaniel Lee, *Lucius Junius Brutus*, ed. John Loftis (Lincoln: University of Nebraska Press, 1967), 2.216–21.

14 Aphra Behn, prologue to *The Feigned Courtesans* (1679).

15 Charles Gildon, *The Lives and Characters of the English Dramatick Poets. Also an Exact Account of all the Plays that were ever yet printed in the English Tongue; their Double Titles, the Places where Acted, the Dates when printed, and the Persons to whom Dedicated; with Remarks and Observations on most of the said Plays. First begun by Mr. Langbain, improv'd and continued down to this Time, by a Careful Hand* (1699), p. 111.

16 Nicholas Rowe, epilogue to *Jane Shore* (1714).

17 Thomas Otway, *The Orphan* in *The Works of Thomas Otway*, ed. J. C. Ghosh (Oxford: Clarendon Press, 1932), 5.468–469.

18 John Banks, *Vertue Betray'd: Or, Anna Bullen* (1682), reprinted for the Augustan Reprint Society (Los Angeles: William Andrews Clark Memorial Library, 1981), p. 74.

19 Thomas Southerne, *The Fatal Marriage: Or, the Innocent Adultery* in *The Works of Thomas Southerne*, ed. Robert Jordan and Harold Love (Oxford: Clarendon Press, 1988), 1.3.197–201.

20 John Dennis, "To Judas Iscariot, *Esq*; On the present State of the Stage" in *The Critical Works of John Dennis*, ed. Edward Niles Hooker (Baltimore: The Johns Hopkins Press, 1943), II, 166.

21 John Vanbrugh, *The Relapse: Or, Virtue in Danger*, ed. Curt A. Zimansky (Lincoln: University of Nebraska Press, 1970), 4.3.79.

22 Nicholas Brady, *The Rape: Or, the Innocent Imposters* (1692), p. 25.

23 John Dryden, *Amboyna*, in *The Works of John Dryden*, ed. H. T. Swedenberg, Jr., *et al.*, 20 vols., in progress (Berkeley: University of California Press, 1994), vol. XII, 4.5.13–14.

12

PAT GILL

Gender, sexuality, and marriage

The plots of Restoration drama begin, develop, and end in concerns about gender, sexuality, and marriage. The demarcation of masculine and feminine domains, the desire of one sex for the other, and the institutions charged with legitimizing both, become the amusing foils or dire impasses that comprise the action and envelop the characters of the plays of this era. Other cultural concerns are neither ignored nor dismissed; rather, the social, political, historical, and personal are imagined and played out primarily through this narrow dramatic focus. Gender, sexuality, and marriage emerge as comically or tragically disordered states whose permutations must be worked through in order to achieve personal goals, to consolidate families, to re-establish social order, to restore political stability, and to secure cultural cohesion. The reliance on such constricted and redundant dramatic tropes is rare if not unique in English theatrical history.

Although all of Restoration drama is preoccupied with gender, sexuality, and marriage, the comedy of manners is perhaps the most exemplary.[1] A type of drama that observes with satiric amusement the deportment, wit, and morality of contemporary society, the comedy of manners flirts with a number of developing and unresolved social tensions. In comic fashion, the plays broach and endeavor to resolve serious cultural concerns, such as the definition of gender roles, the regulation of sexual behavior, the characteristics of class, and the compatibility of marriage partners. Despite the profligate activities of their heroes, a number of whom espouse a nonchalantly libertine creed, these comedies are socially conservative. Engaging in the conventional censure of hypocrisy and fear of cuckoldry in historically specific ways, comedies of manners sketch out a new model of marriage as a witty, cultivated alliance of elegant, like-minded individuals. The balanced unions accordingly produced nonetheless firmly uphold established social hierarchies. The consolidations of the sparkling couples in the last act augur the prospect of savvy, obliging spouses who rule well-bred, refined households. The agitated insistence of social discord in the comic world of these plays serves as a caveat, however, hinting nervously at the precarious nature of this celebrated future civility.

Comedies of manners serve as eloquent testimonies that the Restoration did not restore a past way of life. Dissenting religions, increasing social mobility, the public's growing moral rigidity, and the developing ethos of business, all become satiric grist for the mill as the comedies define and distribute the possession of status, power, masculinity, and women. The alignment of stable gender roles and sexual selections, affirmed and financed by suitable marriages, generates the busy plots of these plays. The comedies describe these social phenomena in comically diminished and caricatured ways, and all characters endure playful jibes at little foibles of vanity or small follies of deportment. The hatred evoked by scheming, salacious women and the contempt elicited by fops in these plays, however, seem in excess to the threats they pose in the Restoration comedies. This excess seems to belie the always successful reduction of these characters in the dramas, suggesting perhaps that they reflect social forces not so easily managed in Restoration life. The rake-hero is on his way out as a viable social and dramatic figure, and all of his triumphs in these plays cannot stop the movement of history past him.

In contrast to comedies of manners, farces and intrigue or libertine comedies seem less concerned with gender stability, sexual control, and traditional moral standards. The vicissitudes of gender, sexuality, and marriage dominate the dramatic action, but the rapid pace of farces and continuous contrivances of intrigue comedies prevent the moral explorations pursued at times in comedies of manners and pathetic dramas. The social, economic, and familial alliances afforded by marriage implicitly ground farces and intrigue comedies, defining the stakes of the seductions, cuckoldings, incompatible partners, forced unions, and (frequently foiled) trysts that sustain their often frantic action. Intrigue comedies emphasize sexual and gender misbehavior, usually poking fun at those who hope to control or to cajole, rather than to evoke, the sexual desire of another. These plays are generally more chaotic, farcical, and risqué than manners comedies; the heroines are more compromised, the heroes less refined and secure, and the endings more morally ambiguous.

Thomas Southerne's rough and nasty *Sir Anthony Love* (1690) and Aphra Behn's *The Rover* (1677) and *Sir Patient Fancy* (1678) serve well as representative models of the cynical tenets and cursory sentiments of intrigue or libertine comedy. *Sir Anthony Love's* rapid pace, preposterous situations, and numerous shallow characters, its reliance on absurd contrivances and increasing complications, are hallmarks of this type of comedy. The titular hero, a cross-dressing, sword-fighting woman of means, thwarts and promotes a number of unions, secure in her knowledge of the venality of humankind. The play broadly and crudely satirizes social mores, and it could be argued that the remarkable Sir Anthony functions in some ways as a comic moral scourge. Like other scourges, she remains aloof from social and sexual encounters even as she directs and performs in them. She enables the man she loves to wed another, a quiet acknowledgment that her anomalous character must always remain marginal, that her unorthodox enactment of gender can never be recast to fit into the final marital scheme of things. Gender misconduct, sexual improprieties, and the business of marriage determine the plot of this fascinating play; all are satirized and all, at least tacitly, are celebrated. The intriguing title-character pricks skillfully with both sword and wit, exposing corruption while enacting it, and demanding moral conclusions while calling each into question.

Behn's plays indulge in a good deal of sexual frolic and gender playfulness as well, but unlike Southerne's play, unnatural women are those who sacrifice love for money and power, not those who have strong sexual yearnings, dress in male garb, or seem at home in masculine domains. Behn's plays observe with stinging derision the foolish actions of fops, lechers, and Whiggish businessmen, but it is forced marriages and marriages of interest that generally propel the plots of these plays. In the involved intrigues of these rollicking comedies, male and female protagonists confront and live out hard choices, often sacrificing love for financial security. In *The Town Fop* (1676), for instance, economic considerations separate and estrange young lovers, and in *The Lucky Chance* (1686) lusty young women discontentedly endure unsatisfying marriages to rich and silly old husbands. The unhappy, mismatched alliances serve as gentle rebukes to any who would forfeit true love for financial gain. The bedroom tricks, cuckoldings, and illicit rendezvous in Behn's plays depict a tawdry world in which furtive pleasures and illicit amours serve as compromised solutions to unalterable circumstances. In this harsh environment, material needs seem always at odds with passionate desires, and the amusing sexual arrangements that end the plays never quite obscure the sordid nature of the compromises. There is a grittiness in Behn's plays that cannot be found in the manners comedies of Etherege, Congreve, Wycherley, Durfey, Farquhar, and Southerne. Even for heroes and heroines life always entails numerous personal concessions and social capitulations.

Behn's distribution of gender attributes corresponds to that found in manners comedies, but the disposition of punishments and rewards for suspect female behavior differs substantially. Women who betray their loyal lovers suffer dearly for it, but those who steal, lie, and cuckold for true love escape grievous reprisals. The women in Behn's raucous comedies and farces prove sexually desirable and desiring; their virtue lies in their faithfulness to their lover, not in their chastity. The rake-heroes who populate these plays tend to be coarser and ruder than their brothers in the manners comedy. The wildly popular Willmore, the title-character of *The Rover*, for example, is a drunken lout willing to seize by rape what he cannot obtain by persuasion. The witty, virtuous heroine Hellena pursues him successfully, but at best she catches a gregarious, self-centered scoundrel who promises her neither love nor loyalty. Time and again Behn's plays couple intelligent, alluring, faithful women with affable rogues who hurt and deceive them, suggesting that this unequal and burdensome pairing is simply the gendered way of the world.

Unlike the comedies of manners, Behn's comedies do not explore definitions of proper masculinity, natural female vice, and ideal feminine virtue, but rather inquire into problems of incompatible marriages and contending claims of love and money. Not surprisingly, the plays neither suggest that women who act on their desires reveal inveterate corruption nor do they condemn out of hand women who marry for money and security rather than love. Sexual desire grounded in love explains if not justifies the illicit behavior of many of her male and female characters in the intrigue comedies, and women are no more or less culpable in their strayings than their male counterparts. The social vicissitudes of gender, such as the economic vulnerability of women, and the frequently raucous conflicts of desire, demand, and need often occupy center stage in Behn's plays, but moral distinctions based on gender difference rarely find their way into the wings.

Comedies of manners prove to be far less tolerant of fallen females. Indeed, these characters undergo some of the most scathing satire found in the plays. Even good-natured, morally lax women, Bellinda of *The Man of Mode* (1676), for example, and Mrs Fainall of William Congreve's *The Way of the World* (1700), reap the promise of dreary, strained futures at the end of their plays. In the comedies of manners, women fall into three general categories: sexually active hypocrites who scheme, betray, entrap, and deceive; naive or ignorant young women who seem potentially amenable to seduction; and charming virgins who possess wealth and wit. Vain, silly, and neglected women engage in self-debasing amorous escapades; dangerous, devious women use sex as a means to power and money; and worthy women wittily withhold. The successful heroines of these plays circumvent the illicit lures of the rake-heroes, shrewdly reserving themselves for the last-act assurance of marriage and respectability. But the closer female characters come to behaving like rakes – the more seductive their speech and duplicitous their actions – the more threatening they are to the traditional realms of masculine social and discursive power. Intelligent, sexually versed women comfortably inhabit these two masculine domains and so transgress cultural categories, calling gender and sexual boundaries into question in the process. Their dual natures as secretly fallen women, equally at home in respectable and iniquitous surroundings, provoke severe dramatic remedies. Restoration comedies of manners domesticate these cunning ladies by unmasking them, by showing them to be merely women and therefore vulnerable to public shame and scorn.

In my book *Interpreting Ladies*, I argue that these satiric moments of unmasking are structurally analogous to hostile, obscene jokes.[2] Sigmund Freud explains that an obscene narrative operates like a power play to confirm the (masculine) tellers as subjects in control and to fix the objects or butts of the jest in a passive (feminine) position.[3] The satire in Restoration comedies functions precisely in this gendered manner – it links masculinity with discursive and sexual prowess and femininity with linguistic and sexual vulnerability. Those women who trespass far into masculine cultural domains are generally forcibly returned to their "proper" feminine spheres. Publicly exposed and humiliated, their most private secrets revealed for all the amused onlookers to see, these women are quite literally ob-scene by the end of the play, exiting in a huff, vowing empty threats of revenge. Often the final pairing of the heroine and hero rises from the ashes of the degraded remains of the publicly denounced hypocrite, so that the culminating moments of the plays include the fall of one woman and the rise of the next.

In the witty, fast-paced discursive romp of Restoration comic satire, the ridicule and exposure of sexualized females reflect a concern with what has now come to be called gender identity. That these artful women are depicted as *naturally* debased reflects the dramas' failure to resolve this concern conclusively. The tacit assessment of women found in the comedy of manners is a resoundingly poor one. Although the heroines shine in these plays, their exemplary and fabulous natures stand in stark contrast to those of women with feet of clay. These latter characters, often enterprising hypocrites determined to get what they feel to be a fair share of pleasure and power, never earn the narratives' sympathy. They are always returned to their proper subordinate place, and the challenge they pose to masculine authority is decisively squelched.

The plays never harp or hammer, however, and it is only on closer inspection that the antagonism and insistence of the satiric assaults on defiant women seem excessive. Nonetheless, when looked at a little more closely, these satiric assaults reveal a significant confusion, even a contradiction, in the plays' dramatized understandings of the social nature of gender. The plays suggest that the Olivias, Loveits, Cockwoods, Touchwoods, and Marwoods of their dramatic worlds behave both as unfeminine, masculinized deviants and as typical women, untrustworthy and promiscuous. Yet the contradiction implicit in characters who both do and don't behave as their gender seems to demand raises the question of what constitutes this proper place.

In general, comedies of manners introduce an amiable rake-hero, disclose his past or present sexual intrigues, and then bring on a heroine who wins his heart with her beauty, wit, and verve, and his hand with her breeding, money, and honesty. Obstacles appear to this happy merger of course, usually in the form of obdurate parents or inconvenient pre-engagements. The clever machinations and remarkable contrivances devised by the rake-hero to remove these obstacles comprise the principal dramatic action, interrupted and complicated by one or two farcical subplots that either assist or complement the rake's progress. The comedies end in the promise of a witty marriage between the rich young beauty and the heretofore resolutely single rake-hero, a marriage of intellectual equals whose guarded admissions to one another seem to suggest genuine affection. Although irreverent and pleasure-seeking, the rakish protagonist nonetheless betrays a clear preference for the established class dictates and customary social decorum embodied in the heroine. If he is a Hobbesian "natural man," he is one whose nature is thoroughly refined by arch reworkings of conventional cultural mores, and whose elegant discourse is underwritten by accepted social codes.[4]

Before his implied reformation in the last act, a rake-hero lies without remorse as he assiduously pursues his desires. An experienced gallant whose pride rivals his passion, the rake-hero not only succeeds in winning the lovely heiress but also often manages to settle old scores and resolve his friends' amorous dilemmas. The conventional (double) standard that celebrates feminine chastity applauds a masculine virtue of quite another sort. An accomplished rake-hero makes assignations, breaks hearts, and converses amiably with equal ease. He seduces women with dazzling self-assurance, enticing some into bed and others to help him, wittingly or unintentionally, with his schemes. The prototype of this beguiling character, the witty, seductive Dorimant of Sir George Etherege's *The Man of Mode*, lives an entertaining life comprised of social diversions and private, illicit entertainments. As cruel and vain as he is charming, he glibly seduces and abandons women who unwisely engage with him on his own terms. For Dorimant, as for his rake successors, the discursive way of the world is masculine and predatory. Ardent testimony of future devotion is the rake's customary means to an immediate, circumscribed end. "Think on your oaths, your vows and protestations, perjured man" (2.2.224–25), an outraged Mrs Loveit demands of Dorimant:

> *Dorimant*: I made 'em when I was in love.
> *Mrs. Loveit*: And therefore ought they not to bind? Oh impious!
> *Dorimant*: What we swear at such a time may be a certain proof of present passion, but to say truth, in love there is no security to be given for the future. (2.2.226–31)

Dorimant's cruel explanation mortifies Loveit and seduces her best friend Bellinda at the same time. One of the remarkable properties of rakes' seductive discourse is its power to divide and conquer women. The degradation of one lover serves to raise the hopes and flatter the vanity of the next. Although Dorimant's professions of love do not differ in form or content from one conquest to the next, they nonetheless make each addressee believe she is special, unlike all the others who went before. Three acts later, a sadder but wiser Bellinda ruefully asks, "Do all men break their words thus?" "Th'extravagant words they speak in love" Dorimant acknowledges, adding, "'tis as unreasonable to expect we should perform all we promise then, as do all we threaten when we are angry – " (5.2.334–37).[5] Dorimant's considerable charms distract Bellinda from the perfectly obvious. She recognizes her consecutive relation to the cast off Mrs Loveit only after Dorimant's diminished interest makes her position as sexual conquest clear to her.

Rake-heroes' facile manipulation of seductive language undoes a number of gullible women in Restoration plays. Yet heroines of these comedies cannot simply be the opposite of the seduced women. The latter reject advances because they are wise to the heroes' charms or oblivious to their virility. By contrast, a heroine distinguishes herself from silly or fallen women by her skillful admission of the rake's declaration of love and simultaneous deflection of its damaging force. She is good at verbal thrust and parry, but her special proficiency is in ingeniously reserving both her personal affirmation and her person, two exercises in negative action that her fallen sisters never master. The delightful heroine Harriet of *The Man of Mode* teases and adroitly mimics the rake-hero Dorimant, acknowledging through her sly imitations her deep appreciation of his seductive power. Although animated and inventive, Harriet never deviates a hairsbreadth from the rules of decorum or the wishes of her mother. At the close of the play, this dutiful daughter prepares to return to the country with that vigilant matriarch, refusing to admit her inclination for Dorimant until he has made a public profession of his own. Unlike any woman he has met before, Harriet never lets down her guard. She captures him with her stunning self-possession, her beguiling scruples, and her witty propriety.

> *Dorimant*: To be with you I could live there: and never send one thought to London.
>
> *Harriet*: Whate'er you say, I know all beyond High Park's a desert to you, and that no gallantry can draw you farther.
>
> *Dorimant:* That has been the utmost limit of my love – but now my passion knows no bounds, and there's no measure to be taken of what I'll do from anything I ever did before.
>
> *Harriet:* When I hear you talk thus in Hampshire, I shall begin to think there may be some little truth enlarged upon.   (5.2.162–73)

Some critics regard the heroine as the lesser half of the hero, as a fitting partner who shares, although always to a slighter degree, the rake-hero's witty perceptions, skepticism, libertine attitudes, and "naturalistic" tendencies, while other writers point to the heroine's many orthodox qualities and the hero's appreciation of them.[6] The heroines in these plays may be cagey and enticing, but they are never conclusively duplicitous or impure. They are always technically "honest," the term punningly carrying the full weight of its two meanings, truthful and chaste. The easy, provocative interchanges between the heroes and these canny virgins tease but do not seriously dispute the orthodox moral and social considerations on which their attraction is based. Ideal embodiments of proper social form, heroines are lively, decorous, and decent, and the heroes finds them irresistible. Their intended marriage in the final act, however playfully conveyed, sketches out a social order based on class affiliation, sanctioned by proper gender roles, and maintained by regulated heterosexual desire.

Heroines of these urbane comedies combine verbal sophistication with sexual innocence. Although a heroine deftly take parts in repartee and appears uncannily attuned to the workings of the world in which she lives, her dramatic position is surprisingly static. While other characters frantically scheme, manipulate, and submit, she remains collected and often inactive. Like Penelope, a Restoration heroine conducts herself and manages others with exquisite circumspection. In some cases, her tantalizing noncommittal allows others foolishly to think themselves favored by her, and while she may allow their mistaken notions to proceed unchecked to further her own aims, she never obligates herself in any way. Her refusal to commit herself by word or deed often invites misinterpretation, but it keeps her free not only from the corrupt machinations but also from the corrupting deliberations around her. Imprudent conversation can prove as dangerous as incautious associations to a heroine. A Restoration manners heroine walks a fine linguistic line: she engages in provocative banter but never indecorous innuendo. "Criminal conversation" is a Restoration term for adultery, and the implicit puns on conversation and honesty in manners comedy repeatedly link verbal activities to sexual ones.[7] Indeed, one indication of a woman's fallen, hardened nature is her dexterity in the false rhetoric of love.

The "virtuous gang" in William Wycherley's *The Country Wife* (1675) perfectly illustrate the debased nature of women whose linguistic duplicity matches that of rakes, while Olivia in Wycherley's *The Plain-Dealer* (1676) reveals with cold precision the dangerous power and influence of a woman skilled in seductive language. These dishonest females divorce the notion of honor from any moral reference; honor collapses into reputation, and reputation suffers not from private iniquity but from public indiscretion. In a marvelous syllogism, Lady Fidget of *The Country Wife* argues that adultery with a private citizen is not a crime. A man who is not a gentleman, she reasons blithely, lacks the attributes of procured status or noble birth necessary to harm women of quality. In this self-justifying formula, the woman's higher social status negates her illicit amour with a common man. "'Tis not an injury to a husband till it be an injury to our honours," Lady Fidget explains, "so that a woman of honour loses no honour with a private person" (2.1.456–59).[8] Rectitude and honesty have no place in Lady Fidget's resourceful but specious interpretation of honor. She and her virtuous gang manipulate terms to their own social advantage and sexual pleasure, and while their spunky inventiveness might be vindicated if not esteemed in the twentieth century, it is soundly satirized in the seventeenth. In a clearly gender-determined dramatic convention, the sexual bravado and amorous guile of rake-heroes become sexual rapaciousness and hypocrisy in women.

The stunningly businesslike Olivia of *The Plain-Dealer* endures a far more stringent reproof than her droll sisters above. Expertly juggling a diverse assortment of men, she flatters them by mirroring back their every opinion, procuring their money and jewels with seasoned ease. Learning too late of his ill-use, the fop Novel laments that Olivia "stands in the drawing room like the glass, ready for all comers to set their gallantry by her, and, like the glass too, lets no man go from her unsatisfied with himself" (4.2.112–15).[9] Revealing his susceptibility to this flattering mirror, Manly, the eponymous hero of the play, tells a friend that Olivia's

> tongue, as well as face, ne'er knew artifice; nor ever did her words or looks contradict her heart. She is all truth and hates the lying, masking, daubing world as I do, for which I love her and for which I think she dislikes not me. For she has often shut out of her conversation for mine the gaudy, fluttering parrots of the town, apes and echoes of men only, and refused their common-

place pert chat, flattery and submissions, to be entertained with my sullen
bluntness and honest love"   (1.1.653–60).

This encomium reveals not only the depth of Manly's misapprehension, but
also the criteria of a proper consort, criteria embodied in the bemused,
dedicated heroine Fidelia. Although *The Plain-Dealer* heartily mocks
Manley's stubborn conviction and faulty judgments, it wholeheartedly
reaffirms the value of his ideals. Olivia's deceitful simulation of these ideal
traits clearly makes her a monstrous and menacing character. Recounting
her counterfeited reverence of Manley, the wily deceiver merrily reveals her
base nature, confessing conspiratorially to her two foppish devotees: "I
knew he loved his own singular moroseness so well as to dote upon a copy
of it; wherefore I feigned an hatred to the world too that he might love me
in earnest" (4.2.250–53). Like Horner of *The Country Wife*, Olivia uses
art and affectation masterfully; unlike that artful poseur, however, she is
brutally exposed and punished.

Manly makes out quite well at the end of *The Plain-Dealer*. His chagrin
and disgrace are redeemed at face value as the lovely Olivia's mocking
reflection of Manly turns back on itself. In a near-literal equivalent of being
caught with her pants down, Olivia is apprehended in her private chambers, rudely exposed before all as a cheat and fraud. Olivia's dismayed cry
of "What means this!" quickly gives way to her unhappy admission: "Oh,
'tis too sure, as well as my shame! which I'll go hide forever" (5.3.89–90).
Unmasked and figuratively naked before all, she banishes herself from the
jeering company. The solicitous and virtuous Fidelia is ready to fill the
vacancy, eagerly offering Manly a fresh self-image, along with her estate,
her family's status, her virtue, and her agreeable reflection of his honest
ways. As she surrenders all she owns to Manly, she tells him that she had
abandoned her affluent life and "multitudes of pretenders" in order to
pursue his love. "I left," she explains, "to follow you, sir, having in several
public places seen you and observed your actions thoroughly, with admiration, when you were too much in love to take notice of mine, which yet
was but too visible" (5.3.173–82). Fidelia's adoring speech restores Manly
fully; he is resurrected through and in her eyes as his original self.

The enigmatic Angelica enacts just such a Fidelia-like redemptive man-
euver in the final act of *Love for Love* (1695). Before ridiculing Sir
Sampson Legend for his ludicrous pretensions to her hand, she tells his
astounded son Valentine: "Had I the World to give you, it cou'd not make
worthy of so generous and faithful a Passion: here's my Hand, my Heart
was always yours, and struggl'd very hard to make this utmost Trial of
your Virtue" (5.1.608–10).[10] In one quick summation, Valentine's an-

guished and uncertain performance as a lover and a man has been ratified and rewarded. Angelica's coolly distant and disdainful air converts to honeyed compliance. Rather gratuitously instructing the already chastened Sir Sampson, Angelica tells him: "Learn to be a good Father, or you'll never get a second Wife. I always lov'd your Son, and hated your unforgiving Nature. I was resolv'd to try him to the utmost; I have try'd you too, and know you both. You have not more Faults than he has Virtues; and 'tis hardly more Pleasure to me, that I can make him and myself happy, than that I can punish you" (5.1.622–27).

The last-act self-revelations of Fidelia and Angelica complement the forced exposures of the fallen women. Unlike a number of heroines in the comedies of manners, these two women actively engage in amending the ways of their world. This unusually energetic activity is explained as self-protective facades, ruses to stave off the moral dangers of a corrupt world. As a cross-dressed cabin boy, Fidelia seemed quite at ease as the sardonically perceptive commentator on the sexual and moral foibles of humankind, an attitude and knowledge she seems to shed, however, with her masculine dress. Angelica's nonchalant comportment as the cruel teaser of Valentine and sarcastic taunter of her silly elders transforms into a compelled charade as she dissolves into sweet submission in the final lines. Although the metamorphoses take Manly and Valentine by surprise, the narratives take care to show that these put-upon heroes are men of substance who deserve this favorable turn of events. The timely reversals of fortunes that unite heroes to their heroines re-establish proper gender and sexual hierarchies and consolidate all with the pledge of marriage.

The dramatic interest in the gender protocol and sexual activities of women reflects a more pressing dramatic concern with the gender protocol and sexual prerogatives of men. In the comedies of manners, real rakes don't do business, they don't become salacious old men, and they don't eat quiche. Manly of *The Plain-Dealer* and Mirabel of *The Way of the World* equate their concern about and disapproval of their lovers' willingness to receive fops and fools with the conviction that those casual associations serve as unflattering reflections on the heroes themselves. Reviling the effeminate dress and manner of Olivia's two suitors, an infuriated Manly proclaims, "I take not your contempt of me worse than your esteem or civility for these things here" (2.1.631–33). In response to Fainall's question "Are you jealous as often as you see Witwoud entertained by Millamant?" a peevish Mirabel replies, "Of her understanding I am, if not her person" (1.1.616–64).[11] Heroines perform important identificatory services for heroes, mirroring back heroes' flattering sense of themselves and refracting the notice of fools. As Olivia in *The Plain-Dealer* demonstrates cogently, the results of an awry reflection can be devastating, at least temporarily, for the hero.

Comedies of manners defend an ideal of aristocratic, urbane English masculinity. The menaces to this standard include not only conniving, competent women, but also Frenchified fops, rich, libidinous old men, and aspiring businessmen. The comedies work in very obvious ways to feminize this socially-ominous triad of young fops, old lechers, and greedy businessmen. Rake-heroes distinguish themselves from all three. The fit composite of aristocratic composure and manly virility, the hero sets his identity against these fatuous contenders and fixes it securely in the admiration of a worthy young heroine. It is the heroine who authenticates the hero; her attraction to him indicates his preeminence over the fops and lechers who mimic him and the businessmen who find making money more rewarding than making love.

Unwittingly complicitous in their own exposure, these silly characters court sexual ripostes that disclose their various incapacities. Their absurd self-promotion suggests that their undoing is well-earned. Fops inadvertently reveal the inadequacy of their sexual performance, the fictional status of their alleged intrigues, or the (disease-generated) flagging of their sexual desire. In like fashion, lechers fall into comic traps that lay bare their unseemly desires either by foiling their plans, leaving the old fools bitterly unsatisfied, or by fulfilling them in an unwanted and humiliating manner. In the pattern of the obscene joke, with the disclosure of inadequate masculinity, the victims' sexual organs are metaphorically unveiled and again, like those of women, found to be lacking or in some way smaller and less potent than those of real men. Manners comedy emasculates all these fools; it ridicules, exposes, and deforms, simultaneously making the clever hero appear discerning and sexually powerful.

The incompetent, misguided follies of these substandard males comically complement the confident, aggressive sexual and social assays of defective females – those hypocritical and depraved ladies of fashion, lascivious elderly matrons, and loose, litigious widows who behave in inappropriately masculine ways. Like these women, fops, lechers, and businessmen are also ridiculed and discredited. Lacking the winning traits of the heroes, these characters haplessly demonstrate their unflattering kinship to those discontented women, proving themselves in the process to be either inferior or disreputable. Their own puerility obscures the spectators' recognition of the overdetermined hostility of these comic attacks. Both the excesses of aggressive women and the deficiencies of inadequate men represent imitations of attitudes celebrated in the rake-hero's refined manhood; both are doomed to fail; and for both the cost of humiliating failure is high. That the plays consistently introduce and then link the three male types – fops, old lechers, and businessmen – aligning them with feminine traits while contrasting them to aggressive women, attest to the strain the male trio places on traditional definitions of masculine behavior.

In demonstrating the hero's overall superiority, *The Man of Mode*, for instance, takes pains to illustrate the contrasting deficiencies of the lecherous Old Bellair as well as those of the foolish Sir Fopling, and Congreve's *Love for Love* unfolds in detail the misbegotten delusions of potent appeal harbored by Sir Sampson Legend. Flawed versions of the rake-heroes, fops and lechers attempt clumsy imitations of rakish seductions that almost always end in their own embarrassment. Like those bad imitators, businessmen too are routinely unmasked and disgraced. Having sacrificed their "natural" masculine appetites to economic enterprise, businessmen prove themselves to be money-grubbing fools who deserve to be cozened and cuckolded.

In Wycherley's *The Country Wife*, Sir Jaspar Fidget recruits the presumably impotent Horner to escort Lady Fidget and her friends about the town. Always too busy to attend to his wife himself, Sir Jaspar allows his keen interest in business to blind him to the sexual cravings and activities of his spouse. In the infamous china scene, as Sir Jaspar unwittingly hands over his wife to Horner for an amorous interlude, the irrepressible Horner pretends general annoyance with such cooperative husbands:

> A pox! can't you keep your impertinent wives at home? Some men are troubled with the husbands, but I with the wives; but I'd have you to know, since I cannot be your journeyman by night, I will not be your drudge by day, to squire your wife about, and be your man of straw, or scarecrow only to pies and jays, that would be nibbling at your forbidden fruit.   (4.3.)[12]

Horner's feigned indignation conveys a real warning. Men whose primary concerns lie elsewhere than the tending of their most valuable possessions will earn the consequences of this misapplied regard, either by marrying or creating wives who dissemble and betray.

Counterpoints to businessman, fops serve as another unacceptable masculine alternative that must be defeated by the superior intelligence and clever rhetoric of rake-heroes by the time the play is over. As satiric portrayals of overtly feminized masculine behavior, fops indicate a particular historical anxiety about the traditional definition of masculinity, an anxiety concomitant with the rise of the bourgeois class and the expanding prospect of social mobility. Restoration life seems to have provided opportunities for a more fluid sexuality than its comedies approve of or allow.[13] The fops who preen and parade across Restoration stages are not depicted as homosexual, if by that one means sexually attracted to members of the same sex. They are not portrayed as heterosexual either, if by that one means sexually attracted to members of the opposite sex. They *are* heterosexual threats, however. The threat lies in their ability to attract and marry backward, silly, and pretentious women of great fortunes, thereby depriving the rake-heroes – the representatives of appropriate English masculinity – of opportunities for securing financial maintenance. Although a comic business, marriage is an important social and economic matter in Restoration plays, as it was in Restoration life, and the potential marital success of fops both affronts and imputes established notions of heterosexual interactions.

The unrelentingly derisive onslaught against fops in manners comedy can be attributed to the very real peril fops pose in relation to the consolidation of masculine characteristics. At issue is the composition of an authentic English male, a composition determined by elegant dress, cultured demeanor, true wit, and libertine social philosophy, characteristics fops affect if not fathom. When the maid Pert in *The Man of Mode* defends Fopling on the grounds that he is just as handsome and as great a gallant as Dorimant, Mrs Loveit impatiently rejects the comparison. Loveit knows full well that Fopling is not equal to Dorimant, but she also recognizes that for some, he's close enough. While it seems clear that the hero is far superior to these other men, there is a nagging insistence about this apparent superiority that belies the confident characterization. Dorimant can still be jealous of a fool like Fopling. Although unquestionably comic inferiors, these characters possess a menacing social potency that the plays are careful first to establish and then to defuse. It is no accident that Dorimant insists that Loveit publicly denounce and humiliate Sir Fopling.

Fops may not particularly care for women, but they understand them. Like women, fops like to gossip, primp, and play cards. And significantly, fops' ability to speak beguilingly to certain credulous young women can rob expectant beaus of great fortunes. In Congreve's *Love for Love*, the provincial Miss Prue strays rather quickly from the path of virtue, aided by the step-by-step directions of delicate fop Tattle. "All well-bred Persons Lie," Tattle explains to this eager trail blazer:

> Besides, you are a Woman; you must never speak what you think; Your words must contradict your thoughts; but your Actions may contradict your words. So, when I ask you if you can Love me, you must say no, but you must Love me too. If I tell you are Handsome, you must deny it, and say I flatter you. But you must think yourself more Charming than I speak you, and like me for the Beauty which I say you have as much as if I had it myself. If I ask you to Kiss me, you must be angry, but you must not refuse me. If I ask you for

more, you must be more angry – but more complying; and as soon as ever I make you say you'll cry out, you must be sure to hold your Tongue.

(2.1.663–76)

In this disquisition, women are obliged at all times to conform to the code of pretense, a code with which Tattle seems perfectly at home. If one rigorously follows Tattle's guidelines, no amorous affirmation should be taken at face value and no sexual check complied with.

Later, further abetting her fall into knowledge, Tattle asks Miss Prue, "And won't you show me, pretty Miss, where your Bed-Chamber is?" (702–03):

> *Miss Prue*: No, indeed won't I: but I'll run there, and hide myself from you behind the Curtains.
> *Tattle*: I'll follow you.
> *Miss Prue*: Ah, but I'll hold the Door with both Hands, and be angry – and you shall push me down before you come in.
> *Tattle*: No, I'll come in first, and push you down afterwards.
> *Miss Prue*: Will you? Then I'll be more angry, and more complying.
> *Tattle*: Then I'll make you cry out.
> *Miss Prue*: Oh, but you shan't, for I'll hold my Tongue. (2.1.704–16)

Tattle's lesson inculcates in Miss Prue the one absolute of feminine discourse: a woman can never mean "no." All the women in the play live by this maxim and use it in more or less skillful ways to get what they want. Miss Prue is delighted to find that she can indicate her sexual willingness while denying it, that she is relieved of verbal compliance and, hence, moral responsibility. Tattle reads Miss Prue perfectly; he knows how to cajole and to illustrate, and his extravagant manner tempts and delights her. More to the point, he seems not only to approve but to practice precisely the same coy, immoral relations he rehearses for this avid sexual tyro. An easy and effective tutor, Tattle acts quickly to test Miss Prue's rote understanding of this doctrine of feminine compliance. Tattle is both too like a successful rake and too like a hypocritical prude. His comfortable residence in both gender categories makes him a disturbing gender anomaly. Although punished at the end of the play – he is tricked into marrying his counterpart, the scheming, aggressively licentious, and poor Mrs Frail – his seductive skill is neither undone nor contained.

In play after play in late seventeenth-century comedy, fops serve as both comic foils and sexual threats to the rake's progress. They never succeed against the rake, but they are not amateurs in country matters. Their effeminate, Frenchified behavior affords them an access to women that the rakes (and, through them, the plays themselves) disdain but nonetheless seem jealous of and worried about. The heroes' utter conviction in their own superior understandings neither eclipses nor appeases their apprehensions of women's negligent tolerance of these affected blockheads. The extraordinary capacity of fops to disconcert testifies to a deep-seated unease that is never completely assuaged by the acquisition of the heroine or by embarrassing the coxcomb, an unease that derives from fundamental questions about proper masculine conduct, natural (that is, normative) sexual relations, and established social dogma.

Although I have concentrated on comedies in discussing gender, sexuality and marriage, heroic and pathetic dramas are equally attentive to these issues.[14] Shifting gender definitions, complicated or deviant sexual entanglements, and unhappy or unsuitable marriages function dramatically as causes, means, and results in these plays. They become metaphors for, as well as the consequence of, political turmoil, social unrest, and moral confusion. In the overwrought dramas of Thomas Otway and Nathaniel Lee especially, male siblings and patriarchs struggle among themselves for the sexual possession of women who are, or are comparable to, sisters and daughters. Sexual obsessions undermine potent leadership and explode familial boundaries. Male rivalries that always end in bloodshed pit brothers, fathers, and friends in battles that cause social and state upheaval. Marriage serves to inflame rather than quench illicit desires. Passionate testimonies of trust and fondness collapse into ecstatic avowals of enmity, generating unspoken and unresolved erotic tensions. The flip side of the polished, carefully tempered, and wittily circumscribed clarifications of gender, sexuality, and marriage in manners comedies, pathetic dramas relate what happens when clarification ceases, when gender roles shift or breakdown, and when sexual desire runs amok.

In Restoration drama, questions of gender, sexuality, and marriage generate the narrative action; issues of gender, sexuality, and marriage inform the subtext; and solutions proposed in terms of gender, sexuality, and marriage comprise the outcomes. The plays dramatize contests over the control and meaning of these terms and categories, a contest all the more significant because of circumstances beyond the control of the dramatic action: the historical interplay between a refined social realm and a newly developing bourgeois sphere informed in part by sentimental apprehensions and private moral convictions. As the brittle, irreverent, and promiscuous comedies give way to dramas exploring the effects of conscience and moral convictions, the relation of gender, sexuality, and marriage is reconfigured and the categories are revised.[15] The banter and appeal of a witty, well-meaning beauty seem more the stuff of tragedy than comedy as the eighteenth century begins, leading not to marriage but disgrace and death, as in Nicholas Rowe's *The Tragedy of Jane Shore* (1714). The dissolute conduct of a staunch libertine begets equally debauched behavior in his wife, as a morally upright, clever younger brother wins the hand of a somewhat silly but amiable young woman, revealing in the process the true qualities necessary to be a tender husband in Richard Steele's play of that name. Sophisticated, amusing intercourse and liberal exchanges among men and women who value style and status make an encore appearance in John Gay's splendid satiric comedy, *The Beggar's Opera* (1728), where highwaymen and prisoners, prostitutes and jailer's daughters, ape their betters in language and appearance, thoroughly mocking and degrading the hackneyed, clearly unacceptable principles they espouse. As the Restoration comes to an end, the rake-hero becomes the foil of kinder, gentler males who succeed by moral persuasion, and the sharp, seductive heroine succumbs to repentant or innocent distress, or hardens into depravity.

NOTES

1 The accuracy or validity of the category "comedy of manners" has been disputed by some, but I find Arthur M. Scouten's definitional distinction still quite useful. See Scouten's "Notes toward a History of Restoration Comedy," *PQ*, 45.1 (January 1966), 62–70. For a forceful argument against this grouping of the comedies, see Robert Hume, *The Development of English Drama in the Late Seventeenth Century* (Oxford: Clarendon Press, 1976), pp. 32–62.

2 *Interpreting Ladies: Women, Wit, and Morality in the Restoration Comedy of Manners* (Athens: University of Georgia Press, 1994). This book provides further elaborations of the ways in which particular comedies use satire to expose, humiliate, and privilege characters.

3 Sigmund Freud, *Jokes and Their Relation to the Unconscious*, trans. and ed. James Strachey (New York: Norton: 1960), pp. 140–58.

4 Thomas Fujimura in *The Restoration Comedy of Wit* (Princeton University Press, 1952) first introduced the Hobbesian notions of naturalism, skepticism, and wit into the discussion of Restoration drama, arguing that the keenly witty, libertine rake-hero embodied Hobbesian principles of human behavior.

5 This and all subsequent references to the text are taken from *The Man of Mode*, in *The Plays of Sir George Etherege*, ed. Michael Cordner (Cambridge University Press, 1982).

6 For differing accounts of the characteristics of the heroine, see R. C. Sharma, *Themes and Conventions in the Comedy of Manners* (New Delhi: Asia Publishing House, 1965); Virginia Ogden Birdsall, *Wild Civility: the English Comic Spirit on the Restoration Stage* (Bloomington: Indiana University Press, 1971); Donald Bruce, *Topics of Restoration Comedy* (New York: St. Martin's Press, 1974); and Harold Weber, *The Restoration Rake-Hero: Transformations in Sexual Understanding in Seventeenth-Century England* (Madison: University of Wisconsin Press, 1986).

7 For a brief delineation of the sexual connotations of the terms "honesty" and "conversation," see the *Oxford English Dictionary* (Oxford University Press, 1979).

8 William Wycherley, *The Country Wife*, *The Plays of William Wycherley*, ed. Peter Holland (Cambridge University Press, 1981).

9 This and all subsequent references to the text are taken from *The Plain-Dealer*, *The Plays of William Wycherley*.

10 This and all subsequent references to the text are taken from *Love for Love*, *The Comedies of William Congreve*, ed. Anthony G. Henderson (Cambridge University Press, 1982).

11 *The Way of the World*, *The Comedies of William Congreve*.

12 *The Country Wife*, *The Plays of William Wycherley*.

13 Kristina Straub, *Sexual Suspects: Eighteenth-Century Players and Sexual Ideology* (Princeton University Press, 1992) analyzes how public perceptions of the immorality of actors and actresses influenced gender expectations in the eighteenth century.

14 See chapter 11, above.

15 See Straub, *Sexual Suspects*.

13

MICHAEL CORDNER

Playright versus priest: profanity and the wit of Restoration comedy

A controversy which erupted in the final years of the seventeenth century threatened the survival of theatre in England. At its peak, the poet laureate, Nahum Tate, drew up "A Proposal for Regulating the Stage & Stage-Players," describing it as "valuable only in case it is decided not to suppress the theatres entirely." A character in George Farquhar's novel, *Adventures of Covent-Garden* (1698), similarly predicted that "in the Battel between the Church and the Stage" "the *Theatre* must down."[1] Such grim prophecies recalled the playhouses' mid-century fate, when a parliamentary edict in 1642 had heralded an eighteen-year ban on theatrical performances.

The attack which gave impetus to this new campaign – Jeremy Collier's *A Short View of the Immorality, and Profaneness of the English Stage* (1698) – was the first book-length assault on the theatre by an English author to be published since William Prynne's infamous *Histriomastix* (1633). Pro-stage writers quickly dubbed Collier a "Younger *Histrio-Mastix*"[2] and asserted that the drama's old enemies were once again venturing into the daylight. Propagandists for the post-1660 playhouses were adept at associating anti-stage invective with insurrection and regicide, citing as proof the undeniable fact that the Parliament which closed the playhouses had also executed Charles I. Collier's recent escapades lent credence to the accusation. He was a nonjuring clergyman – that is, one who, after James II's loss of his throne in the 1688 Revolution, refused to acknowledge the legitimacy of the monarchy of William III and Mary. He wrote against the new régime, was twice imprisoned for his opposition to it, and in 1696 granted absolution on the scaffold to men condemned to death for complicity in a plot to assassinate William. His action implied that the deed for which they were to suffer was no sin. As a consequence he was outlawed. Thomas Tenison, Archbishop of Canterbury, condemned his behavior as "highly schismatical and seditious, dangerous both to the church and state, and contrary to the true doctrine and spirit of the

Christian religion."[3] The claim that anti-theatricalism and regicide went hand in hand seemed once more to have been vindicated.

Collier's attack on the stage, however, proved popular and went through four editions in a year and a half. According to John Oldmixon, it "with many aton'd for the Crime he had been guilty of, in giving Absolution to impenitent Traytors; the religious part of the Town cry'd it up, and some of the wealthy ones rewarded him."[4] Those wooed into altering their judgment of Collier included that same Thomas Tenison, Archbishop of Canterbury, who had earlier denounced him, but who now sent him a public letter of congratulation. More remarkably still, William III himself granted Collier a nolle prosequi, which rendered him immune from further prosecution for his past offense.[5] This astonishing alliance between erstwhile foes made clear the formidable nature of the forces massing against the playhouse.

The task of the stage's defenders was rendered more difficult by the tactics Collier adopted. Earlier anti-theatrical pamphleteering had employed very broad brush-strokes. The actor might, for instance, be denounced as "the Devils Factor, that by a strange delusion sends men laughing to hell" and the theatres characterized as places where men "*sport themselves to hear the* Vassals of the Devil *scoffing* religion, & blasphemously *abusing phrases of holy* Scripture *on their* stages, *as familiarly as they use their* Tobacco-pipes *in their* bibing-houses."[6] But specific examples of the malpractices the players allegedly committed were almost never provided. Collier transformed that situation. By packing the *Short View* with carefully selected quotations from recent plays, he provided plentiful chapter and verse in a field where generalized assertion had previously been the norm. He was well aware of the strength of his chosen strategy and rebuked those who replied to him, if they proved unwilling, or unable, to match him in the closeness of his attention to particular passages of dialogue.

Whatever his tactical innovations, Collier was swimming with the tide in mounting an attack on the contemporary drama. The early to mid-1690s produced a rich crop of anti-theatrical invective. In 1694, James Wright argued that "Plays should be (and have always been in the best Reform'd and most Civilized Times) Moral Representations, but now most of our New Comedies are become the very Pictures of Immorality." Sir Richard Blackmore charged the playwrights with abandoning the drama's traditional duty to praise virtue and discountenance vice: "The Stage was an Outwork or Fort rais'd for the Protection and Security of the Temple; but the Poets that kept it have revolted and basely betray'd it, and, what is worse, have turn'd all their *Force* and discharg'd all their *Artillery* against the Place their Duty was to defend."[7] Such views were also echoed by men in authority. In a crucially influential sermon, John Tillotson, Tenison's predecessor as Archbishop of Canterbury, pronounced a fierce anathema on the contemporary drama:

> as the Stage now is, they [i.e. plays] are intolerable, and not fit to be permitted in a *civilized*, much less in a *Christian* Nation. They do most notoriously minister both to infidelity and vice. By the prophaneness of them, they are apt to instill bad Principles into the Minds of Men, and to lessen the awe and reverence which all Men ought to have for God and Religion: and by their lewdness they teach vice, and are apt to infect the minds of Men, and dispose them to lewd and dissolute Practices.
>
> And therefore I do not see how any Person pretending to Sobriety and Virtue, and especially to the pure and holy Religion of our blessed Saviour, can without great guilt, and open contradiction to his holy Profession, be present at such lewd and immodest plays, much less frequent them, as too many do, who yet would take it very ill to be shut out of the Communion of Christians, as they would most certainly have been in the first and purest Ages of Christianity.[8]

This unyielding statement was often cited during the subsequent controversy. Anti-theatrical campaigners even organized the reprinting of the relevant paragraphs and their distribution "among Ladies of Quality, &c."[9]

Tillotson explained that he had taken up his theme "in compliance with their Majesties pious Proclamation, for the discountenancing and suppressing of Prophaneness and Vice."[10] As early as February 1689, William made clear his attachment to "a General Reformation of the Lives and Manners of all Our Subjects, as being that which must Establish Our Throne, and Secure to Our People Religion, Happiness and Peace."[11] Tony Claydon has recently documented the concerted propaganda effort which was mounted to link the new régime with ideas of godly rule and a rigorous reformation of manners. Ecclesiastical promotion came swiftly to clerics, including Tillotson, who, before 1688, had specialized in "jeremiads" analyzing "England as a nation falling deeper and deeper into sin."[12]

From the early Restoration, a potent strain of pulpit oratory had been obsessed with "the pathology of national piety." A state church which celebrated God's mercy as evidenced in the return of the monarchy in 1660 was inevitably perturbed by the speed with which the promises of spiritual amendment made at the Restoration in gratitude for that mercy had been discarded. In the eyes of the clergy the England of Charles II was not a godly society; and their awareness of this drove them to predictions of "the imminent dissolution of society and nation" and of the danger of God's wrath again being visited on the country: "Even the increasingly partisan tone of Anglican preaching in the years of Tory reaction [in the early 1680s] could not drown out the persistent demand for moral reform."[13] The contemporary drama was awarded a prominent place among the symptoms of national apostasy. In a sermon preached before Charles II in 1667, Edward Stillingfleet, who enjoyed rapid promotion after the 1688 Revolution, regretted that "among persons of civility and honour above all others" religion should be made "the sport of Entertainments" and "the common subject of Plays and Comedies."[14]

Building on the Williamite espousal of the project of a national reformation of manners, Stillingfleet solicited a letter from Queen Mary in July 1691, in which she exhorted the Middlesex magistracy to a fiercer implementation of the laws against vice. Stillingfleet's initiative was prompted by five gentlemen who had formed themselves into a voluntary society in London – the first of those Societies for Reformation of Manners which spread rapidly across the country during the next decade.[15] These societies set out to gather evidence on the basis of which convictions might be obtained and, to this end, provided their members with "an abstract of laws against profaneness and debauchery," "books of blank warrants," and "a booklet of rules for giving information to magistrates."[16] Their primary obsession was with public rather than private vice, one of their apologists asserting that "Vice when it is private and retired is not attended with those provoking circumstances as when it revels in your streets and in your markets and bids defiance to God and Religion in the face of open day."[17] It was therefore inevitable that the theatres would feature prominently on their list of targets. By 1694 they were petitioning William and Mary "*That the public Play-Houses may be suppressed.*"[18]

The societies encouraged their activists to be precise and detailed in their gathering of evidence against malefactors. It was Collier, however, who taught them how a similarly exact list of charges might be assembled against the playhouses. The thoroughness of his use of quotations from playtexts embarrassed, on particular points of detail, dramatists who otherwise adamantly refused to admit the justice of his complaints. William Congreve, generally disdainful in his response, still conceded that the use of the name of Jesus in an oath in his second comedy, *The Double Dealer* (1693), was objectionable: "I had my self long since condemn'd it, and resolv'd to strike it out in the next Impression." John Vanbrugh, too, agreed that Berinthia's use in a speech advocating adultery, in *The Relapse* (1696), of a formula "often us'd at the close of a Sermon" – "consider of what has been said, and heaven give you grace to put it in practice" (4.2.59–60) – "perhaps might as well have been let alone."[19] Such victories were celebrated by Collier's allies and admitted by the playhouses' sager defenders. Edward Filmer, for instance, stressed that many of the passages Collier identified "are indeed extreamly scandalous, impious, and wicked." In defending the theatre, he continued, he was defending a theatre purged from all such excesses.[20]

Admitting miscalculations of this kind carried danger for the playhouses. Surveying a clutch of extracts which included Berinthia's appropriation of a sermon phrase, Collier noted that "There are few of these last Quotations, but what are plain Blasphemy, and within the *Law*."[21] The use of blasphemous language was indeed a criminal offense. Collier's disciples acted on his hint, and individual actors were successfully prosecuted for having spoken "many Profane, Vicious, & immoral Expressions" in, among other plays, Vanbrugh's *The Provok'd Wife* (1697) and Congreve's *Love for Love* (1695).[22] Their attention was not confined to published scripts; knowing that actors' improvisations in the heat of performance might exceed what the dramatists had set down for them, reformers who had attended the playhouses for this purpose offered in evidence lines which have no equivalent in the printed texts.[23] Their persecutors also emphasized that actors convicted of such crimes were guilty not just of breaking the laws of the land but also of defying the theatrical patents by which they were permitted to act, since the latter uniformly outlawed all profanity and blasphemy.

In replying to the *Short View*, dramatists therefore tried to concede as little as possible. Vanbrugh might admit that it would have been better not to allow Berinthia her sermon-phrase; but he immediately sought to limit the significance of that concession:

> A known Pulpit-Expression sounds loose upon the Stage, though nothing is really affronted by it; for that I think in this Case is very plain, to any body that considers, who it is that speaks these words, and her manner of doing it. There's nothing serious in't, as if she wou'd perswade either *Amanda* or the Audience that Heaven approv'd what she was doing: 'Tis only a loose Expression, suitable to the Character she represents, which, throughout the Play, sufficiently shews, she's brought upon the Stage to Ridicule something that's off on't.
>
> These three or four last Quotations Mr. *Collier* says are downright Blasphemy, and within the Law. I hope the Reader will perceive he says wrong.[24]

Vanbrugh was a highly intelligent man, but he scarcely demonstrates that here. Asserting that Berinthia does not seek to persuade anyone that heaven approves adultery is irrelevant, since the blasphemous wit of the passage depends upon her jokingly appropriating the language of religion to validate an action which she and the audience both know Christianity would never condone. It is in the deliberate mismatch of pulpit language to a blithely amoral proposal that the humor of her speech resides. Similarly, alleging that the phrase is "only a loose Expression, suitable to the Character she represents" evades the question of an audience's likely response to such wit. Collier is sure that the deftness of her manoeuver invites spectators to laugh in complicity. Vanbrugh implicitly denies this, but does not attempt to disprove the charge directly.

Congreve also resorted to dubious arguments in coping with his tormentor. In the *Short View*, Collier singled out a passage from his first comedy:

> In the *Old Batchelour, Vain-love* asks *Belmour, could you be content to go to Heaven?*
> Bell. *Hum, not immediately in my Conscience, not heartily.*
> – This is playing I take it with Edge-Tools. To go to Heaven in jeast, is the way to go to Hell in earnest.[25]

Congreve counterattacked:

> In the *Old Batchelour* (says he) *Vainlove asks* Bellmour, *Could you be content to go to Heav'n?*
> Bell. *Hum, not immediately, in my Conscience not Heartily —*
> Here Mr. *Collier* concludes this Quotation with a dash, as if both the Sense and the Words of the whole Sentence, were at an end. But the remainder of it in the Play *Act. 3. Scene 2.* is in these words — *I would do a little more good in my generation first, in order to deserve it.*
>
> I think the meaning of the whole is very different from the meaning of the first half of this Expression. 'Tis one thing for a Man to say positively, he will not go to Heaven; and another to say, that he does not think himself worthy, till he is better prepared. But Mr. *Collier* undoubtedly was in the right, to take just as much as would serve his own turn. The Stile of this Expression is Light, and suitable to Comedy, and the Character of a wild Debauchee of the Town; but there is a Moral meaning contain'd in it, when it is not represented by halves.[26]

This is a vivid example of the lengths to which Collier sometimes drove the dramatists. By completing the quotation, Congreve simply makes matters worse, since the sexual pun in "generation" is obvious and undeniable. In the process, he also adds another instance of profaneness to the tally, since the "do ... good in my generation" phrase derives from the "prayer for a sick child," added to the service for the visitation of the sick in the *Book of Common Prayer* in 1662. The dramatist who elsewhere required "the impartial Reader" not "to pass any Sentence or Censure upon" any of his dialogue "alienated from the Character by which it is spoken; for in that place alone, and in his Mouth alone, can it have its proper and true

Significance"[27] is here hoist with his own petard. On the lips of Bellmour, of whose capacities as a cuckolder we are given graphic proof, such language is necessarily another instance of that smiling misapplication of the vocabulary of piety in which Berinthia indulged. As she dressed adultery in sermon-dialect, so Bellmour professes to believe that a place in the Christian heaven can be earned by persistent devotion to the pleasures of fornication. It is language, as Congreve says, suitable to "a wild debauchee," an example of that profaneness which, the moralists testified, nowadays "in conversation passes for sprightliness and wit."[28] The dialogue he had written cannot be satisfactorily defended against a charge of impiety; but, given the nature of the crisis in which he was embroiled, it was tactically imperative for Congreve to make, at the least, a formal show of doing so.

The constraints which fettered him need no longer inhibit us. Modern scholarship, however, has sometimes puzzlingly committed itself to re-fighting old battles and asserting that Congreve was, after all, in the right. Aubrey Williams, for example, has quoted the exchange over the Bellmour speech as an example of unfair quotation by the clergyman.[29] In his reading, Congreve's comedies are devout expositions of the work of divine providence in human affairs, and the clergyman brings discredit on his calling by his obtuse failure to comprehend this. Williams emphasizes the "large body of shared cosmological assumptions" which were, in his view, the common property of late seventeenth-century society, as also "the religious modes of thought to which everyone in the age had been habituated since childhood." In his account, this generated a uniform belief in a providentialist view of human history, the imprint of which is as evident in Restoration comedy as in Milton's *Paradise Lost*.[30]

Williams's theories seem to me to be based on one fundamental mis-conception. He fails to distinguish between common possession of a language and identical use of that language. Ambitious blasphemy requires a thorough indoctrination in the faith which furnishes the inspiration and materials for the blasphemer's impiety. Collier was gloomily certain that the playwrights were indeed well acquainted with the Bible and the Prayer Book; it was their use of that knowledge that appalled him. What he believed he saw before him was a theatre in which characters could, for example, play with the notion that their actions were devilish without expressing, or evoking in the audience, the horror he judged apt to such a thought. The reformers recognized only too clearly the closeness of the drama's language to their own and, *pace* Williams, were correspondingly angry about the sea-change it had undergone in its passage from pulpit to stage.

The rhetoric in which that fury was expressed was frequently hyperbolical; but this does not prevent the reformers', and especially Collier's, interrogation of textual detail from being potentially illuminating to us. No previous body of material raises such precisely targeted questions about the nature of the laughter particular comic texts were likely to provoke in performance. The campaigners' claim that the theatres had been guilty of "*teaching* the World *a sort of profane and immodest Wit in conversation*" grows from a widespread belief among the moral reformers that they lived "in an Age that ranks Seriousness among the Vices, and Raillery among the Virtues."[31] Such fears surface powerfully in the early days of the Restoration. In 1667, for instance, Sir William Temple contrasted Waller's poetry with that produced by the post-1660 generation: "all the wit he and his company spent, in heightening love and friendship, was better employed, than what is laid out so prodigally by the modern wits, in the mockery of all sorts of religion and government"; and in 1675 John Fell complained that "this Age of ours has somwhat of mockery for its particular Genius" and that his contemporaries found "no faculty more recommending than the being dextrous in turning serious things to Ridicule."[32] The pious acknowledged the dangers such modish facetiousness posed for their faith; in Swift's words, "Religion, like all other Things, is soonest put out of Countenance by being ridiculed."[33] They also warned that such fooling could breed a hardening in the soul which would make an individual's chances of salvation terrifyingly slender. Anthony Horneck applied such thoughts directly to the contemporary stage: "how apt upon these Occasions they are to laugh at those Sins, which require Rivers of Tears, and to smile at the Jest they hear, which deserves their most rigid Censures."[34] It was for this reason that Collier dubbed the playhouse the "Seat of the Scornful."[35]

The response of Vanbrugh and Congreve was to assert that their playwriting served ethical goals which directed and controlled their use of mockery. In Congreve's account,

> Men are to be laugh'd out of their Vices in Comedy; the Business of Comedy is to delight, as well as to instruct: And as vicious People are made asham'd of their Follies or Faults, by seeing them expos'd in a ridiculous manner, so are good People at once both warn'd and diverted at their Expence.

Vanbrugh preached the same doctrine:

> The Stage is a Glass for the World to view it self in; People ought therefore to see themselves as they are; if it makes their Faces too Fair, they won't know they are Dirty, and by consequence will neglect to wash 'em ...[36]

In 1690s comedy, therefore, scorn is harnessed to entirely moral ends and never has the impudence to target religion.

I would like now to test the validity of the dramatists' self-defense, and the implications of the reformers' accusations for our reading today of the plays they indicted, by exploring Vanbrugh's greatest comedy, *The Provok'd Wife* (1697), a work regarded with especial abhorrence by the anti-stage campaigners. Vanbrugh's plot focuses on Sir John and Lady Brute, locked in a mutually unsatisfactory marriage, and both seeking solace for their dissatisfaction elsewhere, the husband in alcoholism, atheism, and street marauding, the wife in possible adultery with Constant, a solicitous gallant. In the *Short View*, Collier took issue with numerous passages in *The Provok'd Wife*. It was, he claimed, "particularly rampant and scandalous" in its use of swearing. Sir John and his cronies were furnished "with a Drunken Atheistical Catch"; Rasor, Sir John's servant, perpetrated "a Jest upon Religion"; and Lady Brute launched into outright blasphemy.[37] Vanbrugh claimed that Collier's handling of his text demonstrated his characteristic "foul play,"[38] a charge which inspired Collier to more extended attacks in his next diatribe against the stage.

Since Vanbrugh could not deny the presence of profanity in his text, his defense had to rest on the claim that it was used to satiric effect – to expose the speaker, not to entertain the audience with its impiety. This is an argument easiest to sustain in respect of Sir John, who fully justifies Vanbrugh's choice of surname for him. The clergy conventionally defined religion as "Our Prerogative above the Beasts" and argued that "if it be Religion which distinguishes Man from the Brute Creatures, ... the Atheist who is fallen from it, must be reckon'd amongst them."[39] The atheist was even credited with a desire to erase the crucial distinctions which separated man from beast. Richard Burridge, a convert from unbelief, testified that "Too often have I seem'd to grudge the poor brute Animals their Irrationality, and to share with them, endeavour'd by a Sensuality to degrade my self into a Beast, or, at least, to become as like one as Humanity would permit me."[40] Sir John's nightly descent into an alcoholic stupor combines with the overt defiance of religion in which he and his atheistical drinking partners indulge to make them textbook examples of the condition the sermonizers excoriated.

Irony is clearly predominant in Vanbrugh's portrait of Sir John. His career is a network of inconsistencies and self-contradictions. Obsessed with his own rank and the privileges this affords him, he can yet drunkenly proclaim "Confusion to all order!" (3.2.2). Exiting from one scene shouting "Liberty and property" (3.2.67–8), he re-enters to participate in a robbery. Ideologically muddled, he is also casually destructive; his gang's rampaging leaves offstage victims severely wounded, if not dead. When Collier complained that "Sir *John's* Character has some Strokes of Discouragement, but he's made pretty easy at last and brought to no Pennance,"[41] at least one pro-stage writer plausibly replied that "Truly, I think his whole Character is one continued Punishment; and I wou'd no more chuse Sir John's Circumstances for the pleasure of his Libertinism, than I wou'd Mr Collier's for the pleasure of Lashing on't."[42]

The aspect of Sir John's impiety which most enraged the reformers was his rabid anti-clericalism – a vice to which, they claimed, the theatres were also addicted. The 1690s produced numerous complaints about the disrespect paid by comedy to "Clergy of all Opinions (thereby insinuating Religion to be but a meer Trade at best)." One campaigner alleged that the mere inclusion of a comic priest in a play ensured playhouse applause; and in a 1673 comedy a tyro dramatist had been given matching advice: "in all you write reflect upon religion and the Clergy; ... believe me this one piece of art has set off many an indifferent Play."[43] Habitual portrayal of priests as fleshly and hypocritical, it was urged, could have grave consequences for the religion they professed, since "Who will believe those are sins, as they exclaim in the Pulpit, if they themselves all the week after walk in them with delight?"[44]

This belief which Sir John shares triggers his most flamboyant escapade. In preparation for his gang's nightly battle with the watch, he dons a parson's gown, so that, as Lord Rake proposes, "though the blows fall upon you, the scandal may light upon the church" (4.1.33–34).[45] Collier had himself written a book entitled The Office of Chaplain Enquir'd Into, and Vindicated From Servility and Contempt (1688). So his fury at Vanbrugh's scenes is easy to predict. Vanbrugh replied that Sir John's clerical masquerade "put the Audience in mind, that there were Laymen so wicked, they Cared not what they did to bring Religion in Contempt, and were therefore always ready to throw dirt upon the Pilots of it."[46] To which we may respond by asking why, if the scenes' satirical design was so secure, did Vanbrugh in due course feel the need to rewrite them, replacing incidents in which he "made a Rake talk like a Rake, in the borrow'd Habit of a Clergyman" with ones in which "he clapt the same Debauchee, into the Undress of a Woman of Quality."[47] That decision suggests that the incongruous combination of dissolute behavior and sanctified dress produced in performance comic results which caused offense to more than the narrow cadre represented by Collier and his fellow zealots.

The masquerade scenes end surprisingly. Arrested by the watch, a drunken Sir John is brought before a justice. The sight of this raucous and lewd parson shocks and grieves the law's officials; but their distress does not lessen their respect for the church as an institution. Instead, they conspire to hush up the whole affair, so that the church will not be disadvantaged by it. Far from doing a little to weaken Christianity's detested power, Sir John has contrived to demonstrate the unshakeable deference with which many still regard it. Vanbrugh, in effect, suavely reassures those who felt that constant images of priestly fallibility would undermine the church's foundations that their worries are excessive. But there is no glorious victory for the church here either, merely a conspiracy by the secular authorities to ensure that the truth about it does not get out. The justice and watch, after all, remain convinced that they have been dealing with a genuine priest.

Defending his handling of Lady Brute taxed Vanbrugh more severely. Sir John's maltreatment of her puts her virtue under strain, and accordingly her first soliloquy toys with thoughts of adulterous revenge: "Perhaps a good part of what I suffer from my husband may be a judgement upon me for my cruelty to my lover. Lord, with what pleasure could I indulge that thought, were there but a possibility of finding arguments to make it good" (1.1.57–61). By "judgement" she means "divine punishment"; so she is already experimenting with the kind of impiety which Berinthia exploited. As yet, however, she lacks the latter's poise. Her second sentence, in effect, declares that there are no "arguments" which would "make it good." Tempted she may be; but religion still has the power to inhibit her actions.

Vanbrugh emboldens her thinking in three extraordinary duologues with her niece Bellinda. No previous Restoration comedy had charted with comparable deftness the growing intimacy between two women. They start diffidently, each concealing secrets they hope the other has not guessed. But they gradually learn to hold nothing back. For Lady Brute this involves speaking more frankly about the attractions adultery holds for her:

Lady Brute: ... In short, Bellinda, he has used me so barbarously of late, that I could almost resolve to play the downright wife – and cuckold him.
Bellinda: That would be downright indeed.
Brute: Why, after all, there's more to be said for't than you'd imagine, child. I know according to the strict statute of the law of religion I should do wrong, but if there were a Court of Chancery in heaven, I'm sure I should cast him.
Bellinda: If there were a House of Lords you might.
Lady Brute: In either I should infallibly carry my cause. Why, he is the first aggressor, not I.
Bellinda: Ay, but you know we must return good for evil.
Lady Brute: That may be a mistake in the translation. Prithee be of my opinion, Bellinda, for I'm positive I'm in the right; and if you'll keep up the prerogative of a woman, you'll likewise be positive you are in the right, whenever you do anything you have a mind to. But I shall play the fool, and jest on, till I make you begin to think I'm in earnest. (1.1.84–101)

This exchange clearly identifies wit as the weapon which may finally permit her to override religious prohibitions. Vanbrugh allows her to be brilliantly inventive in her use of it; that "mistake in the translation" riposte, for instance, is a wonderful gift to any actress. But he also makes her immediately apologize for her daring. Her attempt to pass it off as a mere joke, however, does not fool Bellinda, who is well aware how much of her true feelings Lady Brute has just confessed. Witplay, poised "'twixt jest and earnest" (3.3.138), enables in this play the voicing of desires which could not otherwise be articulated so directly. The jesting surface partially conceals the serious intent; it also allows the speaker to accommodate herself to ideas which attract but also unnerve her.

The process is taken further in the women's late night duologue in Act 3. Warming to their task, they confess how the flesh prevails with them over the spirit: "were there no men in the world, o' my conscience I should be no longer a-dressing than I'm a-saying my prayers; nay, though it were Sunday" (3.3.33–35). Vanbrugh is again fashioning his dialogue out of the materials of pulpit rhetoric, where the life of the worldly and the fashionable is constantly denigrated in similar terms, with devotion to dress, for example, being weighed against devotion to God, and so on and on.[48] The women's admission of their habituation to worldly priorities climaxes with an exchange especially calculated to provoke the pious:

> *Both*: Ha ha ha ha ha.
> *Bellinda*: Our confession is so very hearty, sure we merit absolution.
> *Lady Brute*: Not unless we go through with't and confess all. So, prithee, for
> the ease of our consciences, let's hide nothing.
> *Bellinda*: Agreed.
>
> (3.3.48–53)

The penitent admission of sinfulness plays a crucial role in the Christian conception of salvation. But a confession unaccompanied by a resolution to achieve "utter excision" of the sins confessed is mere mockery. As one popular work put it, "We look on it as a high pitch of impiety boastingly to avow our sins, and it deserves to be consider'd whether this kind of confessing have not affinity with it."[49] Vanbrugh's ladies go further. Their confession is itself both a form of boast and an acknowledgment of a state of affairs which they have no intention of altering.

They now turn to anatomizing how the public decorums defining acceptable female behavior demand that no trace of what they have just confessed should be deducible from their conduct of themselves in society. They wittily exemplify the dilemmas this poses from the situation which now unites everyone who is present in the playhouse – that is, how members of an audience react when the stage dialogue turns unnervingly frank and potentially blush-provoking. In the process, they anatomize a classic double bind. At such moments, they note, the male spectators will observe the female spectators carefully. If the latter laugh, "that's telling truth, and owning we understand the jest" (3.3.81–82), and, hence, an admission of immodesty, since prevailing notions of female modesty decreed that its possessors should lack the knowledge to decode such jokes. But not laughing will also confess that they know what is being alluded to, since "if we did not understand the thing, we should naturally do like other people" (3.3.86–87). The situation described is also, of course, being enacted, since laughing at and with the ladies' confessional wit would itself be an act of self-declaration for the ladies in the audience.

Lady Brute and Bellinda press boldly onwards:

> *Bellinda*: For my part I always take that occasion to blow my nose.
> *Lady Brute*: You must blow your nose half off then at some plays.
> *Bellinda*: Why don't some reformer or other beat the poet for't?
> *Lady Brute*: Because he is not so sure of our private approbation as of our public thanks. Well, sure there is not upon earth so impertinent a thing as women's modesty.
> *Bellinda*: Yes; men's fantasque, that obliges us to it. If we quit our modesty, they say we lose our charms, and yet they know that very modesty is affectation, and rail at our hypocrisy. (3.3.77–97)

Lady Brute's second speech here is resonant indeed. She assumes that the campaign for theatre reform – which, if successful, might secure the silencing of such scenes as this – will not command the private approval of ladies like her, but that, given the nature of their society, they are sure cravenly to offer it their public support. Vanbrugh again challenges his audience to acknowledge by their response that his character speaks for them.

Vanbrugh's answer to Collier's rebuking of this passage is singularly unconvincing:

> Here are two Women (not over Virtuous, as their whole Character shews), who being alone, and upon the rallying Pin, let fall a Word between Jest and Earnest, as if now and then they found themselves cramp'd by their Modesty. But lest this shou'd possibly be mistaken by some part of the Audience, less apprehensive of Right and Wrong than the rest, they are put in mind at the same Instant, That (with the Men) if they quit their Modesty, they lose their Charms: Now I thought 'twas impossible to put the Ladies in mind of any thing more likely to make 'em preserve it. [50]

Vanbrugh does not address the way in which the ladies claim to be voicing the general experience of their audience. Nor does he confront Lady Brute's confidence that the female spectators' "private approbation" will not applaud the intervention of a stage-reformer like Collier, whatever public lip-service they may pay to the justice of his cause. He also ignores Belinda's crisp denunciation of the bad faith with which men manipulate the demand that women behave with impeccable modesty. And, finally, by taking it for granted that for ladies the worst disaster is to "lose their Charms," he merely reiterates his two characters' assertion that the imperatives of the flesh weigh more heavily with them than those of the spirit. The brilliance of his writing here is simply not defensible in any terms Collier would accept. Attempting to do so leaves Vanbrugh looking sophistical and fumbling.

Lady Brute grows progressively bolder during these encounters. But Vanbrugh ends her story anti-climactically. In Act 5, Sir John returns unexpectedly, *"all dirt and bloody"* (5.2.19), to interrupt aunt and niece in a tête-à-tête with Constant and his friend Heartfree. Nothing more compromising than card-playing has occurred, but Sir John leaps to the obvious conclusion. Before the two gallants' presence is revealed, Lady Brute is grimly manhandled by her surly husband who concludes his offensive embraces by jeeringly announcing that "now you being as dirty and as nasty as myself, we may go pig together." Her humiliated aunt's passivity here astonishes Bellinda: "If I were in her pickle, I'd call my gallant out of the closet, and he should cudgel him soundly" (5.2.58–61). Vanbrugh models this incident on the conclusion of Thomas Otway's *The Soldiers' Fortune* (1680), where a husband is reduced to giggling compliance with his fate when his cuckolder holds a sword at his throat. In imitation of his predecessor, Constant, too, will in due course threaten Sir John with his sword, but his paradoxical aim will be to browbeat him into conceding that "nothing has passed but an innocent frolic" (5.2.81). At this crisis Lady Brute's immediate and overwhelming instinct is to patch up a domestic truce with the husband she abhors, and Constant follows her lead. She has not attained the tough independence of spirit needed to translate private skepticism into immodest action. Able to map with stunning clarity the slenderness of the hold religion exercises on her innermost thoughts, she remains too socially conditioned to breach decorum and modesty completely and embrace defiant adultery with Constant. Like her husband, she is in the end a failed rebel against marriage, religion, and respectability.

Vanbrugh's writing for his provoked wife in these final scenes is inevitably devoid of the skeptical wit and blasphemous humor which lent adrenalin and zest to her duologues with Bellinda. As she scrambles to re-erect a façade of marital respectability, she can no longer afford to indulge the profane freethinking which earlier solicited and won the audience's laughter. In depriving his actress of one of her role's strongest resources, Vanbrugh is taking great risks here. But the play's conclusion is also rigorously logical and hard-headed. In retrospect, it also looks prophetic, since it pre-echoes the fate which would soon overtake Vanbrugh himself. Within a year of its first performance, he would find himself compelled to deny in public the true nature of the laughter his comedy was designed to provoke. It was not only rebellious wives who might be forced by late seventeenth-century society to feign a modesty they did not possess. Vanbrugh's masterpiece thus offers one of the richest and most dramatically purposeful exploitations of the profanity endemic in Restoration comedy. The defeat it inflicts on Lady Brute, however, predicts the revenge the pious were about to have on the playhouses. After Collier's onslaught, no eighteenth-century dramatist would dare imitate Vanbrugh's relish for exploring and provoking the laughter of impiety.

NOTES

1 Joseph Wood Krutch, "Governmental Attempts to Regulate the Stage after the Jeremy Collier Controversy," *PMLA* 38 (1923), 161; George Farquhar, *Adventures of Covent-Garden, Works of George Farquhar*, ed. Shirley Strum Kenny, 2 vols. (New York: Oxford University Press, 1988), II, 269.

2 Charles Gildon, *Phaeton: or, The Fatal Divorce. A Tragedy* (London, 1698), sig. C1r.

3 Edward Cardwell, ed., *Documentary Annals of the Reformed Church of England* (Oxford, 1839), II, 346.

4 John Oldmixon, *The History of England, During the Reigns of King William And Queen Mary, Queen Anne King George I* (London, 1735), p. 192.

5 Narcissus Luttrell, *A Brief Historical Relation of State Affairs From September 1678 to April 1714*, 6 vols. (Oxford, 1857), IV, 427; Colley Cibber, *An Apology for the Life of Colley Cibber*, ed. B. R. S. Fone (Ann Arbor: University of Michigan Press, 1968), p. 151.

6 L. S., *Essayes and Characters* (1661), quoted by T. S. Graves, "Notes on Puritanism and the Stage," *SP* 18 (1921), 168; Lewis Bayly, *The Practice of Piety* (London, 1685), sig. A3r.

7 [James Wright], *Country Conversations* (London, 1694), p. 4; Sir Richard Blacknore, "Preface to *King Arthur, An Heroick Poem*," in J. E. Spingarn, ed., *Critical Essays of the Seventeenth Century Vol. III 1685–1700* (Oxford: Clarendon Press, 1908), pp. 229–30.

8 John Tillotson, "Sermon CLX. The Evil of Corrupt Communication," *Works*, 3rd edn. (London, 1722), II, 399.

9 A. J. Turner, "The Jeremy Collier Stage Controversy Again," *N&Q* 218 (1973), 410.

10 Tillotson, *Works*, II, 392.

11 *His Majesties Letter To The Lord Bishop of London* (London, 1689), p. 4.

12 Tony Claydon, *William III and The Godly Revolution* (Cambridge University Press, 1996), pp. 65–66.

13 John Spurr, *The Restoration Church of England, 1646–1689* (New Haven and London: Yale University Press, 1991), pp. 234, 238, and 246.

14 Edward Stillingfleet, "Sermon II. Preached before the King. *March* 13. 1666/7," *Works*, 6 vols. (London, 1710), I, 26.

15 Craig Rose, "Providence, Protestant Union and Godly Reformation in the 1690s," *Transactions of the Royal Historical Society*, 6th Series, 3 (1993), 165.

16 Dudley W. R. Bahlman, *The Moral Revolution of 1688* (New Haven: Yale University Press, 1957), pp. 54–55.

17 T. C. Curtis and W. A. Speck, "The Societies for the Reformation of Manners: a Case Study in the Theory and Practice of Moral Reform," *L&H* 3 (March 1976), 56.

18 *Proposals for a National Reformation of Manners* (London, 1694), p. 14.

19 William Congreve, *Amendments of Mr. Collier's False and Imperfect Citations, &c.* (London, 1698), p. 37; John Vanbrugh, *A Short Vindication of The Relapse and The Provok'd Wife From Immorality and Prophaneness* (London, 1698), p. 27. Act, scene and line references for Vanbrugh's plays are to the texts in Sir John Vanbrugh, *Four Comedies*, ed. Michael Cordner (Harmondsworth: Penguin, 1989).

20 Edward Filmer, *A Defence of Plays: or, The Stage Vindicated* (London, 1707), sig. A3v and p. 39.

21 Jeremy Collier, *A Short View of the Immorality, and Profaneness of the English Stage* (London, 1698), p. 84.

22 James G. McManaway, "Unrecorded Performances in London about 1700," *TN* 19 (1964–65), 68. On the legal situation, see Calhoun Winton, "The London Stage Embattled: 1695–1710," *TSL* 19 (1974), 11.

23 James G. McManaway, "Unrecorded Performances," p. 69; T. C. Duncan Eaves and Ben D. Kimpel, "The Text of Congreve's *Love for Love*," *The Library*, 5th Series, 30 (1975), 334–36.

24 Vanbrugh, *A Short Vindication*, pp. 27–28.

25 Collier, *A Short View*, p. 62.

26 Congreve, *Amendments*, pp. 37–38.

27 Ibid., pp. 9–10.

28 John Sheffield, Duke of Buckingham, "Of Vulgar Errors," *Works*, 3rd edn. (London, 1740), II, 291.

29 Aubrey Williams, "No Cloistered Virtue: Or, Playwright versus Priest in 1698," *PMLA* 90 (1975), 243.

30 Aubrey Williams, "Of 'One Faith': Authors and Auditors in the Restoration Theatre," *SLitI* 10 (1977), 58–59.

31 Arthur Bedford, *A Serious Remonstrance In Behalf Of the Christian Religion* (London, 1719), p. 5; [W. Darrell], *A Gentleman Instructed In the Conduct of a Virtuos and Happy Life*, 2nd edn. (London, 1704), sig. A5v. For a helpful exploration of this subject, see Roger D. Lund, "Irony as Subversion: Thomas Woolston and the Crime of Wit," in Roger D. Lund, ed., *The Margins of Orthodoxy: Heterodox Writing and Cultural Response, 1660–1750* (Cambridge University Press, 1995), pp. 170–94.

32 W. Baptist Scoones, ed., *Four Centuries of English Letters* (London, 1880), p. 123; John Fell, *The Character of the Last Daies. A Sermon Preached before the King* (Oxford, 1675), p. 19.

33 Jonathan Swift, "Upon Sleeping in Church," *Irish Tracts, 1720–1723, and Sermons*, ed. Herbert David and Louis Landa (Oxford University Press, 1948), p. 214.

34 Anthony Horneck, *Sirenes: or Delight and Judgment* 2nd edn. (London, 1680), quoted by [George Ridpath], *The Stage Condemn'd* (London, 1698), p. 83.

35 Jeremy Collier, *A Second Defence Of The Short View* (London, 1700), p. 36.

36 Congreve, *Amendments*, p. 8; Vanbrugh, *A Short Vindication*, p. 46.

37 Collier, *A Short View*, pp. 57, 77–78, and 83.

38 Vanbrugh, *A Short Vindication*, p. 23.

39 Samuel Crossman, *The Young Mans Monitor* (London, 1664), p. 91; John Howard, *The Evil of Our Dayes* (London, 1698), pp. 17–18.

40 Richard Burridge, *Religio Libertini* (London, 1712), p. 15.

41 Collier, *A Defence of the Short View*, p. 128.

42 *Some Remarks Upon Mr. Collier's Defence of his Short View of the English Stage, &c.* (London, 1698), p. 16.

43 [Wright], *Country Conversations*, p. 12; *Rabshaketh Vapulans* (London, 1691), p. 2; Joseph Arrowsmith, *The Reformation* (London, 1678), p. 48.

44 [William Ramesay], *The Gentlemans Companion* (London, 1672), p. 22.

45 For an account of the contemporary background to these scenes, see Michael Cordner, "Anti-Clericalism in Vanbrugh's *The Provoked Wife*," *N&Q* 226 (1981), 212–14.

46 Vanbrugh, *A Short Vindication*, p. 53.

47 Cibber, *Apology*, p. 309.

48 James Ellesby, *The Great Danger And Uncertainty Of A Death-Bed Repentance* (London, 1693), p. 17.

49 *The Causes Of The Decay of Christian Piety* (London, 1667), p. 147.

50 Vanbrugh, *A Short Vindication*, p. 9.

14

ROBERT MARKLEY

The canon and its critics

Since its own time, Restoration drama has been controversial, provoking radically different judgments about its aesthetic value and moral significance. Critical debates reach back at least as far as 1698 when the High Tory churchman, Jeremy Collier, published a scathing indictment of Restoration comedy for its immorality and contempt for authority; various defenders of the drama, including playwrights such as William Congreve, countered these charges by arguing that comedy satirizes vice and vanity to secure the socioeconomic stability premised on feminine virtue and masculine property rights.[1] The terms of this controversy have persisted for three hundred years – Collier and his critical descendants argue that Restoration comedy is obscene, blasphemous, and heartless; its champions claim that it offers timeless insights into the human condition or tellingly satirizes the vices and follies of its era. If these responses to the drama often tell us more about their authors than about the plays themselves, they also describe a contentious history of efforts to domesticate a morally suspect theatre by assimilating Restoration comedy to larger critical and ideological paradigms.[2]

Any attempt to understand the fate of Restoration drama in the hands of its critics must begin by recognizing that generalizations about the more than five hundred extant plays written between 1660 and 1700 are, in part, defensive reactions to a body of drama that seems paradoxically both to challenge its audiences' pretensions to virtue, honor, and faith and ultimately to reinforce the institutions of marriage, property, and patrilineal inheritance. In an important sense, debates about the nature and achievement of Restoration drama are bound inextricably to problems of deciding what constitutes the canon; attitudes toward the drama depend, in large measure, on which plays are available in recent editions to be read and which plays are revived in the theatre. Frequently, generalizations about the drama of the period have been based on only a handful of comedies – particularly those by Etherege, Wycherley, and Congreve – that are considered more or less independently of their histories on the seventeenth-century stage. By overlooking or simplifying the complex problems of patronage, playhouse politics, adaptation, performance, and even theatrical success or failure, many critics have consigned successful playwrights, such as Elkanah Settle, to near-oblivion while celebrating those dramatists, such as Congreve and Dryden, who can be recuperated as serious artists concerned with timeless problems of human existence. The result is that, over time, two occasionally overlapping canons have emerged: the first consists of plays that are revived in the theatre, adapted, and revived again; the other is composed of works, such as Dryden's heroic tragedies, deemed to have significant literary value, even though they rarely have been produced since 1700. The ways in which these two canons have been reshaped during the past three centuries demonstrate that Restoration plays, even when they are abstracted from their theatrical contexts, resist sweeping critical pronouncements.

In his Dedication to *The Way of the World* (1700), Congreve declared that "Poetry ... is sacred to the Good and Great" – that is, to the interlocking values that sustain the moral and political order.[3] His comment suggests the extent to which contemporary playwrights seemed compelled to justify their works as expressions of loyalty to a political order still haunted by the spectre of the closing of the theatres during the Interregnum and portray themselves as standardbearers of a satiric art that instructs as well as entertains.[4] Literature, critics in the seventeenth century routinely claimed, ought to inculcate morality, but because it enthralls its audiences by holding a mirror up to a flawed human nature, it risks depicting evil, seditious, and provocatively amoral characters who can seduce the innocent or unsuspecting into imitating their dangerous actions. To guard against the threat of moralists wielding neo-classical theory, then, Restoration playwrights and critics insist in their prefaces and dedications that the drama serves a moral function: it ridicules vice and ultimately upholds female chastity and patrilineal authority.

In practice, however, dramatists had to negotiate between the theatrical value of challenging social conventions for comic effect and the need to reassure audiences that property and privilege, secured through the chastity of wives and potential wives, will be sustained. In the theatre, audiences can respond emotionally and often in complicated ways to entertaining but amoral or "immoral" figures such as Horner or Angelica Bianca; these characters allow us to suspend temporarily – or even question – the moral judgments we may hold outside the theatre and thereby experience vicariously the thrill of seeing others acting on our socially forbidden desires. These spectacles encourage the audience both to identify with and to distance themselves from what they see onstage; because watching or reading a play is a complex social experience, drama resists attempts to reduce it to a static display of moral, religious, or political meaning. This is, in brief, Aphra Behn's response to the moralists of her time, and it remains a useful counterweight to the tendency of most critics to read their own values into seventeenth-century plays.[5]

The history of Restoration drama criticism can be read, in part, as an effort to reconcile the pleasure that audiences experience in the playhouse to larger systems of beliefs about the moral and ideological functions of art. In trying to make Restoration drama conform to particular models or approaches, critics often simplify the difficulties that dramatists face in trying to make a radical theatrical practice serve the ends of a conservative ideology. Those determined to see Restoration comedy as a "systematic attempt ... to associate vice with those things which men value and desire most, and virtue with every thing ridiculous and degrading" find that they are reading "comedy ... written by blackguards for blackguards"; others who see the drama as a providentialist road map in an orthodox Christian society discover evidence of divine justice at work any time the hero gets the girl and her money; and yet others, who emphasize libertinism of the age, find Hobbesian self-interest dominating the genre.[6] Paradoxically, what such assessments share is the tendency to see Restoration comedy as all of a piece throughout; by assuming that playwrights as different as Behn, Congreve, and Vanbrugh are all trying to write the same kind of "comedy of manners," these critics collapse generic and political differences among dramatists and consequently overlook gaps and inconsistencies within the critical tradition.

In writing about the drama, critics since the eighteenth century voice principles, invoke values, and make assumptions that underlie their read-ings of individual playwrights and, implicitly or explicitly, the tradition of Restoration drama as a whole. Not surprisingly, we can chart in their observations larger currents of thought about theatrical history, aesthetic theory, and the literary politics of their own times. In 1711, Richard Steele launched a moralistic broadside, in Collier's vein, against Etherege's *The Man of Mode* (1676), which had been revived at Drury Lane earlier that year: "The whole celebrated Piece," he declares, "is a perfect Contradiction to good Manners, good Sense, and common Honesty."[7] If the play "is built upon the Ruin of Virtue and Innocence," then its "utmost Corruption and Degeneracy" has both moral and social dimensions (II, 280). In Steele's mind, Etherege is guilty of violating codes of gentlemanly decorum as well as morality by having Dorimant banter with an Orange-Woman; the hero, according to Steele, is both "a direct Knave in his designs, and a Clown in his Language" (II, 278–79). By attacking Etherege's sins against "good Manners" and "good Sense," Steele attempts to base his criticism of *The Man of Mode* on what he wants his readers to see as timeless social and moral values. To invoke absolute standards of behavior, for Steele, is to put into practice the Horatian maxim that art should both entertain and instruct.

Such attempts to impose transhistorical standards on specific works, however, never truly succeed because critics, like dramatists, cannot step outside of history to offer definitive, objective judgments. In contrast to his condemnation of Etherege, Steele calls Congreve's *Love for Love* (1695) "one of the finest comedies that ever appeared upon the *English* Stage" (II, 242). Valentine, who, at the beginning of the play, has had several illegitimate children and squandered his fortune pursuing Angelica, seems no more an exemplar of virtue than Dorimant. Congreve's hero, however, by winning Angelica's hand in marriage, is reintegrated into a system of gentlemanly conduct and stable property relations; Dorimant, given a month's probation by Harriet at the end of *The Man of Mode*, retains the potential to demonstrate that his reformation is merely another role in which he has half-lost himself. The reformation of Congreve's rake coincides with, and, in an important sense, is predicated on, the successful transference of the Legend estate from tyrannical father to deserving son. For Steele, eager to advance the cause of a morally instructive drama, Etherege is a safe target; a supporter of the Stuarts, he had died abroad sometime after 1690. Congreve, however, was very much alive in 1711 and a prominent member of the Whig intelligentsia; appointed by Queen Anne as a patentee of the Queen's Theatre, Haymarket in 1705, he was commissioner of wine licenses from 1705 to 1714, and, after 1714, Secretary to the Island of Jamaica.

Steele's very different responses to two playwrights traditionally considered part of the same comic tradition may serve as a cautionary example for literary historians who want to generalize about previous views of the drama. Critics writing in the same era and ostensibly employing the same literary and moral standards often reach opposed conclusions about Restoration playwrights. In 1758, an anonymous reviewer for *The London Chronicle* called *Love for Love* "the best comedy, either antient or modern, that ever was written to please upon the stage"; in contrast, Samuel Johnson declares that "it is acknowledged with universal conviction that the perusal of [Congreve's] works will make no man better; and that their ultimate effect is to represent pleasure in alliance with vice."[8] The difference between "pleas[ing] upon the stage" and the "universal conviction" that Congreve's works are, at best, amoral reflects different conceptions of what drama – or any art – is supposed to do. For moralists, plays which fail to reinforce "those obligations by which life ought to be regulated" promote the corruption that Johnson finds endemic in Restoration England.[9]

The "universal conviction[s]" that Johnson invokes, however, are themselves historically specific. They represent the values that he feels he must deploy in order to resist the degeneration of literature in his own era. Although he praises Congreve's comedies for having "merit of the highest kind" (II, 228), Johnson finds in Restoration culture the roots of the corrupting influences of patronage and politics which he decries in his own era.[10] He criticizes Dryden, in this respect, for his willingness to become "profitably employed in flattery and controversy" (I, 384), even though his predecessor retains his personal morality and integrity: "Dryden has never been charged with any personal agency unworthy of a good character," the biographer declares; "he abetted vice and vanity only with his pen" (I, 398). This distinction between the individual and the writer allows Johnson to distance himself from the corruption of a patronage system which doomed his predecessors to surrender their art to "vice and vanity." If Dryden is given to "meanness and servility in hyperbolical adulation" of his patrons, he is guilty primarily of "accommodating himself to the corruption of the times" (I, 404). In effect, then, Johnson projects onto Restoration poets and playwrights the struggle he himself experienced in trying to maintain a sense of artistic integrity while participating in a literary marketplace that often encouraged time-serving, flattery, and opportunism. In his mind, this battle between poetry and politics was one which Restoration playwrights – dependent on an irrevocably dissolute Court – were bound to lose.

Johnson's comments on Congreve and Dryden disclose as well his and his culture's continuing ambivalence about theatrical spectacles. In the eighteenth century, the discrepancies between the audience's experience in the theatre and after-the-fact pronouncements about the moral lessons that drama should inculcate are often striking. The reviewer for *The London Chronicle* on 22 February 1757 describes the scene from a revival of Behn's comedy, *The Rover*, in which Blunt is duped by Lucetta, a prostitute, who gets him to undress so that she can steal his money and clothes:

> [Blunt] takes off his Breeches in the Sight of the Audience, whose diversion is of a complicated Nature on this Occasion. The Ladies are first alarmed; then the Men stare: The Women put up their Fans. – "My Lady Betty, what is the Man about?" – "Lady Mary, sure he is not in earnest!" – Then peep thro' their Fans – "Well, I vow, the He creature is taking off his odious Breeches – He-he – Po! – is that all – the "Man has Drawers on." – Then, like Mrs.

Cadwallador in the new Farce – "Well, to be sure, I never saw any Thing in the Shape of it." – Meanwhile, the Delight of the Male Part of the Audience is occasioned by various Operations of this Phoenomenon on the Female Mind. – "This is rare Fun, d–n me – Jack, Tom, Bob, did you ever see any thing like this? – Look at that Lady yonder – See, in the Stage Box – how she looks half-averted," etc., etc. It is a Matter of Wonder that the Upper Gallery don't call for an Hornpipe, or, "Down with the Drawers," according to their usual Custom of insisting upon as much as they can get for their Money. But to be a little serious, it should be remembered by all Managers that this Play was written in the dissolute Days of Charles the Second; and that Decency at least is, or ought to be, demanded at present.[11]

This account of Behn's play in the theatre reveals disjunctions between mid eighteenth-century standards of "Decency" which "ought to be" maintained and the responses of women and men in the audience to a spectacle that comically undermines the moral views that they hold – or are supposed to hold – outside the theatre. The women in the audience know more than they should; the men watch the ladies more than the play. Behn's satire of masculine sexual presumption in Blunt's gullibility is appropriated by the critic to satirize women caught between revealing their sexual desire and the blushes that indicate that they have internalized standards of proper feminine behavior. For the male reviewer, Behn's pandering to female desire reveals that the seductive attraction of Restoration comedy is not yet dead. The women's "alarm" at the spectacle of a man in his drawers gives way to ventriloquized critiques of the actor's body as falling short of their notion of what an ideal male sex object should be – articulated in their question "is that all[?]" and one-liners about the "Shape" in the actor's drawers. The women respond both to the spectacle of fallen breeches and to their recognition that they, too, are on display; putting their fans in front of their faces registers both their fascination with the male body and their awareness that their interest and knowledge violates conventions of feminine modesty. Their "looks" are irrevocably "half-averted" because Behn's play, as this reviewer recognizes, puts audience members in the position of observing a reversal of gender positions: women gazing at the "Shape" of the male body. The men's delight, then, lies in the "rare Fun" of seeing satiric commonplaces about women's sexual hypocrisy confirmed, of witnessing the somatic effects of desire struggling against the social dictates of "the Female Mind." The male members of the audience, as the reviewer describes the scene, can enjoy the spectacle of "half-averted" female desire without having to worry about women's sexual license threatening the transmission of property through marriage. The critic's caution to "all Managers," in this respect, reflects a wariness not only of Behn's seductiveness but of theatrical spectacles, "written in the dissolute Days" of the Restoration, that mock the strictures of a moral economy that exists outside the theatre.

If critics who accept the idea that drama is supposed to instruct as well as delight believe that "rare Fun" must always be contained, theatre managers who need to sell tickets must entertain audiences without offending them. Their need to produce new plays and to adapt old ones to entice people into the theatres means that the repertoire of plays – the theatrical canon – is always changing. By the second half of the eighteenth century, some of the stalwart moneymakers from the Restoration struck audiences as old-fashioned, if not immoral, and many of these plays faded from view. The thirty-four volumes of John Bell's *British Theatre* (second edition, 1790–97) gives us a good sense of what constituted the "canon" at the time because Bell prints texts that are "Regulated from the Prompt-Books" (as the title-page of each play declares) of eighteenth-century performances at either Drury Lane, the Theatre Royal, or Covent Garden. None of Etherege's or Behn's plays are reprinted by Bell. The only play of Wycherley's is Isaac Bickerstaff's adaptation of *The Plain Dealer*; the only plays of Dryden's are *All for Love*, *The Spanish Fryar*, and *Oedipus*, which he coauthored with Nathaniel Lee. But Bell includes all five of Congreve's plays, all of Vanbrugh's, and all of George Farquhar's. There are seven plays by Colley Cibber, six tragedies by Nicholas Rowe, and a scattering of Restoration tragedies: Otway's *Venice Preserv'd*, Lee's *Theodosius*, and Thomas Southerne's *Oroonoko*. The only woman playwright represented is Susannah Centlivre; three of her comedies – *A Bold Stroke for a Wife*, *The Busy Body*, and *The Wonder: a Woman Keeps a Secret* – are reprinted, though with backhanded comments by Bell. He calls *A Bold Stroke* "such a kind of work, as any woman fertile in expedient might conceive, and any woman, conversant with language in a slight degree, might write"; in his brief preface to *The Busy Body*, Bell declares, "I know, positively, no one of her plays which, morally speaking, may not do mischief; but they have bustle, they have business."[12] As this list indicates, Restoration comedies had been largely replaced by the works of early eighteenth-century playwrights. By the early nineteenth century, Elizabeth Inchbald's edition of English drama had removed most of these early eighteenth-century plays as well.[13]

In 1840, Leigh Hunt issued the first standard edition of four "major" Restoration playwrights, *The Dramatic Works of Wycherley, Congreve, Vanbrugh, and Farquhar* (London, 1840). In his influential review of Hunt's edition, Macaulay launched a fierce attack on these dramatists, calling Restoration comedy "a disgrace to our language and our national character" and castigating "the comic poet [as] the mouthpiece of the most deeply corrupted part of a corrupt society" (III, 158, 172). Operating on the assumption that the moral corruption of the Restoration penetrates to the core of its drama, Macaulay set about demolishing the view that Wycherley and his contemporary playwrights were satirists out to scourge the vices of their age. Whereas William Hazlitt in 1819 had praised Wycherley's *The Plain Dealer* as "worth ten volumes of sermons ..." because "it shews the immorality and hateful effects of duplicity, by shewing it fixing its harpy fangs in the heart of an honest and worthy man," Macaulay denounced Manly, the play's hero, as "the greatest rascal that is to be found, even in [Wycherley's] own writings," an embodiment of "nauseous libertinism and ... dastardly fraud" (III, 186).[14] To buttress his attack, the Whig MP and Cabinet Minister embraced the arch-Tory Collier, who was arrested in 1692 for refusing to accept the legitimacy of William's kingship and again in 1695 when he publicly granted absolution to conspirators condemned for plotting to assassinate the king (III, 197–99). According to Macaulay, Collier's condemnation in *Short View* is "truly heroic" in its righteous indignation; the rejoinders by Vanbrugh and Congreve, among others, are "a complete failure" (III, 202, 205). Macaulay appropriates Collier's rhetoric to condemn what he sees as the playwrights' diabolical commitment to the paradoxical extremes of raucous libertinism and, in Wycherley's case, unthinking royalism. In this regard, his attack on Restoration comedy needs to be read in the context of his magisterial *History of England, from the Ascension of James the Second* (1848–57). In this six-volume work, he describes seventeenth-century English history as cyclical, alternating between periods of ascendancy by two equally dangerous threats to a stable sociopolitical order: a tyrannical monarchism and an unruly democracy.[15] In his view, then, the Restoration dramatists threaten the stability of the nation by pandering to "the most deeply corrupted part of a corrupt society" – a profligate aristocracy which wanted to monopolize political power and to defy the moral and religious strictures that safeguard social order by reining in humankind's propensity to vice.

By forcefully reasserting the principle that drama should be judged by its moral effects, Macaulay's attack seeks to counter early nineteenth-century views that Restoration comedy has few, if any, consequences for playgoers or readers. Writing twenty years before Macaulay at a time when Restoration plays were revived infrequently, Charles Lamb had argued that the "artificial comedy" of Wycherley and Congreve represents "a speculative scene of things, which has no reference whatever to the world that is."[16] This "Utopia of gallantry, where pleasure is duty, and the manners perfect freedom" offers an idealized vision of upper-class existence – pleasure without political or economic consequences (II, 280–81). Rejecting the theory that audiences imitate the immoral behavior they see on stage, Lamb maintains that the wish fulfillment of comedy cannot be "translated into real life" – a view that may reflect his limited experience of a body of drama that he declared "is quite extinct on our stage" (II, 282; II, 275). The "undivided pursuit of lawless gallantry," he concedes, if "universally acted upon" outside the theatre, would "reduce this frame of things to a chaos. But no such effects are produced, in *their* world" (II, 282). The imaginary realm of Restoration comedy, in his mind, seems less an escapist fantasy than a kind of thought experiment: what would the relations between the sexes look like if the "frame" of masculine privilege and feminine virtue did not exist? Because Lamb rejects Platonic theories of art as exemplar, he can argue that, in Restoration comedy,

> No reverend institutions are insulted by [the characters'] proceedings – for they have none among them. No peace of families is violated – for no family ties exist among them. No purity of the marriage bed is stained – for none is supposed to have a being. No deep affections are disquieted, no holy wedlock bands are snapped asunder – for affection's depth and wedded faith are not of the growth of that soil. There is neither right nor wrong, – gratitude or its opposite, – claim or duty, – paternity or sonship. (II 282)

Lamb's rhetoric of "paternity and sonship" invokes the same system of values as Macaulay's moralistic condemnations of Restoration comedy but imagines the theatre as a venue to evade the responsibilities that such a system entails. The "reverend institutions" of family, marriage, love, and property that Macaulay wants to protect, Lamb renders immune from theatrical corruption. But rather than labeling the comedy "a superficial literature" that is "transitory, unstable, and episodic,"[17] Lamb figures this "Utopia of gallantry" as the repressed unconscious of a social system that insists on "half-averted" looks, on exciting and then straitjacketing female desire to maintain the interanimating logics of feminine virtue and masculine property. In this respect, Restoration comedy offers a means to gain access to a realm that exists beyond or before moral necessity. "We have not the courage," says Lamb, "to imagine a state of things for which there is neither reward nor punishment. We cling to the painful necessities of shame and blame. We would indict our very dreams" (II, 283). The "courage" of Restoration comedy, in this regard, lies not in desecrating the "painful necessities" which Johnson and Macaulay see as the foundation of social morality but in dramatizing "a state of things" in which such "necessities" do not obtain. Such "dreams" of unrepressed desire paradoxically become both the justification for a repressive morality and the expression of a utopian longing for a pre-social sexuality. By detaching the drama from the dire consequences imagined by moralists such as Macaulay, Lamb anticipates efforts by some recent critics to suggest that the theatre allows female dramatists and spectators to imagine ways to evade, if not resist, masculinist constructions of women and their role in society.[18]

Although Lamb challenges moralistic views of the drama by arguing that Restoration comedy discloses a utopian desire as the political unconscious of a sexually repressive, class-based society, he nonetheless tends to abstract plays from their theatrical contexts. Like many other eighteenth and nine-teenth-century commentators, he largely ignores historical evidence which indicates that Restoration dramatists and audiences viewed the theatre not as a site for thematic exercises or embodiments of particular philosophies but as entertaining and often complex representations of social existence. By the middle of the twentieth century, critics often wrote as though the conflicts they had inherited from their nineteenth-century predecessors offered them only a handful of options to explain the form and function of late seventeenth-century comedy: Macaulay's attack on its immorality, Lamb's defense of its amorality, and Hazlitt's view of its satiric function. Scholarship on Restoration drama accordingly took two directions: theatre historians produced a significant body of work to describe the material conditions under which the drama was produced while literary critics, influenced by the New Criticism, began to question whether debates about the morality of the drama could provide a compelling rationale to secure a place for Etherege, Wycherley, and Congreve in the larger canon of English literature. If the comedy were criminal, trivial, or straightforwardly satiric in ridiculing fops, cuckolds, and termagants, what claims could it make on teachers, students, and scholars as a significant field of literary study?

In the 1950s, formalist critics argued that Restoration drama indeed met the standards of transcendent aesthetic significance – a unity of form and function – that had come to define the canon of great literature. Dale Underwood, for example, sought to harness the critical traditions repre-sented by Macaulay and Lamb to argue that Etherege's comedies brilliantly reconcile the foundational oppositions of western culture – those of "Christianity and Christian humanism, the 'heroic' tradition, the honest-man tradition, and the tradition of courtly love," on the one hand, and those of "philosophical and moral libertinism, Machiavellian and Hobbe-sian concepts as to the nature of man" on the other.[19] This dialectic, others maintained, manifested itself in the plays of Etherege, Wycherley, and Congreve in the form of wit; defined as "intellectual superiority in perception and knowledge, and consequently acumen, penetration, and sophistication," the wit of the Restoration rake-hero became the very consciousness of this effort to balance the oppositions of human nature.[20] Wit, in other words, defined the ironic distance of the hero from the vice and folly around him; he could participate in the fashionable social world, but because his "intelligence, elegance, and taste ... are intellectual and aesthetic, and not principally social" virtues, he could always escape from the charges of being immersed in the corruption on which he comments.[21] This tendency to see the comedy as a strategy for coping with an often absurd world engendered a number of New Critical readings in the 1950s, 60s, and 70s that argued for different ways to unify the drama: some, such as Norman Holland's efforts to examine the imagistic cast of Restoration language, were quite perceptive; others, such as Williams's attempts to argue that Restoration comedy in general, and Congreve's works in particular, exhibit a providentialist faith that audiences readily comprehended, were more problematic.[22]

In different ways, then, the criticism of Underwood, Fujimura, Holland, and Williams maintains that playwrights were engaged in intentional efforts to forge and convey profound insights about existence to audiences as attuned to the aesthetic dimensions of art as they were to the social codes of the theatre. But as John Palmer, one of the more perceptive critics of the early twentieth century recognized in criticizing after-the-fact moral condemnations of Restoration comedy, "the poet's work [is] conditioned by the period in which he lives, the moral laws which his moods and characters *unconsciously* obey."[23] In emphasizing our unconscious complicity to "moral laws," Palmer anticipates the advent of a criticism, often explicitly materialist and feminist, that draws on a sophisticated notion of ideology to extend formalist inquiries and explore questions about the cultural work that the theatre performs, the audiences it attracts and the tensions that it both exploits and mediates.

Feminist critics such as Catherine Gallagher and Pat Gill maintain that the New Critics' effort to describe the aesthetic significance of Restoration drama often reproduces "unconsciously" as well as explicitly masculinist values and assumptions.[24] Because previous generations of males tend to share their culture's paternalistic views of women as characters and authors, they characteristically ignore a significant tradition of women dramatists, whose comic stock-in-trade was turning the gendered world of late seventeenth-century society upside down. Rather than simply recovering women writers such as Delariviére Manley and Catherine Trotter by editing their texts and analyzing their plays, recent feminist critics argue that the construction of gender and class roles is one of the crucial socioideological functions of the drama.[25] Derek Hughes suggests more gener-

ally that almost "all important dramatists vigorously support some liberation of women, yet it is a liberation which, magically, fails to threaten or
erode any socially acceptable male privilege."[26] The drama, in this view,
offers playwrights and audiences a venue to protest gender inequalities and
yet contains that protest so that unruly women do not disrupt the transmission of property among males. For Hughes as well as Gill, then, the
masculinist reinscription of women in Restoration drama describes the
workings of ideology itself. Ideology does not exist simply as overt forms of
repression (malevolent guardians and jealous husbands) or false consciousness (heroines who want to be married off to fools or who prize their
chastity too cheaply); instead it (re)enacts the processes by which subjects
in the seventeenth century (and the twentieth) comply with a system of
values that they often experience as repressive, absurd, or hypocritical. In
this regard, in depicting this comedy of interpellation, Restoration drama
offers a portrayal of social life that, far from being an escapist fantasy or an
attenuated philosophical exercise, is paradoxically too close to its audiences' fascination with fashion, sex, and intrigue to be esconsed safely
within the exclusive precincts of canonical literature. In other words, an
ideological interpretation of Restoration drama challenges the very standards by which the New Critics sought to define and celebrate literary
value.

In large measure, the revaluation of Restoration drama in the 1980s and
1990s has both responded to and provoked reconsiderations of what
constitutes the canon of Restoration drama. Rather than a set catalogue of
those dramatists celebrated by nineteenth-century commentators, recent
critics have suggested that historically the canon has been more unsettled
than we have assumed and that therefore our understanding of the canon
should be more attuned to plays that were popular on the late seventeenth-
century stage. The most significant aspect of this revaluation of both the
theatrical and literary canons since 1988 has been the (re)emergence of
Aphra Behn as a major playwright. In the mid-1970s, only one of her plays,
The Rover, was in print; to read the rest of her plays, one had to find
Montague Summers's 1915 edition of her works. Twenty years later,
multiple editions of her plays are available in paperback as well as all of her
poems and short fiction, and Janet Todd has edited her complete works.
According to the *MLA Bibliography*, between 1994 and 1996 twenty-six
articles were published on Behn's plays (and this excludes numerous articles
on the poems and fiction); in comparison there were ten articles published
on Congreve's plays in this period, six on Wycherley's, and three on
Etherege's. A rough count suggests that *The Rover* may be the most widely
revived Restoration play on stages in Great Britain and the United States.

Behn's rising fortunes as a dramatist, as Hutner argues, is indicative of a sea-change in our perception of the period as a whole.[27]

Since her own day, Behn has been a convenient target for moralistic critics and, in many respects, the victim of conceptions of literature that depend on – and celebrate – the political and social values of middle-class economic morality, sentimental benevolence, and individualist psychology.[28] As the reviewer for *The London Chronicle* recognized in 1757, she challenges some of the fundamental tenets by which the stage and social life more generally "ought to be regulated." In terms of her Tory politics, aristocratic apologetics, and feminist sexual ideology, Behn is historically on the losing side, a marginalized figure because her work resists the critical values and cultural assumptions that have informed our notions of what constitutes "great" literature, particularly those discourses of domestic morality and repressed sexuality that seek to contain feminine desire. As both a political writer and a feminist, Behn frustrates attempts to incorporate her work within progressivist ideologies of class and gender; her distrust of factionalism leads her to promote an idealized vision of a benevolently monarchical order which paradoxically frees women from the demands of the patrilineal ideology on which it ultimately depends. Behn's comedies savage the Puritan ideology of self-denial that both historically and conceptually underlies the construction of the gendered self – the construction of woman as other and as object – that is crucial to a sexual ideology which insists on the indivisibility of feminine chastity and feminine identity.[29]

If Behn's plays attack comically the constraints of internalized morality and feminized virtue, they also challenge the masculinist literary tradition that Underwood and Fujimura invoke as the basis for praising her male counterparts. Because she writes outside of – and against – the economy of repression Behn is able to present her heroines as desiring subjects who can attain – within the parameters that her plays describe – what they desire. In this regard, her dramatizing of feminine desire dialectically reinscribes masculine sexuality as both dangerous and desirable. Her heroes – Willmore in *The Rover*, parts one and two, and Wilding in *The City Heiress* – become their plays' dominant sex symbols: both the objects of desire and the infinitely desiring males. Their sexuality is presented by Behn as a manifestation of their inherent, literally in-born, gentlemanly good nature which leads them to embrace both Royalist loyalties and libertine lifestyles; wenching, drinking, and spending money are "natural" manifestations of their inherent virtue. Conversely, penury and abstinence from women and liquor signal a form of ideological repression, a hypocritical self-policing that internalizes standards of Puritanical self-righteousness. In this regard, her plays offer her audiences an implicit – and, in some cases, explicit –

invitation to remain in a golden age of Cavalier loving and carousing, in which heroes get their women but escape or forestall the responsibilities of marriage. Characteristically, then, Behn's heroes are usually exiled Cavaliers or gentlemen out to repair their lost fortunes; because they are temporarily exiled from England or their estates, they paradoxically are freed from the immediate demands of patrilineal ideology – to marry and to father heirs. Even as her heroes embody the good nature and loyalty that endear them to Royalists, they remain outside of the economy of money and patrilineal succession that forces women to act as means for the exchange of property among men.

Behn's emphasis on the polemical nature of comedy and on its potential for allowing women to act on their desires distinguishes her work from the plays of her predecessors in the 1670s, notably Etherege and Wycherley. Whereas they both exploit and call into question conventions of wit comedy, Behn reinvests ideals of libertine behavior with a political significance that she invokes explicitly in dedicating the second part of *The Rover* to the Duke of York. The play was written, Behn tells us in her dedication, at his behest in 1681 when he was in "voluntary Exile" to appease the "ill-gotten Power, and worse-acted Greatness of the Rabble" during the Exclusion Crisis.[30] She compares the plight of her royal patron to the circumstances of her own hero, the Rover: "he is a wanderer too," she tells the duke, "distrest; belov'd, tho unfortunate, and ever constant to Loyalty." He was, Behn continues, "driven from his Native Country with You, forc'd as You were to fight for his Bread in a strange Land, and suffer'd with You all the Ills of Poverty, War and Banishment" (VI, 229). The parallels she draws between her hero's wanderings in the 1650s and the duke's exile in 1681 depict the Rover as a sexualized embodiment of the duke's virtues, the avatar, like Behn's other Royalist heroes, of "a Prince of ... Illustrious Birth and God-like Goodness" (VI, 228). In this regard, her comedies of the 1680s seek to reclaim the figure of the rake from the ambiguous forms of ironic existence to which he had evolved in the mid 1670s. In Willmore, Behn presents a dialectical portrait of the rake as both libertine and Royalist, at once anti-authoritarian and passionately committed to king, country, and class. If Wycherley and Etherege render the identity of their heroes as ironic, dialogic, Behn decenters notions of identity – of the moral and, she assumes, Puritanical self – to offer culturally based depictions of identity that seek to transcend the constraints of "Custom." The divisiveness of patrilineal ideology dramatized, for example, in *The Country Wife* is subsumed in Behn's foregrounding of mutual desire between the sexes, a vision of unrepressed sexuality that produces and is produced by a political ethos of idyllic royalism.

The feminist interpretations of Behn's plays that have become popular, then, are suggestive of the ways in which Restoration drama is now being read. The comedies, in particular, not only display a conscious set of beliefs and firmly held socioeconomic principles but stage the complexities of living in a society where conventional values are simultaneously mocked and upheld. Restoration rake-heroes typically do not convert in act five to an unwavering faith in moral probity but reach an accommodation with the values that they have spent the better part of five acts violating precisely because they recognize them to be necessary social constructions. At the end of *The Man of Mode*, Harriet tells Dorimant, now protesting his undying love, "Though I wish you devout, I would not have you turn fanatic" (5.2.150–60).[31] This distancing of devotion from fanaticism, cast in a religious rhetoric that may be itself part put-on, captures concisely the double-edged existence that Dorimant embodies – the suggestion that we are all performers at risk of being taken in by our own performances. In this regard, Etherege's comedies, even more than Behn's, stage the paradox of social existence as conformity without ultimate belief; characters surrender to the fantasy of desire without consequences precisely because they see that this fantasy both structures and must be excluded from the "painful necessities" on which the social order depends.[32]

The reemergence of Behn after three centuries suggests the extent to which contemporary critics see their interests in gender and ideology as a means to recover the lived experience of the theatre during the Restoration period. Many of these critics recognize self-consciously that they cannot stand apart from the plays and playwrights they analyze and that therefore criticism of the drama, like any other intellectual activity, is implicated in the complex history of our own times. In an interesting way, then, the criticism of the drama in the 1990s returns us to questions that Collier and Congreve debated: what lessons have we learned from these plays? How willing are we to offer ourselves as the targets as well as the interpreters of Restoration satire? Yet if Behn's current popularity signals, in some respects, a radical revision of the canon, this revolution in thinking is hardly complete. The standard anthology of Restoration and eighteenth-century drama is almost sixty years old and contains no plays by women dramatists.[33] Although *The Rover* is enjoying success on stage, there seems to be little impetus to revive Behn's other comedies, such as *The Rover*, part 2, in which Willmore chooses the prostitute La Nuche over the wealthy heiress. Ironically, it may be that the question of reworking the canon – of thinking through the problems of an anthology which might give equal play to Behn, John Crowne, and Congreve, requires yet another substantive rethinking of our expectations about the functions of dramatic art in a feminist and new historicist age.

NOTES

1 Jeremy Collier, *A Short View of the Immorality and Profaneness of the English Stage* (London, 1698); William Congreve, *Amendments of Mr. Collier's False and Imperfect Citations* (London, 1698).

2 See John Harwood, *Critics, Values, and Restoration Drama* (Carbondale: Southern Illinois University Press, 1982).

3 *The Complete Plays of William Congreve*, ed. Herbert Davis (University of Chicago Press, 1967), p. 392.

4 See Harriett Hawkins, "The 'Example Theory' and the Providentialist Approach to Restoration Drama: Some Questions of Validity and Applicability," *ECent* 24 (1983), 103–14.

5 Laurie Finke, "Aphra Behn and the Ideological Construction of Restoration Literary Theory," in Heidi Hutner, ed., *Rereading Aphra Behn: History, Theory, and Criticism* (Charlottesville: University Press of Virginia, 1993), pp. 17–43. See also Harriett Hawkins, *Likenesses of Truth in Elizabethan and Restoration Drama* (Oxford: Clarendon, 1972).

6 Thomas Babington Macaulay, *Critical and Historical Essays*, ed. Israel Gollancz (1843; repr. London: Dent, 1900), III, 160; Sir Leslie Stephen, *English Literature and Society in the Eighteenth Century* (1904; repr. London: Duckworth, 1947), p. 59; Aubrey Williams, *An Approach to Congreve* (New Haven: Yale University Press, 1979); Harold Weber, *The Restoration Rake-Hero: Transformations in Sexual Understanding in Seventeenth-Century England* (Madison: University of Wisconsin Press, 1986).

7 *The Spectator*, ed. Donald F. Bond (Oxford; Clarendon Press, 1965), I, 280.

8 Quoted in James Agate, ed., *The English Dramatic Critics: an Anthology 1660–1932* (London: Arthur Barker, 1933), p. 28; Johnson, *Lives of the Poets*, ed. George Birkbeck Hill (Oxford: Clarendon Press, 1905), II, 222.

9 Johnson, *Lives*, II, 222.

10 On Johnson and the politics of patronage, see Dustin Griffin, *Literary Patronage in England, 1660–1800* (New York: Cambridge University Press, 1996), pp. 220–45.

11 Quoted in Agate, ed., *English Dramatic Critics*, p. 32. On this revival of *The Rover* in the eighteenth century, see Jane Spencer, "*The Rover* and the Eighteenth Century," in Janet Todd, ed., *Behn Studies* (Cambridge University Press, 1996), pp. 84–106.

12 John Bell, ed., *British Theatre*, 34 vols., 2nd edn. (London, 1790–97), XII, vii; XVI, v.

13 Elizabeth Inchbald, ed., *The British Theatre*, 25 vols. (London, 1808).

14 *Complete Works of William Hazlitt*, ed. P. P. Howe (London: Dent, 1931), VI, 77. Cf. VI, 70–91 and 374–75.

15 See Joseph Hamburger, *Macaulay and the Whig Tradition* (University of Chicago Press, 1976), pp. 73–114.

16 Charles Lamb, "On the Artificial Comedy of the Last Century," in *The Life and*

Works of Charles Lamb, ed., Alfred Ainger, 12 vols. (London: Macmillan, 1899), II, 281. Cf. 277–89.

17 Henry Ten Eyck Perry, *The Comic Spirit in Restoration Drama* (New Haven: Yale University Press, 1925), pp. 131, 132

18 See Jane Spencer, "'Deceit, Dissembling, all that's Woman': Comic Plot and Female Action in *The Feigned Courtesans*," in Hutner, ed., *Rereading Aphra Behn*, pp. 86–101; and, in the same volume, Heidi Hutner, "Revisioning the Female Body: Aphra Behn's *The Rover*, parts I and II," pp. 102–20.

19 Dale Underwood, *Etherege and the Seventeenth-Century Comedy of Manners* (New Haven: Yale University Press, 1957), p. 8.

20 Thomas Fujimura, *The Restoration Comedy of Wit* (Princeton University Press, 1952), p. 19.

21 Ibid., p. 27.

22 Norman Holland, *The First Modern Comedies: The Significance of Etherege, Wycherley, and Congreve* (Cambridge, Mass.: Harvard University Press, 1959); Williams, *Approach to Congreve*.

23 John Palmer, *The Comedy of Manners* (London: G. Bell and Sons, 1913), p. 289 (italics added).

24 Catherine Gallagher, "Who Was That Masked Woman? The Prostitute and the Playwright in the Comedies of Aphra Behn," (1988), repr. in Hutner, ed., *Rereading Aphra Behn*, pp. 65–85; and Pat Gill, *Interpreting Ladies: Women, Wit, and Morality in the Restoration Comedy of Manners* (Athens: University of Georgia Press, 1994).

25 See Kristina Straub, *Sexual Suspects: Eighteenth-Century Players and Sexual Ideology* (Princeton University Press, 1991).

26 Derek Hughes, *English Drama 1660–1700* (Oxford: Clarendon Press, 1996), p. 24.

27 Hutner, "Rereading Aphra Behn: an Introduction," in *Rereading Aphra Behn*, p. 1–11.

28 The following paragraphs condense and extend points I have made in "'Be impudent, be saucy, forward, bold, touzing, and leud': the Politics of Masculine Sexuality and Feminine Desire in Behn's Tory Comedies," in J. Douglas Canfield and Deborah C. Payne, eds., *Cultural Readings of Restoration and Eighteenth-Century English Theater* (Athens: University of Georgia Press, 1995), pp. 114–40. See also Peggy Thompson, "Closure and Subversion in Behn's Comedies," in Katherine M. Quinsey, ed., *Broken Boundaries: Women and Feminism in Restoration Drama* (Lexington: University of Kentucky Press, 1996), pp. 71–88.

29 See Nancy Armstrong, *Desire and Domestic Fiction: a Political History of the Novel* (New York: Oxford University Press, 1987), pp. 3–27, 59–95.

30 *The Works of Aphra Behn*, ed. Janet Todd, 7 vols. (Columbus: Ohio State University Press, 1996), VI, 228.

31 *The Plays of Sir George Etherege*, ed. Michael Cordner (Cambridge University Press, 1982).

32 On the role of fantasy, see Slavoj Žižek, *The Sublime Object of Ideology* (London: Verso, 1989).

33 *British Dramatists from Dryden to Sheridan*, ed. George H. Nettleton and Arthur E. Case; rev. George Winchester Stone (1939; 2nd edn. Carbondale: Southern Illinois University Press, 1975).

In compiling the following selective bibliography, several principles have been followed. First, minor articles and notes have not been included. Second, individual chapters in anthologies or collections of essays have not been included; however, the reader will find the title of the anthology or collection listed in section 3. Finally, modern collections of plays are indicated under the names of individual dramatists; single play titles are not included.

1 Reference works

Backscheider, Paula R., ed. *Restoration and Eighteenth-Century Dramatists: First Series*. Dictionary of Literary Biography 80. Detroit: Gale Research Incorporated, 1989.
Restoration and Eighteenth-Century Dramatists: Second Series. Dictionary of Literary Biography 84. Detroit: Gale Research Incorporated, 1989.
Danchin, Pierre, ed. *The Prologues and Epilogues of the Restoration, 1660–1700: a Complete Edition*. Nancy: Publications Université Nancy II, 1981–88.
Harbage, Alfred B. *Annals of English Drama 975–1700*. Philadelphia: University of Philadelphia Press, 1940.
Highfill, Philip H., Jr., Kalman A. Burnim, and Edward A. Langhans. *A Biographical Dictionary of Actors, Actresses, Musicians, Dancers, Managers, and Other Stage Personnel in London, 1660–1800*. 16 vols. Carbondale: Southern Illinois University Press, 1973–93.
Langhans, Edward A, ed. *Restoration Promptbooks*. Carbondale: Southern Illinois University Press, 1981.
Loftis, John, Richard Southern, Marion Jones and A. H. Scouten. *The Revels History of Drama in English, Volume 5: 1660–1750*. London: Methuen, 1976.
Mann, David D., Susan Garland Mann, and Camille Garnier. *Women Playwrights in England, Ireland, and Scotland 1660–1823*. Bloomington: Indiana University Press, 1996.
Milhous, Judith, and Robert D. Hume, eds. *A Register of English Theatrical Documents 1660–1737*. 2 vols. Carbondale: Southern Illinois University Press, 1992.
Thomas, David, ed. *Restoration and Georgian England, 1660–1788*. Theatre in Europe: a Documentary History. Cambridge University Press, 1989.
Van Lennep, William, *et al. The London Stage, 1660–1800: a Calendar of Plays,*

Entertainments, and Afterpieces. 5 parts. Carbondale: Southern Illinois University Press, 1960–68.

Wiley, Autrey Nell, ed. *Rare Prologues and Epilogues 1642–1700.* Port Washington, N.Y.: Kennikat Press, 1970.

2 Bibliographies

Armistead, J. M. *Four Restoration Playwrights: a Reference Guide to Thomas Shadwell, Aphra Behn, Nathaniel Lee, and Thomas Otway.* Boston: G. K. Hall, 1984.

"Thomas Southerne: Three Centuries of Criticism." *Bulletin of Bibliography* 41 (1984): 216–37.

Ashley, L. R. N. "Colley Cibber: a Bibliography." *RECTR* 6 (1967): 14–27, 51–57.

Bartlett, Laurence. *William Congreve: a Reference Guide.* Boston: G. K. Hall, 1979.

Canfield, J. Douglas. "A Tentative Twentieth-Century Bibliography on Rowe's Tragedies," in *Nicholas Rowe and Christian Tragedy.* Gainesville: University Presses of Florida, 1977.

Davies, Neville H. "Davenant, Dryden, Lee and Otway." In Stanley Wells, ed., *English Drama (Excluding Shakespeare): Select Bibliographical Guides.* Oxford University Press, 1975.

Ham, Roswell Gray. *Otway and Lee: Biography from a Baroque Age.* New Haven: Yale University Press, 1931.

James, Eugene Nelson. *George Farquhar: a Reference Guide.* Boston: G. K. Hall, 1986.

Latt, David J., and Samuel Holt Monk. *John Dryden: a Survey and Bibliography of Critical Studies, 1895–1974.* Minneapolis: University of Minnesota Press, 1976.

Link, Frederick M, ed. *English Drama, 1660–1800: a Guide to Information Sources.* American Literature, English Literature and World Literatures in English 9. Detroit: Gale Research Company, 1976.

Lyles, Albert M., and John Dobson, comps. *The John C. Hodges Collection of William Congreve in the University of Tennessee Library: a Bibliographical Catalog.* Knoxville: University of Tennessee Press, 1970.

Macdonald, Hugh. *John Dryden: a Bibliography of Early Editions and of Drydeniana.* Oxford University Press, 1939.

Mann, David D. *Sir George Etherege: a Reference Guide.* Boston: G. K. Hall, 1981.

O'Donnell, Mary Ann. *Aphra Behn: an Annotated Bibliography of Primary and Secondary Sources.* Garland Reference Library of the Humanities 505. New York: Garland, 1986.

Stratman, Carl J., ed., and Edmund A. Napieralski and Jean E. Westbrook, comps. *Restoration and 18th Century Theatre Research Bibliography, 1961–1968.* Troy, N.Y.: Whitston Publishing Company, 1969.

Stratman, Carl J., David G. Spencer, and Mary Elizabeth Devine, eds. *Restoration and Eighteenth Century Theatre Research: a Bibliographical Guide, 1900–1968.* Carbondale: Southern Illinois University Press, 1971.

Winship, George Parker. *The First Harvard Playwright: a Bibliography of the Restoration Dramatist John Crowne.* Cambridge, Mass.: Harvard University Press, 1922.

3   General critical studies and collections of criticism

Avery, Emmett L. "Rhetorical Patterns in Restoration Prologues and Epilogues." In Max F. Schulz, William D. Templeman, and Charles R. Metzger, eds., *Essays in American and English Literature Presented to Bruce McElderry, Jr.* Athens: University of Georgia Press, 1986.

"The Restoration Audience." *PQ* 45 (1966): 54–61.

Backscheider, Paula R. *Spectacular Politics: Theatrical Power and Mass Culture in Early Modern England.* Baltimore: Johns Hopkins University Press, 1993.

Betterton, Thomas. *The History of the English Stage from the Restoration to the Present Time.* London, 1741.

Bevis, Richard W. *English Drama: Restoration and Eighteenth Century, 1660–1789.* Longman Literature in English Series. New York: Longman Press, 1988.

Bevis, Richard W. ed. *Eighteenth Century Drama: Afterpieces.* London: Oxford University Press, 1970.

Birdsall, Virginia Ogden. *Wild Civility: the English Comic Spirit on the Restoration Stage.* Bloomington: Indiana University Press, 1970.

Boswell, Eleanore. *The Restoration Court Stage, 1660–1702.* Cambridge, Mass.: Harvard University Press, 1932.

Braunmuller, A. R., and J. C. Bulman. *Comedy from Shakespeare to Sheridan: Change and Continuity in the English and European Dramatic Tradition.* Newark: University of Delaware Press, 1986.

Braverman, Richard. *Plots and Counterplots: Sexual Politics and the Body Politic in English Literature, 1660–1730.* Cambridge Studies in Eighteenth-Century English Literature and Thought 18. Cambridge University Press, 1993.

Brown, John Russell and Bernard Harris, eds. *Restoration Theatre.* New York: Capricorn Books, 1965. Reprinted, 1967.

Brown, Laura. *English Dramatic Form, 1660–1760: an Essay in Generic History.* New Haven: Yale University Press, 1981.

"The Defenseless Woman and the Development of English Tragedy." *SEL* 22 (1982): 429–43.

Browning, J. D., ed. *The Stage in the 18ᵗʰ Century.* Publications for the McMaster University Association for Eighteenth-Century Studies 9. New York: Garland, 1981.

Bruce, Donald. *Topics of Restoration Comedy.* New York: St. Martin's Press, 1974.

Bruns, Edward. *Restoration Comedy: Crises of Desire and Identity.* New York: St. Martin's Press, 1987.

Callow, Simon. *Acting in Restoration Comedy.* Acting Series and BBC Master Class. New York: Applause Theatre Books, 1991.

Canfield, J. Douglas. *Tricksters and Estates: On the Ideology of Restoration Comedy.* Lexington: University of Kentucky Press, 1997.

Word as Bond in English Literature from the Middle Ages to the Restoration. Philadelphia: University of Pennsylvania Press, 1989.

"The Ideology of Restoration Tragicomedy." *ELH* 51 (1984): 447–64.

Canfield, J. Douglas, and Deborah C. Payne, eds. *Cultural Readings of Restoration and Eighteenth-Century English Theatre.* Athens: University of Georgia Press, 1995.

Chase, Lewis Nathaniel. *The English Heroic Play: a Critical Description of the Rhymed Tragedy of the Restoration*. Columbia University Studies in English and Comparative Literature. New York: Russell & Russell, 1903. Reprinted, 1965.

Cibber, Colley. *An Apology for the Life of Colley Cibber*. 2 vols. Ed. B. R. S. Fone. Ann Arbor: University of Michigan Press, 1968.

Clark, Sandra, ed. *Shakespeare Made Fit: Restoration Adaptations of Shakespeare*. London: Everyman, 1997.

Cordner, Michael, Peter Holland, and John Kerrigan, eds. *English Comedy*. Cambridge University Press, 1994.

Corman, Brian. *Genre and Generic Change in English Comedy, 1660–1710*. University of Toronto Press, 1993.

Cunningham, John E. *Restoration Drama*. Literature and Perspective. London: Evans Brothers, 1966.

Dobrée, Bonamy. *Restoration Comedy, 1660–1720*. Oxford: Clarendon Press, 1924. Reprinted, 1955.

    Restoration Tragedy, 1660–1720. Oxford: Clarendon Press, 1929. Reprinted, 1954.

Dobson, Michael. *The Making of the National Poet: Shakespeare, Adaptation and Authorship, 1660–1769*. Oxford: Clarendon Press, 1992.

Downes, John. *Roscius Anglicanus*. Ed. Judith Milhouse and Robert D. Hume. London: Society for Theatre Research, 1987.

Ellehauge, Martin. *English Restoration Drama: its Relation to Past English and Contemporary French Drama, from Jonson Via Molière to Congreve*. Copenhagen: Levin & Munksgaard, 1933. Reprinted, 1974.

Elwin, Malcolm. *Handbook to Restoration Drama*. New York: Kennikat Press, 1928. Reprinted, 1966.

Finney, Gail, ed. *Look Who's Laughing: Gender and Comedy*. Studies in Humor and Gender 1. Langhorn, Penn.: Gordon & Breach, 1994.

Freehafer, John. "The Formation of the London Patent Companies in 1660." *TN* 20 (1965): 6–30.

Fritz, Paul and Richard Norton, eds. *Women in the Eighteenth Century*. Toronto: Samuel Stevens Hakkert, 1976.

Fujimura, Thomas H. *The Restoration Comedy of Wit*. Princeton University Press, 1952. Reprinted, 1968.

Gagen, Jean Elisabeth. *The New Woman: her Emergence in English Drama, 1600–1730*. New York: Twayne, 1954.

Gilder, Rosamond. *Enter the Actress: the First Women in the Theatre*. Boston: Houghton Mifflin, 1931. Reprinted, 1971.

Gildon, Charles. *A Comparison Between the Two Stages: a Late Restoration Book of the Theatre*. Preface by Arthur Freeman. New York: Garland, 1973.

Gill, Pat. *Interpreting Ladies: Women, Wit, and Morality in the Restoration Comedy of Manners*. Athens: University of Georgia Press, 1994.

Harbage, Alfred. *Cavalier Drama: an Historical and Critical Supplement to the Study of the Elizabethan and Restoration Stage*. New York: Russell & Russell, 1964.

Harwood, John T. *Critics, Values, and Restoration Comedy*. Carbondale: Southern Illinois University Press, 1982.

Hawkins, Harriet. *Likenesses of Truth in Elizabethan and Restoration Drama.* Oxford: Clarendon Press, 1972.

"The 'Example Theory' and the Providentialist Approach to Restoration Drama: Some Questions of Validity and Applicability." *ECent* 24 (1983): 104–14.

Hendricks, Margo, and Patricia Parker, eds. *Women, "Race," and Writing in the Early Modern Period.* London: Routledge, 1994.

Holland, Norman. *The First Modern Comedies: the Significance of Etherege, Wycherley, and Congreve.* Cambridge, Mass.: Harvard University Press, 1959.

Holland, Peter. *The Ornament of Action: Text and Performance in Restoration Comedy.* Cambridge University Press, 1979.

Hotson, Leslie. *The Commonwealth and Restoration Stage.* Cambridge, Mass.: Harvard University Press, 1928.

Howe, Elizabeth. *The First English Actresses: Women and Drama, 1660–1700.* Cambridge University Press, 1992.

Hughes, Derek. *English Drama, 1660–1700.* Oxford: Clarendon Press, 1996.

Hughes, Leo. *A Century of English Farce.* Princeton University Press, 1956.

"Attitudes of Some Restoration Dramatists Towards Farce." *PQ* 19 (1940): 268–87.

Hume, Robert D. *The Development of English Drama in the Late Seventeenth Century.* Oxford: Clarendon Press, 1976.

The Rakish Stage: Studies in English Drama, 1660–1800. Carbondale: Southern Illinois University Press, 1983.

Hume, Robert D. ed. *The London Theatre World, 1660–1800.* Carbondale: Southern Illinios University Press, 1980.

Jeffares, Norman A., ed. *Restoration Comedy.* London: Folio Press, 1974.

Jose, Nicholas. *Ideas of the Restoration in English Literature, 1660–1671.* London: Macmillan, 1984.

Kavenik, Frances M. *British Drama, 1660–1779: a Critical History.* Twayne's Critical History of British Drama. New York: Twayne, 1995.

Kenny, Shirley Strum, ed. *British Theatre and the Other Arts, 1660–1800.* London: Associated University Presses, 1984.

"Humane Comedy." *MP* 75 (1977): 29–43.

"Perennial Favorites: Congreve, Vanbrugh, Cibber, Farquhar, and Steele." *MP* 73 (1976) S4–S11.

King, Thomas A. "Reconstructing the First English Actresses." *DR* 36 (1992): 78–102.

Knutson, Harold C. *The Triumph of Wit: Molière and Restoration Comedy.* Columbus: Ohio State University Press, 1988.

Krutch, Joseph Wood. *Comedy and Conscience after the Restoration.* Columbia University Studies in English and Comparative Literature. New York: Columbia University Press, 1924.

Langbaine, Gerard. *Momus Triumphans; or, The Plagiaries of the English Stage and the Lives and Characters of the English Dramatick Poets. The English Stage: Attack and Defense, 1577–1730.* New York: Garland Publishers, 1973.

Leacroft, Richard. *The Development of the English Playhouse.* Ithaca: Cornell University Press, 1973.

Levin, Carole, and Patricia A. Sullivan, eds. *Political Rhetoric, Power, and*

Renaissance Women. SUNY Series in Speech Communication. Albany: State University of New York Press, 1995.

Lewcock, Dawn. "Computer Analysis of Restoration Staging, 1661–1694." *TN* 47 (1993): 20–29, 141–56, and 48 (1994): 103–15.

Loftis, John. *Comedy and Society from Congreve to Fielding.* Stanford Studies in Language and Literature 19. Stanford University Press, 1959.

The Politics of Drama in Augustan England. Oxford: Clarendon Press, 1963.

The Spanish Plays of Neoclassical England. New Haven: Yale University Press, 1973.

Loftis, John, ed. *Restoration Drama: Modern Essays in Criticism.* New York: Oxford University Press, 1966.

Loftis, John, Richard Southern, Marion Jones, and A. H. Scouten. *The Revels History of Drama in English, Volume V: 1660–1750.* London: Methuen, 1976.

Lynch, Kathleen M. *The Social Mode of Restoration Comedy.* New York: Macmillan, 1926. Reprinted, 1965.

McCabe, Richard A. *Incest, Drama, and Nature's Law, 1550–1700.* New York: Cambridge University Press, 1993.

McCollum, John I. *The Restoration Stage.* Boston: Houghton Mifflin, 1961. Reprinted, 1973.

McDonald, Margaret Lamb. *The Independent Woman in the Restoration Comedy of Manners.* Salzburg: University of Salzburg, 1976.

Maguire, Nancy Klein. *Regicide and Restoration: English Tragicomedy, 1660–1671.* Cambridge University Press, 1992.

Maguire, Nancy Klein, ed. *Renaissance Tragicomedy: Explorations in Genre and Politics.* New York: AMS Press, 1987.

Markley, Robert, and Laurie Finke, eds. *From Renaissance to Restoration: Metamorphoses of the Drama.* Cleveland: Bellflower Press and Case Western Reserve University, 1984.

Marsden, Jean. *The Re-Imagined Text: Shakespeare, Adaptation and Eighteenth-Century Literary Theory.* Lexington: University Press of Kentucky, 1995.

Marshall, Geoffrey. *Restoration Serious Drama.* Norman: University of Oklahoma Press, 1975.

Mauss, Katherine E. "'Playhouse Flesh and Blood': Sexual Ideology and the Restoration Actress." *ELH* 46 (1979): 595–617.

Mignon, Elizabeth. *Crabbed Age and Youth: the Old Men and Women in the Restoration Comedy of Manners.* Durham, N.C.: Duke University Press, 1947.

Milhous, Judith, and Robert D. Hume. *A Register of English Theatrical Documents 1660–1737.* 2 vols. Carbondale: Southern Illinois University Press, 1991.

Producible Interpretation: Eight English Plays, 1675–1707. Carbondale: Southern Illinois University Press, 1985.

Miner, Earl, ed. *Restoration Dramatists: a Collection of Critical Essays.* Englewood Cliffs, N.J.: Prentice-Hall, 1966.

Muir, Kenneth. *The Comedy of Manners.* Hutchinson University Library: English Literature. London: Hutchinson, 1970.

Nettleton, George Henry. *English Drama of the Restoration and Eighteenth Century (1642–1780).* New York: Macmillan, 1914. Reprinted, 1968.

Nicoll, Allardyce. *A History of Restoration Drama 1660–1700*. Cambridge University Press, 1928.

Noyes, Robert Gale. *Ben Jonson on the English Stage, 1660–1776*. Cambridge, Mass.: Harvard University Press, 1935.

The Neglected Muse: Restoration and Eighteenth-Century Tragedy in the Novel (1740–1780). Brown University Studies 24. Providence, R.I.: Brown University Press, 1958.

Owen, Susan J. *Restoration Theatre and Crisis*. Oxford: Clarendon Press, 1996.

Palmer, John. *The Comedy of Manners*. New York: Russell & Russell, 1914. Reprinted, 1962.

Perry, Henry Ten Eyck. *The Comic Spirit in Restoration Drama: Studies in the Comedy of Etherege, Wycherley, Congreve, Vanbrugh, and Farquhar*. New Haven: Yale University Press, 1925. Reprinted, 1962.

Powell, Jocelyn. *Restoration Theatre Production*. Theatre Production Studies. London: Routledge & Kegan Paul, 1984.

Quinsey, Katherine M., ed. *Broken Boundaries: Women and Feminism in Restoration Drama*. Lexington: University Press of Kentucky, 1996.

Redmond, James, ed. *Drama, Sex and Politics*. Themes in Drama 7. Cambridge University Press, 1985.

Roach, Joseph R. *The Player's Passion: Studies in the Science of Acting*. Ann Arbor: University of Michigan Press, 1993.

Roberts, David. *The Ladies: Female Patronage of Restoration Drama 1660–1770*. Oxford English Monographs. Oxford: Clarendon Press, 1989.

Rosenfeld, Sybil. *Strolling Players and Drama in the Provinces 1660–1765*. New York: Octagon Books, 1970.

Rothstein, Eric. *Restoration Tragedy: Form and the Process of Change*. Madison: University of Wisconsin Press, 1967. Reprinted, 1978.

Rothstein, Eric, and Frances M. Kavenik. *The Designs of Carolean Comedy*. Carbondale: Southern Illinois University Press, 1988.

Schneider, Ben Ross, Jr. *The Ethos of Restoration Comedy*. Urbana: University of Illinois Press, 1971.

Schofield, Mary Anne, and Cecilia Macheski, eds. *Curtain Calls: British and American Women and the Theatre, 1660–1820*. Athens: Ohio University Press, 1991.

Scott, Virginia. *The Commedia dell'arte in Paris, 1644–1697*. Charlottesville: University Press of Virginia, 1990.

Singh, Sarup. *Family Relationships in Shakespeare and the Restoration Comedy of Manners*. New York: Oxford University Press, 1983.

Smith, Dane Farnsworth. *The Critics in the Audience of the London Theatres From Buckingham to Sheridan: a Study of Neoclassicism in the Playhouse, 1671–1779*. University of New Mexico Publications in Language and Literature 12. Albuquerque: University of New Mexico Press, 1953.

Smith, John Harrington. *The Gay Couple in Restoration Comedy*. Cambridge, Mass.: Harvard University Press, 1948. Reprinted, 1971.

Sorelius, Gunnar. *"The Giant Race Before the Flood": Pre-Restoration Drama on the Stage and in the Criticism of the Restoration*. Uppsala: Almquist & Wiksells, 1966.

Spencer, Christopher, ed. *Five Restoration Adaptations of Shakespeare*. Urbana: University of Illinois Press, 1965.

Spencer, Hazelton. *Shakespeare Improved: The Restoration Versions in Quarto and on the Stage*. Cambridge, Mass.: Harvard University Press, 1927.

Sprague, Arthur Colby. *Beaumont and Fletcher on the Restoration Stage*. Cambridge, Mass.: Harvard University Press, 1926.

Staves, Susan. *Players' Scepters: Fictions of Authority in the Restoration*. Lincoln: University of Nebraska Press, 1979.

Stone, George Winchester, Jr., ed. *The Stage and the Page: London's "Whole Show" in the Eighteenth-Century Theatre*. Berkeley: University of California Press, 1981.

Styan, J. L. *Restoration Comedy in Performance*. Cambridge University Press, 1986.

Straub, Kristina. *Sexual Suspects: Eighteenth-Century Players and Sexual Ideology*. Princeton University Press, 1992.

Summers, Montague. *The Playhouse of Pepys*. London: K. Paul, Trench, Trubner and Company, 1935.

The Restoration Theatre. London: K. Paul, Trench, Trubner and Company, 1934. Reprinted, 1964.

Taney, Retta M. *Restoration Revivals on the British Stage, 1944–1979: a Critical Survey*. Lanham, Md.: University Press of America, 1985.

Tave, Stuart M. *The Amiable Humorist: a Study in the Comic Theory and Criticism of the Eighteenth and Early Ninteenth Centuries*. University of Chicago Press, 1960.

Visser, Colin. "The Anatomy of the Early Restoration Stage: *the Adventures of Five Hours* and John Dryden's 'Spanish' Comedies." *TN* 29 (1975): 56–69, 114–19.

Waith, Eugene M. *Ideas of Greatness: Heroic Drama in England*. New York: Barnes & Noble, 1971.

Weber, Harold. *The Restoration Rake-Hero: Transformations in Sexual Understanding in Seventeenth-Century England*. Madison: University of Wisconsin Press, 1986.

Wilcox, John. *The Relation of Molière to Restoration Comedy*. New York: Columbia University Press, 1938. Reprinted, 1964.

Williams, Aubrey. "No Cloistered Virtue: or, Playwright versus Priest in 1968." *PMLA* 90 (1975): 234–46.

Wilson, John Harold. *All the King's Ladies: Actresses of the Restoration*. University of Chicago Press, 1958.

The Court Wits of the Restoration: An Introduction. Princeton University Press, 1948.

A Preface to Restoration Drama. Riverside Studies in Literature L6. Boston: Houghton Mifflin, 1965.

The Influence of Beaumont and Fletcher on Restoration Drama. Columbus: Ohio University Press, 1928. Reprinted, 1967.

Young, Douglas M. *The Feminist Voices in Restoration Comedy: the Virtuous Women in the Play-Worlds of Etherege, Wycherley and Congreve*. Lanham, Md.: University Press of America, 1997.

Zimbardo, Rose A. *A Mirror to Nature: Transformations in Drama and Aesthetics, 1660–1732*. Lexington: University of Kentucky Press, 1986.

4 Biographies and bibliographies of individual authors

BANKS, JOHN (*c.* 1653–1706)

Of unknown origins, John Banks trained for the bar, becoming, in the words of Gerard Langbaine, "a Member of the Honourable Society of New-Inn." He quit law to begin writing for the King's Company in 1677. Banks's first three plays, all heroic dramas, based their plots on stories from antiquity. Subsequently Banks turned to the lives of English historical figures: Mary, Queen of Scots; Anne Boleyn; the Earl of Essex; and Lady Jane Gray. These later plays, all of them popular with female spectators, were written in the "pathetic" mode and are often seen as precursors to the "she-tragedies" Nicholas Rowe would write in the early eighteenth century. Banks evidently targeted his plays for women: six are dedicated to titled women. Banks married Elizabeth Thompson in 1691 and died, perhaps impoverished, in 1706.

Studies:

Wykes, David. "The Barbinade and the She-Tragedy: On John Banks's *The Unhappy Favourite.*" In Douglas Lane Patey and Timothy Keegan, eds., *Augustan Studies: Essays in Honor of Irvin Ehrenpreis.* Newark: University of Delaware Press, 1985.

BEHN, APHRA (*c.* 1640–1689)

The circumstances of Behn's early life are vague. She may have been born in Kent; she may have lived in Surinam for a while, as she claimed in her novella, *Oroonoko* (1688). Behn probably married a Dutch merchant in the early 1660s; he seems to have died around 1665. Charles II employed her as a spy in Antwerp during the Second Dutch War; she remain unpaid and was imprisoned for debt. Her writing career began in 1670 with *The Forced Marriage; or, The Jealous Bridegroom.* Behn went on to write between eighteen and twenty more plays, most of them comedies. Although attacked in some lampoons for presuming to write (and publish), Behn quickly gained entry to inner social and theatrical circles: she numbered the Earl of Rochester, Nell Gwyn (the King's "Protestant whore"), the leading tragic actress Elizabeth Barry, and the writers John Dryden, Edward Ravenscroft, Thomas Otway, and Sir George Etherege among her friends. Behn's intense Toryism is evident throughout her writings, and she often directed her most pointed barbs against Whigs and Republicans. Toward the end of her life, Behn turned to writing prose romances and poetry. Behn died in straitened circumstances and is buried in Westminster Abbey.

Works:

Summers, Montague, ed. *The Works of Aphra Behn.* 6 vols. New York: Phaeton Press, 1915. Reprinted, 1967.

Todd, Janet, ed. *The Works of Aphra Behn.* 7 vols. Columbus: Ohio State University Press, 1992–96.

Studies:

Batten, Charles L., Jr. "The Source of Aphra Behn's *The Widow Ranter.*" *RECTR* 13.1 (1974): 12–18.

Carver, Larry. "Aphra Behn: the Poet's Heart in a Woman's Body." *PLL* 14 (1978): 414–24.

Copeland, Nancy. "'Once a whore and ever'? Whore and Virgin in *The Rover* and its Antecedents." *Restoration* 16.1 (1992): 20–27.

Cotton, Nancy. "Aphra Behn," in *Women Playwrights in England, c. 1363–1750.* London: Associated University Presses. 1980.

Day, Robert Adams. "Muses in the Mud: the Female Wits Anthropologically Considered." *WS* 7 (1980): 61–74.

DeRitter, Jones. "The Gypsy, *The Rover*, and the Wanderer: Aphra Behn's Revision of Thomas Killigrew." *Restoration* 10.2 (1986): 82–92.

Diamond, Elin. "Gestus and Signature in Aphra Behn's *The Rover.*" *ELH* 56 (1989): 519–41.

Duffy, Maureen. *The Passionate Shepherdess: Aphra Behn 1640–89.* London: J. Cape, 1977.

Franceschina, John. "Shadow and Substance in Aphra Behn's *The Rover*: the Semiotics of Restoration Performance." *Restoration* 19.1 (1995): 29–42.

Gallagher, Catherine. "Who Was That Masked Woman? The Prostitute and the Playwright in the Comedies of Aphra Behn." *WS* 15 (1988): 23–42.

Gardiner, Judith Kegan. "Aphra Behn: Sexuality and Self-Respect." *WS* 7 (1980): 67–78.

Hill, Rowland M. "Aphra Behn's Use of Setting." *MLQ* 7 (1946): 189–203.

Hutner, Heidi, ed. *Rereading Aphra Behn: History, Theory, and Criticism.* Feminist Issues. Charlottesville: University Press of Virginia, 1993.

Kaufman, Anthony. "The Perils of Florinda": Aphra Behn, Rape, and the Subversion of Libertinism in *The Rover, Part 1.*" *RECTR* 11.2 (1996): 1–21.

Kubek, Elizabeth Bennett. "'Night Mares of the Commonwealth': Royalist Passion and Female Ambition in Aphra Behn's *The Roundheads.*" *Restoration* 17.2 (1993): 88–103.

Link, Frederick M. *Aphra Behn.* Twayne's English Author Series 63. New York: Twayne, 1968.

Musser, Joseph F., Jr. "'Imposing Nought But Constancy in Love': Aphra Behn Snares *The Rover.*" *Restoration* 3:1 (1979): 17–25.

Nash, Julie. "'The Sight on't Would Beget a Warm Desire': Visual Pleasure in Aphra Behn's *The Rover.*" *Restoration* 18.2 (1994): 77–87.

Owen, Susan J. "'Suspect My Loyalty When I Lose My Virtue': Sexual Politics and Party in Aphra Behn's Plays of the Exclusion Crisis, 1678–83." *Restoration* 18.1 (1994): 37–47.

Root, Robert L., Jr. "Aphra Behn, Arranged Marriage, and Restoration Comedy." *W&L* 5 (1977): 3–14.

Sackville-West, V. *Aphra Behn: The Incomparable Astrea.* Representative Women. New York: Viking Press, 1928.

Taetzsch, Lynne. "Romantic Love Replaces Kinship Exchange in Aphra Behn's Restoration Drama." *Restoration* 17.1 (1993): 30–38.

Todd, Janet. *Aphra Behn Studies.* Cambridge University Press, 1996.

Witmer, Anne, and John Freehafer. "Aphra Behn's Strange News from Virginia." *LC* 34 (1968): 7–23.

Woodcock, George. *Aphra Behn: the English Sappho.* Montreal: Black Rose Books, 1989.

BETTERTON, THOMAS (*c.* 1635–1710)

Betterton is better known for his acting and management of companies than for his writing. Nonetheless, in 1669 he altered Webster's *Appius and Virginia* to *The Roman Virgin*. Around this time he also revised Molière's *Georges Dandin* into *The Amorous Widow* and, the following year, produced *The Woman Made a Justice*. The first two plays were printed long after their première; the third play was never printed, indicating Betterton's utter disinterest in publication.

Studies:

Gildon, Charles. *The Life of Betterton, the Late Eminent Tragedian.* London, 1710.
Milhous, Judith. *Thomas Betterton and the Management of Lincoln's Inn Fields, 1695–1708.* Carbondale: Southern Illinois University Press, 1979.
   "Thomas Betterton's Playwriting." *BNYPL* 77 (1974): 375–92.
   "An Annotated Census of Thomas Betterton's Roles, 1659–1710." *TN* 29 (1975): 33–45, 85–94.

BOYLE, ROGER, EARL OF ORRERY (1621–1679)

Born to Richard Boyle, first Earl of Cork, and his second wife, Katherine Fenton, at Linsmore Castle, Waterford, Ireland, Boyle is known more for his distinguished military career than his literary contributions. He attended Trinity College, Dublin, between 1630 and 1635 but never received a degree. Although Boyle fought in Ireland on Cromwell's behalf, he never professed loyalty to him and worked instead for the restoration of Charles II. In 1641 Boyle married Margaret Howard (1623–89), the third daughter of Theophilus Howard, second Earl of Suffolk; they had seven children. Boyle is credited with introducing the rhymed heroic play onto the Restoration stage; indeed, his first play, *The General* (1661), resulted from a debate among the court wits as to whether or not the French fashion for rhymed drama could work on the English stage. Boyle wrote a total of nine plays.

Works:

Clark, William Smith, II, ed. *The Dramatic Works of Roger Boyle, Earl of Orrery.* 2 vols. Cambridge University Press, 1937.

Studies:

Clark, William S. "Further Light upon the Heroic Plays of Roger Boyle, Earl of Orrery." *RES* 2 (1926): 206–11.
   "The Published but Unacted Heroic Plays of Roger Boyle, Earl of Orrery." *RES* 2 (1926): 280–83.
Lynch, Kathleen M. "Conventions of Platonic Drama in the Heroic Plays of Orrery and Dryden." *PMLA* 44 (1929): 456–71.
   Roger Boyle, First Earl of Orrery. Knoxville: University of Tennessee Press, 1965.
Maguire, Nancy Klein. "Regicide and Reparation: the Autobiographical Drama of Roger Boyle, Earl of Orrery." *ELR* 21 (1991): 257–82.
Mill, L. J. "The Friendship Theme in Orrery's Plays." *PMLA* 53 (1938): 795–806.
Pebworth, Ted Larry. "The Earl of Orrery and Cowley's *Davideis*: Recovered Works and New Connections." *MP* 76 (1978): 136–48.

CARYLL, JOHN (1625–1711)

Diplomat and secretary to Mary of Modena and an envoy to Rome, Caryll, born to a Roman Catholic family from Sussex, authored one tragedy – *The English Princess; or The Death of Richard III* (1667) – and one comedy – *Sir Salomon* (1670). He also translated Ovid, Virgil and versions of the Psalms.

Studies:

Taylor, Richard C. "The Originality of John Caryll's *Sir Salomon*." *CompD* 20 (1986): 261–69.

CAVENDISH, WILLIAM, DUKE OF NEWCASTLE (1592–1676)

William Cavendish, perhaps less known today than his second wife, Margaret, was profoundly important to literary history, but less for his own plays than for his patronage of Shirley, Dryden, Jonson, and Shadwell. Born to Sir Charles Cavendish of Nottinghamshire, he attended St. John's College, Cambridge. Cavendish so generously supported the King during the Civil War period, when many of the Royalists lived abroad, that he was often quite poor himself. He met his second wife while in exile in Paris. When they returned to London after the Restoration, both began careers as writers. Cavendish collaborated on a number of minor comedies such as *Sir Martin Mar-All* with John Dryden.

Studies:

Perry, Henry Ten Eyck. *The First Duchess of Newcastle and her Husband as Figures in Literary History*. Harvard Studies in Ennglish 4. 1918. Reprinted, 1968.

Trease, Geoffrey. *Portrait of a Cavalier: William Cavendish, First Duke of Newcastle*. New York: Taplinger, 1979.

CENTLIVRE, SUSANNA (1669?–1723)

The facts of Centlivre's birth and youth are hazy. It is likely she was born to William Freeman and his wife, Anne. Centlivre left home at the age of fifteen. Until she married Joseph Centlivre, a royal cook, in 1707, she enjoyed a series of youthful adventures: for a while, disguised as a boy, she lived with a student at Cambridge; she contracted some sort of relationship with one Mr. Fox; she later lived with a Mr. Carroll (who was killed in a duel). Centlivre enjoyed a long and successful career as a playwright at a time when few women wrote for the stage. She wrote a total of nineteen plays, three of them farces. Among her most popular plays were *The Gamester* (1705), *The Busy Body* (1709), *The Wonder: a Woman Keeps a Secret* (1714), and *A Bold Stroke for a Wife* (1718). Her plays are known for their lively plots and deft comedy; Centlivre's plays also garnered a reputation for being eminently "actable" and many famous actors appeared in original productions and revivals. An ardent Whig, Centlivre numbered Nicholas Rowe, Richard Steele, and George Farquhar among her literary (and political) friends.

Works:

The Dramatic Works of the Celebrated Mrs. Centlivre, With a New Account of Her Life. 3 vols. London: J. Pearson, 1760–61. Reprinted, 1872.

Frushell, Richard C., ed. *The Plays of Susanna Centlivre*. Eighteenth Century English Drama. 3 vols. New York: Garland, 1981.

Studies:
Anderson, Paul Bunyan. "Innocence and Artifice: or, Mrs. Centlivre and *The Female Tatler*." *PQ* 16 (1937): 358–75.
Bateson, F. W. *English Comic Drama, 1700–1750*. Oxford: Clarendon Press, 1929.
Bowyer, John Wilson. *The Celebrated Mrs. Centlivre*. Durham, N.C.: Duke University Press, 1952.
Cotton, Nancy. *Women Playwrights in England, c. 1363–1750*. Lewisburg, Penn.: Bucknell University Press, 1980.
Frushell, Richard C. "Marriage and Marrying in Susanna Centlivre's Plays." *PLL* 22 (1986): 16–38.
Lock, F. P. *Susanna Centlivre*. Twayne's English Author Series 254. Boston: Twayne, 1979.

CIBBER, COLLEY (1671–1757)

A controversial figure throughout his life, Cibber was a well-known theatre manager and actor as well as a playwright. Born to Jane Colley and Caius Gabriel Cibber – the latter famous for his sculptures over Bethlehem Hospital – Cibber attended the free school of Grantham. In 1690 Cibber joined the United Company, where he quickly distinguished himself in comic roles. Throughout his career Cibber was known for his ability to perform fops, although he also insisted on playing tragic roles, such as Richard III, for which he was less suited. He remained at Drury Lane after the defection of Betterton and the other actors and helped bolster the company by writing his first comedy, *Love's Last Shift* (1696). Cibber went on to write and adapt more plays – twelve comedies, six tragedies, one tragicomedy, one farce, and several musical and operatic entertainments – but increasingly he assumed managerial responsibilities, serving between 1710 and 1732 as one of the actor-managers of Drury Lane. Cibber was named Poet Laureate in 1730, an appointment that earned him the enmity of Alexander Pope, among others; Cibber was to engage in a war of words with the poet for several years. Cibber did not enjoy happy relations with his actors or his family: for many years he lived apart from his wife, Katherine Shore (married in 1693), and two of his children, Theophilus and Charlotte, humiliated him with their exploits.

Works:
Hayley, Rodney L., ed. *The Plays of Colley Cibber*. Eighteenth Century English Drama. 2 vols. New York: Garland, 1980.

Studies:
Ashley, Leonard R. N. *Colley Cibber*. Twayne's English Author Series 17. New York: Twayne, 1965. Reprinted, 1989.
Barker, Richard Hindry. *Mr. Cibber of Drury Lane*. Columbia University Studies in English and Comparative Literature 143. New York: Columbia University Press, 1939.
Brown, Richard E. "The Fops in Cibber's Comedies." *ELWIU* 9 (1982): 31–41.

Dixon, Peter, and Rodney Hayler. "*The Provoked Husband* on the Nineteenth-Century Stage." *NCTR* 8 (1980): 1–16.

Fone, B. R. S. "*Love's Last Shift* and Sentimental Comedy." *RECTR* 9.1 (1970): 11–23.

Galef, David. "Love, Convention, and Character in Cibber's *The Careless Husband*." *Restoration* 14.2 (1990): 82–90.

Hughes, Derek. "Cibber and Vanbrugh: Language, Place, and Social Order in *Love's Last Shift*." *CompD* 20 (1986–87): 287–304.

"Vanbrugh and Cibber: Language, Place, and Social Order in *The Relapse*." *CompD* 21 (1987): 62–83.

Hume, Robert D. "Marital Discord in English Comedy from Dryden to Fielding." *MP* 74 (1977): 248–72.

Kenny, Shirley Strum. "Humane Comedy." *MP* 75 (1977): 29–43.

Koon, Helene. *Colley Cibber: a Biography*. Lexington: University Press of Kentucky, 1986.

Parnell, Paul E. "Equivocation in Cibber's *Love's Last Shift*." *SP* 57 (1960): 519–34.

Potter, Lois. "Colley Cibber: the Fop as Hero." In J. C. Hilson, M. M. B. Jones, J. R. Watson, eds., *Augustan Worlds: Essays in Honour of A.R. Humphreys*. Leicester University Press, 1978.

Vance, John A. "Power and Conversion in Cibber's *The Careless Husband*." *Restoration* 7.2 (1983): 68–74.

Wanko, Cheryl. "Colley Cibber's *The Rival Queans*: a New Consideration." *RECTR* 3.2 (1988): 38–52.

CONGREVE, WILLIAM (1670–1729)

Born in Bardsey in Yorkshire to an ancient and respected family, Congreve grew up and was educated in Ireland. He first attended Kilkenny College from 1682–86, transferring to Trinity College, Dublin at the end of that period. In 1691 he moved to London where he attended Middle Temple, one of the Inns of Court. It was during this period that he was introduced to fashionable London society, especially literary and theatrical circles. In 1693 Congreve's first comedy, *The Old Bachelor* was produced at the Theatre Royal in Drury Lane; he went on to write three more comedies, including his masterpiece, *The Way of the World* (1700), and one tragedy, *The Mourning Bride* (1697). In 1698 Congreve responded to Jeremy Collier's attack on the immorality of the stage, an attack that singled out Congreve and Vanbrugh. After 1700 Congreve wrote several more pieces for the stage, including a libretto for *Semele*, but no more full-length plays. Congreve never married but was supposedly involved with the actress, Anne Bracegirdle. Later in life he embarked on a long-term love affair with Henrietta, Duchess of Marlborough; their union most likely produced a daughter, Mary, in 1723. Congreve numbered among his friends Dryden, Pope, Southerne, Catharine Trotter, and the publisher, Jacob Tonson. He is buried in Westminster Abbey.

Works:
Davis, Herbert, ed. *The Complete Plays of William Congreve*. Curtain Playwrights. University of Chicago Press, 1967.

Henderson, Anthony G., ed. *The Comedies of William Congreve*. Plays by Renaissance and Restoration Dramatists. Cambridge University Press, 1982.

Summers, Montague, ed. *The Complete Works of William Congreve*. 4 vols. New York: Russell & Russell, 1923. Reprinted, 1964.

Studies:

Avery, Emmett L. *Congreve's Plays on the Eighteenth-Century Stage*. New York: Modern Language Association of America, 1951.

Braverman, Richard. "Capital Relations and *The Way of the World*." *ELH* 52 (1985): 133–58.

Corman, Brian. "Johnson and Profane Authors: the Lives of Otway and Congreve." In Paul J. Korshin, ed., *Johnson After Two Hundred Years*. Philadelphia: University of Pennsylvania Press, 1986.

"'The Mixed Way of Comedy': Congreve's *The Double-Dealer*." *MP* 71 (1974): 356–65.

"*The Way of the World* and Morally Serious Comedy." *UTQ* 44 (1975): 199–212.

Deitz, Jonathan E. "Congreve's Better Way to Run the World." *PLL* 11 (1975): 367–79.

Dobrée, Bonamy. *William Congreve*. Bibliographical Series of Supplements to British Book News on Writers and Their Work 58. London: Longmans, Green, 1963.

Erickson, Robert A. "Lady Wishfort and the Will of the World." *MLQ* 45 (1984): 338–49.

Gagen, Jean. "Congreve's Mirabell and the 'Idea' of the Gentleman." *PMLA* 79 (1964): 422–27.

Gosse, Anthony. "Collier, Congreve and the Patriarchalist Debate." *ECLife* 4 (1978): 83–86.

"Plot and Character in Congreve's *Double-Dealer*." *MLQ* 29 (1968): 274–88.

Hinnant, Charles H. "Wit, Propriety, and Style in *The Way of the World*." *SEL* 17 (1977): 373–86.

Hoffman, Arthur W. "Allusion and the Definition of Themes in Congreve's *Love for Love*." In Louis L. Martz and Aubrey Williams, eds., *The Author in His Work: Essays on a Problem in Criticism*. ELS Monograph Series 58. New Haven: Yale University Press, 1978.

Congreve's Comedies. Victoria: University of Victoria, 1993.

Hurley, Paul J. "Law and the Dramatic Rhetoric of *The Way of the World*." *SAQ* 70 (1971): 191–202.

Jarvis, F. P. "The Philosophical Assumptions of Congreve's *Love for Love*." *TSLL* 14 (1972): 423–34.

Kaplan, Deborah. "Learning 'to Speak the English Language': *The Way of the World* on the Twentieth-Century American Stage." *TJ* 49 (1997): 301–21.

Kaufman, Anthony. "Language and Character in Congreve's *The Way of the World*." *TSLL* 15 (1973): 411–27.

Kimball, Sue L. "Games People Play in Congreve's *The Way of the World*." In Donald Kay, ed., *A Provision of Human Nature: Essays on Fielding and Others in Honor of Miriam Austin Locke*. University of Alabama Press, 1977.

Kraft, Elizabeth. "Why Didn't Mirabell Marry the Widow Languish?" *Restoration* 13.1 (1989): 26–34.

Kroll, Richard W. F. "Discourse and Power in *The Way of the World*." *ELH* 53 (1986): 727–58.

Loftis, John E. "Congreve's *Way of the World* and Popular Criminal Literature." *SEL* 36 (1996): 561–78.

Lynch, Kathleen M. *A Congreve Gallery*. Cambridge, Mass.: Harvard University Press, 1951. Reprinted, 1967.

McCarthy, B. Eugene. "Providence in Congreve's *The Double-Dealer*." *SEL* 19 (1979): 407–19.

McComb, John King. "Congreve's *The Old Bachelour*: a Satiric Anatomy." *SEL* 17 (1977): 361–72.

Morris, Brian. *William Congreve*. London: Ernest Benn, 1972.

Mueschke, Paul, and Miriam Mueschke. *A New View of Congreve's "The Way of the World."* University of Michigan Contributions in Modern Philology 23. Ann Arbor: University of Michigan Press, 1958.

Nolan, Paul T. "*The Way of the World*: Congreve's Moment of Truth." *SSJ* 25 (1959): 75–95.

Novak, Maximillian E. "Congreve's *The Old Bachelor*: from Formula to Art." *EIC* 20 (1970): 182–99.

William Congreve. Twayne's English Author's Series 112. New York: Twayne, 1971.

Peters, Julie Stone. *Congreve, the Drama, and the Printed Word*. Stanford University Press, 1990.

Roper, Alan. "Language and Action in *The Way of the World, Love's Last Shift*, and *The Relapse*." *ELH* 40 (1973): 44–69.

Rosowski, Susan J. "Thematic Development in the Comedies of William Congreve: the Individual in Society." *SEL* 16 (1976): 387–406.

Rump, Eric. "Sheridan, Congreve and The School for Scandal." In James Morwood and David Crane, eds., *Sheridan Studies*. Cambridge University Press, 1995.

Snider, Alvin. "Professing a Libertine in *The Way of the World*." *PLL* 25 (1989): 376–97.

Thomas, David. *William Congreve*. English Dramatists. New York: St. Martin's Press, 1992.

Thompson, James. "Congreve's Dramatic Songs: 'O I am glad we shall have a Song to divert the Discourse.'" *PQ* 62 (1983): 367–82.

"Reading and Acting in *Love for Love*." *ELWIU* 7 (1980): 21–30.

Van Voris, W. H. *The Cultivated Stance: the Designs of Congreve's Plays*. Dublin: Dolmen Press, 1965.

Weber, Harold. "Disguise and the Audience in Congreve." *MLQ* 46 (1985): 368–89.

"The Rake-Hero in Wycherley and Congreve." *PQ* 61 (1982): 143–60.

Williams, Aubrey L. *An Approach to Congreve*. New Haven: Yale University Press, 1979.

"No Cloistered Virtue: Or, Playwright versus Priest in 1698." *PMLA* 90 (1975): 234–46.

"Political Justice, the Contrivances of Providence, and the Works of William Congreve." *ELH* 35 (1968): 540–65.

"The 'Utmost Tryal' of Virtue and Congreve's *Love for Love*." *TSL* 17 (1972): 1–18.

Williams, Aubrey and, Maximillian E. Novak. *Congreve Consider'd: Papers Read at a Clark Library Seminar, December 5, 1970*. William Andrews Clark Memorial Library Seminar papers. Los Angeles: University of California, 1971.

COWLEY, ABRAHAM (1618–1667)

Son of a wealthy London stationer, Cowley attended the Westminster School as a King's Scholar and Trinity College, Cambridge, as a Fellow. A prolific writer from the age of ten, he wrote two romantic epics by fifteen and both a pastoral drama and a Latin comedy by twenty. But his poetry remains his most respected work. During the Civil War, he left Cambridge for Oxford to support the Royalist cause, eventually exiling himself to France in 1644 and becoming Queen Henrietta Maria's secretary. Cowley returned to England in 1656, became a physician and was arrested for spying, but was released after publically submitting to Cromwell. Charles II never rewarded him for the spying nor punished him for his submission to Cromwell. His most popular drama, written in exile, was *The Guardian* (1650).

Works:

Calhoun, Thomas O., Laurence Heyworth, and Allan Pritchard, eds. *The Collected Works of Abraham Cowley*. 2 vols. Newark: University of Delaware Press, 1989.

Grosart, Alexander B., ed. *The Complete Works in Verse and Prose of Abraham Cowley*. Chertsey Worthies' Library. 2 vols. 1881. Reprinted, New York: AMS Press, 1967.

Studies:

Hinman, Robert B. *Abraham Cowley's World of Order*. Cambridge, Mass.: Harvard University Press, 1960.

Langley, T. R. "Abraham Cowley's 'Brutus': Royalist or Republican?" *YES* 6 (1976): 41–52.

Nethercot, Arthur H. "Abraham Cowley as Dramatist." *RES* 4 (1928): 1–24.

    Abraham Cowley: The Muse's Hannibal. London: H. Milford, Oxford University Press, 1931. Reprinted 1967.

Taaffe, James G. *Abraham Cowley*. Twayne's English Authors Series 115. New York: Twayne Publishers, 1972.

CROWNE, JOHN (1641–1712)

Although he grew up in the parish of St. Martins-in-the-Fields, London, Crowne spent his adolescence in Nova Scotia and then America. He was one of the first students to matriculate at Harvard, studying there from 1657 through 1660 but not taking a degree. He accompanied his father back to England in 1661 but refused to return to America, largely because he found Puritanism (or so he claimed) oppressive. Crowne's first play, *Juliana; or, The Princess of Poland* (1671), combines heroic tragedy and romance, but he went on to work in various genres, including tragedy, such as *The Destruction of Jerusalem*, comedy, such as the popular *Sir Courtly Nice*, and even one masque, *Calisto* (1675). He was a favorite of Charles II and influential courtiers, such as the Earl of Rochester, but contemporary accounts represent him as a reluctant sycophant.

Works:

Maidment, James, and W. H. Logan, eds. *The Dramatic Works of John Crowne.* 4 vols. Edinburgh: William Paterson, 1873–74.

McMullin, B. J., ed. *The Comedies of John Crowne: a Critical Edition.* The Renaissance Imagination 4. New York: Garland Publishers, 1984.

Studies:

Canfield, J. Douglas. "*Regulus* and *Cleomenes* and 1688: from Royalism to Self-Reliance." *ECLife* 12 (1988): 67–75.

Hirt, A. "A Question of Excess: Neo-Classical Adaptations of Greek Tragedy." *Costerus* 3 (1972): 55–119.

Hughes, Charlotte B. *John Crowne's Sir Courtly Nice: a Critical Edition.* Studies in English Literature 14. The Hague: Mouton, 1966.

Kaufman, Anthony. "Civil Politics – Sexual Politics in John Crowne's *City Politiques.*" *Restoration* 6.2 (1982): 72–80.

MacDonald, Joyce Green. "'Hay for the Daughters': Gender and Patriarchy in *The Miseries of Civil War* and *Henry VI.*" *CompD* 24 (1990): 193–216.

McMullin, B. J. "The Songs from John Crowne's *Justice Buisy, or the Gentleman-Quack.*" *RES* 28 (1977): 168–75.

Sengupta, Shivaji. "Biographical Notes on John Crowne." *Restoration* 6.1 (1982): 26–30.

"Shakespeare Adaptations and Political Consciousness: 1678–1682." *MHLS* 4 (1981): 58–67.

Wilson, John Harold, ed. *City Politiques.* Regents Restoration Drama Series. Lincoln: University of Nebraska Press, 1967.

DAVENANT, SIR WILLIAM (1606–1668)

Also D'Avenant. The son of an Oxford innkeeper and not, as rumored by Davenant himself, the illegitimate son of Shakespeare, Davenant became one of the most important figures in the Restoration theatre. As a boy, he was employed as a page to the Duchess of Richmond. By 1629 Davenant turned to writing plays and poetry; he enjoyed the patronage of Fulke-Greville and eventually caught the eye of Queen Henrietta-Maria, whose patronage he also enjoyed. In 1633 Davenant wrote the popular comedy, *The Wits,* and he became the unofficial Poet Laureate after Jonson retired from the position. During the Civil War, Davenant supported the Royalists and earned a knightship at the siege of Gloucester in 1643. Between 1650 and 1652 Davenant was imprisoned in the Tower for his ties to the Royalists. Davenant managed several times during the Interregnum to evade the ban on theatre by staging operas and musical entertainments. Upon the Restoration, he received one of two patents to manage a new company (the Duke's Company), giving him and Thomas Killigrew a virtual monopoly over all theatrical productions in London. Although Davenant wrote several comedies and adapted a number of plays, including several by Shakespeare, he is recognized more today for his innovations in staging, including the development of movable scenery and the training of actresses. He is buried at Westminster Abbey.

Works:
Maidment, James, and W. H. Logan, eds. *The Dramatic Works of Sir William D'Avenant.* 5 vols. Edinburgh: W. Paterson, 1872–74. Reprinted, 1964.

Studies:
Auberlen, Eckhard. *"The Tempest* and the Concerns of the Restoration Court: a Study of *The Enchanted Island* and the Operatic *Tempest." Restoration* 15.2 (1991): 71–88.

Blaydes, Sophia B., and Philip Bordinat. *Sir William Davenant: an Annotated Bibliography, 1629–1985.* Garland Reference Library of the Humanities 525. New York: Garland Publishers, 1986.

Bordinat, Philip. "William Davenant and the Caroline Masque." *BWVACET* 3.2 (1976): 1–18.

Bordinat, Philip, and Sophia B. Blaydes. *Sir William Davenant.* Twayne's English Authors Series 303. Boston: Twayne Publishers, 1981.

Clare, Janet. "The Production and Reception of Davenant's *Cruelty of the Spaniards in Peru." MLR* 89 (1994): 832–41.

Collins, Howard S. *The Comedy of Sir William Davenant.* Studies in English Literature 24. The Hague: Mouton, 1967.

Dobson, Michael. "'Remember First to Possess His Books': the Appropriation of *The Tempest,* 1700–1800." *ShS* 43 (1991): 99–107.

Dyson, Peter. "Changes in Dramatic Perspective: From Shakespeare's *Macbeth* to Davenant's." *SQ* 30 (1979): 402–07.

Guffey, George R. "Politics, Weather, and the Contemporary Reception of the Dryden-Davenant *Tempest." Restoration* 8.1 (1984): 1–9.

Harbage, Alfred. *Sir William Davenant, Poet Venturer, 1606–1668.* Philadelphia: University of Pennsylvania Press, 1935. Reprinted, 1971.

Harvey, A. D. "Virginity and Honour in *Measure for Measure* and Davenant's *The Law Against Lovers." ES* 75.2 (1994): 123–32.

Kroll, Richard. "Emblem and Empiricism in Davenant's *Macbeth." ELH* 57 (1990): 835–64.

McCarthy, William. "D'avenant's Prefatory Rhetoric." *Criticism* 20 (1978): 128–43.

Nethercot, Arthur H. *Sir William Davenant: Poet Laureate and Playwright-Manager.* University of Chicago Press, 1938. Reprinted, 1967.

Raddadi, Mongi. *Davenant's Adaptations of Shakespeare.* Uppsala: Almquist & Wiksells, 1979.

Scouten, Arthur H. "The Premiere of Davenant's Adaptation of *Macbeth.*" In W. R. Elton and William B. Long, eds., *Shakespeare and Dramatic Tradition: Essays in Honor of S. F. Johnson.* Newark: University of Delaware Press, 1989.

Shershow, Scott Cutler. "Windings and Turnings: the Metaphoric Labyrinth of Restoration Dramatic Theory." *CompD* 26 (1992): 1–18.

Spencer, Christopher. "Macbeth and Davenant's *The Rivals." SQ* 20 (1969): 225–29.

Wikander, Matthew H. "'The Duke My Father's Wrack': the Innocence of the Restoration *Tempest" ShS* 43 (1991): 91–98.

Young, Bruce W. "The Language of *Macbeth*: a Comparison of Shakespeare's and Davenant's Versions." *ISJR* 60 (1986): 431–43.

DRYDEN, JOHN (1631–1700)

Born in Northamptonshire to Parliamentary supporters, Dryden was educated at Westminster School where he was taught by Richard Busby, also the teacher of Christopher Wren, John Locke, Robert Hooke, and Matthew Prior. He matriculated from Trinity College, Cambridge in 1650 and took his B.A. in 1654. He married Lady Elizabeth Howard, sister to Sir Robert Howard, in 1663. Five years later Dryden was named as the first official Poet Laureate; he also became Historiographer Royal in 1670. Both the originator of several satires and attacks on other authors as well as the victim of similar attacks, Dryden enjoyed a lengthy career notable, even by Restoration standards, for controversy and tumult. Many attacks focused on Dryden's shifting political and religious allegiances; in 1686, for instance, he converted to Roman Catholicism, a move interpreted by some observers as an attempt to ingratiate himself with the newly crowned James II. Over the course of his life, Dryden wrote twenty-seven plays in various genres, as well as poems and prefaces. Dramatically Dryden is best known for his innovations in the part-verse, part-prose tragicomedy, as well as his attempts in the 1660s at heroic drama. Dryden is buried in Westminster Abbey.

Works:

Summers, Montague, ed. *Dryden: the Dramatic Works*. London: The Nonesuch Press, 1931–32. Reprinted, 1968.

H. T. Swedenberg, Jr., *et al.* eds. *The Works of John Dryden*. 20 vols, in progress. Berkeley: University of California Press, 1956–.

Studies:

Allen, Ned B. *The Sources of John Dryden's Comedies*. New York: Gordian Press, 1935. Reprinted, 1967.

Alssid, Michael W. "The Design of Dryden's *Aureng-Zebe*." *JEGP* 64 (1965): 452–69.

"The Perfect Conquest: a Study of Theme, Structure and Characters in Dryden's *The Indian Emperor*." *SP* 59 (1962): 539–559.

Armistead, J. M. "Dryden and the Occult as Dramatic Code: *Tyrannick Love*." *PLL* 24 (1988): 367–83.

"Dryden's *King Arthur* and the Literary Tradition: a Way of Seeing." *SP* 85 (1988): 53–72.

"Egypt in the Restoration: a Perspective on *All for Love*." *PLL* 22 (1986): 139–53.

"The Higher Magic in Dryden's *Conquest of Granada*." *PLL* 26 (1990): 478–88.

Banks, Landrum. "Dryden's Baroque Drama." In Thomas Austin Kirby and William John Olive, eds., *Essays in Honor of Esmond Linworth Marilla*. Baton Rouge: Louisiana State University Press, 1970.

Barbeau, Anne T. *The Intellectual Design of John Dryden's Heroic Plays*. New Haven: Yale University Press, 1970.

Bhattacharya, Nandini. "Ethnopolitical Dyamics and the Language of Gendering in Dryden's *Aureng-Zebe*." *CultCrit* 25 (1993): 153–76.

Bowers, Fredson. "The 1665 Manuscript of Dryden's *Indian Emperour*." *SP* 48 (1951): 738–60.

Bredvold, Louis I. *The Intellectual Milieu of John Dryden: Studies in Some Aspects of Seventeenth-Century Thought*. Ann Arbor: University of Michigan Press, 1934. Reprinted, 1956.

Brooks, Harold F. "Dryden's *Aureng-Zebe*: Debts to Corneille and Racine." *RLC* 46 (1972): 5–34.

Brown, Laura S. "The Divided Plot: Tragicomic Form in the Restoration." *ELH* 47 (1980): 67–79.

Bywaters, David. *Dryden in Revolutionary England*. Berkeley: University of California Press, 1991.

Coltharp, Duane. "'*Pleasing Rape*': the Politics of Libertinism in *The Conquest of Granada*." *Restoration* 21.2 (1997): 15–31.

Davison, Dennis. *Dryden*. Literature in Perspective. London: Evans Brothers, 1968.

Dobrée, Bonamy. *John Dryden*. London: Longmans, Green, 1956. Revised, 1961.

Eliot, T. S. *John Dryden: the Poet, the Dramatist, the Critic*. New York: Haskell House, 1966.

Evans, David R. "'Private Greatness': the Feminine Ideal in Dryden's Early Heroic Drama." *Restoration* 16 (1992): 2–19.

Flores, Stephan P. "Negotiating Cultural Prerogatives in Dryden's *Secret Love* and *Sir Martin Mar-all*." *PLL* 29 (1993): 170–96.

Frank, Marcie. "Fighting Women and Loving Men: Dryden's Representation of Shakespeare in *All for Love*," In Jonathan Goldberg, ed., *Queering the Renaissance*. Durham, N.C.: Duke University Press, 1994.

Fujimura, Thomas H. "The Appeal of Dryden's Heroic Plays." *PMLA* 75 (1960): 37–45.

Gagen, Jean. "Love and Honor in Dryden's Heroic Plays." *PMLA* 77 (1962): 208–20.

Gardner, William Bradford. "John Dryden's Interest in Judicial Astrology." *SP* 47 (1950): 506–21.

Garnett, Richard. *The Age of Dryden*. London: G. Bell and Sons, 1895. Reprinted, 1971.

Harth, Phillip. *Contexts of Dryden's Thought*. University of Chicago Press, 1968.
　Pen for a Party: Dryden's Tory Propaganda in Its Contexts. Princeton University Press, 1993.
　"Religion and Politics in Dryden's Poetry and Plays." *MP* 70 (1973): 236–42.

Hinnant, Charles H. "*All for Love* and the Heroic Ideal." *Genre* 16 (1983): 57–74.

Hopkins, David. *John Dryden*. British and Irish Authors. Cambridge University Press, 1986.

Hughes, Derek. "*Aphrodite katadyomene*: Dryden's Cleopatra on the Cydnos." *CompD* 14 (1980): 35–45.
　Dryden's Heroic Plays. Lincoln: University of Nebraska Press, 1981.
　"The Unity of Dryden's *Marriage a la Mode*." *PQ* 61 (1982): 125–42.

Jager, Eric. "Educating the Senses: Empiricism in Dryden's *King Arthur*." *Restoration* 11 (1987): 107–16.

King, Bruce. *Dryden's Major Plays*. Biography and Criticism 6. London: Oliver & Boyd, 1966.

"Dryden's *Marriage a la Mode*." *DramS* 4 (1965): 28–37.

"Dryden, Tillotson, and *Tyrannic Love*." *RES* 16 (1965): 364–77.

King, Bruce, ed. *Twentieth Century Interpretations of "All for Love."* Twentieth Century Interpretations. Englewood Cliffs, N.J.: Prentice-Hall, 1968.

King, Robert I. "*Res et Verba*: the Reform of Language in Dryden's *All for Love*." *ELH* 54 (1987): 45–61.

Kinsley, James, and Helen Kinsley, eds. *Dryden: the Critical Heritage*. The Critical Heritage Series. New York: Barnes & Noble, 1971.

Kirsch, Arthur C. *Dryden's Heroic Drama*. Princeton University Press, 1965. Reprinted, 1972.

"The Significance of Dryden's *Aureng-Zebe*." *ELH* 29 (1962): 160–74.

Kloesel, Lynn F. "The Play of Desire: Vulcan's Net and Other Stories of Passion in *All for Love*." *ECent* 31 (1990): 227–44.

Kropf, Carl R. "Patriarchal Theory in Dryden's Early Drama." *EiT* 6 (1987): 41–48.

"Political Theory and Dryden's Heroic Tragedies." *EiT* 3 (1985): 125–38.

Law, Richard. "The Heroic Ethos in John Dryden's Heroic Plays." *SEL* 23 (1983): 389–98.

Loftis, John. "Exploration and Enlightenment: Dryden's *The Indian Emperour* and its Background." *PQ* 45 (1966): 71–84.

Love, Harold. "Dryden, Durfey, and the Standard of Comedy." *SEL* 13 (1973): 422–36.

Lynch, Kathleen M. "Conventions of Platonic Drama in the Heroic Plays of Orrery and Dryden." *PMLA* 44 (1929): 456–71.

MacCallum, Hugh. "'A Track of Glory': Dryden's *Don Sebastian* and the Tragedy of Heroic Leadership." *Restoration* 19 (1995): 43–54.

Mace, Dean T. "Dryden's Dialogue on Drama." *JWCI* 25 (1962): 87–112.

MacMillan, Dougald. "The Sources of Dryden's *The Indian Emperour*." *HLQ* 13 (1950): 355–70.

Martin, Leslie H. "The Consistency of Dryden's *Aureng-Zebe*." *SP* 70 (1973): 306–28.

McHenry, Robert W., Jr. "Betrayal and Love in *All for Love* and *Berenice*." *SEL* 31 (1991): 445–61.

McKeon, Michael. "Marxist Criticism and *Marriage a la Mode*." *ECent* 24 (1983): 141–62.

Miner, Earl, ed. *John Dryden*. Writers and Their Background. Athens: Ohio University Press, 1972.

Moore, Frank Harper. "Heroic Comedy: a New Interpretation of Dryden's *Assignation*." *SP* 51 (1954): 585–98.

The Nobler Pleasure: Dryden's Comedy in Theory and Practice. Chapel Hill: University of North Carolina Press, 1963.

Moore, John Robert. "Political Allusions in Dryden's Later Plays." *PMLA* 73 (1958): 36–42.

Myers, William. *Dryden*. London: Hutchinson, 1973.

Newman, Robert S. "Irony and the Problem of Tone in Dryden's *Aureng-Zebe*." *SEL* 10 (1970): 439–58.

Osborn, James Marshall. *John Dryden*. Gainesville: University of Florida Press, 1965.

Owen, Susan J. "The Politics of John Dryden's *The Spanish Fryar; or, the Double Discovery*." *English* 43 (1994): 97–113.

Pendlebury, B. J. *Dryden's Heroic Plays: A Study of Origins*. New York: Russell & Russell, 1967.

Rosenthal, Laura. "'A Kind Mistress is the Good Old Cause': the Gender of the Heir in *Marriage a la Mode*." *JDTC* 5 (1990): 39–48.

Sherwood, Margaret Pollock. *Dryden's Dramatic Theory and Practice*. Yale Studies in English 4. New York: Russell & Russell, 1966.

Smith, David Nichol. *John Dryden*. The Clark Lectures of English Literature, 1948–49. Cambridge: Cambridge University Press, 1950. Reprinted, 1966.

Swedenberg, H. T., Jr. *Essential Articles for the Study of John Dryden*. The Essential Articles Series. Hamden, Conn.: Archon Books, 1966.

Thompson, James. "Dryden's *Conquest of Granada* and the Dutch Wars." *ECent* 31 (1990): 211–26.

Vance, John A. "Antony Bound: Fragmentation and Insecurity in *All for Love*." *SEL* 26 (1986): 421–38.

Visser, Colin. "John Dryden's *Amboyna* at Lincoln's Inn Fields, 1673." *RECTR* 15.1 (1976): 1–11, 32.

Wallace, John M. "Dryden and History: a Problem in Allegorical Reading." *ELH* 36 (1969): 265–90.

Wasserman, George R. *John Dryden*. Twayne's English Author's Series 14. New York: Twayne, 1964.

Winterbottom, John A. "The Development of the Hero in Dryden's Tragedies." *JEGP* 52 (1953): 161–73.

"The Place of Hobbesian Ideas in Dryden's Tragedies." *JEGP* 57 (1958): 665–83.

"Stoicism in Dryden's Tragedies." *JEGP* 61 (1962) : 868–83.

Zebouni, Selma Assir. *Dryden: a Study in Heroic Characterization*. Baton Rouge: Lousiana State University Press, 1965.

DUFFETT, THOMAS (fl. 1678)

According to popular accounts, Duffett began life as a milliner in the New Exchange before he turned to playwriting. Little is known of his life. His first effort, *The Spanish Rogue*, premièred at the King's Company in 1674. Perhaps best known is Duffett's *The Mock Tempest, or The Enchanted Castle* (1676), a burlesque of the Davenant/Dryden operatic adaptation of *The Tempest* that was playing at the rival playhouse. So "scurrilous" was this play that, when it was staged in Dublin, several ladies left in disgust. In addition to penning half-a-dozen comedies, Duffett also produced a small book of poems, songs, prologues and epilogues (1676).

Works:

DiLorenzo, Ronald Eugene, ed. *Three Burlesque Plays of Thomas Duffett: The Empress of Morocco, The Mock-Tempest, Psyche Debauch'd*. Iowa City: University of Iowa Press, 1972.

Studies:
Lewis, Peter Elvet. "The Three Dramatic Burlesques of Thomas Duffett." *DUJ* 63 (1966): 149–56.
West, Michael. "Dryden's *MacFlecknoe* and the Example of Duffett's Burlesque Dramas." *SEL* 18 (1978): 457–64.

DURFEY, THOMAS (1653–1723)

Born in Devonshire in 1653, Durfey was probably the descendent of French Huguenot refugees. He produced his first three plays in 1676: a heroic drama and two comedies. Comedy, especially broad, farcical comedy, proved to be Durfey's particular strength. He also became well known as a writer of songs and ballads. After 1688 he benefitted from Henry Purcell's help in setting the songs in his plays to music. Durfey's plays were enjoyed by Charles II, but he lost the patronage of James II. He recovered patronage when Anne ascended the throne; George II and Queen Caroline saw revivals of Durfey's plays. Known for frequenting the taverns and coffeehouses around London, Durfey numbered among his friends several well-known writers, including Richard Steele and Joseph Addison. He is interred in St. James's Church, London.

Works:
Vaughn, Jack A., ed. *Two Comedies [by Thomas D'Urfey]*. Rutherford: Fairleigh Dickinson University Press, 1976.

Studies:
Graham, C. B. "The Jonsonian Tradition in the Comedies of Thomas D'Urfey." *MLQ* 8 (1947): 47–52.
Knowles, Jack. "Thomas D'Urfey and Three Centuries of Critical Response." *Restoration* 8 (1984): 72–80.
Love, Harold. "Dryden, Durfey, and the Standard of Comedy." *SEL* 13 (1973): 422–36.
Lynch, Kathleen M. "Thomas D'Urfey's Contribution to Sentimental Comedy." *PQ* 9 (1930): 249–59.
Wheatley, Christopher J. "'Power like New Wine': the Appetites of Leviathan and Durfey's *Massaniello*." *SECC* 22 (1992): 231–51.
    "Thomas Durfey's *A Fond Husband*, Sex Comedies of the Late 1670s and Early 1680s, and the Comic Sublime." *SP* 90 (1993): 371–90.

ETHEREGE, SIR GEORGE (c. 1636–1692)

Information about Etherege's early life is vague; his father probably fled to France in 1644 to escape political upheavals at home, dying abroad in 1650. Thus it is likely Etherege spent his youth in France before his grandfather assumed his guardianship. Supposedly Etherege was educated at Cambridge, but evidence is inconclusive. His grandfather in 1654 apprenticed him to an attorney; four years later he was admitted to study law as a member of Clement's Inn. In 1663 Etherege left the law to begin work on his first play, *The Comical Revenge* (1664). This play, enduringly popular with audiences, established Etherege as a member of the group of wits surrounding Charles II, a group that included Sir Charles Sedley, and John Wilmot, Earl of Rochester. In 1668 Etherege produced his second play, *She Would If She Could*, which proved less successful with audiences. That same year Etherege was appointed a Gentleman of the Privy Chamber in Ordinary; he also became secretary to Sir Daniel Harvey, the ambassador to Turkey. Etherege accompanied Harvey to Constantinople, not returning to London until 1671. It is his final play, *The Man of Mode* (1676) for which Etherege is best known. Etherege quit writing for the stage, marrying a wealthy widow in 1680 and receiving a knighthood. He served as envoy to James II in Ratisbon between 1685 and 1689. He died in Paris as a Jacobite exile.

Works:

Brett-Smith, H. F. B., ed. *The Dramatic Works of Sir George Etherege.* The Percy Reprints 6. 2 vols. Oxford: B. Blackwell, 1927. Reprinted, 1971.

Cordner, Michael, ed. *The Plays of Sir George Etherege.* Plays by Renaissance and Restoration Dramatists. Cambridge University Press, 1982.

Studies:

Barnard, John. "Point of View in *The Man of Mode.*" *EIC* 34 (1984): 285–308.

Berglund, Lisa. "The Language of the Libertines: Subversive Morality in *The Man of Mode.*" *SEL* 30 (1990): 369–86.

Berman, Ronald. "The Comic Passions of *The Man of Mode.*" *SEL* 10 (1970): 459–68.

Borkat, Roberta F. S. "Vows, Prayers, and Dice: Comic Values in *The Man of Mode.*" *UDR* 12 (1976): 121–31.

Brown, Harold Clifford, Jr. "Etherege and the Comic Shallowness." *TSLL* 16 (1975): 675–90.

Brown, Laura S. "The Divided Plot: Tragicomic Form in the Restoration." *ELH* 47 (1980): 67–79.

Bruder, C. Harry. "Women in the Comedies of Sir George Etherege." *PAPA* 10.2 (1984): 1–11.

Canfield, J. Douglas. "Religious Language and Religious Meaning in Restoration Comedy." *SEL* 20 (1980): 385–406.

Corman, Brian. "Interpreting and Misinterpreting *The Man of Mode.*" *PLL* 13 (1977): 35–53.

Cox, R. S., Jr. "Richard Flecknoe and *The Man of Mode.*" *MLQ* 29 (1968): 183–89.

Davies, Paul C. "The State of Nature and the State of War: a Reconsideration of *The Man of Mode.*" *UTQ* 39 (1969): 53–62.

Fisher, Judith W. "The Power of Performance: Sir George Etherege's *The Man of Mode.*" *RECTR* 10.1 (1995): 15–28.

Gagen, Jean. "The Design of the High Plot in Etherege's *The Comical Revenge.*" *RECTR* 1.2 (1986): 1–15.

Hayman, John G. "Dorimant and the Comedy of a *Man of Mode.*" *MLQ* 30 (1969): 183–97.

Henshaw, Wandalie. "Sir Fopling Flutter; or the Key to *The Man of Mode.*" *EiT* 3 (1985): 98–107.

Hughes, Derek. "Play and Passion in the *Man of Mode.*" *CompD* 15 (1981): 231–57.

Hume, Robert D. "Reading and Misreading *The Man of Mode.*" *Criticism* 14 (1972): 1–11.

Huseboe, Arthur R. *Sir George Etherege.* Twayne's English Authors Series 446. Boston: Twayne, 1987.

Krause, David. "The Defaced Angel: a Concept of Satanic Grace in Etherege's *The Man of Mode.*" *DramaS* 7 (1969): 87–103.

Markley, Robert. *Two-Edg'd Weapons: Style and Ideology in the Comedies of Etherege, Wycherley and Congreve.* Oxford: Clarendon Press, 1988.

Martin, Leslie H. "Past and Parody in *The Man of Mode.*" *SEL* 16 (1976): 363–76.

McCamic, Frances Smith. *Sir George Etherege: a Study in Restoration Comedy (1660–1680).* Folcraft, 1931. Reprinted, 1974.

Morrow, Laura. "The Right Snuff: Dorimant and the Will to Meaning." *Restoration* 14 (1990): 15–21.

Neill, Michael. "Heroic Heads and Humble Tails: Sex, Politics, and the Restoration Comic Rake." *ECent* 24 (1983): 115–39.

Plank, Jeffrey. "Augustan Conversion of Pastoral: Waller, Denham, and Etherege's *The Man of Mode.*" *ELWIU* 12 (1985): 189–99.

Staves, Susan. "The Secrets of Genteel Identity in *The Man of Mode*: Comedy of Manners vs. the Courtesy Book." *SECC* 19 (1989): 117–28.

Thompson, James. "Lying and Dissembling in the Restoration." *Restoration* 6 (1982): 11–19.

Underwood, Dale. *Etherege and the Seventeenth-Century Comedy of Manners.* Yale Studies in English 135. New Haven: Yale University Press, 1957.

Weber, Harold. "Charles II, George Pines, and Mr. Dorimant: The Politics of Sexual Power in Restoration England." *Criticism* 32 (1990): 193–219.

Wess, Robert. "Utopian Rhetoric in *The Man of Mode.*" *ECent* 27 (1986): 141–61.

Wilkinson, D. R. M. "Etherege and a Restoration Pattern of Wit." *ES* 68 (1987): 497–510.

Young, Douglas M. *The Feminist Voices in Restoration Comedy: The Virtuous Women in the Play-Worlds of Etherege, Wycherley, and Congreve.* Lanham, Md.: University Press of America, 1997.

Zimbardo, Rose A. "Toward Zero/Toward Public Virtue: The Conceptual Design of Dramatic Satire before and after the Ascension of William and Mary." *ECLife* 12.3 (1988): 53–66.

FARQUHAR, GEORGE (*c.* 1677–1707)

Farquhar was born in Londonderry, Ireland, to an Anglican clergyman who, as tradition would have it, was burned out of his possessions by Jacobites during the uprisings which followed the Glorious Revolution. There is some speculation that Farquhar served in the Battle of the Boyne in 1690; if so, he would have been twelve or thirteen. Farquhar entered Trinity College, Dublin, in July of 1694. He left in 1696 without a degree and became an actor in Joseph Ashbury's troupe at the Smock Alley Theatre in Dublin. He played many roles, although his thin voice was a disadvantage. After an accident occurred on stage during a duel, he swore off acting. Farquhar left for London in 1697 or 1698; in December of 1698 his first play, *Love and a Bottle*, opened in Drury Lane. It was his next play, *The Constant Couple; or a Trip to the Jubilee* (1699), that secured Farquhar's reputation. So popular did this play prove that Farquhar reused the characters in his next play, *Sir Harry Wildair: Being the Sequel of the Trip to the Jubilee* (1701). Some time between 1703 and 1704 Farquhar married an army widow with three children; the couple had two daughters of their own. In March of 1704 Farquhar left the stage for the military, having secured a lieutenant's commission; he probably became a recruiting officer by June, an experience he would put to good use in his play of the same name. Farquhar is best known for his final two plays, *The Recruiting Officer* and *The Beaux' Stratagem*. Farquhar died young of a wasting fever and is buried at St. Martin's-in-the-Fields.

Works:

Ewald, Alexander Charles, ed. *The Dramatic Works of George Farquhar*. 2 vols. London: John C. Nimmo, 1892.

Stonehill, Charles, ed. *The Complete Works of George Farquhar in 2 Volumes*. London: The Nonesuch Press, 1930. Reprinted, 1976.

Studies:

Berman, Ronald. "The Comedy of Reason." *TSLL* 7 (1965): 162–68.

Canfield, J. Douglas. "Religious Language and Religious Meaning in Restoration Comedy." *SEL* 20 (1980): 385–406.

Connely, Willard. *Young George Farquhar: the Restoration Drama at Twilight*. London: Cassell, 1949.

Cope, Jackson I. "*The Constant Couple*: Farquhar's Four-Plays-in-One." *ELH* 41 (1974): 477–93.

Farmer, A. J. *George Farquhar*. London: Longmans, 1966.

Hughes, Derek. "Body and Ritual in Farquhar." *CompD* 31 (1997): 414–35.

"Who Counts in Farquhar?" *CompD* 31 (1997): 7–27.

James, Eugene Nelson. "The Burlesque of Restoration Comedy in *Love and a Bottle*." *SEL* 5 (1965): 469–90.

Kenny, Shirley Strum. "George Farquhar and 'The Bus'ness of a Prologue.'" *ThS* 19 (1978): 139–54.

"Humane Comedy." *MP* 75 (1977): 29–43.

Kimball, Sue L. "'Ceres in her harvest': the Exploded Myths of Womanhood in George Farquhar's *The Beaux' Stratagem*." *RECTR* 3.1 (1988): 1–9.

Larson, Milton A. "The Influence of Milton's Divorce Tracts on Farquhar's *Beaux' Stratagem*." *PMLA* 39 (1924): 174–78.

McVeagh, John. "George Farquhar and Commercial England." *SVEC* 217 (1983): 65–81.

Milhous, Judith, and Robert D. Hume. "*The Beaux' Stratagem*: a Production Analysis." *TJ* 34 (1982): 77–95.

Olshen, Barry N. "*The Beaux' Stratagem* on the Nineteenth-Century London Stage." *TN* 28 (1974): 70–80.

Rogers, J. P. W. "The Dramatist vs. the Dunce: George Farquhar and John Oldmixon." *RECTR* 10.2 (1971): 53–58.

Rothstein, Eric. "Farquhar's *Twin-Rivals* and the Reform of Comedy." *PMLA* 79 (1964): 33–41.
George Farquhar. Twayne's English Author Series 58. New York: Twayne, 1967.
Roper, Alan. "*The Beaux' Strategem*: Image and Action." In Earl Miner, ed., *Seventeenth-Century Imagery: Essays on Uses of Figurative Language from Donne to Farquhar.* Berkeley: University of California Press, 1971.
Wertheim, Albert. "Bertolt Brecht and George Farquhar's *The Recruiting Officer.*" *CompD* 7 (1973): 179–90.

FLECKNOE, RICHARD (d. 1678)

Today Flecknoe is best known for being the object of Dryden's ridicule in the mock-epic fragment, *MacFlecknoe*; however, this former Jesuit did produce some poetry, four plays, and dramatic criticism. To the derision of his contemporaries, Flecknoe saw only one of his plays, *Love's Kingdom*, actually staged (1664). According to Gerard Langbaine, "it had the misfortune to miscarry in the Representation." Some biographers think Flecknoe may have been Irish; still others think he was the nephew of Fr. William Flecknoe, S. J., and a native of Oxford. If the latter account is true, then it is likely Flecknoe was sent to one of the Jesuit colleges abroad before he left to pursue a more worldly existence.

Studies:
Canfield, J. Douglas. "Richard Flecknoe's Early Defense of the Stage: An Appeal to Cromwell." *RECTR* 2.2 (1987): 1–7.
Cox, R. S., Jr. "Richard Flecknoe and *The Man of Mode.*" *MLQ* 29 (1968): 183–89.

GILDON, CHARLES (1665–1723/4)

Born to a Roman Catholic family in Dorsetshire, Gildon relinquished the priesthood for the pleasures of London. Having spent his paternal estate, he made an imprudent (and unhappy) marriage to mend his fortunes. Gildon wrote three tragedies, *The Roman Bride's Revenge* (1697), *Phaeton, or The Fatal Divorce* (1698), and *Love's Victim, or The Queen of Wales* (1701). Gildon also altered *Measure for Measure* in addition to publishing Behn's last play, *The Younger Brother; or, The Amorous Jilt.* Today Gildon is perhaps best known for his dramatic criticism, *A Comparison between the two Stages* (1702). Gildon expressed his religious and philosophical skepticism in early writings; however, he later recanted those beliefs in *The Deist's Manual, or Rational Enquiry into the Christian Religion* (1705). Gildon also engaged in a war of words with Alexander Pope, thus earning himself a place in *The Dunciad*.

Works:
Backscheider, Paula R., ed. *The Plays of Charles Gildon.* Eighteenth-Century English Drama. New York: Garland, 1979.

HOWARD, EDWARD (fl. 1668)

A son of the Earl of Berkshire and therefore brother-in-law to John Dryden. Edward Howard is best known for the infamous political drama, *The Change of Crowns*

(1667), which offended court sensibilities. Charles II shut down the production and briefly imprisoned the actor, John Lacy, who played the role of Asinello, a country gentleman horrified by court corruption. Like his brother, Robert Howard, he quarreled with Dryden over literary matters, criticizing rhymed tragedy and praising Jonsonian-style comedy; indeed, two plays he published in 1671, *The Women's Conquest* and *The Six Days Adventure*, both featured prefaces aimed at Dryden. Shadwell lampooned Edward, along with his brother Robert, in *The Sullen Lovers*; Edward was depicted as "Poet Ninny."

HOWARD, JAMES (fl. 1674)

The youngest son of the Earl of Berkshire and brother to Lady Elizabeth Howard, the wife of John Dryden, James Howard wrote two plays, *All Mistaken, or The Mad Couple* (1672) and *The English Mounsieur* (1674). He also adapted *Romeo and Juliet*, although it was never printed. Little else is known.

HOWARD, SIR ROBERT (1626–1698)

Sixth son of the Earl of Berkshire and brother-in-law to John Dryden, Robert Howard attended Magdalen College, Cambridge. For his loyalty during the Civil War, he was rewarded with the post of Auditor of the Exchequer, a position that made him quite wealthy. Howard earned many enemies for his obstinacy and pride: Shadwell portrayed him as Sir Positive At-all in *The Sullen Lovers*, and the Duke of Buckingham evidently depicted him as Bilboa in the original version of *The Rehearsal*. Robert Howard wrote six plays, some of them, like *The Committee* (1665) and *The Indian Queen* (1665) tremendously popular with audiences. He collaborated with Dryden, his brother-in-law, in the mid-sixties, but the two men eventually fell out over the legitimacy of rhymed drama. Howard is also known for his translation of the fourth book of *The Aenead* (1660).

Studies:
Oliver, H. J. *Sir Robert Howard, 1626–1698: a Critical Biography*. Durham, N.C.: Duke University Press, 1963.
Roscioni, Gian Carlo. "Sir Robert Howard's 'Skeptical Curiosity.'" *MP* 65 (1967): 53–59.

KILLIGREW, SIR THOMAS (1612–1683)

Born to a distinguished old family, Killigrew was a page to Charles I and later a close friend to Charles II. He wrote a few plays before the Restoration, including the popular farce, *The Parson's Wedding* (1640). During the Interregnum Killigrew traveled abroad with the royal family, writing closet dramas to amuse Queen Henrietta Maria and her entourage. After the Restoration Killigrew used his connections to the royal family to secure one of two theatrical patents, giving him and William Davenant a virtual monopoly over London theatre. Although he competed with Davenant for audiences and copied his innovations in staging, Killigrew never took his company, the King's Company, that seriously. Indeed, the company folded after twenty years of family mismanagement, and the remaining actors were joined to the Duke's Company to form a new enterprise in 1682, the United Company.

Works:
Comedies and Tragedies. New York: B. Blom, 1967.

Studies:
DeRitter, Jones. "The Gypsy, *The Rover*, and The Wanderer: Aphra Behn's Revision of Thomas Killigrew." *Restoration* 10.2 (1986): 82–92.
Harbage, Alfred. *Thomas Killigrew: Cavalier Dramatist, 1612–83.* New York: B. Blom, 1930. Reprinted, 1967.

LACY, JOHN (1622?–1681)

Born in Yorkshire, Lacy became one of the most popular actors of the Restoration. The facts of his early life are vague. Lacy may have been apprenticed to John Ogilby, the printer of fine-quality books, or he may have been a dancing master before becoming a lieutenant. Not disputed, though, is the extent of Lacy's acclaim. Pepys, seeing Lacy perform the role of Teague in *The Committee*, a role for which he was celebrated, described him as "beyond imagination." Charles II ordered a portrait of Lacy in his three best-known roles: Teague in *The Commitee*; Mr. Scruple in *The Cheats*; and M. Galliard in *The Variety*. Lacy wrote three farces, the first two of which were extraordinarily popular: *The Dumb Lady, or The Farriar made Physitian* (1672); *The Old Troop, or Monsieur Ragou* (1672); and *Sir Hercules Buffoon*. The last play was staged and printed after Lacy's death.

Works:
Maidment, James, and W. H. Logan. *The Dramatic Works of John Lacy, Comedian.* Edinburgh: W. Paterson, 1875. Reprinted, 1967.

Studies:
Scheil, Katherine West. "*Sauny the Scot: or, The Taming of the Shrew*: John Lacy and the Importance of Theatrical Context in the Restoration." *Restoration* 21.2 (1997): 66–81.

LEE, NATHANIEL (*c.* 1645–1692)

The son of Richard and Elizabeth Lee, Nathaniel attended the Westminster School and then Trinity College, Cambridge, where he earned a B.A. in 1669. After graduation Lee attempted acting; he soon after began writing tragedy. His first play, *The Tragedy of Nero* was performed at Drury Lane on 16 May 1674. Lee wrote or collaborated on thirteen plays, four of them overwhelmingly popular with audiences. Over the course of his career, Lee turned from writing rhymed heroic tragedies – the sort of plays popular in the 1660s – to blank-verse tragedies featuring pathetic and tortured heroes. These plays often featured homicidal or suicidal endings, in addition to a heightened dramatic language that expressed the anguish of his heroes and ill-fated lovers. Lee collaborated with John Dryden on two plays,

Oedipus (1678) and *The Duke of Guise* (1682). *Lucius Junius Brutus* (1680) was banned for "very Scandalous Expressions & Reflections upon the Government" at the height of the Exclusion Crisis. Between 1684 and 1689, Lee was confined to Bedlam after a mental breakdown. He died during a drinking binge three years after his release.

Works:

Stroup, Thomas B., and Arthur L. Cooke, eds. *Works.* 2 vols. Metuchen, N.J.: Scarecrow Reprint Corporation, 1954–55. Reprinted, 1968.

Studies:

Armistead, J. M. "Hero as Endangered Species: Structure and Idea in Lee's *Sophonisba.*" *DUJ* 71 (1978): 35–43.

"Lee, Renaissance Conventions, and the Psychology of Providence: the Design of *Caesar Borgia.*" *ELWIU* 4 (1977): 159–73.

Nathaniel Lee. Twayne's English Authors Series 270. Boston: Twayne, 1979.

"Occultism in Restoration Drama: Motives for Revaluation." *MLS* 9.3 (1979): 60–67.

"The Tragicomic Design of *Lucius Junius Brutus*: Madness as Providential Therapy." *PLL* 15 (1979): 38–51.

Barbour, Frances. "The Unconventional Heroic Plays of Nathaniel Lee." *TSLL* 20 (1940): 109–16.

Birley, Robert. "Nathaniel Lee: *The Rival Queens.*" In *Sunk Without Trace: Some Forgotten Masterpieces Reconsidered.* London: R. Hart-Davis, 1962.

Brown, Richard E. "Heroics Satirized by 'Mad Nat. Lee.'" *PLL* 19 (1983): 385–401.

Cooke, A. L., and Thomas B. Stroup. "The Political Implications in Lee's *Constantine the Great.*" *JEGP* 49 (1950): 506–15.

Hammond, Antony. "The 'Greatest Action': Lee's *Lucius Junius Brutus.*" In Antony Coleman and Antony Hammond, eds., *Poetry and Drama, 1570–1700: Essays in Honour of Harold F. Brooks.* London: Methuen, 1981.

Hume, Robert D. "The Satiric Design of Nat. Lee's *The Princess of Cleve.*" *JEGP* 75 (1976): 117–38.

Kastan, David Scott. "*Nero* and the Politics of Nathaniel Lee." *PLL* 13 (1977): 125–35.

Owen, Sue. "'Partial Tyrants' and 'Freeborn People' in *Lucius Junius Brutus.*" *SEL* 31 (1991): 463–82.

Parker, Gerald D. "'History as Nightmare' in Nevil Payne's *The Siege of Constantinople* and Nathaniel Lee's *Lucius Junius Brutus.*" *PLL* 21 (1985): 3–18.

Verdurmen, J. Peter. "*Lucius Junius Brutus* and Restoration Tragedy: the Politics of Trauma." *JES* 19 (1989): 81–98.

Vieth, David M. "Psychological Myth as Tragedy: Nathaniel Lee's *Lucius Junius Brutus.*" *HLQ* 39 (1975): 57–76.

MANLEY, DELARIVIÉRE (*c.* 1672–1724)

Born in the Channel Islands to Sir Roger Manley, a former cavalier and military governor who published translations from the Dutch, a history of the English rebellion, and a continuation of a Turkish history. Manley was sent away to study languages – French, Spanish, Italian, and Latin – with a Huguenot minister; she returned before mastering the last three. After her father's death, she married her cousin (and ward) John Manley in what proved to be a bigamous union. Her estate squandered by her husband, Manley tried to support herself by being a retainer to Barbara Villiers, Duchess of Cleveland (one of the aging mistresses of Charles II); ultimately, she turned to writing as a means of support. Her first play – and only comedy – *The Lost Lover; or, The Jealous Husband* premièred at Drury Lane in 1696. She went on to write three heroic tragedies, *The Royal Mischief* (1696), *Almyna; or, The Arabian Vow* (1706), and *Lucius, the First Christian King of Britain* (1717). Manley also wrote "secret histories," such as the scandalous *New Atalantis*, as well as political pamphlets. Manly lived with the printer John Barber from 1711 to her death; she is buried in the Church of St. Benet at Paul's-Wharf.

Studies:

Clark, Constance. *Three Augustan Women Playwrights*. New York: P. Lang, 1986.
Day, Robert Adams. "Muses in the Mud: The Female Wits Anthropologically Considered." *WS* 7.3 (1980): 61–74.
Katz, Candace Brook. "The Deserted Mistress Motif in Mrs. Manley's *Lost Lover*, 1696." *RECTR* 16.1 (1977): 27–39.
Needham, Gwendolyn B. "Mary de la Rivière Manley, Tory Defender." *HLQ* 12 (1949): 253–288.
"Mrs. Manley: An Eighteenth-Century Wife of Bath." *HLQ* 14 (1951): 259–84.
Palomo, Dolores. "A Woman Writer and the Scholars: A Review of Mary Manley's Reputation." *W&L* 6.1 (1978): 36–46.

MOTTEUX, PETER ANTHONY (1663–1718)

A French Huguenot born in Rouen, Motteux moved to London after the revocation of the Edict of Nantes in 1685. Facile in languages, Motteux quickly mastered English and soon was editing *The Gentleman's Journal; or The Monthly Miscellany*. He also did translations of Cervantes and Rabelais. His best-known plays include *Love's a Jest* (1696) and *Beauty in Distress* (1698). Opera interested Motteux, and he tried his hand at semi-operatic works, such as the 1699 adaptation of *The Island Princess*; he also introduced to the London stage its first completely-sung Italianate opera. After mixed genre plays were banned from the stage in 1708, Motteux turned to business. He died under peculiar circumstances in a London brothel.

Studies:

Cunningham, Robert Newton. *Peter Anthony Motteux, 1663–1718: a Biographical and Critical Study*. Oxford: B. Blackwell, 1933.

OLDMIXON, JOHN (c. 1673–1742)

Oldmixon was born at Axbridge in Somerset and educated privately. He wrote some plays (including the tragedy *The Governor of Cyprus* in 1703), poems, and pastorals, but is really more famous as a Whig historian and a political pamphleteer. Pope attacked him twice, in *The Dunciad* and *Peri Bathous*.

Works:

Oldmixon, John. *Reflections on the Stage.* New York: Garland Publishers, 1699. Reprinted, 1972.

Studies:

Rogers, J. P. W. "The Dramatist vs. the Dunce: George Farquhar and John Oldmixon." *RECTR* 10.2 (1971): 53–58.

OTWAY, THOMAS (1652–1685)

Born in Sussex and educated at Winchester and Christ College, Oxford, Otway got his start in theatre thanks to Aphra Behn, who gave him a part to act in one of her plays. His acting was not well-received, and he turned to playwriting. His two most popular tragedies, *Venice Preserv'd* (1682) and *The Orphan* (1680), were revived for over a hundred years. Otway's early plays – *Alcibiades* (1675) and *Don Carlos* – (1676) – were written in the prevailing fashion of heroic couplets. Like Lee and Dryden, though, Otway eventually turned to prose for his most popular tragedies. Otway also wrote two excellent (and under-appreciated) comedies: *Friendship in Fashion* (1678) and *The Souldiers Fortune* (1680), in addition to a smattering of poetry. Throughout his life Otway struggled with poverty, and the themes of patronage and financial security run throughout his works. Otway died at thirty-three, the victim of poverty and alcoholism. He left no family, only debts to his booksellers, his vintner, even the actors who performed in his plays.

Works:

Ghosh, J. C., ed. *The Works of Thomas Otway: Plays, Poems, and Love-letters.* 2 vols. Oxford: Clarendon Press, 1932. Reprinted, 1968.

Summers, Montague, ed. *The Complete Works of Thomas Otway.* 3 vols. London: The Nonesuch Press, 1926.

Studies:

Berman, Ronald. "Nature in *Venice Preserv'd.*" *ELH* 36 (1969): 529–43.

Bywaters, David. "Venice, its Senate, and its Plot in Otway's *Venice Preserv'd.*" *MP* 80 (1983): 256–63.

DePorte, Michael. "Otway and the Straits of Venice." *PLL* 18 (1982): 245–57.

Durant, Jack D. "'Honor's Toughest Task': Family and State in *Venice Preserv'd.*" *SP* 71 (1974): 484–503.

Ham, Roswell Gray. *Otway and Lee: Biography from a Baroque Age.* New Haven: Yale University Press, 1931.

Harth, Phillip. "Political Interpretations of *Venice Preserv'd.*" *MP* 85 (1988): 345–62.

Hauser, David R. "Otway Preserved: Theme and Form in *Venice Preserv'd.*" *SP* 55 (1958): 481–93.

Hughes, Derek W. "A New Look at *Venice Preserv'd.*" *SEL* 11 (1971): 437–57.

Munns, Jessica. *Restoration Politics and Drama: the Plays of Thomas Otway, 1675–1683.* Newark: University of Delaware Press, 1995.

PAYNE, HENRY NEVIL (1672–1700)

Although he wrote several plays, Payne is more famous for his career as a spy and conspirator. After the Glorious Revolution, Payne became an agent for King James. In 1690 he was arrested for his part in planning the Montgomery plot, for which he was imprisoned and tortured for ten years. He gained release from prison in 1700 due to his ailing health, but died soon after. He was the last man legally tortured in Scotland. Payne produced two tragedies and a comedy: *The Fatal Jealousy* (1673); *The Morning Ramble* (1673); and *The Siege of Constantinople* (1675).

Studies:

Parker, Gerald D. "'History as Nightmare' in Nevil Payne's *The Siege of Constantinople* and Nathaniel Lee's *Lucius Junius Brutus*." *PLL* 21.1 (1985): 3–18.

PHILIPS, KATHERINE (1632–1664)

Also known by her pseudonym "The Matchless Orinda." Daughter of the merchant John Fowler, she married Colonel James Philips at the age of sixteen. Better known as a poet than a playwright, Philips translated two of Pierre Corneille's tragedies, *Pompey* (1663) and *Horace* (1664). The latter play was unfinished at her death, and the poet Sir John Denham completed the final act. Philips was much admired by other writers, and she organized a salon for the discussion of religion and poetry. A severe case of smallpox led to her death in her early thirties.

Studies:

Shifflett, Andrew. "'How Many Virtues Must I Hate': Katherine Philips and the Politics of Clemency." *SP* 94 (1997): 103–35.

PIX, MARY GRIFFITH (1666–1709)

Little is known about Pix's early life. At eighteen she married the merchant-tailor George Pix in London; by thirty she was writing for the stage. Pix wrote seven tragedies and six comedies, several of them, such as *Ibrahim* (1696) and *The Innocent Mistress* (1696) popular with audiences. Pix is best known as a member of the triumvirate of female playwrights who débuted in the London theatrical season of 1695–96. However, unlike either Catharine Trotter or Delarivière Manley, Pix led a fairly staid existence. Lampoons refer to her corpulence and her fondness for good wine and company, but in general she seems to have been well liked. Her professional relationships were equally genial. She, Trotter, and Manley wrote commendatory poems praising each other's work, and William Congreve mentored her in the craft of playwriting.

Studies:

Finke, Laurie A. "The Satire of Women Writers in *The Female Wits*." *Restoration* 8 (1984): 64–71.
McLaren, Juliet. "'Presumptuous Poetess, Pen-Feathered Muse': the Comedies of

Mary Pix." In Anne Messenger, ed., *Gender at Work: Four Women Writers of the Eighteenth-Century*. Detroit: Wayne State University Press, 1990.

RAVENSCROFT, EDWARD (1654?–1697)

Born to an ancient family, Ravenscroft trained at the Middle Temple but, like so many other Restoration dramatists, he turned his attention from legal matters to the theatre. His first play, *Mamaouchi, or The Citizen Turned Gentleman* (1671), was a hit with audiences as well as the Court. Ravenscroft worked in a variety of dramatic forms, ranging from farce in the manner of *commedia dell'arte* (the 1677 *Scaramouche*) to Spanish intrigue comedy (the 1676 *Wrangling Lovers*) to tragicomedy (the 1677 *King Edgar and Alfreda*) to Shakespearean adaptation (the 1678 *Titus Andronicus*.) Best known of Ravenscroft's plays is *The London Cuckolds* (1682), so enduringly popular that it became customary to stage it on the Lord Mayor's Day. Ravenscroft engaged in a series of quarrels with Dryden, a literary feud that undoubtedly led to the decline of his dramatic reputation posthumously.

Studies:

Meekins Jeanne S. "Evidence for Performance of *The London Cuckolds, The Maid's Tragedy* and *Oedipus* in 1685–1686." *ThS* 23.1 (1982): 101–03.

Pedicord, Harry William. "Revivals of Restoration Comedies in London." *Restoration* 3.2 (1979): 66–68.

Thorson, James L. "Authorial Duplicity: a Warning to Editors." *AEB* 3 (1979): 79–96.

Tibbetts, Robert A. "Queer Foliation in *The London Cuckolds*." *PBSA* 71 (1977): 486–87.

Velz, John W. "Topoi in Edward Ravenscroft's Indictment of Shakespeare's *Titus Andronicus*." *MP* 83.1 (1985): 45–50.

ROWE, NICHOLAS (1674/6–1718)

Born in Bedfordshire and educated at the Westminster School, Rowe in 1691 entered the Middle Temple and studied in his father's law chambers. Rowe married his first wife, Antonia Parsons, in 1693. He completed his studies quickly and was called to the bar in 1696. Although Rowe practiced law for several years, he became interested in writing, initially exchanging verses with Anne Finch and dabbling in some imitations of Horace. By 1700 he had given up his Temple chambers in order to turn his full attention to writing. Rowe's first play, *The Ambitious Stepmother*, was in production by December. Rowe penned eight plays, all of them tragedies with the exception of *The Biter* (1705); *Jane Shore* (1714) and *The Fair Penitent* (1703) are by far the best known. Rowe invented the term "she-tragedy" to describe his dramas, which often feature victimized women seeking redemption. In theme and form, these plays recall the pathetic tragedies written by Lee and Otway during the 1670s and early 1680s. Rowe is also famous for producing the first new edition of Shakespeare's works since the 1623 folio; he added stage directions and act and scene designations, many of them still retained by editors today. Rowe also held government posts: he served as the Secretary of State for Scotland from 1709 to 1711 and as Poet Laureate from 1715 until his death. His first wife died in 1712;

Rowe married again, to one Anne Devenish, in 1716. He is buried in Westminster Abbey.

Studies:

Aikens, Janet E. "To Know Jane Shore 'think on all time backward'," *PLL* 18 (Summer 1982): 258–77.

Brown, Laura. "The Defenseless Woman and the Development of English Tragedy." *SEL* 22 (1982): 429–43.

Burns, Landon C. *Pity and Tears: the Tragedies of Nicholas Rowe.* University of Salzburg, 1974.

Canfield, J. Douglas. *Nicholas Rowe and Christian Tragedy.* Gainesville: University Presses of Florida, 1977.

Cohen, Derek. "Nicholas Rowe, Aphra Behn, and the Farcical Muse." *PLL* 15 (1979): 383–95.

Dammers, Richard H. "Female Characterization in English Platonic Drama: a Background for the Eighteenth Century Tragedies of Nicholas Rowe." *RECTR* 1.2 (1986): 34–41.

"The Female Experience in the Tragedies of Nicholas Rowe." *W&L* 6.1 (1978): 28–35.

DeRitter, Jones. "'Wonder Not, Princely Gloster, at the Notice This Paper Brings You': Women, Writing, and Politics in Rowe's *Jane Shore*." *CompD* 31 (1997): 86–104.

Hagstrum, Jean H. *Sex and Sensibility: Ideal and Erotic Love from Milton to Mozart.* University of Chicago Press, 1980.

Hesse, Alfred W. "Who Was Bit by Rowe's Comedy *The Biter*?" *PQ* 62 (1983): 477–85.

Kearful, Frank J. "The Nature of Tragedy in Rowe's *The Fair Penitent*. *PLL* 2 (1966): 351–60.

Sherry, Richard J. "'Restoring and Preserving . . . Learning': Rowe's *Ulysses*, 1705." *RECTR* 3.1 (1988): 10–19.

Sutherland, James R. "Introduction" to *Three Plays: Tamerlane, The Fair Penitent, Jane Shore, by Nicholas Rowe.* London: Scholartis, 1929.

Tumir, Vaska. "She-Tragedy and its Men: Conflict and Form in *The Orphan* and *The Fair Penitent*." *SEL* 30.3 (1990): 411–28.

SEDLEY, SIR CHARLES (*c.* 1639–1701)

Descended from an ancient Kentish family, Sedley was educated at Wadham College, Oxford, where he was elected fellow in 1656 but never took a degree. Today Sedley is best known as one of the court wits surrounding Charles II. He wrote verse that was much admired at the time for its ease and elegance, as well as four plays: *Antony and Cleopatra* (1677); *Bellamira* (1687); *The Mulberry Garden* (1668); and, after his death, *Beauty the Conqueror, or The Death of Marc Anthony* (1702). Although Sedley's youth was fairly dissolute, he nonetheless took umbrage at the Stuart dynasty after his daughter became the mistress of the Duke of York, the future James II. Sedley numbered Dryden and Rochester among his close friends.

Studies:

Pinto, V. de Sola. *Sir Charles Sedley, 1639–1701: a Study in the Life and Literature of the Restoration.* London: Constable, 1927.

SETTLE, ELKANAH (1648–1724)

Known as the "city poet," Settle was born in Dunstable and attended for a short time Trinity College, Oxford. Settle wrote fifteen plays, most of them tragedies, and for a while he upstaged the aging dramatist, John Dryden, with such hits as *The Empress of Morocco* (1673). The two men engaged in a pamphlet war. Settle, in early life a devoted Whig, wrote political writings in support of the Earl of Shaftesbury and against Roman Catholics, a position he eventually recanted. He was named City Poet in 1691 and received a pension for an annual panegyric to celebrate the festival of the Lord Mayor. Reduced circumstances toward the end of his life forced Settle to write drolls for the yearly Bartholomew Fair. He died, impoverished, in the Charterhouse.

Studies:

Brown, Frank Clyde. *Elkanah Settle: his Life and Works.* University of Chicago Press, 1910.

Doyle, Anne T. *Elkanah Settle's "The Empress of Morocco" and the Controversy Surrounding It: a Critical Edition.* Satire and Sense. New York: Garland, 1987.

SHADWELL, THOMAS (1641?–1692)

Born in Norfolk to a Royalist family, Shadwell attended Gonville and Caius College, Cambridge, for two years followed by a stint at the Middle Temple. In the early 1660s Shadwell married Anne Gibbs, one of the first actresses on the English stage; he also made the acquaintance of William Cavendish, Duke of Newcastle, who was to prove an important patron. Shadwell was also a skilled musician, having been trained by John Jenkins, musician in ordinary to Charles I and Charles II. Shadwell's first play, *The Sullen Lovers*, premièred in 1668 at the Duke's Company, the company for which Shadwell would write most of his plays. Shadwell quickly proved to be a popular playwright: he went on to write thirteen more plays, many of them adaptations of Molière, until his Whig politics forced him from the stage. A long-standing feud with John Dryden may also have contributed to Shadwell's banishment from the stage. After 1688, when the political climate proved more hospitable, Shadwell once again wrote for the stage, producing another five plays. He succeeded Dryden – demoted for his conversion to Roman Catholicism – as poet laureate in 1689. Plagued by ill health, Shadwell died either of vascular disease or of the "gout." He is buried in Westminster Abbey. Although remembered today largely as the butt of Dryden's satire in *MacFlecknoe*, Shadwell was an accomplished and well-known comic playwright during the Restoration.

Studies:

Bancroft, Vicky. "'A Desperate Ill, Must Have a Desperate Cure': Cross-Dressing in the Plays of Thomas Shadwell." *Restoration* 20 (1996): 165–74.

"Wycherley's *The Plain Dealer* and Shadwell's *A True Widow.*" *RECTR* 4.1 (1989): 49–51.

Combe, Kirk. "Introduction: Considering Shadwell." *Restoration* 20.2 (1996): 88–100.

Corman, Brian. "Thomas Shadwell and the Jonsonian Comedy of the Restoration." In Robert Markley and Laurie Fink, eds., *From Renaissance to Restoration: Metamorphoses of the Drama.* Cleveland: Bellflower Press, 1984.

Dunne, Sara Lewis. *"The Woman Captain*: Shadwell's Juvenalian Menu." *Restoration* 20.2 (1996): 189–94.

Love, Harold. "Shadwell, Rochester and the Crisis of Amateurism." *Restoration* 20 (1996): 119–34.

Munns, Jessica. "'The Golden Days of Queen Elizabeth': Thomas Shadwell's *The Lancashire Witches* and the Politics of Nostalgia." *Restoration* 20 (1996): 195–216.

Ross, John C. "Theatricality and Revolution Politics in *The Squire of Alsatia* and *Bury-Fair.*" *Restoration* 20 (1996): 217–35.

Zomchick, John P. "Force, Contract, and Power in *The Woman-Captain.*" *Restoration* 20 (1996): 175–88.

SOUTHERNE, THOMAS (1660–1746)

Born in Ireland to a Dublin brewer, Southerne attended Trinity College, Dublin, before entering the Middle Temple in London. As with many other Restoration playwrights, Southerne shifted from the law to the theatre, writing his first play, *The Loyal Brother, or, The Persian Prince* in 1682, a tragedy in the pathetic mode of John Banks, Thomas Otway, and Nathaniel Lee. Dryden helped the aspiring playwright, supplying the prologue and epilogue. Southerne's Tory politics were evident in the play – which was produced at the height of the Exclusion Crisis – and he became affiliated with a group of Tory playwrights that included John Crowne, John Dryden, Aphra Behn, and Thomas Otway. Southerne wrote another tragedy before a brief sojourn in the army. After his return, he wrote several comedies, including the immensely popular *Sir Anthony Love* (1690) and the darkly troubling *The Wives' Excuse.* Southerne is perhaps best known for his stage adaptation of Aphra Behn's novella, *Oroonoko*; his redaction remained in the stage repertoire for one hundred fifty years. In 1696 Trinity College, Dublin, awarded Southerne his M.A. degree. He also married a widow, Agnes Atkyns, around this time. Southerne, who lived until eighty-six, wrote a total of ten plays, producing his final one at the age of sixty-seven. He numbered among his friends such literary luminaries as John Dryden, Aphra Behn, Jonathan Swift, and Alexander Pope.

Studies:

Cordner, Michael. "Marriage Comedy after the 1688 Revolution: Southerne to Vanbrugh." *MLR* 85 (1990): 273–89.

Drougge, Helga. "Love, Death and Mrs. Barry in Thomas Southerne's Plays." *CompD* 27 (1993/94): 408–25.

"'We'll Learn that of the Men': Female Sexuality in Southerne's Comedies." *SEL* 33 (1993): 545–63.

Hume, Robert D. "The Importance of Thomas Southerne." *MP* 87 (1990): 275–90.

Jordan, Robert. "Inversion and Ambiguity in *The Maid's Last Prayer.*" *Restoration* 15.2 (1991): 99–110.

Root, Robert L., Jr. *Thomas Southerne.* Twayne's English Authors Series 315. Boston: Twayne, 1981.

Thompson, Peggy J. "Facing the Void in *The Wives Excuse; or Characters Make Themselves.*" *PLL* 31 (1995): 78–98.

Weber, Harold. "The Female Libertine in Southerne's *Sir Anthony Love* and *The Wives Excuse.*" *EiT* 2 (1984): 125–139.

TATE, NAHUM (1652–1715)

Most likely born in Ireland to a family of Irish clergymen, Tate entered Trinity College, Dublin, in 1668; during the early 1670s he moved to London. Tate's first play, which blends the fourth book of the *Aeneid* with the history of Brutus, the founder of New Troy (London), premièred in 1678. Tate went on to write another original play, *The Loyal General* (1679), before turning his hand to the adaptations for which he is best known. Tate's most notorious adaption is that of *King Lear* (1681) – Lear and Cordelia live happily ever after – although he also adapted plays by Aston Cokaine, Ben Jonson, and John Fletcher. Conservative in his literary principles and modest in his demeanor, Tate nonetheless attempted a variety of genres over the course of his lifetime. In addition to writing and adapting plays, Tate translated a variety of works (Heliodorus to poems on syphilis), scribbled birthday and commemorative poems for the monarch, penned pastoral dialogues on moral subjects, produced a new edition of the Psalms, and wrote the libretto for an opera. Indeed, it is this latter enterprise for which Tate today is perhaps best known: the libretto for Purcell's opera, *Dido and Aeneas* (1689). After Shadwell died in 1692, Tate was awarded the Laureateship; he was appointed Historiographer Royal in 1702. Despite these honors, Tate suffered ill health and poverty in his later years. He died in the Mint in 1715.

Studies:

Anselment, Raymond A. "Fracastoro's Syphilis: Nahum Tate and the Realms of Apollo." *BJRL* 73 (1991): 106–18.

Black, James. "An Augustan Stage History: Nahum Tate's *King Lear.*" *RECTR* 6.1 (1967): 36–54.

"The Influence of Hobbes on Nahum Tate's *King Lear.*" *SEL* 7 (1967): 377–85.

Green, Lawrence D. "'Where's My Fool?' – Some Consequences of the Omission of the Fool in Tate's *Lear.*" *SEL* 12 (1972): 259–74.

Mack, Maynard. *King Lear in Our Time.* Berkeley: University of California Press, 1965.

Odell, George C. D. *Shakespeare from Betterton to Irving.* New York: C. Scribner's, 1920.

Price, Curtis Alexander. *Henry Purcell and the London Stage.* Cambridge University Press, 1984.

Spencer, Christopher. *Nahum Tate.* Twayne's English Authors Series 126. New York: Twayne, 1972.

"A Word for Tate's *King Lear.*" *SEL* 3 (1963): 241–51.

TROTTER, CATHERINE (1679–1749)

Later Cockburn. Born to a navy captain whose death left his family in straitened circumstances, Trotter from an early age displayed a precocious aptitude for logic, languages, and verse. She published her first work, a prose romance entitled *Olinda's Adventures*, when she was only fourteen and her first play, a stage adaptation of Behn's romance, *Agnes de Castro*, when sixteen. Trotter became known as one of the so-called "female wits" along with Delarivière Manley and Mary Pix. Over the next decade, she would write three more tragedies and a comedy, *Love at a Loss* (1701). Trotter left the theatre after 1707, perhaps stung by the reaction to her last play, *The Revolution of Sweden* (1706). Influenced by the writings of Bishop Gilbert Burnet, she also converted from Catholicism to Anglicanism around this time. Trotter married Patrick Cockburn in 1708 and gave up writing until 1726 when she began a defense of Locke. She devoted her later years to theological and philosophical writings. Trotter numbered William Congreve, George Farquhar, and Delarivière Manley among her friends.

Works:

Steeves, Edna L., ed. *The Plays of Mary Pix and Catherine Trotter.* Eighteenth Century English Drama. 2 vols. New York: Garland, 1982.

Studies:

Clark, Constance. *Three Augustan Women Playwrights.* New York: Peter Lang, 1986.

Finke, Laurie A. "The Satire of Women Writers in *The Female Wits.*" *Restoration* 8.2 (1984): 64–71.

VANBRUGH, SIR JOHN (1664–1726)

The son of a London woman, Elizabeth Barker, and a man of Flemish extraction, Giles Vanbrugh, John Vanbrugh is known as much for his architectural brilliance as for his sparkling comedies. Little is known about Vanbrugh's early education, although it is possible he acquired some architectural training in France in 1683. He received a military commission from his kinsman, the Earl of Huntingdon, in 1685 but soon resigned it. From 1688 to 1692 he was imprisoned in various French prisons in Calais, Paris, and Vincennes for openly supporting the Glorious Revolution of 1688. Vanbrugh turned to writing for the theatre in 1696, producing *The Relapse*, a sequel to Colley Cibber's popular comedy, *Love's Last Shift.* Vanbrugh's comedy, an overwhelming success, may very well have saved the faltering Drury Lane company. The next year he wrote *The Provok'd Wife*, although this play went to the rival company headed by Thomas Betterton, the great actor and manager. Like *The Relapse*, it proved immediately popular and stayed in the repertoire for the next seventy-five years. Vanbrugh also adapted several plays, among them *Aesop*, taken from Edmé Boursault's *Les Fables d'Esope, The Country House*, taken from Florent Carton Dancourt's *La Maison de campagne*, and *The Pilgrim*, taken from John Fletcher's play of the same name. In all, Vanbrugh adapted and/or wrote eleven plays. Vanbrugh shifted his attentions to architecture in 1699; over the next two decades he would produce such monumental edifices as Castle Howard, Blenheim Palace, and Seaton Delaval. Vanbrugh retained his interest in theatre, though, designing and managing the Haymarket opera house, an ill-fated venture, and supporting various operatic projects. Vanbrugh was an active member of the Kit-Cat Club, a society of prominent Whig politicians and literati, and he numbered many prominent men among his friends. At the age of fifty-four Vanbrugh finally married: Henrietta Maria, second cousin to the Duchess of Newcastle, in 1719. He died seven years later.

Works:

Dobrée, Bonamy and Geoffrey Webb, eds. *The Complete Works of Sir John Vanbrugh*. 4 vols. London: The Nonesuch Press, 1927–28.

Studies:

Berkowitz, Gerald M. "Sir John Vanbrugh and the Conventions of Restoration Comedy." *Genre* 6 (1973): 346–61.

  Sir John Vanbrugh and the End of Restoration Comedy. Amsterdam: Editions Rodopi, 1981.

Chiappelli, Carolyn. "The Single-Plot Structure of Vanbrugh's *The Relapse*." *EM* 28–29 (1979–80): 207–25.

Cordner, Michael. "Time, the Churches, and Vanbrugh's Lord Foppington." *DUJ* 77 (1984): 11–17.

Drougge, Helga. "'The Deep Reserves of Man': Anxiety in Vanbrugh's *The Relapse*." *SEL* 34 (1994): 507–22.

Faller, Lincoln B. "Between Jest and Earnest: the Comedy of Sir John Vanbrugh." *MP* 72 (1974): 17–29.

Gill, James E. "Character, Plot, and the Language of Love in *The Relapse*: a Reappraisal." *Restoration* 16 (1992): 110–25.

Harley, Graham D. "Squire Trelooby and *The Cornish Squire*: a Reconsideration." *PQ* 49 (1970): 520–29.

Hughes, Derek. "Cibber and Vanbrugh: Language, Place, and Social Order in *Love's Last Shift*." *CompD* 20 (1986–87): 287–304.

  "Vanbrugh and Cibber: Language, Place, and Social Order in *The Relapse*." *CompD* 21 (1987): 63–83.

Kenny, Shirley Strum. "Humane Comedy." *MP* 75 (1977): 29–43.

Kropf, C. R. "*The Relapse* and the Sentimental Mask." *JNT* 1 (1971): 193–99.

Malek, James S. "Comic Irony in Vanbrugh's *The Relapse*." *CLAJ* 26 (1983): 353–61.

McCormick, Frank. "The Unity of Vanbrugh's *A Journey to London*." *DUJ* 76 (1984): 187–94.

Mueschke, Paul, and Jeannette Fleisher. "A Re-evaluation of Vanbrugh." *PMLA* 49 (1934): 848–89.

Olshen, Barry N. "The Original and 'Improved' Comedies of Sir John Vanbrugh: their Nineteenth-Century London Stage History." *RECTR* 13:1 (1974): 27–52.

Van Niel, Pieter Jan. "*The Relapse* – Into Death and Damnation." *ETJ* 21 (1969): 318–32.

VILLIERS, GEORGE, SECOND DUKE OF BUCKINGHAM (1628–1687)

At times the most powerful politician during the Restoration, Buckingham was born to the first Duke, the principal favorite of James I. Seven months old when his father was assassinated, Buckingham and his brother were raised in the royal family as companions to the princes. Buckingham left Trinity College, Cambridge, to join the Royalist forces against the Parliamentarians. For much of the Civil War, he lived abroad, although he returned to England in 1657 to wed Mary Fairfax, largely to recover his lands. Between his lands, positions, and pensions, he became the wealthiest man in England during the Restoration. As with other courtier-writers, Buckingham followed a collaborative model of authorship; he also adapted plays. In 1663 or 1664 he apparently collaborated with Charles Saint-Evremond and Louis d'Aubigny on the closet drama, *Sir Politick Would-Be*, an adaptation of Ben Jonson's *Volpone*. He revised John Fletcher's play, *The Chances*, which saw performance in 1664 and print in 1682. With Sir Robert Howard he wrote *The Country Gentleman*, a satire of Sir William Coventry that eventually toppled him from power. The play, banished from the stage and suppressed from print, was thought lost until a scribal manuscript was discovered twenty years ago. It is *The Rehearsal* (1671), though, for which Buckingham is best known. Thought to be a satire of Dryden and heroic drama, the play was written by Buckingham and Sir Robert Howard and proved popular well into the eighteenth century. Buckingham's political and personal fortunes were always tumultuous. He killed the husband of his mistress, the Countess of Shrewsbury, in a notorious duel. Impeached by the House of Commons in 1674, Buckingham briefly retired to Yorkshire. In 1675 Buckingham forged a political alliance with Anthony Ashley Cooper, the Earl of Shaftesbury, to create an opposition party. He was imprisoned in 1677, although he was enormously popular with the people. In 1681 he again retired to country life. Buckingham is known for promoting religious toleration, an unpopular position at the time, as well as for his interest in the "new science," as exemplified by his membership in the Royal Society.

Studies:

Chapman, Hester W. *Great Villiers: a Study of George Villiers, Second Duke of Buckingham, 1628–1687*. London: Secker & Warburg, 1949.

Gravitt, G. Jack. "The Modernity of *The Rehearsal*: Buckingham's Theatre of the Absurd." *CollL* 9 (1982): 30–38.

O'Neill, John H. *George Villiers, Second Duke of Buckingham*. Twayne's English Authors Series 394. Boston: Twayne, 1984.

Smith, Dane Farnsworth. *The Critics in the Audience of the London Theatres from Buckingham to Sheridan: a Study of Neoclassicism in the Playhouse, 1671–1779*. Albuquerque: University of New Mexico Press, 1953.

Stocker, Margarita. "Political Allusion in *The Rehearsal*." *PQ* 67 (1988): 11–35.

WALLER, EDMUND (1606–1687)

The son of a wealthy landowner, Waller was born in Buckinghamshire and educated at Eton and King's College, Cambridge. He entered Parliament first as a member of the opposition, earning a reputation for his oratorical skills, but converting to the

Royalist side after a few years. He made use of those oratorical skills mostly in his many volumes of poetry, occasionally authoring dramas. He married a wealthy heiress in 1631, but she died three years later. He later remarried in 1644. In 1643, he faced prison, fine and banishment for his participation in a plot to seize London for Charles I. Waller, however, made peace with Cromwell in 1657, which did not seem to hurt him at all at the Restoration. Dryden and others expressed great regard for Waller both as a poet and as a statesman.

Studies:
Gilbert, Jack G. *Edmund Waller.* Twayne's English Authors Series 266. Boston: Twayne, 1979.

WILMOT, JOHN, EARL OF ROCHESTER (1647–1680)

The dissolute son of Henry Wilmot, the first Earl, John was born in Oxfordshire and educated at Burford Grammar School and Wadham College, Oxford. He was admitted as a commoner in 1660 and left, with a M.A., in 1661 to embark on a grand tour of Europe with Sir Andrew Balfour, the botanist. At seventeen Rochester was presented at court, where he rapidly became a popular member of the group of wits surrounding Charles II. Better known for his romantic and erotic verse than his forays into the drama, Rochester nevertheless adapted Fletcher's play, *Valentinian* and may have authored the notorious pornographic play, *Sodom.* Rochester was a patron to several dramatists, including John Dryden, Nathaniel Lee, Thomas Otway, and Elkanah Settle. He had an affair with the famous actress, Elizabeth Barry, and was good friends with Aphra Behn and Nell Gwynn. Rochester died at thirty-three, the victim of hard drinking and venereal disease. He is buried in Spelsbury Church in Oxfordshire.

Studies:
Burns, Edward, ed. *Reading Rochester.* New York: St. Martin's Press, 1995.
Carver, Larry. "Rochester's *Valentinian.*" RECTR 4.1 (1989): 25–38.
Vieth, David M., ed. *John Wilmot, Earl of Rochester: Critical Essays.* New York: Garland, 1988.

JOHN WILSON (1626–1695?)

Born in London to the distinguished Anglican divine, Aaron Wilson, John Wilson attended Exeter College, Oxford and, later, Lincoln's Inn for legal training. He was called to the bar in 1652. From 1666 to 1680 he served his patron, the Duke of Ormonde, as Recorder of Londonderry. Of Wilson's four plays, the best known is *The Cheats* (1663). He also wrote *Andronicus Comnenius* (1664), *The Projectors* (1665), and *Belphegor; or the Marriage of the Devil* (Dublin 1677–78; London 1690). In addition to drama, Wilson translated the *Moriae Encomium; or The Praise of Folly* of Erasmus, and he wrote three political tracts during the 1680s and 1690s in defense of absolute monarchy. Like Dryden, he ended his literary career as a translator. Wilson died, probably in 1695, in the parish of St. Martin-in-the-Fields.

Works:
Maidment, James, and W. H. Logan, eds. *The Dramatic Works of John Wilson.* Edinburgh: William Paterson, 1874; rpt. 1967.

Studies:
Hammond, Anthony. "John Wilson and the Andronicus Plays: a Reconsideration." *YES* 4 (1974): 112–19.

Lesko, Kathleen M. "A Rare Restoration Manuscript Prompt-book: John Wilson's *Belphegor*, Corrected by the Author." *SB* 32 (1979): 215–19.

Nahm, Milton C. "John Wilson and His 'Some Few Plays.'" *RES* 14 (1938): 143–54.

Willard, Thomas Spaulding. "John Wilson's Satire of Hermetic Medicine." In Marie Mulvery Roberts and Roy Porter, eds., *Literature and Medicine During the Eighteenth Century.* London: Routledge, 1993.

WYCHERLEY, WILLIAM (1641–1715)

Born to an ancient Shrophire family, Wycherley was sent by his ardent Royalist father to France for his education. There he met Julie d'Angennes, Marquise de Montausier, from whom he imbibed *précieuse* teachings on Platonic love. In 1660 Wycherley returned to England and attended Queen's College, Oxford for a very brief period; by November he had enrolled in the Inner Temple. He never completed his legal training. Wycherley published his first work, a mock-heroic poem entitled *Hero and Leander, in Burlesque* in 1669. His first piece for the theatre, *Love in a Wood* (1671), brought Wycherley to the attention of the court and proved immensely popular with audiences. The next year Wycherley produced *The Gentleman Dancing-Master* (printed in 1673), also popular with audiences. However, his final two plays, *The Country Wife* (1675) and *The Plain Dealer* (1676), both brilliant satires of Restoration culture, secured Wycherley's reputation for posterity. He lived for another forty years, but never again wrote for the stage. A brain fever contracted in 1677 ruined Wycherley's health and creativity; an imprudent marriage in 1679 to the debt-ridden Countess of Drogheda plunged him into deep financial woes and lost him royal patronage. In 1682 he was committed to Newgate Prison for debt; he was transferred to the Fleet, where he remained for four years until James II cleared his debts. Wycherley brought out a collection of his poems in 1704 and lived modestly until the end of his life. At the age of seventy-four he married again – his first wife died in 1685 – but he died eleven days later. Throughout his life, Wycherley moved in prominent literary circles. He numbered Dryden, Congreve, Southerne, and Dennis among his friends, and he used his influence to promote the young Alexander Pope, newly arrived on the London scene at the age of seventeen.

Works:
The Complete Plays of William Wycherley. Ed. Gerald Weales. Garden City: Doubleday, 1966.

The Plays of William Wycherley. Ed. Arthur Friedman. Oxford: Clarendon Press, 1979.

The Plays of William Wycherley. Ed. Peter Holland. Cambridge: Cambridge University Press, 1981.

Studies:

Bancroft, Vicky. "Wycherley's *The Plain Dealer* and Shadwell's *A True Widow*." *RECTR* 4.1 (1989): 49–51.

Berman, Ronald. "Wycherley's Unheroic Society." *ELH* 51 (1981): 465–78.

Bode, Robert F. "A Rape and No Rape: Olivia's Bedroom Revisited." *Restoration* 12.2 (1988): 80–85.

"'Try Me, at Least': the Dispensing of Justice in *The Plain Dealer*." *RECTR* 4.1 (1989): 1–24.

Burke, Helen M. "Wycherley's 'Tendentious Joke': the Discourse of Alterity in *The Country Wife*." *ECent* 29.3 (1988): 227–41.

Cohen, Derek. "The Alternating Styles of *The Plain Dealer*." *RECTR* 2.1 (1987): 19–37.

"*The Country Wife* and Social Danger." *RECTR* 10.1 (1995): 1–14.

"The Revenger's Comedy: A Reading of *The Country Wife*." *DUJ* 76.1 (1983): 31–36.

Ford, Douglas. "*The Country Wife*: Rake Hero as Artist." *Restoration* 17.2 (1993): 77–84.

Friedson, A. M. "Wycherley and Moliere: Satirical Point of View in *The Plain Dealer*." *MP* 64 (1967): 189–97.

Hallett, Charles A. "The Hobbesian Substructure of *The Country Wife*." *PLL* 9 (1973): 380–95.

Hawkins, Barrie. "*The Country Wife*: Metaphor Manifest." *RECTR* 11.1 (1996): 40–63.

Hughes, Derek. "*The Plain Dealer*: A Reappraisal." *MLQ* 43.4 (1982): 315–36.

Hynes, Peter. "Against Theory? Knowledge and Action in Wycherley's Plays." *MP* 94 (1996): 163–89.

Mann, David D. "The Function of the Quack in *The Country Wife*." *Restoration* 7.1 (1983): 19–22.

Marshall, W. Gerald. "The Idea of Theatre in Wycherley's *The Gentleman Dancing-Master*." *Restoration* 6.1 (1982): 1–10.

"Wycherley's Drama of Madness: *The Plain Dealer*." *PQ* 59.1 (1980): 26–37.

"Wycherley's 'Great Stage of Fools': Madness and Theatricality in *The Country Wife*." *SEL* 29.3 (1989): 409–29.

"Wycherley's *Love in a Wood* and the Designs of Providence." *Restoration* 3.1 (1979): 8–16.

Matalene, H. W. "What Happens in *The Country Wife*." *SEL* 22.3 (1982): 395–411.

Matlack, Cynthia. "Parody and Burlesque of Heroic Ideals in Wycherley's Comedies: a Critical Reinterpretation of Contemporary Evidence." *PLL* 8 (1972): 273–86.

McCarthy, Eugene B. *William Wycherley: a Biography*. Athens: Ohio University Press, 1979.

Morrow, Laura. "Phenomenological Psychology and Comic Form in *The Plain Dealer*." *RECTR* 3.2 (1988): 1–10.

Neill, Michael. "Horned Beasts and China Oranges: Reading the Signs in *The Country Wife*." *ECLife* 12.2 (1988): 3–17.

Payne, Deborah C. "Reading the Signs in *The Country Wife*." *SEL* 26.3 (1986): 403–19.

Rogers, Katharine M. *William Wycherley*. Twayne's English Authors Series 127. New York: Twayne, 1972.

Thompson, James. *Language in Wycherley's Plays: Seventeenth-Century Language Theory and Drama*. University: Univeristy of Alabama Press, 1984.

"Ideology and Dramatic Form: The Case of Wycherley." *SlitI* 17.1 (1984): 49–62.

"Providence and Verbal Irony in *The Country Wife*." *SoAR* 47.4 (1982): 37–42.

Thompson, Peggy. "The Limits of Parody in *The Country Wife*." *SP* 89.1 (1992): 100–14.

Velissariou, Aspasia. "Gender and the Circulation of Money and Desire in Wycherley's *The Plain-Dealer*." *Restoration* 18.1 (1994): 27–36.

"Patriarchal Tactics of Control and Female Desire in Wycherley's *The Gentleman Dancing-Master* and *The Country Wife*." *TSLL* 37.2 (1995): 115–26.

Vernon, P. F. *William Wycherley*. Bibliographical Series of Supplements to British Book News on Writers and Their Works. London: Longmans, Green, 1965.

Weber, Harold. "Horner and His 'Women of Honour': The Dinner Party in *The Country Wife*." *MLQ* 43.2 (1982): 107–20.

"The Rake-Hero in Wycherley and Congreve." *PQ* 61.2 (1982): 143–60.

Zimbardo, Rose A. *Wycherley's Drama: a Link in the Development of English Satire*. Yale Studies in English 156. New Haven: Yale University Press, 1965.

INDEX

AEB-9455